CWNA ™

Certified Wireless Network Administrator
Official Study Guide

(Exam PW0-100)

THIRD EDITION

Planet3 Wireless

McGraw-Hill/Osborne
New York Chicago San Francisco Lisbon London Madrid
Mexico City Milan New Delhi San Juan Seoul Singapore Sydney Toronto

McGraw-Hill/Osborne
2600 Tenth Street
Berkeley, California 94710
U.S.A.

To arrange bulk purchase discounts for sales promotions, premiums, or fund-raisers, please contact McGraw-Hill/Osborne at the above address. For information on translations or book distributors outside the U.S.A., please see the International Contact Information page immediately following the index of this book.

CWNA Certified Wireless Network Administrator
Official Study Guide (Exam PW0-100) Third Edition

1234567890 JPI JPI 019876543

ISBN 0-07-225538-2

Publisher	Editorial Director	Indexer
Brandon A. Nordin	Gareth Hancock	Jack Lewis
Vice President & Associate Publisher	**Author**	**Computer Designers**
Scott Rogers	Joshua Bardwell	Scott Turner
	Devin Akin	
Acquisitions Editor	**Technical Editors**	**Illustrator**
Timothy Green	Criss Hyde	Scott Turner
Project & Copy Editor	**Proofreader**	**Series Design**
Kevin Sandlin	Arnold Friedman	Scott Turner

The CWNP® Program

The CWNP Program is the industry standard for wireless LAN training and certification, and is intended for individuals who administer, install, design, troubleshoot, and support IEEE 802.11 compliant wireless networks. Achieving CWNP certification will help you to design, install, and maintain wireless LANs that are more secure, cost-effective, and reliable.

The CWNP Program has three levels of knowledge and certification covering all aspects of wireless LANs.

Foundation

CWNA covers a broad range of wireless networking topics. Your CWNA certification will get you started in your wireless career by ensuring you have the skills to successfully administer a wireless LAN.

Advanced

CWSP advances your career by ensuring you have the skills to successfully secure wireless networks from hackers.. CWSP offers the most thorough information available on how attacks occur and how to secure your wireless network from them.

CWAP ensures you have the skills to maximize the performance of a wireless network and reduce the time spent troubleshooting problems. You will be able to confidently analyze and troubleshoot any wireless LAN system using any of the market leading software and hardware analysis tools.

Expert

CWNE credential is the final step in the CWNP Program. By successfully completing the CWNE practical examination, network engineers and administrators will have demonstrated that they have the most advanced skills available in today's wireless LAN market.

I would like to dedicate my contribution to this book to my father, Joseph Bardwell, who sparked my interest in computers and networking and who continues to encourage, aid, and support me in all aspects of my life, both professional and personal. I am enormously privileged and thankful to have been allowed to follow in his footsteps.

Thanks also to Anita Lenk for her professional guidance from the beginning of my career onward.

Joshua Bardwell

We at Planet3 Wireless would like to dedicate this book to our Lord Jesus Christ. It is through Him that we have had the talent, time, encouragement, and strength to work many long months in preparing this text. Our goal through the creation of this book and through all things that He allows us to do going forward is to glorify Him. We acknowledge His hand in every part of our company, our work, and our friendships. We would also like to thank our families who have been amazingly supportive, our friends who have encouraged us, and everyone that contributed to this book in any way.

"I can do all things through Christ, who strengthens me." – Philippians 4:13

Acknowledgements

Planet3 Wireless, Inc. would like to acknowledge and thank the following people for their tireless contributions to this work:

Joshua Bardwell, whose in-depth understanding of wireless LAN technology has been a great asset to the CWNP Program since its earliest days. Joshua has a unique way of conveying difficult material in a simple way so that even beginners understand. Joshua's extensive background in WLAN protocol analysis and network architecture makes him highly qualified to teach and write materials such as this study guide, and his continuing support of the CWNP Program over the years has improved its quality significantly.

Devin Akin, whose knowledge of wireless LAN technology and 802.11 standards are renowned in the industry. His talents to convey, teach, write, and edit are an integral part of the CWNP Program and essential in making this the most accurate and comprehensive writing on wireless LANs in today's market.

Criss Hyde, for providing the most detailed review possible. Criss is the only person we know who can find a needle in a haystack on a consistent basis. He has contributed substantially to all Planet3 products published or republished since 2004, and currently holds all CWNP certifications. His thorough understanding of the IEEE 802.11 standards and his ability to comprehend the most difficult concepts astounds all of us.

Scott Turner, who constantly keeps us in line and focused on what is important. Scott's work in formatting, framing, content organization, and graphics creation was indispensable. Scott's eye for detail and his motivation for perfection in everything he does keep us in awe.

Contents at a Glance

Introduction		*xxi*
Chapter 1	Introduction to Wireless LANs	3
Chapter 2	Radio Frequency (RF) Fundamentals	21
Chapter 3	RF Math	47
Chapter 4	Antennas	69
Chapter 5	Antenna Accessories	131
Chapter 6	Spread Spectrum Technology	169
Chapter 7	Wireless LAN Infrastructure Devices	217
Chapter 8	Wireless LAN Organizations and Standards	299
Chapter 9	802.11 Network Architecture	327
Chapter 10	MAC and Physical Layers	363
Chapter 11	Troubleshooting Wireless LAN Installations	393
Chapter 12	Wireless LAN Security	423
Chapter 13	Site Survey Fundamentals	477
Appendix A	Site Survey Access Point Form	549
Appendix B	Site Survey Questionnaire	559
Index		573

Contents

Chapter 1	**Introduction to Wireless LANs**	**3**
	The Wireless LAN Market	2
	History of Wireless LANs	2
	Today's Wireless LAN Standards	4
	Applications of Wireless LANs	5
	Three Main Roles for Wireless LANs	5
	Corporate Data Access and End-User Mobility	6
	Educational/Classroom Use	7
	Health Care	8
	Network Extension to Remote Areas	8
	Industrial – Warehousing and Manufacturing	9
	Building-to-Building Connectivity – Bridging	9
	Last Mile Data Delivery – Wireless ISP	11
	Mobility	12
	Small Office/Home Office - SOHO	13
	Mobile or Temporary Offices (Mobile Office Networking)	14
	Metro Area Wireless LANs	15
	Public Hotspots	16
	Summary	17
	Key Terms	18
	Review Questions	19
Chapter 2	**Radio Frequency (RF) Fundamentals**	**21**
	Radio Frequency Signals	22
	RF Properties	23
	Amplitude	23
	Frequency	25
	Wavelength	26
	Phase	27
	Polarization	29
	RF Behaviors	32
	Gain	33
	Loss	33
	Reflection	35
	Refraction	36

	Diffraction	36
	Scattering	38
	Absorption	39
	Voltage Standing Wave Ratio (VSWR)	39
	VSWR Measurements	40
	Effects of VSWR	41
	Solutions to VSWR	41
	Intentional Radiator	41
	Equivalent Isotropically Radiated Power (EIRP)	42
	Key Terms	44
	Review Questions	45
Chapter 3	**Radio Frequency (RF) Math**	**47**
	Units of Measure	48
	Watt (W)	48
	Milliwatt (mW)	49
	Decibel (dB)	50
	dBm	55
	dBi	59
	Accurate Measurements	62
	dBd	63
	How 802.11 Radios Measure Signal Strength	64
	RSSI	65
	Conclusions	65
	Key Terms	67
	Review Questions	68
Chapter 4	**Antennas**	**69**
	Principles of Antennas	71
	Types of Antennas	72
	Omnidirectional Antennas	72
	Semi-directional Antennas	77
	Highly-directional Antennas	84
	Line of Sight (LOS)	87
	Fresnel Zone	88
	Free Space Path Loss	96
	Link Budget/System Operating Margin	98
	Fade Margin	101
	Antenna Installation	103
	Placement	103
	Mounting	105

Appropriate Use   117
Orientation   117
Alignment   117
Safety   119
Maintenance   121
FCC Rules Regarding Antennas   125
Integral Antennas No Longer Required In UNII-1   125
Unique Connectors Still Required   126
More Flexibility in Antenna Choice   126
Advanced "Smart" Antennas   127
Key Terms   129
Review Questions   130

Chapter 5   Antenna Accessories   131

RF Amplifiers   132
Common Options   135
Configuration & Management   136
Special Stipulations on Amplifiers   137
RF Attenuators   141
Common Options   143
Placement   143
Grounding Rods/Wires   144
Lightning Arrestors   145
Common Options   147
Installation   150
Fiber Optic Cable   150
RF Splitters   151
Choosing an RF Splitter   154
RF Connectors   157
Choosing an RF Connector   158
RF Cables   160
RF "Pigtail" Adapter Cable   162
Frequency Converter   163
Test Kits   165
Key Terms   167
Review Questions   168

Chapter 6   Spread Spectrum Technology   169

Introducing Spread Spectrum   171
Narrowband Transmission   171
Spread Spectrum Technology   173

Common Uses of Spread Spectrum	176
FCC Specifications	176
Frequency Hopping Spread Spectrum (FHSS)	178
How FHSS Works	178
IEEE FHSS Standards	184
FCC Rules affecting FHSS	184
Direct Sequence Spread Spectrum (DSSS)	186
Direct Sequence Systems	186
DSSS Encoding	191
'Encoding' vs. 'Modulation'	196
Summary of DSSS Encoding	196
Orthogonal Frequency Division Multiplexing	197
How OFDM Works	197
OFDM in 802.11a	199
OFDM in 802.11g	201
Summary of OFDM Encoding	203
Packet Binary Convolutional Code (PBCC)	204
Comparing 802.11 Technologies	205
Narrowband Interference	205
System Cost	207
Co-location	208
Equipment compatibility and availability	211
Data rate & throughput	211
Range	212
Security	213
Key Terms	214
Review Questions	215
Chapter 7 Wireless LAN Infrastructure Devices	**217**
Access Points	220
Access Point Modes	222
Common Options	227
Wireless Bridges	243
Modes	244
Aligning Bridges	245
Common Options	246
Wireless Workgroup Bridges	253
Common Options	255
Summary	256
Wireless Routers	256
Wireless LAN Client Devices	257

PC, CF, and SD Cards 258
PCI and Mini-PCI Adapters 260
USB Adapters 262
PCMCIA-to-PCI Adapters 263
Ethernet & Serial Converters 264
Common Options 264
Wireless Residential Gateways 271
Common Options 273
Configuration and Management 273
Enterprise Wireless Gateways (EWGs) 274
Configuration and Management 276
Enterprise Encryption Gateways (EEGs) 278
Configuration and Management 280
Wireless LAN Switches 280
Configuration and Management 283
Access Points with Phased Array Antennas 284
WLAN Mesh Routers 286
Configuration and Management 289
Power over Ethernet (PoE) Devices 290
Common Options 291
Key Terms 297
Review Questions 298

Chapter 8   Wireless LAN Organizations and Standards   299

Federal Communications Commission 301
License-free Bands 302
Industrial Scientific Medical (ISM) Bands 303
Unlicensed National Information Infrastructure Bands 304
Power Output Rules 305
IEEE 311
IEEE 802.11 Base Standard 312
802.11b Supplement 313
802.11a Supplement 314
802.11g Supplement 314
802.11e Supplement 315
802.11F Recommended Practice 315
802.11i Supplement 316
802.11h Supplement 316
802.11j Supplement 317
802.11d Supplement 318
802.11s Supplement 318

Clause Summary   319
Wi-Fi® Alliance   320
    Wi-Fi Protected Access (WPA™)   321
    Wi-Fi Multimedia (WMM)   322
Key Terms   324
Review Questions   325

Chapter 9   802.11 Network Architecture   327

The Basic Service Set   329
    Basic Service Set Identifier   331
    Extended Service Set Identifier   332
Locating a Wireless LAN   333
    Beacons   333
    Passive Scanning   335
    Active Scanning   336
Joining a Wireless LAN   338
    Authentication   339
    Authentication Methods   339
    Association   342
    802.11 State Machine   343
The Distribution System   344
Roaming   346
Power Management Features   352
    Active Mode   352
    Power Save Mode   353
Key Terms   360
Review Questions   361

Chapter 10   MAC and Physical Layers   363

802.11 Frame Transmission   364
    Wireless Frame Types   365
    Maximum Frame Size   366
    CSMA/CA   367
    Carrier Sense   367
    Interframe Spacing   368
    The Contention Window   371
    Collision Handling (Acknowledgements)   375
Distributed Coordination Function   375
Point Coordination Function   376
    The PCF Process   376
    Interaction of PIFS and DIFS   377

	QoS via 802.11e and WMM	378
	802.11e Supplement	379
	Wireless Multimedia (WMM)	381
	Request to Send/Clear to Send (RTS/CTS)	383
	CTS-to-Self	387
	Fragmentation	387
	Dynamic Rate Selection	389
	Key Terms	391
	Review Questions	392
Chapter 11	**Troubleshooting Wireless LAN Installations**	**393**
	Multipath	394
	Effects of Multipath	395
	Troubleshooting Multipath	399
	Solutions for Multipath	400
	Hidden Node	402
	Diagnosing Hidden Node	403
	Solutions for Hidden Node	404
	Near/Far	406
	Troubleshooting Near/Far	407
	Solutions for Near/Far	408
	Throughput	408
	Co-location Throughput	410
	Interference	413
	Narrowband	413
	All-band Interference	415
	Weather	415
	Range Considerations	418
	Transmission Power	418
	Antenna Type	419
	Environment	419
	Key Terms	420
	Review Questions	421
Chapter 12	**Wireless LAN Security**	**423**
	802.11 Security Methods	426
	Wired Equivalent Privacy (WEP)	426
	Temporal Key Integrity Protocol (TKIP)	428
	802.1X/EAP Framework	431
	WPA	438
	WPA2/802.11i	441

                     Summary   442
               Additional Security Methods   442
                  Filtering   442
                  Proprietary Layer 2 Encryption   443
                  Wireless VPNs   443
                  Application-Layer Encryption (SSL & SSH)   447
                  Captive Portals   450
                  Profile-Based Firewalls   452
                  Summary   452
               Attacks on Wireless LANs   452
                  Eavesdropping   453
                  Encryption Cracking   454
                  RF Jamming   457
                  Wireless Hijacking   459
                  Rogue Access Points   460
                  Penetration Attacks   462
               Corporate Security Policy   464
                  General Security Policy   466
                  Functional Security Policy   467
                  Security Recommendations   468
               Key Terms   473
               Review Questions   475

Chapter 13   **Site Survey Fundamentals**   **477**

               What is a Site Survey?   479
               Preparing for a Site Survey   481
                  Facility Analysis   482
                  Existing Networks   483
                  Area Usage & Towers   486
                  Purpose & Business Requirements   489
                  Bandwidth & Roaming Requirements   491
                  Available Resources   493
                  Security Requirements   495
                  Preparation Exercises   496
                  Preparation Checklist   497
               Site Survey Equipment   498
                  Access Point   499
                  PC Card and Utilities   500
                  Laptops & PDAs   504
                  Paper   505
                  Outdoor Surveys   506

Spectrum Analyzer 507
Protocol Analyzer 510
Site Survey Kit Checklist 511
Conducting a Site Survey 514
Indoor Surveys 514
Outdoor Surveys 515
Before You Begin 515
RF Information Gathering 517
Post-Installation Verification 530
Alternative and Supplemental Methods 531
Site Survey Reporting 538
Report Format 539
Key Terms 545
Review Questions 546

Appendix A   Site Survey Access Point Form   549
Appendix B   Site Survey Questionnaire   559
Index   573

Forward

If it were easy, anyone could do it.

It's a fact. Wireless networking is just plain cool. It's cool to be physically disconnected from everything, yet wirelessly connected to the world. Getting into wireless networking is pretty easy - becoming an expert isn't.

There's a lot to learn to become a wireless LAN guru. The people at the CWNP Program and their associates go out of their way to test, verify, and thoroughly understand the inner workings of protocols, standards, and products so they can pass that information on to network engineers.

Wireless networking is the "cell phone" of this decade. 802.11 networking, a.k.a. Wi-Fi®, became an industry standard in the late 1990s and took off like wildfire. The next major change to wireless networking involved the IEEE 802.11i standard, which addressed security. The Wi-Fi Alliance details how the industry implements 802.11i wireless security and has named the implementation "WPA2".

802.11i adds complexity to previously simplistic WLAN security solutions. There is a reason behind this movement: enterprise organizations haven't been comfortable with the level of enterprise-class security available for wireless LANs. This is surprising considering that most secure enterprise wireless LANs are more secure than most organization's wired networks.

So, what does this mean for wireless network engineers? It means that our jobs get more complex and, hopefully, our salaries or billing rates increase. The fact of the matter is that most organizations want very secure wireless networks, they don't want to assume the responsibility for implementing them, and yet they still want them to be easy to use. Security though, while a necessary evil, rarely equates to ease of use.

My point here is this: to get to the hard stuff, like security and analysis, you have to understand the technology basics and how WLAN products evolved. Knowledge about protocols, standards, RF, networking, electronics, and network analysis is valuable when working with wireless networking equipment. You may not use this knowledge every day, but when you need it, you'll be ready. That's what the CWNA does for you, and the CWNP Program approaches it from a vendor-neutral perspective, discussing solutions you'd find or implement in today's enterprise environments.

Becoming a CWNA is a significant step in the right direction toward attaining WLAN guru status. Following the CWNA, the next steps are CWSP (Security), CWAP (Analysis), and eventually the CWNE (Expert). To reach these goals, you'll need dedication, commitment, intelligence, and persistence. You'll want to continue learning about the wireless industry as well. Protocols and standards will emerge and evolve; new wireless solutions will create contention and confusion. You'll need to understand how they impact the wireless solutions you are proposing or have implemented. At some point, you'll need to figure out if they are viable solutions and consider if it is important to become an expert in them as well.

In working with, and mentoring, many friends over the last decade, I've found that in many cases people begin working on a certification because they think it's interesting or it might help jumpstart their career. They become disillusioned when they find out that certifications are difficult and possibly only the first step in a long list of things to accomplish. Many of my friends completed or nearly completed entry level certifications. Many of them never made it to the higher levels. They received an introductory certification like Novell's CNA®, Microsoft's MCP®, or Cisco's CCNA®, but they made no progress toward showing a prospective employer that they were dedicated to becoming an expert in a certain technology or product. When I talk to them now, they often wonder why they can't obtain better paying or more prominent positions.

It's been my experience that certification really does pay off. It opens the door for opportunities into careers that were previously unattainable, or better yet, careers that didn't exist until someone found out about your level of expertise. However, employers don't owe an engineer a salary or a position because he or she accomplished a certain certification - *the engineer has to earn that*. Having the certification to back up your knowledge is an easy way to make yourself known as an expert to the public and to your peers, managers, and executives. I would not be where I am today if it weren't for the hard work I've put in to becoming certified and specialized in networking and especially wireless networking. For me, the bonus in all of this is that I really love what I do.

An article I read recently in Discover Magazine (March 2005, vol. 26, no. 3, p. 50) about Richard Feynman brought home a valid point concerning knowledge specialization and expertise. Richard Feynman (1918-1988) was a prominent American physicist and made the following statement in a letter he wrote to his daughter, Gweneth, concerning his involvement with the commission investigating the Challenger space shuttle accident in 1986:

> "You Gweneth, were quite right - I have a unique qualification - I am completely free, and there are no levers that can be used to influence me - and I am reasonably straight-forward and honest. There are exceedingly powerful political forces and consequences involved here… I disregard them all and proceed with apparent naïve and single-minded purpose to one end, first why, physically the shuttle failed, leaving to later the question of why humans made apparently bad decisions when they did…"

Wireless networking requires a bit of Feynman's modesty. You need to persevere to understand and implement the best technical solution for your customer, regardless of who that customer may be. You need to be prepared to sift through the deluge of information you gather on a daily basis and turn it into knowledge. You need to be uniquely qualified, reasonably straightforward, and honest.

As far as wireless networking goes, stick with it if it's really what you want to do. If it's not, figure out what it is that you really love to do, and then do it to the best of your ability - the money will follow. Just keep this in mind while you're at it, "If it were easy, anyone could do it."

Joel W. Barrett
Wireless Consulting Systems Engineer
Cisco Systems, Inc.

Preface

As is customary, I would like to begin by thanking Devin Akin and Planet3 for giving me the opportunity to participate in producing this version of the CWNA study guide. Although I've published articles and white papers, this is my first book. This is an ambitious project for a first book, and Devin showed enormous faith in me by asking me to co-author it with him.

I've long said that one of the great things about computer networking is that it never gets stale. You can never sit on your laurels in computer networking because there's always some new technology right around the bend that will make everything you know obsolete. Still, around 1998, it seemed like we had achieved some sort of stasis - 10/100 Ethernet was well-established; gigabit Ethernet was new, but was basically just faster Ethernet; everybody had pretty much figured out how switches fit into the network; and so on.

802.11 blew all of that out of the water. Not only is 802.11 much more complex than any LAN standard that came before it, it is also moving much faster. There have been many new developments in 802.11 since it was ratified: 802.11b, 802.11g, 802.11a, 802.1X, and so on. Each of those standards represents a whole new technology that network administrators and designers must learn about. Keeping up with 802.11's developments has been challenging for me. I hope that this study guide helps make that challenge a little bit easier for the reader.

Like the original CWNA study guide, this study guide aims to give the type of information that a "typical WLAN administrator" would need. Deep technical details that might be needed by a protocol analyst are left for the CWAP curriculum. 802.11 has evolved since the first edition of this book, and the "typical WLAN administrator" has continued to educate himself. Therefore, the type of information that we included in this edition is a little bit more technical than in the previous edition.

One of the challenges in writing a book about 802.11 is that, no matter how hard you try, by the time the book gets to the reader's hands, something is out of date. We've tried to make this book as comprehensive a reference on the current state of 802.11 as we can. Even as new technologies are developed and new standards replace or refine the ones in this book, the basic information about designing WLANs should continue to be true. After all, RF waves are RF waves, when all is said and done.

This book alone only provides a starting point for educating yourself about wireless networking. Wireless networking is a deep field, with many nuances that only experience can teach. This study guide should help a beginner get "over the hump," and should help fill in the gaps for even more experienced WLAN administrators and designers. As always, there are some things that you can only learn by doing.

- Joshua Bardwell

Senior RF Analyst and Technical Instructor
Connect802, Inc

Introduction

This CWNA Official Study Guide is intended first to help prepare you to install, manage, and support wireless networks, and second to prepare you to take and pass the CWNA certification exam (PW0-100). As part of the CWNP Training and Certification program, the CWNA certification forms the foundation on which all CWNP program certifications are based. The CWNA certification is widely recognized as the industry standard for wireless LAN technology certification and prepares the student for a career in advanced wireless LAN technology with the higher levels of certification within the CWNP Program.

Your study of wireless networking will involve bringing together two fascinating worlds of technology, because wireless networks conjoin Radio Frequency (RF) and networking technologies. No study of wireless LANs would be complete without first making sure the student understands the foundations of both RF and local area networking fundamentals.

For that reason, we recommend that you obtain a basic level of networking knowledge, as exhibited in the CompTIA Network+™ certification. If you have achieved other certifications such as the Cisco CCNA, then you most likely already have the understanding of networking technologies necessary to move into wireless.

By purchasing this book, you are taking the first step towards a bright future in the networking world. Why? Because you have just jumped ahead and apart from the rest of the pack by learning wireless networking to complement your existing networking knowledge.

The wireless LAN industry continues to grow faster than any other market segment in networking. Many new careers are presenting themselves in support of the added responsibilities network administrators must deal with when they add wireless LANs to their networks. Studying wireless technology now will enable you to compete effectively in today's marketplace.

Who This Book Is For

This book focuses on the technologies and tasks vital to installing, managing, and supporting wireless networks, based on the exam objectives of the CWNA certification exam. You will learn the wireless technology standards, governing bodies, hardware, RF math, RF behavior, security, troubleshooting, and site survey methodology. After you achieve your CWNA certification, you will find this book to be a concise compilation of the basic knowledge necessary to manage wireless LANs.

The best method of preparation for the CWNA certification exam is to attend an official CWNA training course. A list of training centers offering CWNA training is available from the CWNP website at http://www.cwnp.com. If you prefer to study and prepare at your own pace, then this book and the official practice exam from cwnp.com should adequately prepare you to pass the exam.

New To Wireless

If you've been working on wireline networks – LANs, MANs, WANs, etc. – but not yet taken on wireless, then this book and the subsequent certification exam are great introductions into wireless LAN technology. Be careful not to assume that wireless is just like any other form of networking. While wireless LANs certainly serve as an extension to wired LANs, they are a field of study all their own. An individual can spend many more than the standard 40 hours in a week learning and using wireless LAN technology. With wireless LAN security, design, troubleshooting, protocol analysis, and advanced applications such as voice and video over wireless now clearly in focus, the industry is piling on knowledge requirements that wireless LAN administrators must master quickly in order to keep pace. Wireless LANs are reaching into new areas with each passing month that nobody thought they would ever reach. Even if you're one of the few people who does not have wireless on your LAN, you still need to educate yourself about the implications of wireless technologies, if only to detect unauthorized wireless devices on your network (such as a hacker—or employee—installed access point) and respond appropriately if (or when) they appear. If you work with computer networks, there's simply no avoiding wireless. Wireless is here to stay.

Wireless Experts

If you are experienced in wireless networking already, there is substantial material covered in this book that will benefit you. Most people who attend a CWNA class marvel from the first day about how much they *don't* know. If you have been working with wireless LANs for years, be careful you don't assume that you know all there is to know about them. Because wireless technology is evolving so fast, even experts who spend hours each day studying wireless material in order to stay up-to-date find it difficult to keep up with the pace of wireless technology. An unprecedented number of IEEE 802.11 standards have been proposed in the last three years, and many, such as 802.11g, have been ratified in an unusually short time. In addition, vendors have been very eager to bring these standards to market, in some cases releasing products before the standard is even completed! This book will be kept up-to-date as the wireless industry progresses so that the reader always knows that he is receiving the latest information.

While our program was still in its infancy, we were privileged to have some industry experts take part in our testing. We found out very quickly that their status of "expert" was in question. There is such a broad base of knowledge required to be a wireless expert that it will likely feel overwhelming at times. As you will soon see, this book is geared toward the beginner and intermediate reader alike. We hope that it will take you further than you had expected to go when you first picked it up, and we hope that it will open your eyes to a wonderful new field of study.

RF Experienced

Some of you may have worked with RF for years, perhaps in the military, and have moved into the networking industry. Your knowledge and experience is right on track with the evolution of wireless LAN technology, but you have probably never measured your knowledge of these two technologies by taking a certification exam. This measurement is the purpose of the CWNA certification exam. Fields of study like Electrical Engineering, RF Metrology, Satellite Communications, and others typically provide a solid background in radio frequency fundamentals. In this book, we will address specific topics that you may or may not be familiar with, or you may just have to dust off that portion of your memory. Many people have crossed over from careers in radio frequency to careers in Information Technology (IT), but never dreamed where the two fields of study might meet. Wireless LAN technology is the meeting place.

New to Networking

Finally, if you are stepping into the networking world for the very first time, please make sure you have a basic understanding of networking concepts, and then jump right in! The wireless LAN industry is still growing at a phenomenal rate. Wireless networking is replacing and adding to the mobility of conventional network access methods very quickly. We do not pretend to know which technology will ultimately hold the greatest market share. Instead, we cover all currently available wireless LAN technologies. Some technologies, like 802.11b, hold a tremendous market share presently, and those will be covered at length in this book. Again, as the industry and market place change, so will this book in order to stay current.

How Is This Book Organized?

This Official CWNA Study Guide is organized in the same manner as the official CWNA course is taught, starting with the basic concepts or building blocks and developing your knowledge of the convergence of RF and networking technologies.

Each chapter contains subsections that correspond to the different topics covered on the CWNA exam. Each topic is explained in detail, followed by a list of key terms that you should know after comprehending each chapter. Then, we close each chapter with comprehensive review questions that cause you to apply the knowledge you've just gained to real world scenarios.

Finally, we have a complete glossary of wireless LAN terms for continual reference to you as you use your new wireless LAN knowledge on the job.

What's New in this 3rd Edition?

The third edition of this study guide reflects a major re-examination of the topics and material covered by the CWNA program. Whereas the first and second editions focused primarily on 802.11b, this edition takes into account new standards that have been ratified or that are close to ratification: 802.11a, 802.11g, 802.11e, 802.11f, 802.11i, and 802.11n. The third edition takes into account the July 2004 revisions to the FCC's part 15 rules, which, among other things, modify the rules for adding third-party antennas to 802.11 devices.

Many sections that carried over from previous editions have been expanded, including: decibel math (including more examples and calculation of link budget), spread spectrum modulation and coding, 802.11 architecture (MAC and PHY), and 802.11 security (although in-depth discussion on this topic is more appropriate for CWSP, an overview of WPA and EAP types has been added). The section on site surveying has been expanded to include information on predictive, verification, and automatic site survey tools.

The above list is not comprehensive. Each section of the study guide has been evaluated for relevance and technical accuracy, and numerous—too numerous to list—changes and additions have been made throughout the book.

Why Become CWNA Certified?

Planet3 Wireless, Inc. has created a certification program, not unlike those of Cisco, Novell, and Microsoft, that gives networking professionals a standardized set of measurable wireless LAN skills and employers a standard level of wireless LAN expertise to require of their employees.

Passing the CWNA exam proves you have achieved a certain level of knowledge about wireless networking. Where Cisco and Microsoft certifications prove a given level of knowledge about their products, the CWNA exam is proof of achievement about wireless technology that can be applied to any vendor's products. The wireless LAN industry is still in its infancy, much like the world of networking LANs and WANs was in the early 1990s. Learning wireless networking sets you apart from your peers and your competition.

For some positions, certification is a requirement for employment, advancement, or increases in salary. The CWNP program is positioned to be that certification for wireless networking. Imagine if you had CCIE, MCSE, or CNE in 1993! Advancement in wireless technologies will follow the same steps as other certifications – an increase in responsibilities within your organization, perhaps followed by increases in salary.

How Do You Get CWNA Certified?

You get CWNA certified by taking and passing one exam, exam number
PW0-100. Complete information about the exam, including how to
register for and where to take the exam is available at cwnp.com.

The CWNP program consists of multiple levels of certification, beginning
with CWNA. Once you earn your CWNA, you are then eligible to move
up to CWSP and CWAP. Once you register for the exam, you will be
given complete instructions for where to go and what to bring. For
cancellations, please pay close attention to the procedures, which can be
found at the following URL:

http://www.cwnp.com/certifications/exam_registration/exam_policy.html

The best way to prepare for the CWNA exam is to attend a CWNA
training course or to study at your own pace with this book. The CWNA
practice exam provides you with a good idea of the types of questions that
can be found on the real exam. The official CWNA practice exam and
complete information on available training for the CWNA certification
are both available at www.cwnp.com.

As you prepare for the CWNA exam, and the other, more advanced
CWNP certifications, we highly recommend that you practice with
wireless LAN gear. Because enterprise class wireless LAN equipment
typically has many more advanced features than SOHO class equipment,
we recommend that you purchase at least one access point and two
802.11a/b/g PC Cards for building your skills. Obviously this equipment
can be expensive, but there are some avenues like eBay and used
equipment vendors that can aid in keeping costs at a minimum. SOHO
class equipment can familiarize you with the basic features of wireless
LANs in most cases, but the advanced features typically only come with
more expensive equipment.

CWNA Exam Objectives

The CWNA certification exam covering the CWNA objectives will certify that successful candidates know the fundamentals of RF behavior, can describe the features and functions of wireless LAN components, and have the skills needed to install, configure, and troubleshoot wireless LAN hardware peripherals and protocols. A typical candidate should have the CompTIA Network+ certification or equivalent knowledge, although Network+ certification is not required.

The skills and knowledge measured by this examination are derived from a survey of wireless networking experts and professionals. The results of this survey were used in weighting the subject areas and ensuring that the weighting is representative of the relative importance of the content.

This section outlines the exam objectives for the CWNA exam.

 The objectives for the CWNA exam can change at any time. For the most current objectives visit www.cwnp.com.

Radio Frequency (RF) Technologies – 21%

1.1.   RF Fundamentals

    1.1.1.   Define and explain the basic concepts of RF behavior

- Gain
- Loss
- Reflection
- Refraction
- Diffraction
- Scattering
- VSWR
- Return Loss
- Amplification
- Attenuation

- ° Absorption
- ° Wave propagation
- ° Free-space Path Loss
- ° Delay Spread

1.2.   RF Mathematics

    1.2.1.   Understand and apply the basic components of RF mathematics

- ° Watt
- ° Milliwatt
- ° Decibel (dB)
- ° dBm
- ° dBi
- ° dBd
- ° RSSI
- ° System Operating Margin (SOM)
- ° Fade Margin
- ° Link Budget
- ° Intentional Radiator
- ° Equivalent Isotropically Radiated Power (EIRP)

1.3.   RF Signal and Antenna Concepts

    1.3.1.   Identify RF signal characteristics, the applications of basic RF antenna concepts, and the implementation of solutions that require RF antennas

- ° Visual LOS
- ° RF LOS
- ° The Fresnel Zone
- ° Beamwidths
- ° Azimuth & Elevation
- ° Passive Gain
- ° Isotropic Radiator
- ° Polarization
- ° Antenna Diversity

- Wavelength
- Frequency
- Amplitude
- Phase

1.3.2.   Explain the applications of basic RF antenna types and identify their basic attributes, purpose, and function

- Omni-directional / Dipole antennas
- Semi-directional antennas
- Highly-direction antennas
- Phased array antennas
- Sectorized antennas

1.3.3.   Describe the proper locations and methods for installing RF antennas

- Pole/mast mount
- Ceiling mount
- Wall mount

1.4.   RF Antenna Accessories

1.4.1.   Identify the use of the following wireless LAN accessories and explain how to select and install them for optimal performance within FCC regulations

- Amplifiers
- Attenuators
- Lightning Arrestors
- Grounding Rods/Wires
- RF Cables
- RF Connectors
- RF Signal Splitters

802.11 Regulations and Standards - 12%

2.1.   Spread Spectrum Technologies

2.1.1.   Identify some of the uses for spread spectrum technologies

- Wireless LANs

- ° Wireless PANs
- ° Wireless MANs
- ° Wireless WANs

2.1.2. Comprehend the differences between, and explain the different types of spread spectrum technologies
- ° FHSS
- ° DSSS
- ° OFDM

2.1.3. Identify the underlying concepts of how spread spectrum technology works
- ° Modulation
- ° Coding

2.1.4. Identify and apply the concepts which make up the functionality of spread spectrum technology
- ° Co-location
- ° Channels
- ° Carrier Frequencies
- ° Dwell time & Hop time
- ° Throughput vs. Bandwidth
- ° Communication Resilience

2.2. IEEE 802.11 Standard

2.2.1. Identify, explain, and apply the concepts covered by the IEEE 802.11 standard and the differences between the following 802.11 clauses:
- ° 802.11
- ° 802.11a
- ° 802.11b
- ° 802.11d
- ° 802.11e
- ° 802.11F
- ° 802.11g
- ° 802.11h

       ° 802.11i
       ° 802.11j
       ° 802.11n
       ° 802.11s

2.3.   802.11 Industry Organizations and Their Roles

    2.3.1.   Define the roles of the following organizations in providing direction, cohesion, and accountability within the wireless LAN industry

       ° FCC
       ° IEEE
       ° Wi-Fi Alliance

802.11 Protocols and Devices - 14%

3.1.   802.11 Protocol Architecture

    3.1.1.   Summarize the processes involved in authentication and association

       ° The 802.11 State Machine
       ° Open System and Shared Key Authentication
       ° Association, Reassociation, and Disassociation
       ° Deauthentication
       ° Shared Keys
       ° Certificates and PACs

    3.1.2.   Define, describe, and apply the following concepts associated with wireless LAN service sets

       ° BSS & BSSID
       ° ESS & ESSID/SSID
       ° IBSS
       ° Roaming
       ° Infrastructure Mode
       ° Ad Hoc Mode

    3.1.3.   Explain and apply the following power management features of wireless LANs

- PSP Mode
- CAM Mode
- TIM/DTIM/ATIM

3.2. 802.11 MAC & PHY Layer Technologies

    3.2.1. Describe and apply the following concepts surrounding wireless LAN frames

- 802.11 Frame Format vs. 802.3 Frame Format
- Layer-3 Protocol Support by 802.11 Frames

    3.2.2. Identify methods described in the 802.11 standard for locating, joining, and maintaining connectivity with an 802.11 wireless LAN

- Active Scanning (Probes)
- Passive Scanning (Beacons)
- Dynamic Rate Selection

    3.2.3. Define, describe, and apply 802.11 modes and features available for moving data traffic across the RF medium

- DCF vs. PCF modes
- CSMA/CA vs. CSMA/CD protocols
- RTS/CTS and CTS-to-Self protocols
- Fragmentation
- Wireless Multimedia (WMM) certification

3.3. Wireless LAN Infrastructure and Client Devices

    3.3.1. Identify the purpose of the following wireless LAN infrastructure devices and describe how to install, configure, secure, and manage them

- Access Points
- Wireless LAN Bridges
- Wireless LAN Switches
- PoE Injectors and PoE-enabled Switches
- Residential Wireless Gateways
- Enterprise Wireless Gateways
- Enterprise Encryption Gateways

° Wireless LAN Routers

° Remote Office Wireless Switches

° Wireless LAN Mesh Routers

3.3.2. Describe the purpose of the following wireless LAN client devices and explain how to install, configure, secure, and manage them

° PCMCIA Cards

° USB, CF, and SD Devices

° Serial and Ethernet Converters

° PCI and Mini-PCI Cards

° Card Adapters

° Wireless Workgroup Bridges

802.11 Network Implementation - 21%

4.1.   802.11 Network Design, Implementation, and Management

6.1.1.   Identify technology roles for which wireless LAN technology is appropriate

° Corporate data access and end-user mobility

° Network extension to remote areas

° Building-to-building connectivity - Bridging

° Last-mile data delivery - Wireless ISP

° Small Office / Home Office (SOHO) use

° Mobile office networking

° Educational / Classroom use

° Industrial - Warehousing and Manufacturing

° Healthcare - Hospitals and Offices

° Hotspots - Public Network Access

4.2.   802.11 Network Troubleshooting

6.2.1.   Identify and explain how to solve the following wireless LAN implementation challenges

° Multipath

° Hidden Nodes

- ° Near/Far
- ° Narrowband and Wideband RF Interference
- ° System Throughput
- ° Co-channel and Adjacent-channel Interference
- ° Weather

802.11 Network Security - 16%

5.1.   802.11 Network Security Architecture

    5.1.1.   Identify and describe the strengths, weaknesses, appropriate uses, and appropriate implementation of the following 802.11 security-related items:

- ° Shared Key Authentication
- ° WEP
- ° WPA-PSK
- ° Encryption Algorithms
- ° RC4
- ° AES
- ° Key Management Mechanisms
- ° TKIP
- ° CCMP
- ° Access Control and Authentication
- ° 802.1X/EAP framework
- ° EAP types commonly used with 802.11 WLANs
- ° WPA / WPA2
- ° AAA Support
- ° RADIUS
- ° LDAP Compliant/Compatible
- ° Local Authentication Database
- ° MAC Filters

    5.1.2.   Describe the following types of wireless LAN security attacks, and explain how to identify and prevent them where possible

        ° Eavesdropping

        ° RF jamming (Denial of Service)

        ° Man-in-the-middle

        ° Management Interface Exploits

        ° Encryption Cracking

        ° Hijacking

5.1.3. Describe, explain, and illustrate the appropriate applications for the following client-related wireless security solutions

        ° Role-based Access Control

        ° IPSec VPN

        ° PPTP VPN

        ° Profile-based firewalls

        ° Captive Portal

5.1.4. Describe, explain, and illustrate the appropriate applications for the following wireless LAN system security and management features

        ° Rogue AP detection and/or containment

        ° SNMPv3 / HTTPS / SSH

5.2.   802.11 Network Security Analysis Systems, Devices

5.2.1. Identify the purpose and features of the following wireless analysis systems and explain how to install, configure, integrate, and manage them as applicable

        ° Handheld and Laptop protocol analyzers

        ° Distributed Wireless Intrusion Detection Systems (WIDS)

        ° Remote hardware and software sensors

        ° Handheld RF analyzers

5.3.   802.11 Network Security Policy Basics

5.3.1. Describe the following General Security Policy elements

        ° Risk Assessment

        ° Impact Analysis

        ° Security Auditing

5.3.2. Describe the following Functional Security Policy elements
- ° Baseline Practices
- ° Design and Implementation Practices
- ° Physical Security
- ° Social Engineering
- ° Monitoring, Response, and Reporting

802.11 RF Site Surveying - 16%

6.1. 802.11 Network Site Survey Fundamentals

6.1.1. Explain the importance and processes involved in conducting a complete RF site survey

6.1.2. Explain the importance of and proprietary documentation involved in preparing for an RF site survey
- ° Gathering business requirements
- ° Interviewing managers and users
- ° Defining security requirements
- ° Gathering site-specific documentation
- ° Documenting existing network characteristics
- ° Gathering permits and zoning requirements
- ° Indoor- or Outdoor-specific information

6.1.3. Explain the technical aspects and information collection procedures involved in an RF site survey
- ° Interference sources
- ° Infrastructure connectivity and power requirements
- ° RF coverage requirements
- ° Data capacity requirements
- ° Client connectivity requirements

6.1.4. Describe site survey reporting procedures
- ° Customer reporting requirements
- ° Reporting methodology
- ° Security-related reporting
- ° Graphical documentation

        ° Hardware recommendations and bills of material

6.2.   802.11 Network Site Survey Systems and Devices

    6.2.1.   Identify the equipment, applications, and system features involved in performing automated site surveys

        ° Predictive analysis / simulation applications

        ° Integrated virtual site survey features

        ° Self-managing RF technologies

        ° Passive site survey verification tools and/or applications

    6.2.2.   Identify the equipment and applications involved in performing manual site surveys

        ° Site survey hardware kits

        ° Active site survey tools and/or applications

        ° Passive site survey tools and/or applications

        ° Manufacturer's client utilities

Tips for succeeding on the CWNA Exam

Following are some general tips for success on the CWNA Exam:

- Take advantage of the CWNA Practice exam so you will be familiar with the types of questions that you will see on the real exam.
- Arrive at least 15 minutes earlier than your scheduled exam time, and preferably 30 minutes early, so you can relax and review your study guide one last time.
- Read every question very carefully.
- Do not leave any unanswered questions. These count against your score.

Once you have completed the CWNA exam, you will be provided with a complete Examination Score Report, which shows your pass/fail status section by section. Your test scores are sent to Planet3 Wireless, Inc. within 10 working days. If you pass the exam, you will receive a CWNA Certificate and a welcome email with your CWNP ID number within 3 weeks.

Contact information

We are always eager to receive feedback on our courses and training materials. If you have specific questions about something you have read in this book, please use the information below to contact us.

The CWNP® Program
Planet3 Wireless, Inc.
P.O. Box 20063
Atlanta, Georgia 30325
866-GET-CWNE
404-305-0555
http://www.cwnp.com

Direct feedback via email:
feedback@cwnp.com

Introduction to Wireless LANs

CWNA Exam Objectives Covered:

❖ Identify technology roles for which wireless LAN technology is appropriate

- Corporate data access and end-user mobility

- Network extension to remote areas

- Building-to-building connectivity – Bridging

- Last mile data delivery – Wireless ISP

- Small Office / Home Office (SOHO) use

- Mobile office networking

- Educational / Classroom use

- Industrial – Warehousing and Manufacturing

- Health care – Hospitals and Offices

- Hotspots – Public Network Access

In This Chapter

The Wireless LAN Market

Applications of Wireless LANs

In this section, we will discuss the wireless LAN market, an overview of the past, present, and future of wireless LANs, and an introduction to the standards that govern wireless LANs. We will then discuss some of the appropriate applications of wireless LANs. In closing, we will introduce you to the various organizations that guide the evolution and development of wireless LANs.

Knowledge of the history and evolution of wireless LAN technology is an essential part of the foundational principles of wireless LANs. A thorough understanding of where wireless LANs came from and the organizations and applications that have helped the technology mature will enable you to better apply wireless LANs to your organization or your client's needs.

The Wireless LAN Market

The market for wireless LANs seems to be evolving in a similar fashion to the networking industry as a whole, starting with the early adopters using whatever technology was available. The market has moved into a rapid-growth stage, for which popular standards are providing the catalyst. The big difference between the networking market as a whole and the wireless LAN market is the rate of growth. Wireless LANs allow so many flexibilities in their implementation that it is no wonder they are outpacing every other market sector.

History of Wireless LANs

Spread spectrum wireless networks, like many technologies, came of age under the guidance of the military. The military needed a simple, easily implemented, and secure method of exchanging data in a combat environment. This technology eventually made its way into the private sector. Because of its cost, low data rates, and general complexity, early wireless networks were primarily used in special cases where no other solution would do. For example, one of the first private wireless data networks was ALOHAnet, developed at the University of Hawaii to link sites on different islands.

In the mid-to-late-1990s, several wireless technologies were available, including 802.11 and HomeRF. Although cost and complexity of wireless networking was declining fast, it still remained a niche product due to its low data rates and reliability.

The turning point for wireless occurred in the late 1990s, when three things happened. First, the IEEE ratified 802.11b, which increased the maximum data rate for 802.11 from 2 Mbps to 11 Mbps. The 11 Mbps data rate finally brought wireless technologies on par with wired technologies in terms of their ability to carry data and support many users. Second, the Wi-Fi® Alliance (formerly known as WECA) was formed to certify interoperability of wireless local area network (WLAN) products based on IEEE 802.11 specification. The Wi-Fi Alliance helped to make wireless LANs a household item, thus driving the technology into the enterprise because people want the same wireless connectivity at the workplace. Third, some would argue that Cisco Systems' acquisition of Aironet, a maker of 802.11 products, was just as influential in the success of 802.11. Cisco's brand recognition and marketing power brought 802.11 out of the shadows and into the mainstream.

As the cost of wireless technology declined and the quality increased, it became cost-effective for enterprise companies to integrate wireless segments into their network. Wireless technology offered a relatively inexpensive way for corporate campuses to connect buildings to one another without laying copper or fiber cabling. Today, the cost and complexity of wireless technology is low enough that most businesses can afford to implement wireless segments on their network, if not convert completely to a wireless access network, saving the company time and money while allowing the flexibility of roaming.

Households also are benefiting from the low cost and subsequent availability of wireless LAN hardware. Many people are now creating cost-effective wireless networks that take advantage of the convenience of mobility to create home offices or wireless gaming stations. The sales of household wireless networks now outpace those of traditional wired home networks.

As wireless LAN technology improves, the cost of manufacturing (and thus purchasing and implementing) the hardware continues to fall, and the number of installed wireless LANs continues to increase. The standards that govern wireless LAN operation will increasingly stress interoperability and compatibility. As the number of users grows, lack of compatibility may render a network useless, and the lack of interoperability may interfere with the proper operation of other networks.

Today's Wireless LAN Standards

Wireless LANs transmit using radio frequencies, so they are regulated by the same legal regulations that govern other radio transmitters such as HAM radios. The Federal Communications Commission (FCC) regulates the wireless LAN devices' use of the RF spectrum. Meanwhile, the *Institute of Electrical and Electronics Engineers (IEEE)* defines standards for how RF transmissions can be used to carry data. Several accepted operational standards and drafts in the United States have been created and are maintained by the IEEE.

The IEEE standards are created by groups of people that represent many different organizations, including academics, corporate business, military, and the government. Because standards set forth by the IEEE can have such an impact on the development of technology, the standards can take many years to be created and agreed upon, although ratification of 802.11 standards seems to have accelerated greatly in the last few years, probably due to the extreme demand for 802.11 products.

The standards specific to wireless LANs are covered in great detail in Chapter 8. Because these are the standards upon which the latest wireless LANs are built, a brief overview is provided here.

IEEE 802.11 – the original wireless LAN standard that specifies 1 and 2 Mbps data transfer rates using both 2.4 GHz unlicensed radio frequencies (RF) and infrared light-based transmission technologies. The RF technologies include both frequency hopping spread spectrum (FHSS) and direct sequence spread spectrum (DSSS). This standard was ratified by IEEE in 1997, revised in 1999, corrected again in 2001, and finally reaffirmed in 2003.

IEEE 802.11b – modifies 802.11 2.4 GHz DSSS to include faster data transfer rates up to 11 Mbps This standard was the first to be widely promoted as Wi-Fi® by the Wi-Fi Alliance. 802.11b was ratified by IEEE in 1999 as an amendment to the original IEEE 802.11 standard.

IEEE 802.11a – specifies much faster data transfer rate than 802.11b, but lacks compatibility with IEEE 802.11b. 802.11a uses the 5 GHz UNII frequency bands. This standard was ratified by IEEE in 1999 as an amendment to the original IEEE 802.11 standard. Wi-Fi® product certification has been extended to include 802.11a.

IEEE 802.11g – describes data transfer rates as fast as IEEE 802.11a using the same technologies as, and boasts backward compatibility to, 802.11b, allowing incremental upgrades. The 802.11g standard was ratified by the IEEE in June, 2003. Wi-Fi® certification has been extended to include 802.11g.

Emerging technologies will require standards that describe and define their proper behavior. The challenge for manufacturers and standards-makers alike will be to bring their resources to bear on the problems of interoperability and compatibility.

Applications of Wireless LANs

When computers were first built, only large universities and corporations could afford them. Today you may find three or four personal computers in your neighbor's house. Wireless LANs have taken a similar path, first used by large enterprises, and now available to us all at affordable prices. Wireless LANs have enjoyed a very fast adoption rate due to the many advantages they offer over wired LANs, primarily ubiquitous access and the ability to roam within certain boundaries. In this section, we will discuss some of the most common and appropriate uses of wireless LANs.

Three Main Roles for Wireless LANs

802.11 LANs are usually used in an *access role* in which mobile or portable client stations and an immobile access point communicate with one another and, through the access point, communicate to other networks. Data-link technologies commonly used in a similar access role are Ethernet, DSL, dial-up, and cable.

Sometimes 802.11 LANs are used in a *distribution role*. Wireless bridges may be used to carry the traffic from networks attached to their Ethernet ports. Data-link technologies commonly used for distribution are Ethernet, Frame Relay, and ATM.

Due to a lack of speed and resiliency, wireless networks are not typically implemented in the core of a network—the *core role*. Of course, in small networks, there may be no differentiation between the core, distribution, or access layers of the network. The core layer of a network should be fast, stable, able to handle a tremendous amount of traffic with little difficulty, and experience no down time. Wireless LANs do not typically meet these requirements for an enterprise solution.

Corporate Data Access and End-User Mobility

Figure 1.1 illustrates a wireless LAN made up of client stations connected to an access point, which is connected to a wired LAN.

FIGURE 1.1   Access role of a wireless LAN

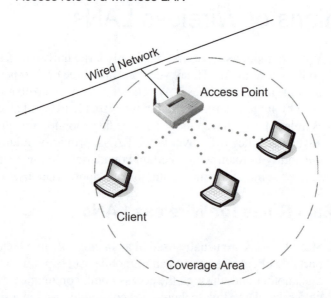

One common usage of wireless LANs is to provide access to corporate resources in areas where wired connectivity would be expensive or inconvenient. In this role, the wireless LAN is simply a means to the end of providing access to the corporate resources—as opposed to a hotspot role, where the wireless LAN could be viewed as the "end" in and of itself.

Wireless LANs offer a specific solution to a difficult problem: mobility. Without doubt, wireless LANs solve a host of problems for corporations and home users alike, but all of these problems stem from the need for freedom from data cables. Cellular solutions have been available for quite some time, offering users the ability to roam while staying connected, but at slow speeds and very high prices. Wireless LANs offer the same flexibility without the disadvantages. Wireless LANs are reasonably fast and inexpensive and can be located almost anywhere.

When considering wireless LANs for use in your network, keep in mind that using them for their intended purpose will provide the best results. Administrators implementing wireless LANs in a core or distribution role should understand exactly what performance to expect before implementing them in this fashion, to avoid having to replace them later. The only distribution role in a corporate network that is definitely appropriate for wireless LANs is building-to-building bridging. In this scenario, wireless *could* be considered as playing a distribution role; however, it will always depend on how the wireless segments are used in the network.

Some Wireless Internet Service Providers (WISPs) use licensed wireless frequencies in a distribution role, but these organizations generally use unlicensed 802.11 frequencies in an access role. For example, the WISP might use a satellite link to get the signal out to a remote access point (licensed frequencies/distribution), and then use 802.11 frequencies to get the signal to the users (unlicensed frequencies/access).

Educational/Classroom Use

Wireless networks are particularly appropriate for classrooms. Although students are not typically mobile during a class (they are sitting in their seats), a wireless network allows students to access resources from their seats, rather than having to use hard-wired workstations. This provides more flexibility in room layout—for example, workstations are sometimes placed facing the wall to avoid having to run cables, forcing students to face away from the teacher. Wireless networks also make it easy for students to take their laptops from class to class.

Health Care

Hospitals and medical offices are another example of the "corporate data access and mobility" application. Doctors' offices use wireless networks in the same ways that other offices do, but health care makes additional demands. Emergency room doctors, for example, are extremely mobile and need rapid access to information. A handheld wireless PC can provide access to medical databases and patient records wherever the doctor might be. Hospitals provide a unique challenge to 802.11 networks, since they often already use proprietary wireless technology that may interfere with 802.11 equipment or vice-versa.

Network Extension to Remote Areas

Wireless networks can serve as an extension to a wired network. There may be cases in which extending the network would require installing additional cabling that is cost prohibitive. You may discover that hiring cable installers and electricians to build out a new section of office space for the network is going to cost tens of thousands of dollars. Or in the case of a large warehouse, the distances may be too great to use Category 5 (Cat5) cable for an Ethernet network. Fiber might have to be installed, requiring an even greater investment of time and resources. Installing fiber also might involve upgrades to existing edge switches.

Wireless LANs can be implemented easily to provide seamless connectivity to remote areas within a building, as illustrated by the floor plan image in Figure 1.2. Because only a modest amount of wiring is necessary to install a wireless LAN, the costs of hiring installers and purchasing Ethernet cable might be completely eliminated.

FIGURE 1.2   Network Extension

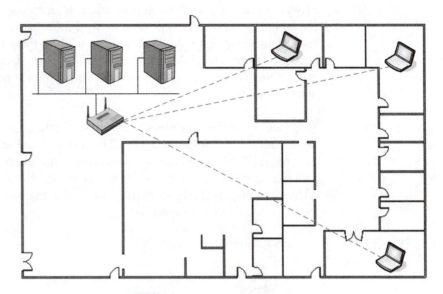

Industrial – Warehousing and Manufacturing

Industrial applications such as warehouses and manufacturing facilities are one common example of the "network extension" application. These facilities often are not wired for Ethernet, and adding wiring would be difficult. A wireless network can be used to extend coverage to the entire warehouse. This type of environment presents unique challenges to a wireless network, since there can be performance issues caused by a lot of metal and RF interference (discussed in Chapter 11).

Building-to-Building Connectivity – Bridging

In a campus environment or an environment with as few as two adjacent buildings, there may be a need to have the network users in each building have direct access to the same computer network. In the past, this type of access and connectivity would be accomplished by running cables underground from one building to another or by renting expensive leased lines from a local telephone company.

Using wireless LAN technology, equipment can be installed easily and quickly to allow two or more buildings to be part of the same network without the expense of leased lines or the need to dig up the ground between buildings. With the proper wireless antennas, many buildings can be linked together on the same network. Certainly there are limitations to using wireless LAN technology, as there are in any data-connectivity solution. However the flexibility, speed, and cost-savings that wireless LANs introduce to the network administrator make them indispensable.

There are two different types of building-to-building connectivity. The first is called point-to-point (PTP). The second is called point-to-multipoint (PTMP). Point-to-point links are wireless connections between only two buildings, as illustrated in Figure 1.3. PTP connections often use semi-directional or highly directional antennas at each end of the link (discussed in Chapter 4).

FIGURE 1.3   Building-to-building connectivity

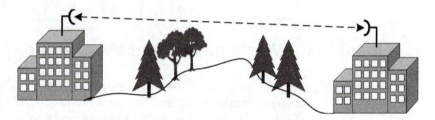

Point-to-multipoint links are wireless connections between three or more buildings, typically implemented in a "hub and spoke" or star topological fashion, where one building is the central focus point of the network. This central building would house the core network, Internet connectivity, and the server farm. Point-to-multipoint links between buildings typically use omni-directional antennas in the central "hub" building and semi-directional antennas on each of the outlying "spoke" buildings.

There are many ways to implement these two basic types of connectivity, as you will undoubtedly see over the course of your career as a wireless LAN administrator or consultant. However, no matter how the implementations vary, they all fall into one of the two previously mentioned categories.

Last Mile Data Delivery – Wireless ISP

Wireless Internet Service Providers (WISPs) are now taking advantage of recent advances in wireless technology to offer last mile data delivery service to their customers. "Last mile" refers to the communication infrastructure—wired or wireless—that exists between the central office of the telecommunications company (telco) or cable company and the end user. Currently the telcos and cable companies own their last mile infrastructure, but with the broadening interest in wireless technology, WISPs are now creating their own wireless last mile delivery service, as illustrated in Figure 1.4.

FIGURE 1.4   Last Mile Service

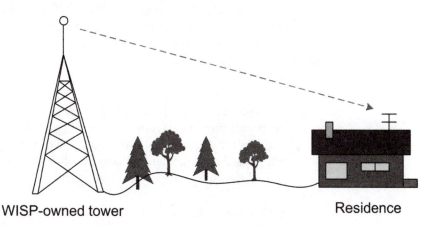

WISP-owned tower   Residence

Consider the case in which both the cable companies and telcos are encountering difficulties expanding their networks to offer broadband connections to more households or businesses. If you live in a rural area, chances are you do not have access to a broadband connection (cable modem or xDSL) and probably will not for quite some time. It is much more cost effective for WISPs to offer wireless access to these remote locations because WISPs will not encounter the same costs a cable company or telco would incur to install the necessary equipment.

WISPs have their own unique set of challenges. Just as xDSL providers have problems going farther than 18,000 feet (5.7 km) from the central office and cable providers have issues with the cable being a shared medium to users, WISPs have problems with rooftops, trees, mountains, lightning, towers, and many other obstacles to connectivity. Certainly WISPs don't have a fail-proof solution, but they have the capability to offer broadband access to users that other, more conventional technologies cannot reach.

Mobility

As an access layer solution, wireless LANs cannot replace wired LANs in terms of data rates (for example, IEEE 802.3 Ethernet at 100 Mbps full duplex versus IEEE 802.11a/g at 54Mbps half-duplex). A wireless environment uses intermittent connections and has higher error rates over what is usually a narrower bandwidth. As a result, applications and messaging protocols designed for the wired world sometimes operate poorly in a wireless environment. The wireless expectations of end users and IT manager are set by the performance and behaviors of their wired networks. What wireless LANs do offer is an increase in mobility (as can be seen in Figure 1.5) as the trade-off for throughput and network reliability.

For example, a parcel delivery company uses wireless technology to update parcel-tracking data immediately upon the arrival of the delivery vehicle. As the driver parks at the dock, the driver's computer has already logged onto the network and transferred the day's delivery data to the central network.

In another example, a nurse in a hospital can wheel a cart of wireless diagnostic equipment into a patient's room and immediately begin monitoring the patient's vital statistics, without having to plug into the hospital's wired network. The patient's information is logged to a computer database automatically.

FIGURE 1.5   Mobility

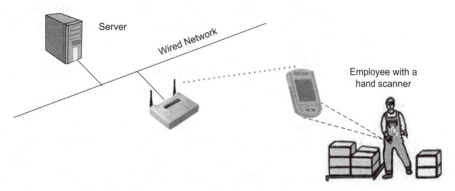

Finally, in warehousing and manufacturing facilities, wireless networks are used to track the storage locations and disposition of products. This data is then synchronized in the central computer for the purchasing and shipping departments. Handheld wireless scanners are becoming commonplace in organizations with employees who move around within their facility processing orders and inventory.

In each of these cases, wireless networks have created the ability to transfer data without requiring the time and manpower to input the data manually at a wired terminal. Wireless connectivity also has eliminated the need for such user devices to be connected using wires that would otherwise get in the way of operations.

Wireless LANs allow users to *roam,* or move physically from one area of wireless coverage to another without losing connectivity or the quality of the connection, just as a mobile telephone customer is able to roam between cellular coverage areas. In larger organizations, where wireless coverage spans large areas, roaming capability has significantly increased productivity simply because users remain connected to the network away from their main workstations.

Small Office/Home Office - SOHO

As an IT professional, you may have more than one computer at your home. And if you do, these computers are most likely networked together so you can share files, a printer, or a broadband connection.

This type of configuration also is utilized by many businesses that have only a few employees. These businesses need to share information between users and a single Internet connection for efficiency and greater productivity.

For these applications – small office-home office, or SOHO – wireless LANs are a very simple and effective solution. Figure 1.6 illustrates a typical SOHO wireless LAN solution. SOHO wireless devices are especially beneficial when office workers want to share a single Internet connection. The alternative, of course, is running wires throughout the office to interconnect all of the workstations. Many small offices are not outfitted with pre-installed Ethernet ports, and only a very small number of houses are wired for Ethernet networks. Trying to retrofit these places with Cat5 cabling usually results in creating unsightly holes in walls and ceilings. With a wireless LAN, users can be interconnected easily and neatly with enough bandwidth to perform useful tasks.

FIGURE 1.6   SOHO Wireless LAN

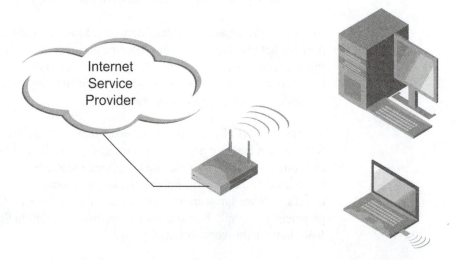

Mobile or Temporary Offices (Mobile Office Networking)

Mobile or temporary offices or classrooms allow users to pack up their computer equipment quickly and move to another location. Due to overcrowded classrooms, many schools now use temporary mobile classrooms. These classrooms usually consist of large, movable trailers that are used while more permanent structures are built. In order to extend the computer network to these temporary buildings, aerial or underground cabling would have to be installed at great expense. Wireless LAN connections from the main school building to the mobile classrooms allow for flexible configurations at a fraction of the cost of alternative cabling. A simple example of connecting remote classroom buildings using wireless LAN connectivity is illustrated in Figure 1.7.

Temporary office spaces also benefit from being networked with wireless LANs. As companies grow, they often find themselves with a shortage of office space, and need to move some workers to a nearby location, such as an adjacent office or an office on another floor of the same building. Installing Cat5 or fiber cabling for these short periods of time is not cost-effective, and usually the owners of the building do not allow removal of the installed cables. With a wireless network, the components can be packed up and moved to the next location quickly and easily.

FIGURE 1.7   A school with mobile classrooms

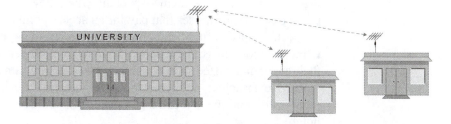

Many groups might use movable networks effectively, including the Super Bowl, the Olympics, circuses, carnivals, fairs, festivals, construction companies, and others. Wireless LANs are well suited to these types of environments.

Metro Area Wireless LANs

Although the coverage area of a single 802.11 access point is only about 100 to 300 feet in an indoor environment, and about 1000 feet in an outdoor environment with line of sight, these limitations have not stopped some entrepreneurs from trying to blanket metropolitan areas with 802.11 coverage and then sell network access. This type of service is intended to provide a high-bandwidth alternative to cellular data service, but so far users seem reluctant to pay for it. Unlike cellular service, which can be used to make phone calls when it is not being used for data, metro wireless LANs have relatively limited use (realistically, how often do you want to check your email while you're walking down the street?). In addition, the number of access points required to provide good coverage over a metropolitan area is large. This requirement results in significant capital outlay that requires a correspondingly large subscriber base in order to achieve profitability. As a result, no metro wireless LAN provider stands out as particularly successful. The best commercial results seem to occur when a city or municipality provides the resources to buy the equipment as a public service for its constituents, and then recoups the cost through tax revenue or other mandatory payments.

Public Hotspots

Public hotspots have been simultaneously one of the most successful and most unsuccessful 802.11 applications. They have been successful at generating a great deal of positive press for 802.11 and good will among the customers who use them (especially when they're free), but there are many cases of businesses that pay for an access point and a DSL connection only to find that nobody is interested in paying them enough to recoup those costs. Few people want to pay $40 per month to check their email at a coffee shop when they could do the same thing at home or work. Nevertheless, public hotspots are popular to business travelers and others who don't have local, high-speed Internet access at the airport or a hotel.

An alternative business model suggests giving the wireless Internet access for free, and then making back your money on additional sales from those who are attracted by the free access.

Summary

Wireless technology has come a long way since its simple military implementations. The popularity and level of technology used in wireless LANs continues to grow at an incredible rate. Wireless LAN equipment manufacturers have created many solutions for our varying wireless networking needs. The convenience, popularity, availability, and cost of wireless LAN hardware provide us all with many different solutions.

With the explosive expansion of wireless technology, manufacturers, and hardware, the role of organizations such as the FCC, IEEE, and the Wi-Fi Alliance will become increasingly important to the removal of barriers of operation between solutions. The laws put in place by regulatory organizations like the FCC, along with the standards provided by promotional and other organizations like IEEE and the Wi-Fi Alliance, will focus the wireless LAN industry and provide a common path for it to grow and evolve over time.

Key Terms

Before taking the exam, you should be familiar with the following terms:

access layer

core layer

distribution layer

FCC

IEEE

IEEE 802.11

IEEE 802.11a

IEEE 802.11b

IEEE 802.11g

last mile

SOHO

WISP

Review Questions

1. Explain the main differences between core, distribution, and access layers of the network, and explain which layer of the network is best suited for 802.11 technologies and why.

2. What was the effect of the Wi-Fi Alliance on the wireless LAN market, and why is this effect important to the future of wireless LAN technologies?

3. Name and describe five common applications for wireless LANs, and explain why the use of wireless LANs makes each of these applications possible, or more efficient than they would be using traditional wired networking.

4. Explain the difference between "mobility" and "portability" as these terms apply to the use of wireless LAN technologies. Describe an application of each.

5. What are the differences between 802.11, 802.11b, 802.11g, and 802.11a? What are their similarities? Which technologies are compatible on the same network? Why?

Radio Frequency (RF) Fundamentals

CWNA Exam Objectives Covered:

❖ Define and apply the basic concepts of RF behavior

- Gain (Amplification)
- Loss (Attenuation)
- Reflection
- Refraction
- Diffraction
- Scattering
- VSWR
- Return Loss
- Absorption
- Wave Propagation

❖ Understand RF signal characteristics, the applications of basic RF antenna concepts, and the implementation of solutions that require RF antennas.

- Frequency
- Wavelength
- Amplitude
- Phase
- Polarization

❖ Understand and apply the basic components of RF mathematics

- Intentional Radiator
- Equivalent Isotropically Radiated Power (EIRP)

In This Chapter

Radio Frequency Signals

RF Properties

RF Behaviors

Voltage Standing Wave Ratio (VSWR)

Intentional Radiator

Equivalent Isotropically Radiated Power (EIRP)

In a wired LAN, the electrical signal travels predictably; it propagates within the wire, with little interference. By contrast, the RF signals used in a WLAN propagate in a much more complex manner, and can be modified in many ways that are not relevant to a wired LAN signal. To understand the propagation of signals in a wireless LAN, an administrator must have a solid foundation in the fundamentals of radio frequency (RF) theory. In this chapter we will discuss the properties of RF radiation and how its behavior in certain situations can affect the performance of a wireless LAN. This knowledge can be used to answer such questions as, "why do stations lose signal whenever they go behind the bookshelf," and "why do I get good signal strength in the hallway, but lose signal strength as soon as I go into a room?"

Radio Frequency Signals

RF signals are high frequency alternating current (AC) signals composed of electromagnetic energy. RF signals are generated as electrical energy by the transmitting radio, passed along a copper wire to the antenna, and then radiated into the air by the antenna. The antenna converts the wired signal to a wireless signal, and vice versa.

If you can imagine dropping a rock into a still pond (Figure 2.1) and watching the concentric ripples flow away from the point where the rock hits the water, then you have an idea of how RF propagates from an antenna. Understanding the behavior of these RF waves is an important part of understanding why and how wireless LANs function. Without this base of knowledge, an administrator would be unable to locate proper installation locations of equipment, and would not understand how to troubleshoot a problematic wireless LAN.

 Since humans don't have senses that are capable of directly perceiving RF energy, when we discuss RF energy, we must resort to analogies. In many cases, these analogies don't fully capture the nuances of what happens to the RF energy, and an RF engineer might take issue with the analogies. But remember that our goal is to give the average network administrator enough knowledge to maintain his or her network, not to make him into an RF engineer.

FIGURE 2.1   Rock into a pond

RF Properties

All radio frequency signals have the properties of *amplitude*, *frequency*, *wavelength*, *phase*, and *polarity*.

Amplitude

In some ways, waves of RF energy are analogous to sound waves. Sound waves are changes in pressure of air. The cone of a loudspeaker creates sound waves by moving back and forth. As it moves forward, it pushes on nearby air molecules, which push on other molecules, and so on, creating a propagating wave front of high pressure. As the loudspeaker cone moves backward, it creates a similar area of negative pressure, which also propagates away from the loudspeaker cone.

With RF waves, instead of a speaker cone vibrating in a loudspeaker, causing waves of high and low air pressure, we have electrons vibrating in an antenna, causing waves of high and low pressure. Physicists don't really know what the medium for electromagnetic energy is. Sound waves move through air, but, as far as we can tell, electromagnetic waves are unique in that they seem to propagate without any medium at all.

Fortunately, as network engineers and not physicists, we don't need to worry about that.

In the same way that we can measure the change in pressure caused by a passing sound wave, we can measure the change in RF energy caused by a passing RF wave. This change is known as the *amplitude* of the signal. The amplitude of an RF signal is analogous to a voltage level in an electrical signal. Higher amplitude signals are more likely to show high signal strength when they are received by an 802.11 station. Although watts are units of power and volts are units of amplitude, we would expect that a station using a higher transmit power (say, 100 mW) would transmit signals with a higher amplitude (voltage) than a station using a lower transmit power (e.g., 30 mW).

FIGURE 2.2   RF Signal Amplitude

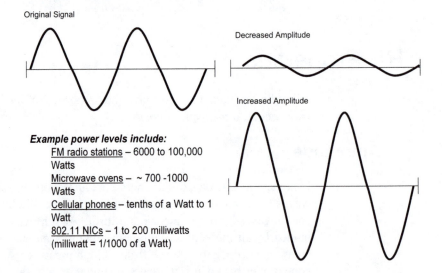

Original Signal

Decreased Amplitude

Increased Amplitude

Example power levels include:
FM radio stations – 6000 to 100,000 Watts
Microwave ovens – ~ 700 -1000 Watts
Cellular phones – tenths of a Watt to 1 Watt
802.11 NICs – 1 to 200 milliwatts
(milliwatt = 1/1000 of a Watt)

Amplitude is the most basic quality of an RF signal. Other qualities of the signal, such as frequency, wavelength, and phase, are all based on variation of the signal's amplitude over time. One quality, polarity, is independent of the signal's amplitude.

Practical Use

The higher the amplitude of an RF signal, the stronger the signal strength an 802.11 receiver will see. Higher amplitude signals can go farther before they become so weak as to be unreceivable. Amplitude can be increased or decreased by increasing or decreasing the power output of a transmitter. As a rule of thumb, an 802.11 transmitter should use just enough power, but not too much.

Frequency

A signal that doesn't change cannot convey any information. Therefore, in order to encode data, it is necessary to change some quality of the signal. Since amplitude is the most basic quality of an RF signal, information is conveyed by changing the amplitude of the RF signal over time. This is referred to as an *alternating current* (AC) signal. By contrast, a signal whose amplitude doesn't change at all over time is referred to as a *direct current* (DC) signal.

FIGURE 2.3   RF Signal Frequency & Wavelength

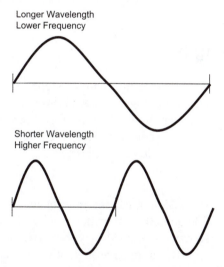

Transmission and reception are easier when the signal oscillates with a more or less regular rhythm. The time between one peak in the signal's amplitude and the next peak is constant from peak to peak. The number of times per second that the signal's amplitude peaks is the frequency of the signal. Frequency is measured in Hertz (abbreviated as Hz). 802.11 transmissions operate at frequencies of around 2.4 or 5.8 GHz (1 GHz = 1,000,000,000 Hz or 1 billion cycles per second). In reality, an 802.11

signal is not perfectly fixed at one particular frequency, but modulates slightly around a central frequency. Again, since a change in the signal is required to convey information, it would be impossible to transmit data if the signal were fixed at one frequency. The slight modulations around the central frequency are interpreted as ones and zeros.

Practical Use

Since signals that oscillate at different frequencies are less likely to interfere with each other, putting transmitters on different frequencies is a common way to increase the number of stations that can coexist in an area. Of course, two stations that want to talk to each other must transmit and receive on the same frequency. Finally, 802.11 network engineers are constrained by the FCC's limits on what frequencies can be used. The 2.4 GHz ISM band (used by 802.11, 802.11b, and 802.11g) and the 5 GHz UNII bands (used by 802.11a) are two sets of frequency ranges that the FCC allows the public to use. Frequencies outside of those ranges require licensing.

Wavelength

The wavelength of an RF signal is a function of the signal's frequency and its propagation speed through space. If a signal's wave front is propagating through space at a certain speed, and we know the amount of time between each peak, then we can calculate how far the signal will have traveled from one peak to the next. That distance is the signal's wavelength.

In a vacuum, RF energy propagates at the speed of light, or about 300,000,000 meters per second. In the earth's atmosphere, it propagates somewhat more slowly, but 300,000 m/s is often used as an approximation. Through other media, electromagnetic energy is slowed enough that the speed of light is no longer a good approximation, and more accurate numbers should be used. For example, in twisted-pair Ethernet cables, electrical signals propagate at about two-thirds the speed of light.

If we assume that an RF signal is propagating at the speed of light, then its wavelength and frequency can be calculated as follows:

wavelength (m) = 300,000,000 m/s / frequency (Hz)

By rearranging this formula, we can calculate frequency from wavelength:

frequency (Hz) = 300,000,000 m/s / wavelength (m)

Therefore, an 802.11 signal with a frequency of 2.4 GHz, or 2,400,000,000 Hz, has a wavelength of:

wavelength = 300,000,000 m/s / 2,400,000,000 Hz
wavelength = 0.125 m
wavelength = 12.5 cm

Practical Use

The most direct way that we interact with wavelength is through the antennae on most 802.11b access points (AP). Antennae are most receptive to signals that have a wavelength equal to the length of the antenna's element. Antenna elements of one-half and one-quarter wavelength are the next best choice. If you measure the length of the antenna on your AP, keep in mind that it is the length of the antenna's internal element that matters, not the length of the rubber or plastic outer sheath (which is invisible to 2.4 GHz radiation).

Phase

Phase is a method of expressing the relationship between the amplitudes of two RF signals that have the same frequency. Phase is measured in degrees (like the degrees of a compass, not the degrees of a thermometer).

If two signals are aligned so that they both reach their peak at the exact same time, we say that they have zero degrees of phase separation. They are completely in phase. If the signals are aligned so that one reaches its peak at the exact same time that the other reaches its trough (lowest amplitude), we say that they have 180 degrees of phase separation. They are completely out of phase. All other possible relationships between the amplitudes of the two signals fall somewhere between these two extremes and have corresponding phase measurements. For example, if the first signal reaches its peak just as the second signal is halfway between its peak and its trough, the signals would be 90 degrees out of phase.

FIGURE 2.4 RF Signal Phase

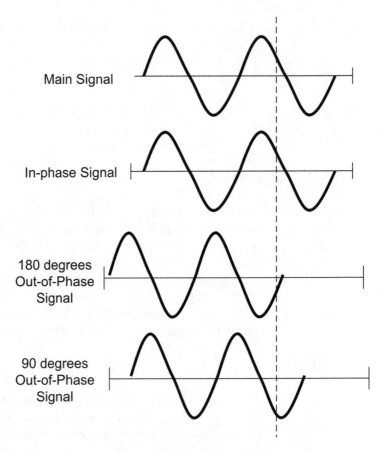

To the WLAN engineer, phase is significant because two signals that are in phase add their energy together, resulting in a stronger signal. Two signals that are 180 degrees out of phase completely cancel each other out, resulting in a null. Signals that are partially in or out of phase strengthen or weaken each other proportionally to their phase relationship.

Although it's not necessary for a WLAN administrator to understand RF signaling to this level, it is interesting to point out that phase is the quality of the signal that is usually manipulated in order to convey information. Early RF transmitters manipulated the signal's amplitude (known as Amplitude Modulation, or AM), which was very simple to build, but not very resistant to corruption. Amplitude Modulation also had limited data rates. Today's transmitters usually use Phase Modulation, which manipulates the signal's phase relative to a reference sine wave. For more information, search the web on the terms "amplitude modulation," "frequency modulation," and "phase modulation."

Practical Use

You probably won't interact directly with the phase of an RF signal, as you would with the frequency or wavelength. Phase becomes relevant when you troubleshoot problems such as multipath interference, where the phase difference of two overlapping signals cancels them out, causing a "dead zone" in the network coverage.

Polarization

A radio wave is actually made of up two fields, one electric and one magnetic. These two fields are on planes perpendicular to each other, as shown in Figure 2.5.

FIGURE 2.5   E-planes and H-planes

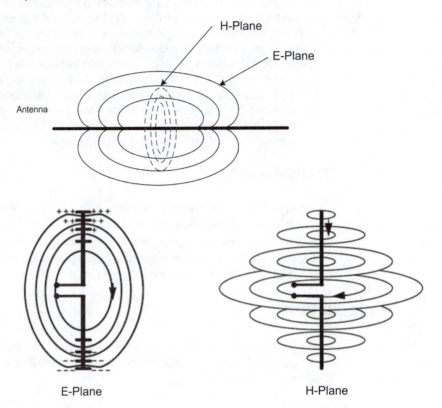

The sum of the two fields is called the electromagnetic field. In the
process known as *oscillation*, energy is transferred back and forth from
one field to the other. The plane that is parallel with the antenna element
is referred to as the "E-plane," whereas the plane that is perpendicular to
the antenna element is referred to as the "H-plane." We are interested
primarily in the electric field since its position and direction with
reference to the Earth's surface (the ground) determines wave
polarization.

Polarization is the physical orientation of the antenna in a horizontal or
vertical position. The electric field is parallel to the radiating elements
(the antenna element is the metal part of the antenna that is doing the
radiating); therefore, if the antenna is vertical, then the polarization is
vertical.

Horizontal polarization – the electric field is parallel to the ground

Vertical polarization – the electric field is perpendicular to the ground

Vertical polarization, which is typically used in wireless LANs, is perpendicular to the Earth's plane. Notice the dual antennas sticking up vertically from most any access point – these antennas are vertically polarized in that position. Horizontal polarization is parallel to the Earth. Figure 2.6 illustrates the effects polarization can have when antennae are not aligned correctly. Antennae that are not polarized in the same way are not able to communicate with each other effectively.

FIGURE 2.6   Polarization

Visible light shining through slits in two pieces of cardboard

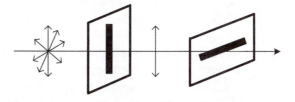

RF radiation transferred between two antennas

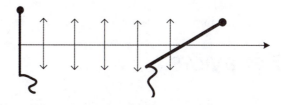

In Figure 2.6, the top part of the diagram shows light shining through two pieces of cardboard with slits cut in them. The direction of the slit represents the polarization of an antenna. Light shining through the first piece of cardboard represents the signal that would be transmitted by that antenna. Light shining through the second piece of cardboard represents the amount of signal that will be received by the second antenna. In this orientation, notice that very little of the transmitted light will be received, but if the antennae were oriented in the same direction, nearly all of the transmitted light would be received.

Practical Use

The designers of the antennae for PCMCIA cards face a real problem. It is not easy to form antennae onto the small circuit board inside the plastic cover that sticks off the end of the PCMCIA card. The polarization of PCMCIA cards and that of access points is sometimes not the same, which is why turning your laptop in different directions sometimes improves reception. PDAs, which usually have a vertically-oriented PCMCIA card, sometimes exhibit good reception in areas where laptops, which usually have a horizontally-oriented PCMCIA card, exhibit bad reception. External, detachable antennae mounted vertically with Velcro to the laptop computer almost always show great improvement over the snap-on antennae included with most PCMCIA cards. In areas where there are a high number of PCMCIA card users, it is sometimes helpful to orient access point antennae horizontally for better reception.

As you consider the effects of polarization on an RF signal, it's important to realize that polarization is not an all-or-nothing thing. For example, matching polarization is very important in a long distance point-to-point link using highly directional antennas. On the other hand, polarization is not as important in indoor links since, even if a signal is polarized in a certain plane, the many reflections that exist in an indoor environment will probably not maintain that polarization. Even if the receiver is not in polarization with the transmitter, there's a good chance the receiver will be in polarization with one of the reflections.

RF Behaviors

Small things can affect an RF signal in unexpected ways. Things as small as a connector not being tight enough, or a slight impedance mismatch on the line, can cause erratic behavior and undesirable results. After transmission, the RF signal can be modified in various ways as it interacts with the environment. The following sections describe these types of behaviors and what can happen to radio waves as they are transmitted.

Gain

Gain, illustrated in Figure 2.7, is the term used to describe an increase in an RF signal's amplitude. Gain can be active, such as when a powered RF amplifier is used to add energy to a signal before transmission, or it can be passive, such as when a high-gain antenna is used to focus the energy of a signal during transmission to increase its power within the beam.

FIGURE 2.7   Power Gain

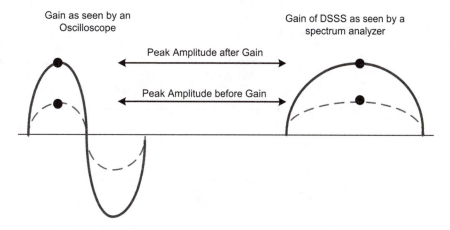

Passive processes also can cause gain after signal transmission. For example, reflected RF signals can combine in phase with the main signal to increase the resultant signal's strength. Increasing the RF signal's strength may have a positive or negative result. Typically, more power is better, but there are cases, such as when a transmitter is radiating power very close to the legal power output limit, where added power would be a serious problem.

Loss

Loss describes a decrease in signal amplitude (Figure 2.8). Many things can cause RF signal loss, both while the signal is still in the cable as a high frequency AC electrical signal and when the signal is propagated as radio waves through the air by the antenna. Resistance of cables and connectors causes loss because of the conversion of the AC electrical signal to heat. Impedance mismatches in the cables and connectors can cause power to be reflected back toward the source. Since some energy is reflected back toward the transmitter, less energy is available to be transmitted, causing a reduction in signal amplitude. As an RF wave moves through any medium, such as a wall, a person, or even the air, some of its energy is lost. Some mediums cause significantly more loss than others—for example, anything containing water will be highly absorptive to 2.4 GHz energy. Loss can be intentionally injected into a circuit with an RF attenuator, which is an accurate resistor that converts high frequency AC to heat in order to reduce signal amplitude at that point in the circuit.

FIGURE 2.8   Power Loss

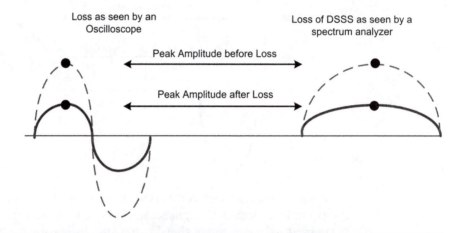

Loss as seen by an Oscilloscope

Loss of DSSS as seen by a spectrum analyzer

Peak Amplitude before Loss

Peak Amplitude after Loss

There are many things that can affect an RF signal between the transmitter and receiver. Gains or losses must be quantifiable in order to be relevant to the implementation of wireless LANs. Chapter 3 will cover quantifiable loss and gain and how to calculate and compensate for them.

Being able to measure and compensate for loss in an RF connection or circuit is important because radios have a receive sensitivity threshold. A sensitivity threshold is defined as the point at which a radio can clearly distinguish a signal from background noise. Since a receiver's sensitivity is finite, the transmitting station must transmit a signal with enough amplitude that the signal is recognizable at the receiver, even after the losses that will inevitably occur during transmission. If excessive losses occur between the transmitter and receiver, the problem must be corrected by removing the objects causing loss, increasing the transmission power, or making the receiver more sensitive.

Gain and loss are measured in units called *decibels* (dB). The specifics of working with decibels are covered in Chapter 3.

Reflection

Reflection, as illustrated in Figure 2.9, occurs when a propagating electromagnetic wave strikes an object that has very large dimensions in comparison to the wavelength of the propagating wave. Reflections occur from the surface of the earth, buildings, walls, and many other obstacles. If the surface is smooth, the reflected signal may remain intact, though there is some loss due to absorption and scattering of the signal.

FIGURE 2.9   Reflection

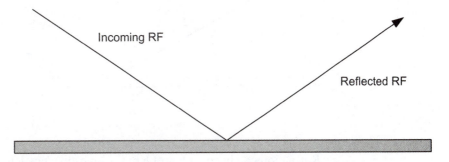

RF signal reflection can cause serious problems for wireless LANs. This reflecting of the main signal from many objects in the area of the transmission is referred to as *multipath*. Multipath can have severe adverse effects on a wireless LAN, such as degrading or canceling the main signal, and causing holes or gaps in the RF coverage area. Surfaces such as lakes, metal roofs, metal blinds, metal doors, and others can cause severe reflection, and hence, multipath.

Reflection of this magnitude is never desirable and typically requires special functionality (antenna diversity) within the wireless LAN hardware to compensate for it.

Refraction

Refraction describes the bending of a radio wave as it passes through a medium of different density. As an RF wave passes into a denser medium (like a pool of cold air lying in a valley), the wave will be bent such that its direction changes. When passing through such a medium, some of the wave will be reflected away from the intended signal path, and some will be bent through the medium in another direction, as illustrated in Figure 2.10.

FIGURE 2.10   Refraction

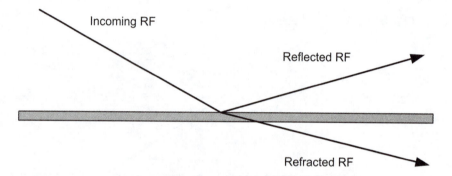

Refraction can become a problem for long-distance RF links. As atmospheric conditions change, the RF waves may change direction, diverting the signal away from the intended target.

Diffraction

Diffraction occurs when the radio path between the transmitter and receiver is obstructed by a surface that has sharp irregularities or an otherwise rough surface. At high frequencies, diffraction, like reflection, depends on the geometry of the obstructing object and the amplitude, phase, and polarization of the incident wave at the point of diffraction.

Diffraction is commonly confused, and improperly used interchangeably, with *refraction*. Care should be taken not to confuse these terms. Diffraction describes a wave bending around an obstacle (Figure 2.11), whereas refraction describes a wave bending as it travels from a medium of one density to a medium of a different density. Taking the rock in the pond example from the beginning of the chapter, now consider a small twig sticking up through the surface of the water near where the rock hit the water. As the ripples hit the stick, they would be blocked to a small degree, but to a larger degree, the ripples would bend around the twig. This illustration shows how diffraction causes RF signal with an obstacle in its path to behave, depending on the makeup of the obstacle. If the object was large or jagged enough, the wave might not bend, but rather might be blocked.

FIGURE 2.11   Diffraction

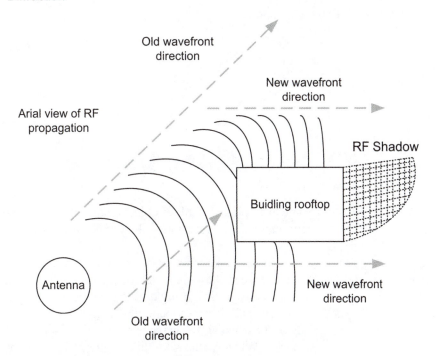

Diffraction is the slowing of the wave front at the point where the wave front strikes an obstacle, while the rest of the wave front maintains the same speed of propagation. Diffraction is the effect of waves turning, or bending, around the obstacle. As another example, consider a machine blowing a steady stream of smoke. The smoke would flow straight until an obstacle entered its path. Introducing a large wooden block into the smoke stream would cause the smoke to curl around the corners of the block, causing a noticeable degradation in the smoke's velocity at that point and a significant change in direction.

Scattering

Scattering occurs when the medium through which the wave travels consists of objects with dimensions that are small compared to the wavelength of the signal, and the number of obstacles per unit volume is large. Scattered waves are produced by rough surfaces, small objects, or by other irregularities in the signal path, as can be seen in Figure 2.12. Scattering can be thought of as lots of little reflections.

FIGURE 2.12 Scattering

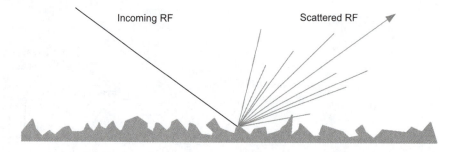

Some examples of outdoor objects that can cause scattering in a mobile communications system include foliage, street signs, and lampposts.

Scattering can take place in two primary ways. First, scattering can occur when a wave strikes an uneven surface and is reflected in many directions simultaneously. Scattering of this type yields many small amplitude reflections and destroys the main RF signal. Dissipation of an RF signal may occur when an RF wave is reflected off sand, rocks, or other jagged surfaces. When scattered in this manner, RF signal degradation can be significant, to the point of intermittently disrupting communications or causing complete signal loss.

Second, scattering can occur as a signal wave travels through particles in the medium, such as heavy dust content. In this case, rather than being reflected off an uneven surface, the RF waves are individually reflected on a very small scale off tiny particles.

Absorption

Absorption occurs when the RF signal strikes an object and is absorbed into the material in such a manner that it does not pass through, reflect off, or bend around the object, as shown in Figure 2.13. Absorption occurs, to one degree or another, whenever an RF signal travels through an object. You can often receive an AP's signal through two or three drywall-over-2x4-stud walls, but a single concrete or cinderblock wall often blocks the signal entirely. This scenario is an example of absorption.

FIGURE 2.13   Absorption

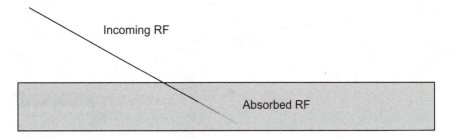

Voltage Standing Wave Ratio (VSWR)

VSWR occurs when there is mismatched *impedance* (resistance to current flow, measured in Ohms) between devices in an RF system. In this context, "mismatched" means that one piece of equipment has a greater or lesser impedance than the piece of equipment to which it is connected. VSWR is caused by an RF signal reflected at a point of impedance mismatch in the signal path. VSWR causes *return loss*, which is defined as the loss of forward energy through a system due to some of the power being reflected back toward the transmitter. If the impedances of the ends of a connection do not match, then the maximum amount of the transmitted power will not be received at the antenna. When part of the RF signal is reflected back toward the transmitter, the signal level on the line varies, instead of being steady. This variance is an indicator of VSWR.

As an illustration of VSWR, imagine water flowing through two garden hoses. As long as the two hoses are the same diameter, water flows through them seamlessly. If the hose connected to the faucet were significantly larger than the next hose down the line, there would be backpressure on the faucet, and even at the connection between the two hoses. This standing backpressure illustrates VSWR, as can be seen in Figure 2.14. In this example, you can see that backpressure can have negative effects, and not nearly as much water is transferred to the second hose as there would have been with matching hoses screwed together properly.

FIGURE 2.14 VSWR - like water through a hose

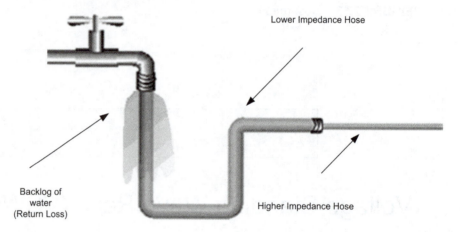

VSWR Measurements

VSWR is a ratio, so it is expressed as a relationship between two numbers. A typical VSWR value would be 1.5:1. The two numbers relate the ratio of impedance mismatch against a perfect impedance match. The second number is always 1, representing the perfect match, whereas the first number varies. The lower the first number (closer to 1), the better impedance matching your system has. For example, a VSWR of 1.1:1 is better than 1.4:1. A VSWR measurement of 1:1 would denote a perfect impedance match, and no voltage standing wave would be present in the signal path.

Effects of VSWR

Excessive VSWR can cause serious problems in an RF circuit. Most of the time, the result is a marked decrease in the amplitude of the transmitted RF signal. However, since some transmitters are not protected against power being applied (or returned) to the transmitter output circuit, the reflected power can burn out the electronics of the transmitter. VSWR's effects are evident when transmitter circuits burn out, power output levels are unstable, and the power observed is significantly different from the expected power. The methods of changing VSWR in a circuit include proper use of proper equipment. Tight connections between cables and connectors, use of impedance-matched hardware throughout, and use of high-quality equipment with calibration reports where necessary are all good preventive measures against VSWR. VSWR can be measured with high-accuracy instrumentation, such as SWR meters, but this measurement is beyond the scope of this text and the job tasks of a network administrator.

Solutions to VSWR

To prevent the negative effects of VSWR, it is imperative that all cables, connectors, and devices have impedances that match each other as closely as possible. Never use 75-Ohm cable with 50-Ohm devices, for example. Most of today's wireless LAN devices have an impedance of 50 Ohms, but it is still recommended that you check each device before implementation, just to be sure. Every device, from the transmitter to the antenna, must have impedances matching as closely as possible, including cables, connectors, antennas, amplifiers, attenuators, the transmitter output circuit, and the receiver input circuit.

Intentional Radiator

As defined by the Federal Communication Commission (FCC), an intentional radiator is an RF device specifically designed to generate and radiate RF signals. In terms of hardware, an intentional radiator will include the RF device and all cabling and connectors up to, but not including, the antenna, as illustrated in Figure 2.15 below.

FIGURE 2.15 Intentional Radiator

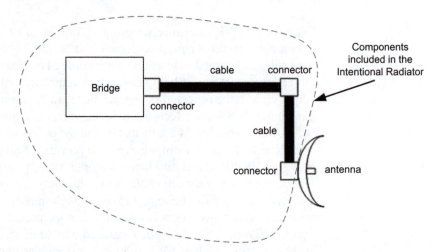

Any reference to "power output of the intentional radiator" refers to the power output at the end of the last cable or connector before the antenna. For example, consider a 30-milliwatt transmitter that loses 15 milliwatts of power in the cable and another 5 milliwatts from the connector at the antenna. The power at the intentional radiator would be 10 milliwatts. As an administrator, it is your responsibility to understand the FCC rules relating to intentional radiators and their power output. Understanding how power output is measured, how much power is allowed, and how to calculate these values are all covered in this book. FCC regulations concerning output power at the intentional radiator are found in Part 47 CFR, Chapter 1, Section 15.247.

Equivalent Isotropically Radiated Power (EIRP)

EIRP is the power actually radiated by the antenna element, as shown in Figure 2.16. This concept is important because it is regulated by the FCC and because it is used in calculating whether or not a wireless link is viable. EIRP takes into account the gain of the antenna (discussed in Chapter 4).

FIGURE 2.16   EIRP

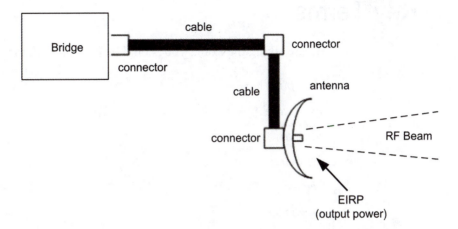

Suppose a transmitting station uses a 10 dBi antenna (which passively amplifies the signal ten-fold by focusing the power in a specific direction) and is fed by 100 milliwatts from the intentional radiator. The EIRP is 1000 mW, or 1 Watt. The FCC has rules defining both the power output at the intentional radiator and the antenna element.

 Failure to comply with FCC rules regarding power output can subject the administrator or the organization (or both) to legal action and fines.

Key Terms

Before taking the exam, you should be familiar with the following terms:

absorption

amplitude

antenna

diffraction

frequency

impedance

phase

polarity

reflection

refraction

scattering

wavelength

VSWR

Review Questions

1. Given that all radio frequency signals have the properties of *amplitude*, *frequency*, *wavelength*, *phase*, and *polarity*, explain how each of these properties is relevant to the implementation and management of an 802.11 wireless LAN.

2. Explain what could cause each of the following RF behaviors in the ongoing management of a wireless LAN:

   A. Gain (Amplification)

   B. Loss (Attenuation)

   C. Reflection

   D. Refraction

   E. Diffraction

   F. Scattering

3. Describe in your own words what VSWR is, how it is measured, how it could occur in a wireless LAN system, and how VSWR can be corrected.

4. Why is it important for the wireless LAN administrator to know and understand all the properties and behaviors of RF?

5. What is the relationship between the intentional radiator and EIRP?

Radio Frequency (RF) Math

CWNA Exam Objectives Covered:

❖ Understand and apply the basic components of RF mathematics:

- Watt
- Milliwatt
- Decibel (dB)
- dBm
- dBi
- dBd
- RSSI
- RF Signal and Antenna Concepts
- Isotropic Radiator

In This Chapter

Units of Measurement

Calculating dB gain and loss

How 802.11 Radios Measure Signal Strength

RSSI

There are several important areas of power calculation in a wireless LAN. They are:

- Power at the transmitting device.
- Loss and gain of connectivity devices between the transmitting device and the antenna – such as cables, connectors, amplifiers, attenuators, and splitters.
- Power at the Intentional Radiator (the last connector before the RF signal enters the antenna).
- Power radiated by the antenna element, known as EIRP.
- Power lost by the signal as it travels through the space between the transmitting and receiving antennae—in other words, the difference between transmitted power and received power.
- Loss and gain of connectivity devices between the receiving antenna and the receiving device.

Consideration of each of these areas is required to determine whether RF links are compliant with the power limitations set by the FCC. Each of these factors must be taken into account when planning a wireless LAN, and all of these factors are related mathematically. The following section explains the units of measure used to calculate power output when configuring wireless LAN devices.

Units of Measure

There are a few standard units of measure that a wireless network administrator should become familiar with in order to be effective in implementing and troubleshooting wireless LANs. We will discuss them all in detail, giving examples of their usage. We will then put them to use in some sample math problems so that you have a solid grasp of what is required as part of the tasks of a CWNA.

Watt (W)

The basic unit of power is a watt. A watt is defined as one ampere (A) of current at one volt (V). As an example of what these units mean, think of a garden hose that has water flowing through it. The pressure on the water line would represent the voltage in an electrical circuit. The water flow would represent the amperes (current) flowing through the garden hose. Think of a watt as the result of a given amount of pressure and a given amount of water in the garden hose. One watt is equal to an ampere multiplied by a volt.

A typical 120-volt plug-in night light uses about 7 watts. On a clear night, this 7 W light may be seen 50 miles (83 km) away in all directions. If we could somehow encode information, such as with Morse code, we could establish a wireless link. Remember, we are only interested in sending and receiving data, not illuminating the receiver with RF energy, as we would illuminate a room with light. You can see that relatively little power is required to form an RF link of great distance.

 We can carry this analogy further by considering how our ability to transmit data with the night light would change if we were on top of a hill looking down on a city, and the night light was in the city. In this case, the "noise" of the city lights would drown out the night light's weaker signal. The same effect occurs with RF noise.

The FCC allows up to 4 watts of power to be radiated from an antenna in a point-to-multipoint wireless LAN connection using unlicensed 2.4 GHz spread spectrum equipment. Four watts might not seem like much – it is much less than a typical night light – but it is enough to send a clear RF data signal for miles.

Milliwatt (mW)

Although the FCC allows up to 4 watts of power to be radiated from an antenna in a point-to-multipoint wireless LAN configuration, 4 watts actually is much more power than most WLANs require to deliver excellent connectivity to the users. Most 802.11 devices use power levels between 1 and 100 milliwatts (mW), where 1 milliwatt equals 1/1000 of a watt. Power levels as low as 1 milliwatt can be used for a small area. PCMCIA clients commonly use power levels of 15 to 30 mW. Access points generally use between 30 and 100 mW of power, depending on the manufacturer, although a few access points support transmit powers up to 250 mW. Only in the case of outdoor connections, such as between buildings or when a very large area needs to be covered, would power levels above about 250 mW be used.

Most of the power levels referred to by administrators will be in mW or dBm. These two units of measure both represent an absolute amount of power and are both industry standard measurements.

Decibel (dB)

Milliwatts are most useful when talking about an RF signal's transmit power, which is relatively high compared to the RF signal's receive power. Milliwatts are less useful when talking about the power of an RF signal at the point of reception (the receive power), which might be as low as 0.0000001 mW. Because the power of an RF signal drops off logarithmically as it propagates, a signal will have become much weaker after propagating for only a short distance.

To gain an intuitive understanding of logarithmic decay, consider the parable of the peasant. The story goes that a King offered the peasant whatever he wanted in reward for some good deed. The peasant asked that, on a chessboard, one grain of rice be placed on the first square, two grains of rice on the second square, four grains on the third square, and so on. The King agreed, not thinking this was very much to ask for at all. Mathematically, the number of grains of rice on a given square, numbered n, is equal to $2^{\wedge}(n-1)$. This means that the 64th square on the board would have $2^{\wedge}63$, or 9,223,372,036,854,775,808 grains of rice! That's about nine billion billion grains of rice! The point of the parable is that exponential growth starts small, but gets very large very fast. Logarithmic decay, such as RF signals experience, is the inverse of exponential growth. Whereas exponential growth gets very large very fast, logarithmic decay causes an RF signal to get very weak very fast.

Since RF signals get very weak very fast, milliwatts are not a good unit for measuring the change in the power of an RF signal. Instead of saying, "this signal is 99.999999 milliwatts weaker than this other signal," it is more intuitive (and easier on the tongue) to say something like, "this signal is 1/10,000th as strong as this other signal." Ratios, or fractions, more accurately reflect the non-linear way in which the signal's power degrades.

The *decibel* is the unit of measurement that is designed specifically to measure power loss. A decibel gives us a standard way of saying, "this signal is such-and-such a fraction of this other signal." In addition, decibels let us add and subtract power more easily than can be done with fractions.

There are two key differences between a decibel and a milliwatt. First, *a decibel always measures the relative strength between two signals,* whereas a milliwatt measures the absolute strength of one signal. If someone were to ask you, "How strong is this signal, in dB?" you couldn't answer. You'd have to reply, "relative to what?" Second, a milliwatt is a linear measurement, whereas a decibel is a logarithmic measurement. Intuitively, it makes sense that we measure RF power gain and loss, which is logarithmic in nature, using a logarithmic unit instead of a linear one. But what does that really mean?

A logarithm is the exponent to which the number 10 must be raised to reach some given value. If we are given the number 1000 and asked to find the logarithm (log), we find that log 1000 = 3 because $10^3 = 1000$. Notice that, in our logarithm, 3 is the exponent.

If you work out some examples, you will see that logarithmic measurements have a curious quality: every time the number goes up by a factor of ten, the logarithm only goes up by one. Here are some examples:

n	*log(n)*
10	1
100	2
1000	3
10000	4

Notice that the numbers in the left column are growing exponentially—each one is ten times the one before it—while the numbers in the right column are growing linearly—each is one greater than the one before it. That's the power of the logarithm: it gives us a linear way of representing logarithmic or exponential functions, such as power loss or gain in an RF signal. It is easier to calculate power gains and losses with linear units.

The right column of the above table is measured in a unit called the *bel*. By subtracting the right-column numbers for two left-column entries, we can find the number of bels between them. So, for example, 10,000 is 2 bels greater than 100. As its metric prefix suggests, a *deci*-bel is equal to one-tenth of a bel. Therefore, 10,000 is 20 decibels greater than 100. Using this information, we can rewrite the table as:

Difference (linear)	dB (logarithmic/relative)
10	10
100	20
1000	30
10000	40

Notice that the left-hand column doesn't have any units. That's because it doesn't matter whether signal A is 10,000 mW greater than signal B, 10,000 volts greater than signal B, or 10,000 *boogles* (an imaginary unit) greater! In all cases, the difference is 40 dB. Because dB measures the relative amounts of two signals, and the two signals are required to have the same units, the units cancel out of the equation. The general formula for calculating the decibel difference between two signals (for example, the power of a transmitted signal and the power at which it was received) is:

$$\text{Power Difference (dB)} = 10 * \log(\text{Power A / Power B})$$

In summary, the decibel is a general-purpose unit for expressing the difference between two measurements. In the context of RF, we use it to measure the gain and loss in signal strength (mW) between two RF signals.

Gain and Loss Measurements

Power gain and loss are usually measured in decibels, not in watts, because gain and loss are relative concepts and a decibel is a relative measurement. Gain or loss in an RF system may be referred to by absolute power measurement (e.g., ten watts of power) or by a relative power measurement (e.g., half of its power), but as the change in power gets greater, and as the power level gets weaker, decibels become much easier to use. Saying that the signal started at 100 mW and it gained 300 mW is easy to understand; saying that the signal started at 100 mW and it was received at 0.000 008 mW is much less intuitive.

When an RF engineer works with gain and loss, he or she needs to be able to do simple gain and loss calculations without pulling out a calculator and using the dB formula shown above. Fortunately, it usually is sufficient to approximate gain and loss numbers, which means that we can take advantage of these helpful shortcuts:

−3 dB	=	half the power in mW
+3 dB	=	double the power in mW
−10 dB	=	one tenth the power in mW
+10 dB	=	ten times the power in mW

In other words:

−3 dB	=	divide power by 2	= / 2
+3 dB	=	multiply power by 2	= * 2
−10 dB	=	divide power by 10	= / 10
+10 dB	=	multiply power by 10	= * 10

We refer to these shortcuts as the 10s and 3s of RF math. If you refer back to the dB formula and check the numbers, you will see that they are approximately right. If "power A" is twice "power B," the result is always 3 dB; if "power A" is 1/10 of "power B," the result is always -10 dB, and so on.

We can then apply these shortcuts to some simple problems:

A signal is transmitted at 100 mW. It travels through a length of coaxial cable that has 3 dB of loss. What is the resulting strength of the signal, in mW?

100 mW	−3 dB	=
100 mW	/ 2	= **50 mW**

A signal is transmitted at 30 mW, after which it goes through an amplifier that adds 10 dB of gain. What is the resulting strength of the signal, in mW?

30 mW	+10 dB =	
30 mW	* 10	= **300 mW**

A signal is transmitted at 100 mW. After passing through a coaxial cable, it is measured with a signal strength of 10 mW. What is the loss of the cable, in dB?

100 mW	/ 10	= 10 mW
100 mW	−10 dB	= **10 mW**

The "rule of 10s and 3s" can be extended to gains and losses that are even multiples of ten and three. For example, a gain of 6 dB is equivalent to two gains of 3 dB; a gain of 30 dB is equivalent to three gains of 10 dB. Here are some examples:

A signal is transmitted at 100 mW. It passes through a coaxial cable that has a loss of 6 dB. What is the resulting strength of the signal, in mW?

100 mW	−6 dB	=	
100 mW	−3 dB	-3 dB	=
100 mW	/ 2	/ 2	= **25 mW**

A signal is transmitted at 30 mW, after which it goes through a 30 dB amplifier. What is the resulting signal power, in mW?

30 mW	+30 dB	=	
30 mW	+10 dB	+10 dB	+ 10 dB =
30 mW	* 10	* 10	* 10 = **30,000 mW**

Finally, one can combine tens and threes to calculate gains and losses for literally any number (although some numbers require such complex mathematical acrobatics that it's quicker to just pull out the calculator). For example:

10 mW	+13 dB	=	
10 mW	+10 dB	+ 3 dB	=
10 mW	* 10	* 2	= 200 mW

20 mW	+27 dB	=		
20 mW	+10 dB	+ 10 dB	+ 10 dB	– 3 dB =
20 mW	* 10	* 10	* 10	/ 2 = 10,000 mW

When calculating power gain and loss, you can always express the number of dBs of gain or loss as a sum of tens and threes. These values give you the ability to quickly and easily calculate RF loss and gain with a fair amount of accuracy without the use of a calculator. For completeness, here is a table showing how to express any amount of gain or loss as tens and threes:

Gain (dB)	Expression as 10s and 3s
1	$+10-9 \ (+10-3-3-3)$
2	$-10+12 \ (-10+3+3+3+3)$
3	$+3$
4	$+10-6 \ (+10-3-3)$
5	$+20-15 \ (+10+10-3-3-3-3-3)$
6	$+6 \ (+3+3)$
7	$+10-3$
8	$+20-12 \ (+10+10-3-3-3-3)$
9	$+9 \ (+3+3+3)$
10	$+10$

Higher numbers can be expressed as combinations of those numbers. As you can see from the table, some changes, such as 1 dB, 2 dB, and especially 5 dB and 8 dB require so much "dividing-by-2" that even this "shortcut" would probably require a calculator, at which point you may as well just do the logarithm.

A final point is that gains and losses are additive. If an access point were connected to a cable whose loss was –2 dB and then a connector whose loss was –1 dB, then these loss measurements would be additive and yield a total of –3 dB of loss. The additive characteristic means that you don't need to calculate gain and loss for each component of an RF transmission chain individually. You can add up the gain and loss for all the components and just calculate that. We will walk through some RF calculations in the coming sections to give you a better idea of how to relate these numbers to actual scenarios.

dBm

A decibel always measures the difference between two signals. For example, when decibels are used to measure gain and loss, they are measuring the difference between the original signal and the resulting signal after the gain or loss. But in some circumstances, it can be convenient to use decibels to measure an absolute power level. For example, if you could use decibels to measure an absolute power level, then you could potentially avoid converting between milliwatts and decibels when doing gain/loss calculations. Instead, you could carry the entire calculation out in decibels, simply by adding and subtracting. As you've probably guessed, there is a way to use decibels to measure absolute power levels: *normalizing the decibel.*

To normalize the decibel means to measure the power level of a signal relative to some arbitrary reference power. Instead of asking, "What is the power level of signal A relative to signal B?" we ask, "What is the power level of signal A relative to a previously-defined, fixed power level?"

For example, we could define the fixed power level to be 1 mW and then calculate the power of other signals relative to 1 mW. A 1 mW signal would be zero dB greater or less than the reference 1 mW signal. A 10 mW signal would be 10 dB greater than the reference 1 mW signal. A 0.01 mW signal would be 20 dB less than the reference 1 mW signal, and so on. The unit that we've just described is called dB-milliwatt, or dBm. Consider these examples:

A certain AP transmits with a power of 100 mW. How many dBm is this?

1 mW	* 10 * 10	= 100 mW
1 mW	+ 10 dB + 10 dB	= 100 mW
1 mW	+ 20 dB	= 100 mW

100 mW = 20 dBm

A certain PCMCIA client transmits with a power of 30 mW. How many dBm is this?

1 mW	* 10	* 3	= 30 mW
1 mW	+ 10 dB	+ 3 dB =	30 mW
1 mW	+ 13 dB		= 30 mW

30 mW = 13 dBm

dBm are convenient because you can add dB gains and subtract dB losses to and from dBm, whereas if you're working in milliwatts, you have to multiply and divide. Addition and subtraction is easier than multiplication and division. Here are some examples:

A certain signal is transmitted at 30 mW. It goes through a run of cable that causes a loss of 2 dB, then an amplifier that gives a gain of 9 dB. What is the resulting signal strength?

Normally, we would solve this problem by taking 30 mW and using the rule of tens and threes to subtract 2 dB, and then add 9 dB. This calculation would be difficult, since –2 dB = +10 – 12. We would have to multiply by 10 to get 300 mW, then divide by two four times to get 150, 75, 37.5, etc. This many calculations becomes tedious. We could simplify the step by combining the –2 dB and 9 dB to get a net gain of 7 dB, but 7 dB is only a little easier to calculate than –2 dB!

Instead, watch how easy the problem is if we convert the milliwatts to dBm first.

1 mW	* 10	* 3	= 30 mW
1 mW	+ 10 dB	+ 3 dB	= 30 mW
1 mW	+ 13 dB		= 30 mW

1 mW = 13 dBm

13 dBm	–2 dB	+ 9 dB	= **20 dBm**

Now, we convert 20 dBm back to milliwatts:

1 mW	+ 20 dB		=
1 mW	+ 10 dB+ 10 dB		=
1 mW	* 10	* 10	= 100 mW

20 dBm = 100 mW

The following is the general equation for converting mW to dBm:

$$P_{dbm} = 10\log_{PmW}$$

This equation can be manipulated to reverse the conversion, now converting dBm to mW:

$$Pmw = \log^{-1}\left(\frac{P_{dbm}}{10}\right)$$

*Note: $\log^{-1}$ denotes the inverse logarithm (inverse log)

 You will not be tested on logarithmic functions using these formulas as part of the CWNA exam. These formulas are provided only for your reference in case they are needed during your administrative tasks. Calculators are not needed on the CWNA exam. However, you should be able to apply the rule of tens and threes as in the examples above. You should also be able to convert simple values such as the ones in the examples from milliwatts to dBm

These rules will allow a quick calculation of milliwatt power levels when given power levels, gains, and losses in dBm and dB. Figure 3.1 shows that the reference point is always the same, but power levels can move in either direction from the reference point, depending on whether they represent a power gain or loss.

FIGURE 3.1   Power Level Chart

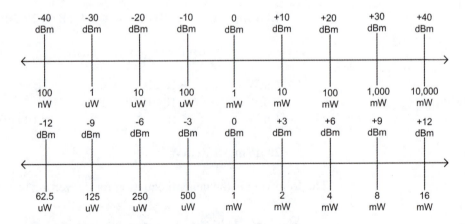

In the top chart of Figure 3.1, gains and losses of 10 dB are shown at each increment. Notice that a gain of +10 dB from the reference point of 1 mW moves the power to +10 dBm (10 mW). Conversely, notice that a loss of –10 dB moves the power to –10 dBm (100 microwatts). On the

bottom chart, the same principle applies. These charts both represent the same thing, except that one is incremented in gains and losses of 3 dB and the other in gains and losses of 10 dB. They have been separated into two charts for ease of viewing. Using these charts, one can easily convert dBm and mW power levels.

dBi

The ideal antenna is referred to as an isotropic radiator. An isotropic radiator transmits energy equally in all directions at 100 percent efficiency. So if, for example, an isotropic radiator were going to transmit 1 mW of power, that 1 mW would be spread evenly over the surface of an ever-expanding sphere centered on the antenna. The sun is an example of a real object that very closely approximates an isotropic radiator, since the energy measured at some distance from the sun is the same no matter where you measure.

FIGURE 3.2   Isotropic Radiation Pattern

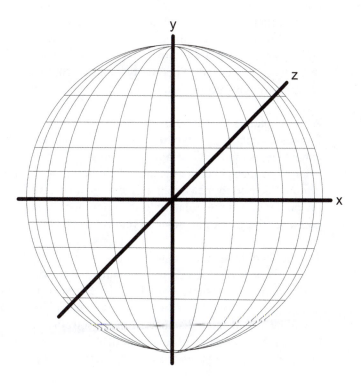

Man-made antennae don't have an isotropic radiation pattern and always radiate more energy in one direction than another. One reason for this characteristic is that the structure of the antenna simultaneously affects the frequencies to which the antenna is most sensitive and the radiation pattern for the antenna. For example, a principle of antenna design says that as an omni-directional dipole antenna gets longer, its radiation pattern gets flatter (more donut-shaped and less spherical). Taken to the extreme, this principle would require an antenna of zero length to get a perfectly spherical (isotropic) radiation pattern. Clearly, a zero-length antenna can't exist.

An antenna element—without the amplifiers and filters typically associated with it—is a passive device. It simply converts the AC electrical energy into RF energy. But the antenna can create the effect of amplification by focusing the energy that it emits.

Just as a lighthouse focuses the light of a bulb to increase its visibility in one direction, while making it less visible in other directions, so does an antenna focus the RF energy that it emits to increase its strength in one (or more) directions, while making it weaker in other directions. The bulb and the antenna emit the same *total* amount of energy, regardless of how that energy is focused. Specific types of antennas and their propagation patterns are covered in Chapter 4.

Antenna gain is measured by comparing the degree to which an antenna focuses its energy relative to an isotropic radiator. As the gain of an antenna goes up, the coverage area narrows so that high-gain antennae offer more focused coverage areas than low-gain antennae. The dBi is the unit that is used to measure the gain of an antenna. Just as dBm measures the power of a signal relative to the reference value of 1 mW, dBi measures the gain of an antenna relative to an isotropic radiator.

To calculate the gain of an antenna, an RF engineer first determines the antenna's *preferred direction* – the direction in which the antenna is designed to focus its energy. Then, the engineer measures the power level at a certain distance from the antenna and calculates what the power level would be at that same distance from an isotropic radiator. The difference between those two power levels, in dBi, is the antenna gain. Therefore, an antenna that emits twice as much energy in its preferred direction, such as an isotropic radiator, would have an antenna gain of 3 dBi. An antenna that emits ten times as much energy in its preferred direction as an isotropic radiator would have an antenna gain of 10 dBi.

Since an antenna always focuses its energy, and since antenna gain is always measured in the direction in which the antenna will focus its energy, it follows that a real antenna will always put more energy in its preferred direction than an isotropic radiator would. Therefore, antenna gain is always positive, never negative, and is always expressed in positive terms. Put another way, real antennae always have some amount of gain over an isotropic radiator.

The dBi measurement is used in RF calculations in the same manner as dB. Units of dBi are relative. For example, consider a 10 dBi antenna with 1 watt of power applied. What is the EIRP (output power at the antenna element)?

> 1 W + 10 dBi (a ten-fold increase) = 10 W

This calculation works in the same fashion as showing gain measured in dB. A gain of 10 dBi multiplies the input power of the antenna by a factor of ten. Like dB, dBi is a relative unit of measure and can be added to or subtracted from other decibel units. For example, if an RF signal is reduced by 3 dB as it runs through a copper cable, and is then transmitted by an antenna with a gain of 5 dBi, the result is an overall gain of +2 dB.

Example

Given the RF circuit in Figure 3.3, determine the power at all marked points in milliwatts.

FIGURE 3.3   Sample wireless LAN configuration

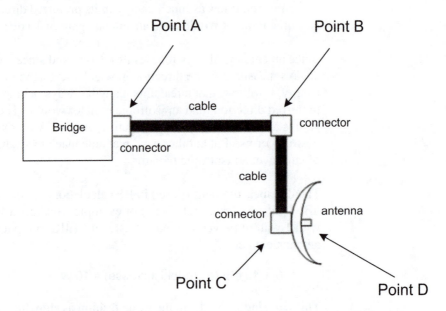

Access Point	Point A	Point B	Point C	Point D
100 mW	−3 dB	−3 dB	−3 dB	+12 dBi
= 100 mW	÷2	÷2	÷2	(x2 x2 x2 x2)
= 100 mW	÷2	÷2	÷2	x16
= 50 mW		÷2	÷2	x16
= 25 mW			÷2	x16
= 12.5 mW				x16
= 200 mW				

Accurate Measurements

Although these techniques are helpful and expedient in some situations, there are times when rounded or even numbers may not be available. In these cases, using the formula is the best way to do RF calculations. Since the decibel is a unit of relative power measurement, a change in power level is implied. If the power level is given in dBm, then change in dB is simple to calculate:

Initial power = 20 dBm
Final power = 33 dBm

Change in power, $\Delta P = 33 - 20 = +13$ dB, the value is positive, indicating an increase in power.

If the power levels are given in milliwatts, the process can become more complicated:

Initial power = 130 mW
Final power = 5.2 W
Change in power,

$$\Delta P = 10 \log \left(\frac{P_f}{P_i} \right)$$

$$= 10 \log \left(\frac{5.2W}{130mW} \right)$$

$$= 10 \log 40$$

$$= 10 * 1.6$$

$$= 16dB$$

You will not be tested on logarithmic functions using these formulas as part of the CWNA exam, but your understanding of power calculations using the 10s and 3s will be tested. These formulas are provided only for your reference in case they are needed during your administrative tasks. Calculators are not needed on the CWNA exam.

dBd

As we discussed in the section on dBi, real antennae always have some amount of gain over an isotropic radiator. Therefore, for some applications, it is more practical to compare the real antenna to a hypothetical "standard" antenna instead of to an isotropic radiator. Just as dBi measures the gain of a real antenna relative to a theoretical perfect (isotropic) radiator, dBd measures the gain of a real antenna relative to a theoretical half-wave dipole antenna (antenna types, including dipole, are discussed in the next chapter). The "standard" antenna used for dBd measurement is a half-wave dipole with a gain of 2.14 dBi. dBd can be converted to dBi by adding 2.14 (e.g., 0 dBd = 2.14 dBi).

In our experience, 802.11 antennae are most commonly measured in dBi, while dBd is more commonly used to measure the gain of UHF or VHF antennas, but you should be aware of the term dBd if you ever experience it in the context of 802.11.

How 802.11 Radios Measure Signal Strength

All 802.11 radios must measure the strength of the signal they are receiving. For example, some cards measure the strength of the signal that is being received from its access point to determine whether it should attempt to roam to a different access point (many cards use more sophisticated metrics in their roaming algorithm). A card also uses the strength of its incoming signals to decide what data rate to use when it transmits. Higher data rates are faster but are also harder to receive. The stronger the signal a station receives, the higher the data rate it will attempt to use when it transmits, since the station will assume that it is closer to its access point. Finally, stations must measure signal strength in order to determine whether any other station is transmitting on the medium, both to determine whether the station should begin receiving and to determine whether it is safe for the station to transmit its own data. If the strength of the ambient RF energy is below a certain threshold, the station will assume that no one is transmitting.

As we think about how 802.11 radios measure signal strength, it is important to keep in mind the reasons *why* the card has to measure signal strength. In each case, all the card has to do is decide if the signal strength is above or below a certain threshold. The card will check several criteria:

- Above the "roaming threshold"? Don't roam.
- Below the "roaming threshold"? Roam.
- Above the "carrier sense threshold"? Start receiving.
- Below the "clear channel threshold"? Okay to transmit.

The implication is that none of these decisions require a large degree of precision, such as would be found in an RF spectrum analyzer.

RSSI

When the card measures signal strength, what representation does it use? Although you might think that a card would report signal strength in mW or dBm, these units are far more precise than the card really needs. The 802.11 standard requires only that the card report signal strength using a simple metric called Received Signal Strength Indicator (RSSI). Ironically, all 802.11 cards measure RSSI in dBm or mW, then use a mathematical formula to convert that to the RSSI value required by 802.11. RSSI is not measured or expressed in any sort of unit, as are dBi and dBm.

Importantly, the 802.11 standard does *not* specify how RSSI should be calculated. Rather, the standard requires only that the card's hardware be capable of reporting RSSI up to the driver. As with any vagueness in a standard, this one has resulted in different implementations between vendors. For example, one vendor may measure RSSI on a scale of 1 to 255, while another vendor may measure RSSI on a scale of 1 to 32. For the first vendor, the "roaming threshold" might be when the signal falls below an RSSI of 75, while for the second vendor, the "roaming threshold" might be 10.

Adding to this inconsistency is the fact that each vendor uses a different mathematical scale to map dBm or mW to RSSI. So, for the first vendor, a signal strength of −10 dBm (0.1 mW) or greater might represent an RSSI of 255, or 100 percent signal strength. The second vendor might choose to map a signal strength of −15 dBm (0.03 mW) or greater to an RSSI of 32, or 100 percent signal strength. This inconsistency has significant implications for the WLAN administrator. Given a −15 dBm signal, the second vendor's card will report 100 percent signal strength while the first vendor's will report less than 100 percent signal strength. You might conclude that the second vendor's card is better than the first vendor's, but in fact, the cards are both receiving exactly the same signal. The vendors are just reporting signal strength differently.

Conclusions

Given this inconsistency, what conclusions can be drawn? First, since cards usually only report RSSI to the drivers, without knowing the formula that the vendor uses to convert dBm into RSSI, it is impossible to do an accurate comparison of the signal strength that two different vendor's cards are seeing. Second, even if you know the formula, and therefore can convert back from RSSI to dBm (as some client manager software does), the granularity of the card's RSSI measurement will limit the accuracy of the reverse-conversion.

For example, an 802.11 card might be able to receive signals from −90 dBm up to about +10 dBm, a range of 100 dBm. If the vendor chooses to map that to an RSSI measurement of 1–32, then conversions back from RSSI to dBm can't have an accuracy of greater than 100 / 32 = 3.125 dBm. In other words, when you convert back from RSSI to dBm, you might be off from the actual original value by as much as 3.125 dBm. That might not sound like much, but remember that a change of 3 dB equals a doubling or halving of signal strength. By comparison, the vendor who chooses to use an RSSI of 1–255 could achieve much better accuracy (better than 0.5 dBm) over the same range of powers.

Key Terms

Before taking the exam, you should be familiar with the following terms:

antenna gain

dB

dBi

dBm

isotropic radiator

logarithm

milliwatts

rule of tens and threes

Review Questions

1. Explain the difference between an absolute measurement of power and a relative measurement, as it applies to antenna output.

2. What unit of measure is used to represent power gain and loss? Why?

3. Explain, in your own words, the "rule of 10s and 3s" and how it applies to wireless LAN implementation and management.

4. What is the general equation for converting mW to dBm?

5. For what reasons does a PC card (or other device receiving the WLAN RF signal) need to measure signal strength?

Antennas

CWNA Exam Objectives Covered:

- ❖ Understand the applications of basic RF antenna concepts and explain implementation of solutions that require RF antennas
  - Visual LOS
  - RF LOS
  - The Fresnel Zone
  - Beamwidths
  - Azimuth & Elevation
  - Passive Gain
- ❖ Understand the applications of basic RF antenna types and identify their basic attributes, purpose, and function
  - Omni-directional / Dipole antennas
  - Semi-directional antennas
  - Highly-directional antennas
  - Phased-array antennas
  - Sectorized antennas
- ❖ Understand and apply the basic components of RF mathematics
  - System Operating Margin
  - Fade Margin
  - Link Budget

In This Chapter

Principles of Antennas

Types of Antennas

Link Budget

Antenna Installation

FCC Rules Regarding Antennas

- ❖ Describe the proper locations and methods for installing
  - Antennas
  - Pole/mast mount
  - Ceiling mount
  - Wall mount
- ❖ Define and explain the basic concepts of RF behavior
  - Free-space Path Loss

Antennas are most often used to increase the range of wireless LAN systems, but proper antenna selection also can enhance the security of a wireless LAN. A properly chosen and positioned antenna can reduce the chances of the signals leaking out of your workspace, and make signal interception extremely difficult. In this chapter, we will explain the radiation patterns of different antenna designs, and how the positioning of the user's antenna makes a difference in signal reception.

There are three general categories into which all wireless LAN antennas fall: omnidirectional, semi-directional, and highly-directional. We will discuss the attributes of each of these groups in depth, as well as the proper methods for installing each kind of antenna. We also will explain coverage patterns, appropriate uses, and address the many different items used to connect antennas to other wireless LAN hardware.

Principles of Antennas

It is not our intention to teach antenna theory in this book, but rather to explain some very basic antenna principles that directly relate to the use of wireless LANs. It is not necessary for a wireless LAN administrator to thoroughly understand antenna design in order to administer the network. A couple of key points that are important to understand about antennas are:

- Antennas convert electrical energy into RF waves in the case of a transmitting antenna, or RF waves into electrical energy in the case of a receiving antenna.
- The physical dimensions of an antenna, such as its length, are directly related to the frequency at which the antenna can propagate waves or receive propagated waves.
- The physical structure of an antenna is directly related to the shape of the area in which it concentrates most of its radiated RF energy.

Some essential points of understanding in administering license-free wireless LANs are: line of sight, the effects of the Fresnel (pronounced "fra-NEL") Zone, and antenna gain through focused beamwidths. These points will be discussed in this chapter.

Types of Antennas

An RF antenna is a device used to convert high frequency (RF) signals on a transmission line (a cable or waveguide) into propagated waves in the air. The RF fields emitted from antennas are called *beams* or *lobes*. There are three generic categories of RF antennas:

- Omnidirectional
- Semi-directional
- Highly-directional

Each category has multiple types of antennas, each having different RF characteristics and appropriate uses. There are many types of antenna mounts, each suited to fit a particular need. After studying this chapter, you will understand which antenna and mount best meets your needs, and why.

Omnidirectional Antennas

An omnidirectional antenna radiates energy equally in all directions around the antenna's vertical axis. The most common type of omnidirectional antenna, and indeed the most common wireless LAN antenna in general, is the dipole antenna. Simple to design, the dipole antenna is standard equipment on most access points.

A dipole antenna consists of multiple elements, the length of which depends on the wavelength to which the antenna is tuned. An antenna is most sensitive to RF signals whose wavelength is an even multiple of the antenna's length, including fractional multiples such as ½ or ¼. A 2.4 GHz dipole antenna typically contains one or more ½-wavelength elements joined together. (½ wavelength at 2.4 GHz is approximately two inches.) As the number of elements increases, so does the gain of the antenna.

For more information on dipole antennas, including instructions on how to make your own from coaxial cable and copper tubing, try a web search on the term *2.4 GHz collinear antenna design*. For best results, search for pages containing all of the individual terms, not the complete phrase (i.e., don't put the phrase in quotes when you search).

The dipole antennas used with wireless LANs are small compared to other dipole antennas like the "rabbit ears" that people sometimes use on top of their TV sets. This is because wireless LAN frequencies are in the 2.4 GHz microwave spectrum instead of the 100 MHz TV spectrum. As the radio frequency gets higher, the wavelength becomes smaller.

A dipole's radiant energy is concentrated into a region that looks like a doughnut, with the dipole vertically through the "hole" of the "doughnut." As discussed in the previous chapter, it is not possible to make an antenna with an isotropic radiation pattern; hence all antennas have some degree of gain. In a dipole antenna, the gain is achieved by pressing down the radiation pattern along the vertical axis. As the gain of the dipole antenna increases, the antenna radiates less energy above and below the antenna, and radiates that energy out horizontally instead. The result is that the antenna's range decreases along the vertical axis and increases proportionally along the horizontal axis.

Passive vs. Active Gain

The type of gain discussed in the previous paragraph is known as *passive gain*, since the total amount of energy that is emitted by the antenna doesn't increase—only the distribution of the energy around the antenna. A general definition of passive gain is: a type of gain that is achieved by designing an antenna so that it focuses more of its energy in a specific direction, as opposed to an isotropic radiator, which radiates its energy equally in all directions. Passive gain is always a function of the antenna, and is independent of the components leading up to the antenna. The alternative to passive gain is *active gain*, which is the type of gain achieved through the use of an amplifier. Active gain increases the total power output of the antenna without changing the shape of its coverage area (except to make it larger).

One disadvantage of active gain compared to passive gain is that an amplifier requires an external power source (the extra power has to come from somewhere), while passive gain does not require an external power source—only a higher gain antenna. But passive gain also has a disadvantage in that, as the gain of an antenna increases, its coverage becomes more and more focused. The highest-gain antennas can't be used for mobile users because their beam is so tight.

The Effect of Passive Gain on Coverage

If a client is directly above or below an access point using a dipole antenna, the client might have very weak signal strength even though it is relatively close to the AP. Ironically, by moving further from the AP into the coverage area of the main lobe, the client can increase its received signal strength.

If a dipole antenna is placed in the center of a single floor of a multistory building, most of its energy will be radiated along that floor, with some significant fraction sent to the floors above and below the access point. Figure 4.1 shows examples of some different types of omnidirectional antennas. Figure 4.2 shows a two-dimensional example of the top view and side view of a dipole antenna.

FIGURE 4.1   Sample omnidirectional antennas

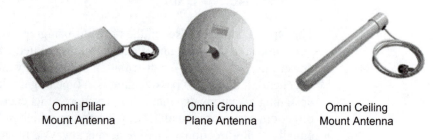

Omni Pillar
Mount Antenna

Omni Ground
Plane Antenna

Omni Ceiling
Mount Antenna

FIGURE 4.2   Coverage area of a low-gain omnidirectional antenna – cutaway view

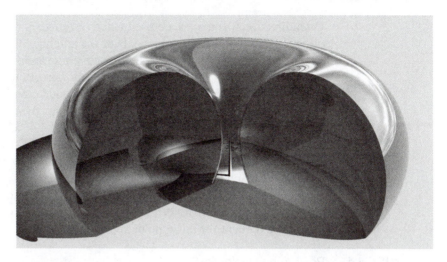

High-gain dipole antennas offer more horizontal coverage area, and reduced vertical coverage area, as can be seen in Figure 4.3. This characteristic can be an important consideration when mounting a higher-gain omni antenna indoors on the ceiling. If the ceiling is too high, the coverage area may not reach the floor (or desktop height), where the client devices are located.

FIGURE 4.3   Coverage area of a high-gain omnidirectional antenna – cutaway view

Usage

Omnidirectional antennas are used when coverage is required in all directions around the horizontal axis of the antenna. Omnidirectional antennas are most effective when large coverage areas are needed around a central point. For example, placing an omnidirectional antenna in the middle of a large, open room would provide good coverage. Omnidirectional antennas are commonly used for *point-to-multipoint* designs with a star topology, as shown in Figure 4.4. Used outdoors, an omnidirectional antenna should be placed on top of a structure (such as a building) in the middle of the coverage area, but not so high that its main lobes don't reach the level at which the client devices will be located. Nor should the structure create an RF "shadow" that would block users close to the building from getting a signal. A flagpole or other mast-type mount is excellent for this type of application.

FIGURE 4.4   Point-to-multipoint link

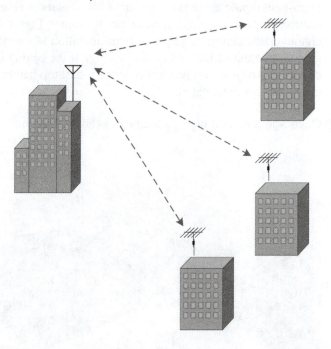

When used indoors the antenna should be placed in the middle of the building or desired coverage area near the ceiling for optimum coverage.

Omnidirectional antennas emit a large coverage area in a circular pattern and are suitable for warehouses or trade shows where coverage is usually from one corner of the building to the other.

The typical access point ships with a dipole antenna with 2 to 5 dBi gain. For the most part, a 2 dBi antenna can be treated as if it were an isotropic radiator. Signal strength directly above and below the antenna will be somewhat weaker than signal strength at the same level with the antenna's center-line, but not so much that it should make a difference in most installations. Dipoles with a gain of about 5 to 8 dBi are still appropriate for situations where the antenna will be mounted above users, but as the antenna gain increases, the vertical tolerance decreases. An 8 dBi antenna mounted on a high flagpole might provide great coverage for users in the third floor of a nearby building, but lesser coverage for users on the ground below its main lobe.

Dipole antennas with a gain above about 8 to 10 dBi have a very flat radiation pattern and are usually not appropriate for applications where the users will be more than a few feet above or below the antenna's center-line. These antennas will have great range, but only within a very small vertical coverage pattern.

In some cases, it is beneficial to tilt the antenna so that it isn't perfectly vertical, causing the main lobe to wash down over the ground below the access point. Tilting an omni antenna is not an ideal solution because half the antenna's coverage ends up going into the sky or the ceiling, where it probably cannot be used. As an alternative to physically tilting the antenna, some dipole antennas come with a few degrees of *downtilt*. That is, the antenna is designed so that the main lobe actually points down in all directions instead of pointing out exactly perpendicular to the antenna. These antennas are designed for cases in which the antenna must be mounted higher above the clients than would normally be desirable.

Semi-directional Antennas

Semi-directional antennas come in many different styles and shapes. Some semi-directional antenna types frequently used with wireless LANs are patch, panel, and yagi (pronounced "YAH-gee") antennas. Patch and panel antennas are generally flat and designed for wall mounting. They typically focus coverage in a horizontal arc of 180 degrees or less (i.e., with relatively little coverage behind the antenna). Yagi antennas look like a long rod with tines sticking out of it, but they are usually encased in a plastic cylinder, so the antenna itself usually cannot be seen. Yagi antennas focus coverage in a "beam" with common vertical and horizontal beamwidths of 90 degrees or less. Beamwidths of 30 degrees or less are the average for this type of antenna. Figure 4.5 shows some examples of semi-directional antennas.

FIGURE 4.5   Sample semi-directional antennas

Yagi Antenna   Patch Antenna   Panel Antenna

These antennas direct the energy from the transmitter significantly more in one particular direction, rather than the uniform, circular pattern that is common with the omnidirectional antenna. Semi-directional antennas often radiate in a hemispherical or cylindrical coverage pattern as can be seen in Figure 4.6.

FIGURE 4.6   Coverage area of a semi-directional antenna

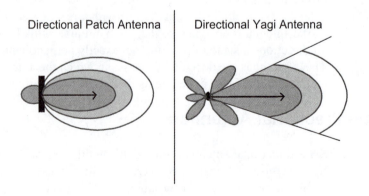

Directional Patch Antenna   Directional Yagi Antenna

It is important to note that, even though these antennas put *most* of their energy in one particular direction, they all have small side-lobes or back-lobes. For example, if you mount a patch antenna on the wall, users on the other side of the wall might be able to receive a signal if they get close enough to the wall. The signal will be very weak, but it will be there. Do not assume that the "cone-shaped" beam you picture coming out of your antenna actually represents the signal that it is sending. The real picture is more complex.

In addition, the quoted beamwidth of an antenna doesn't mean that the signal just stops at the beamwidth. Typically, beamwidth is calculated by measuring the number of degrees off-axis where the beam drops to ½ (or -3 dB) its strength at the zero-degree position. In other words, point the antenna directly at the receiver and measure signal strength. Now, start moving the receiver in a circle around the antenna. As you move off-axis, the signal strength will drop. Continue moving until signal strength measures half of the on-axis strength. The number of degrees around the circle that you moved is the antenna's horizontal beamwidth, meaning a user who is outside of the antenna's beamwidth still might be able to get a signal, albeit a weaker one.

FIGURE 4.7   Beamwidth of an antenna

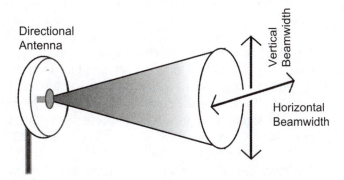

Two vectors must be considered when discussing an antenna's beamwidths: the vertical and the horizontal. The vertical beamwidth is measured in degrees and is perpendicular to the Earth's surface. The horizontal beamwidth is measured in degrees and is parallel to the Earth's surface. The chart below can be used as a quick reference guide for typical beamwidths.

Antenna Type	Horizontal Beamwidth (in degrees)	Vertical Beamwidth (in degrees)
Omnidirectional	360	Ranges from 7–80
Patch/Panel	Ranges from 30–180	Ranges from 6–90
Yagi	Ranges from 30–78	Ranges from 14–64
Parabolic Dish	Ranges from 4–25	Ranges from 4–21

Azimuth and Elevation Charts

Although beamwidth information provides a general sense of an antenna's coverage, an *azimuth and elevation chart* provides a more complete picture (literally). An azimuth and elevation chart is a standard way of representing an antenna's coverage pattern. The azimuth chart shows a top-down view of the antenna's coverage, while the elevation chart shows a side-view of the antenna's coverage. Figure 4.8 shows these charts for two antennas.

A manufacturer creates an azimuth chart by placing the antenna in an RF-shielded room and then transmitting a signal through the antenna. The frequency of the signal is chosen to match the antenna's intended use — i.e., a 2.4 GHz antenna might use a frequency in the exact middle of the 2.4 GHz band. Using a spectrum analyzer, the signal strength (in mW, not RSSI) is measured in a circle around the antenna. If the antenna is omnidirectional, such as a dipole, the signal strength will be roughly the same at all points on the circle; if the antenna is directional, such as a yagi, the signal strength will be higher in front of the antenna than behind or beside the antenna.

The outer ring of the azimuth chart represents the strongest signal strength that was measured, and is typically marked "0 dB." Inner rings represent a signal strength of some number of dB below the strongest signal strength. Note that the azimuth chart does not take the distance from the antenna into account. The chart shows the signal strength of each location *relative to each other location*, not relative to some absolute distance from the antenna or some absolute power level.

FIGURE 4.8   Example Azimuth and Elevation Charts

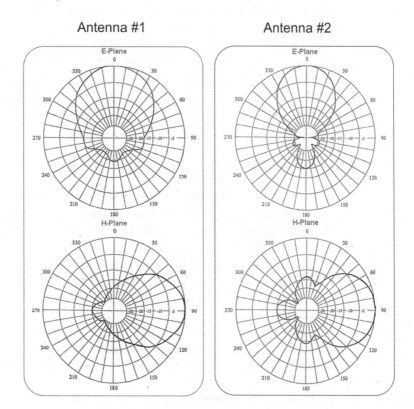

Reading an antenna's azimuth and elevation chart is relatively simple. First, determine which direction the antenna was oriented when it was tested. Common practice is to point the antenna's element at the "zero degree" mark on the azimuth chart and at the "90 degree mark on the elevation chart." Some antennas will have an alignment mark on their base to allow precision alignment when installing. To determine the relative signal strength at some number of degrees of rotation around the antenna, find the radius on the azimuth chart that represents that number of degrees of rotation. The point at which the antenna's coverage line intersects that line represents the number of dB below maximum that the antenna will put out in that direction. For example, Antenna #1 in Figure 4.8 is at approximately –15 dB at 90 degrees. The coverage contour intersects the 90 degree radial at the –15 dB point. By comparison, Antenna #2 is down more than –30 dB at 90 degrees. Its coverage contour is inside the –30 dB circle at that rotation. At 180 degrees (directly behind the antenna), Antenna #1 is down just under –20 dB from the main lobe, while Antenna #2 is down approximately –15 dB. Antenna #2's rear lobe is approximately 5 dB stronger than Antenna #1's.

The elevation chart is created and read exactly the same as the azimuth chart, except that it represents coverage in a circle in the plane that is above, to the front, below, and behind the antenna (a side-view circle), instead of in a circle in the plane that is in front, to the right, behind, and to the left of the antenna (a top-down circle).

Antenna Usage

Semi-directional antennas are ideally suited for short and medium range bridging. For example, two office buildings across the street from one another that need to share a network connection would be a good scenario in which to implement semi-directional antennas. In a large indoor space, if the transmitter must be located in the corner or at the end of a building, a corridor, or a large room, a semi-directional antenna would be a good choice to provide the proper coverage. Yagi antennas are most often used on short to medium length building-to-building bridging up to 2 miles (3.3 km). Patch and panel antennas are more typically used on short range building-to-building and in-building directional links. Figure 4.9 illustrates a link between two buildings using semi-directional antennas.

FIGURE 4.9   Point-to-point link using semi-directional antennas

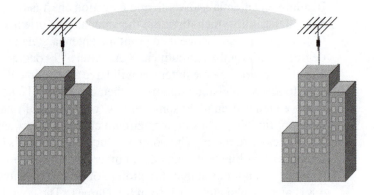

Patch and panel antennas also are available with 180 degree beamwidths, for mounting on an interior wall, where signal leakage to the outside is

undesirable. You sometimes can see these types of antennas in large retail stores. Patch antennas with 180-degree coverage are mounted approximately 15 feet up on each wall of a rectangular store. Since the antennas have a 180-degree coverage pattern, little energy leaks outside the store. Because the antennas are mounted 15 feet up, they are able to send the RF signal over the shelves, while diffraction and reflection provide some coverage in the aisles. If this configuration were combined with a low-gain omnidirectional antenna hanging from the roof, coverage could be increased further still.

Selecting an antenna with appropriately wide or narrow beamwidths is essential in having the desired RF coverage pattern. For example, imagine a long hallway in a hospital, with rooms on both sides. Instead of using several access points with omni antennas, you have decided to use a single access point with a semi-directional antenna, such as a patch antenna.

The access point and patch antenna are placed at one end of the hallway pointing down the hallway. For complete coverage on the floors directly above and below this floor, a patch antenna with a significantly large vertical beamwidth such as 60–90 degrees could be employed. After some testing, you may find that your selection of a patch antenna with 80 degrees vertical beamwidth provides the appropriate coverage.

Once the appropriate vertical beamwidth has been determined, a similar process should be used to determine the necessary horizontal beamwidth to be used. Due to the length of the hallway, testing may reveal that a high-gain patch antenna must be used in order to have adequate signal coverage at the opposite end. Having this high gain, the patch antenna's horizontal beamwidths are significantly narrowed such that the rooms on each side of the hallway do not have adequate coverage. Additionally, the high-gain antenna doesn't have a large enough vertical beamwidth to cover the floors immediately above and below. In this case, you might decide to use two patch antennas: one at each end of the hallway facing each other. They would both be low-gain with wide horizontal and vertical beamwidths, providing coverage to the rooms on each side of the hallway, along with the floors above and below. Due to the low gain, the antennas may each cover only a portion (maybe half) of the length of the hallway.

During an indoor site survey, engineers usually are thinking of how to best locate *omnidirectional* antennas, since they are the kind of antenna that most often come with the equipment. In some cases, semi-directional antennas provide such long-range coverage that they may eliminate the need for multiple access points in a building.

As with omnidirectional antennas, semi-directional antennas may include a certain amount of downtilt in order to avoid having to physically point the antenna down at the users. This is less of an issue with semi-directional antennas than omnidirectional. Physically tilting an omnidirectional antenna essentially eliminates the entire back half of the coverage, which ends up shooting into the sky or the ceiling. The back lobes of semi-directional antennas often are so weak as to be unusable; in this case, eliminating them is not an issue. Figure 4.10 shows an example of a semi-directional antenna mounted on a cell tower, such as might be used by a wireless ISP. The antenna's height provides wide coverage but, because it has no downtilt, might cause the signal to shoot over the customers' heads. Downtilt compensates for this problem.

FIGURE 4.10   Downtilt of semi-directional antennas

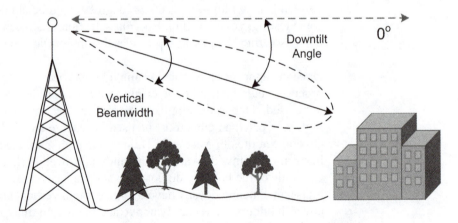

Highly-directional Antennas

Highly-directional antennas emit the most narrow signal beams of any antenna type and have the greatest gain of these three groups of antennas. Two common types of highly directional antennas are parabolic dish and grid. Some models are referred to as parabolic dishes because they resemble small satellite dishes. Others are called grid antennas due to their perforated design for resistance to wind loading. Even though grid antennas have "holes" in them, they are designed so that these holes are invisible to RF energy at the antenna's specified frequency. In other words, a grid antenna is no less receptive of RF energy, even though your intuition might tell you that the RF energy would "leak through the holes."

FIGURE 4.11   Sample of highly-directional antennas

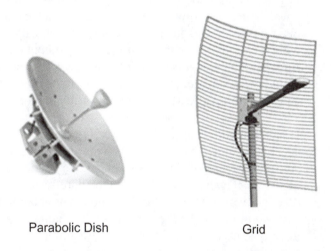

Parabolic Dish   Grid

Figure 4.12 illustrates the radiation pattern of a high-gain antenna. Even in a very high-gain antenna, the same principles of antenna design apply: the energy is being very tightly focused, but there is still some weak radiation in areas outside of the main beam, especially in the side and rear lobes close to the antenna.

FIGURE 4.12   Radiation pattern of a highly-directional antenna

Usage

High-gain antennas do not have a coverage area that client devices can use, so they are never appropriate for mobile users. These antennas are used for point-to-point communication links and can typically transmit at distances up to 35 miles (58 km). Potential uses of highly directional antennas might be to connect two buildings that are miles away from each other and have clear line of sight between them. Additionally, these antennas can be aimed directly at each other within a building in order to "blast" through an obstruction. In some cases, highly directional antennas might be used indoors—for example, to shoot coverage down the aisles of a warehouse or hardware store, where the shelves effectively block any other type of coverage. (This would require many antennas and APs, as well as careful management of the power output of the antennas, to make sure that their side lobes did not interfere with each other.) This setup would be used to get network connectivity to places that cannot be wired and where normal wireless networks will not work.

Highly directional antennas have a very narrow beamwidth and must be accurately aimed at one another. This aiming process can be problematic since the RF line of sight does not have to be the same as the visual line of sight. RF waves might be diffracted, refracted, reflected, etc., in ways that light waves are not. So, the antenna orientation that maximizes signal strength might not be the one where the antennas appear to be pointed directly at each other. The best way to aim highly directional antennas is through trial and error. Move the antenna in small increments, giving the link time to stabilize after each move, and then measure signal strength. Choose the orientation that maximizes signal strength even if it isn't visually the best.

Because of highly directional antennas' small beamwidth, a very small amount of motion such as that caused by wind blowing on the antenna or snow building up on it, can cause enough deviation to significantly degrade the link. Solutions abound, such as very stiff mounts and grid antennas designed to let wind pass through. The best solution of all is to not use a higher-gain antenna than you really need. While to the novice it might seem like the highest-gain antenna possible is the best, in fact a lower-gain antenna might give a more reliable link due to its wider beamwidth. Ask yourself which you'd rather have: 90 percent signal strength that goes down to zero every time the wind blows, or 60 percent signal strength that provides a consistent connection.

Finally, because highly-directional antennas are usually used in point-to-point implementations where the signal isn't subject to very much reflection or multipath, matching the polarization of highly-directional antenna is much more important than it is with omnidirectional antennas (which are commonly used indoors, where the reflections and multipath often make polarization a non-issue). This means that you should not only aim the antennas for maximum signal strength but also give them the same rotation along the axis of the beam.

Line of Sight (LOS)

Visual line of sight (also called simply LOS) is defined as the apparently straight line taken by rays of visible light from the object in sight (the transmitter) to the observer's eye (the receiver). The LOS is an *apparently* straight line because light waves are subject to changes in direction due to refraction, diffraction, and reflection in the same way as RF frequencies. Figure 4.13 illustrates LOS.

FIGURE 4.13 Line of Sight

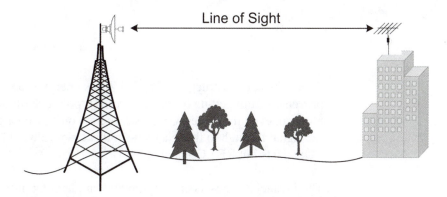

RF works very much the same as visible light within wireless LAN frequencies, with one major exception: RF line of sight also can be affected by blockage of the Fresnel Zone.

Fresnel Zone

The Fresnel Zone is an area centered on the visible LOS between the transmitting and receiving antenna. It can be thought of as being ellipse-shaped—narrow toward the antenna and widest at the midpoint between the antennas. The Fresnel Zone comes about because, even in a highly-directional antenna, the energy of an RF wave is not concentrated in a laser-like beam.

FIGURE 4.14   Fresnel Zone

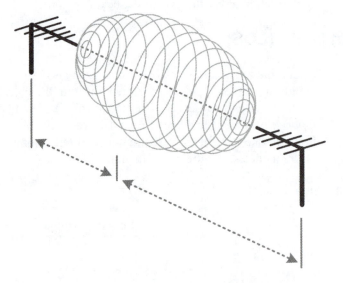

As an obstacle obstructs the Fresnel Zone, energy is absorbed and prevented from getting to the receiver. If too much of the Fresnel Zone is blocked, even if visible LOS exists, there won't be enough energy to get the signal through to the receiver. In this case we would say that visible LOS exists but RF LOS is blocked.

The Fresnel Zone is a consideration when planning or troubleshooting an RF link. The Fresnel Zone is important to the integrity of the RF link because it defines an area around the LOS that can introduce RF signal interference if blocked, as illustrated in Figure 4.15.

FIGURE 4.15   Fresnel Zone Blockage

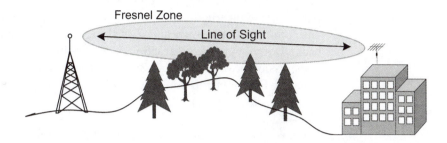

Objects in the Fresnel Zone such as trees, hilltops, and buildings can diffract or reflect the main signal away from the receiver, changing the RF LOS. These same objects can absorb or scatter the main RF signal, causing degradation or complete signal loss.

Obstructions

Considering the importance of Fresnel Zone clearance, we should quantify the degree to which the Fresnel Zone can be blocked. Since a partially blocked RF signal will bend around the obstacle to some degree, and since an RF link often will contain more energy than is absolutely necessary to get a signal through, some blockage of the Fresnel Zone can occur without significant link disruption. Typically, ≤ 40 percent Fresnel Zone blockage introduces a manageable amount of interference into the link. More than 40 percent typically means that the link will be unreliable. It is always suggested to err on the conservative side, allowing no more than 20 percent blockage of the Fresnel Zone. If trees or other growing objects are the source of the blockage, you might want to consider designing the link based on 0 percent blockage because, as the trees grow, they will slowly encroach on the Fresnel Zone.

If the Fresnel Zone of a proposed RF link is more than 20 percent blocked, or if an active link becomes blocked by new construction or tree growth, raising the height of the antennas usually will alleviate the problem. Raising the height of the antennas also will raise the Fresnel Zone, decreasing the degree to which the Fresnel Zone is blocked. In some cases, raising the height of the antennas is not an option. For example, FAA restrictions limit the height of antennas on the ground, on top of buildings, and within a certain distance of airports. Or, perhaps it is something as simple as the antenna already being mounted at the top of the mast and not having the budget to buy a taller tower. In that case removing the obstruction should be your next course of action. Foliage, one common source of Fresnel Zone blockage, often can be trimmed back. If removing the obstruction is not an option, increasing transmission power may work, but it's important to make sure you're not violating FCC transmission power or certified system restrictions (which will be discussed later).

The formula to calculate the "60 percent unobstructed radius" - the minimum clear radius around the visual LOS, is:

$$r = 43.3 \times \sqrt{\frac{d}{4f}}$$

where *d* is the link distance in miles, *f* is the frequency in GHz, and the answer, *r*, is in feet. For example, suppose there is a 2.4000 GHz link 5 miles (8.35 km) in length. The resulting minimum clearance would have a radius of 31.25 feet (9.52 meters). Remember that the radius of the clear zone is 60 percent smaller than the radius of the entire Fresnel Zone. To calculate the radius of the Fresnel Zone itself, substitute 72.2 for 43.3 in the above formula.

Fresnel zone calculations are not part of the CWNA exam. The formula is provided to you for your administrative tasks.

Many references quote the 43.3 multiplier as the radius of the first Fresnel zone, *not* the radius of the "60 percent unobstructed zone". WLAN engineers who use the 43.3 multiplier and then take 60 percent on top of that end up with an unobstructed radius that is 60 percent smaller than it should be. This means that they might think their first Fresnel zone is clear, when it's really not!

This error was discovered by Joseph Bardwell in the process of writing his white paper, "Math and Physics for the 802.11 WLAN Engineer." Details, including derivation of the Fresnel zone formula and confirmation of the conclusion about the 43.3 multiplier, are in the paper.

It may be surprising that the beamwidth (and hence antenna gain) of the antenna is *not* a factor in calculating the radius of the Fresnel Zone. Intuitively it might seem that an antenna that radiates a wider beam (such as a 13 dBi gain Yagi, which might have a 30 degree beamwidth) would have a larger Fresnel Zone than a 24 dBi parabolic dish (which might have a 2–5 degree beamwidth). In fact, that is not the case. The radius of the Fresnel Zone depends only on the distance between the antennas and the frequency of the signal.

Antennas have the advantage of seeing "phases," which is different from how a human would see light. Fresnel Zones are in-phase and out-of-phase areas (zones) around the point source. The First Fresnel Zone is loosely defined as the area between the transmission point source and the end of the first in-phase zone surrounding the point source. Picture in your mind a dot with concentric circles around it. The area between the center dot (called the point source) and the outside of the first ring is considered the First Fresnel Zone (1FZ). Do not block the 1FZ because it is in-phase (additive) with the main transmission signal (the dot).

FIGURE 4.16   Visualizing the Fresnel Zone

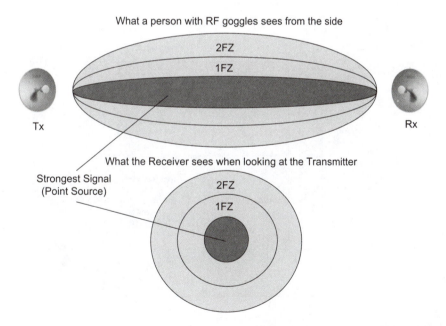

The first zone adds to the main signal amplitude because it is in-phase, and the second zone (2FZ) subtracts from the main signal amplitude because it is out-of-phase. Zones alternate between in-phase and out-of-phase thereafter, as well. It is acceptable – even advantageous – to block the 2FZ, but it is not typical to attempt to block it on purpose.

Imagine standing on a tower at night looking at another tower which had a simple flashlight bulb shining from it. This situation is representative of an omni antenna propagating RF waves. What would you see? You would see a dim dot of light (the point source). If you had binoculars (representative of a high-gain receiving antenna) what would you see? You would see a bright dot of light. If someone took the flashlight reflector out of the flashlight and put it on the other side of the light so that all of the light was reflected toward you, what would you see without the binoculars? You would see a bright dot. What would you see with the binoculars? You would see a very bright dot. The point is that the receiver only sees a point source with in-phase and out-of-phase rings around it, as shown in Figure 4.17. Antenna gain and beamwidth changes only affect perceived intensity (power) of the source – not the Fresnel Zone size.

FIGURE 4.17   How Antennas Perceive RF

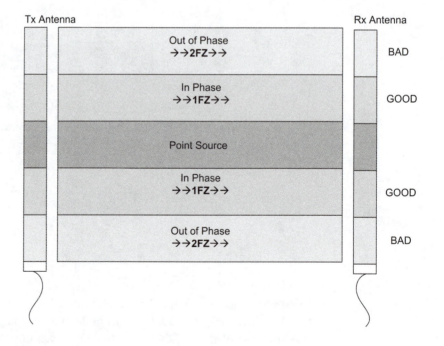

In a case such as that shown in Figure 4.18, buildings are blocking more than 40 percent of the first Fresnel Zone (1FZ).

FIGURE 4.18   Common Fresnel Zone Blockage Scenario

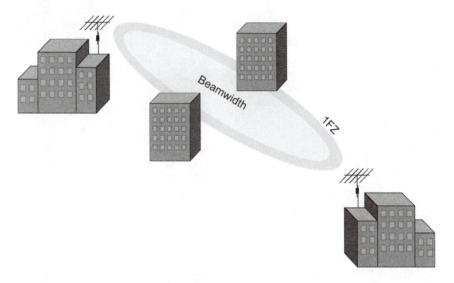

At first glance you would think that the obvious fix is to simply use higher gain antennas, which yield a more tightly focused beam. However this would have no effect on the size of the 1FZ.

FIGURE 4.19 Common Fresnel Zone Blockage Scenario – **WRONG FIX**

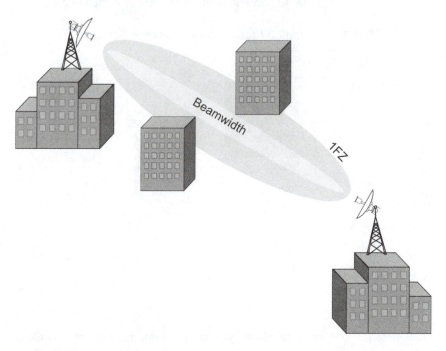

To change the size of the 1FZ in this scenario, you would have to either change the frequency in use or change the distance between the two buildings.

Until now, our Fresnel Zone examples have involved long-distance point-to-point links with medium to high-gain antennas. How does blockage of the Fresnel Zone affect indoor installations, with omnidirectional antennas in the AP and clients and client devices that might physically move around? In most indoor installations RF signals pass through, reflect off, and diffract around many walls, furniture, and other obstructions. The Fresnel Zone is not encroached upon unless the signal is partially or fully blocked. Since the signal takes so many different paths to the user, in an indoor WLAN scenario, the Fresnel Zone really doesn't exist in the same sense. Technically, the Fresnel Zone is always there but, practically speaking, we can ignore it in this situation. In addition, since the environment is constantly changing (people walking around, for example), maintaining a clear Fresnel Zone might not be possible. In a mobile environment, the Fresnel Zone is constantly changing, so the user normally dismisses a loss of connection, thinking that the coverage is simply "bad" where they are located and giving no thought to why the coverage is bad.

Earth Bulge

Given that the Earth is not flat, as the length of an RF link increases, eventually the horizon itself will begin to obstruct the Fresnel Zone. Exactly when this happens depends on the height of the antennas and the length of the RF link. The longer the wireless link, the larger the Fresnel Zone is, and the antennas must be raised accordingly. For indoor links this is not a factor, but earth bulge should be considered any time a point-to-point link of longer than seven miles is being considered. The Fresnel Zone must be at least 60 percent clear (optimally $\geq$ 80 percent) of all obstacles – even the horizon. Figure 4.20 illustrates how Earth bulge can factor into long distance links.

FIGURE 4.20   Earth Bulge

The formula for calculating the *additional* antenna height needed for RF links over 7 miles is:

$$H = \frac{D^2}{8}$$

H = Height of earth bulge (in feet)
D = Distance between antennas (in miles)

The formula for calculating *minimum* antenna height for links over 7 miles is:

$$H = \left(43.3\sqrt{\frac{D}{4F}} \right) + \frac{D^2}{8}$$

H = Height of the antenna (in feet)
D = Distance between antennas (in miles)
F = Frequency in GHz

Free Space Path Loss

Free Space Path Loss (also called Path Loss and Free Space Loss [FSL]) refers to the loss incurred by an RF signal due to "signal dispersion," which is a natural broadening of the wave front. The wider the wave front, the less power can be induced into the receiving antenna. As the transmitted signal propagates, its power level decreases at a rate inversely proportional to the distance traveled, and proportional to the wavelength of the signal. Power level becomes a very important factor when considering link viability.

The Path Loss equation is one of the foundations of link budget calculations. Link budget calculations will be discussed next, but in short, they are the calculations that allow the network designer to know ahead of

$$H = \frac{D^2}{8}$$

time whether the RF link will work or not. Path Loss represents the single greatest source of loss in a wireless system. Below are two formulas for Path Loss.

$$Lp = 36.6 + (20 * \log10(F)) + (20 \log10(D))$$

where

Lp = free-space path loss between antennas (in dB)
F = frequency in MHz
D = path length in miles

or

$$Lp = 32.4 + (20 * \log10(F)) + (20 \log10(D))$$

where

Lp = free-space path loss between antennas (in dB)
F = frequency in MHz

You will not be tested on the Path Loss formula in the CWNA exam, but it is provided for your administrative reference. Instead of calculating the formula by hand, you can find several FSL calculators on the web by searching for "free space loss calculator."

The 6dB Rule

Close inspection of the Path Loss equation yields a relationship that is useful in dealing with link budget issues. Each 6 dB increase in EIRP equates to a doubling of range. Conversely, a 6 dB reduction in EIRP translates into a cutting of the range in half. Below is a chart that provides a rough estimate of the Path Loss for given distances between transmitter and receiver at 2.4 GHz.

Distance	Loss (in dB)
100 meters	80.23
200 meters	86.25
500 meters	94.21
1,000 meters	100.23
2,000 meters	106.25
5,000 meters	114.21
10,000 meters	120.23

 This chart above is provided for your quick reference, and is not tested on the CWNA exam.

Link Budget/System Operating Margin

The *link budget* or *system operating margin* refers to the calculation of the amount of excess signal strength that exists between the transmitter and receiver. It is usually expressed in dB. The link budget is calculated by adding together all of the gains and losses in the path between the transmitter and receiver. For example, in Figure 4.21, you would start with the transmission power, subtract line loss for the cable between the transmitter and the antenna, add antenna gain, subtract free-space loss, add antenna gain at the receiver, and subtract line loss between the receive antenna and the receiver. The result would be the received signal strength, in dBm or mW.

FIGURE 4.21   Link Budget Overview

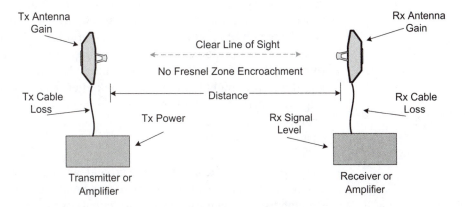

In order to calculate the link budget, you must know the *receive sensitivity* of the receiver. The receive sensitivity is the absolute weakest signal that the radio can reliably receive. To measure the receive sensitivity of a radio, vendors put the card in a shielded room and transmit RF signals of decreasing strength. As the strength decreases, the bit error rate, as calculated by the receiver, increases. A radio's receive sensitivity is defined as the weakest signal that the radio can receive with a bit error rate remaining below a certain threshold. Therefore, a *lower receive sensitivity is better,* since that means that the card can reliably receive a weaker signal.

Receive sensitivity is dependent on the data rate at which the signal is being transmitted. Higher data-rate signals use more complex encoding and modulation methods, and so are more susceptible to corruption. This means that the card's receive sensitivity will almost always go up (get worse) as its data rate goes up. The exception is if different physical-layer technologies are used at higher data rates—an 802.11g card might have a lower (better) receive sensitivity at 6 Mbps (using OFDM) than at 5.5 Mbps (using DSSS), even though 6 Mbps is a higher data rate. For example, a hypothetical 802.11b card might have a receive sensitivity of –95 dBm at 1 Mbps, –93 dBm at 2 Mbps, –90 dBm at 5.5 Mbps, and –87 dBm at 11 Mbps. You can get the actual numbers from your equipment vendor. They are commonly listed on the equipment's box or in its owner's manual.

Link budget specifically refers to the amount of signal strength a station is receiving relative to its receive sensitivity. For example, if the receive sensitivity of a certain 802.11 bridge is –82 dBm and the card measures a signal strength of –50 dBm, the system margin is –82 minus –50, which equals –32 dBm. You can afford to lose approximately another 32 dBm of strength before you lose this particular link. Reality isn't quite that cut-and-dried: you might really lose the link after only 28 dBm of loss, or you might get away with 35 dBm of loss. In general, link budget calculation provides a good guideline for how much loss a given wireless link can sustain before becoming unviable.

Because wireless clients can move around, and because indoor environments have a lot of multipath (potentially causing the signal strength to vary even for a stationary client), we usually don't bother calculating system margin for indoor point-to-multipoint systems. System margin is most useful for long-distance outdoor point-to-point links, such as a wireless bridge link between two buildings, because the signal strength of this type of link is usually more stable.

Calculation of link budget can be complex, especially when there are many components in the RF system. Therefore, many vendors offer spreadsheets that automatically perform the calculations for common combinations of their equipment. One such spreadsheet, from Cisco, is pictured in Figure 4.22.

FIGURE 4.22   Link Budget Calculation Utility Example

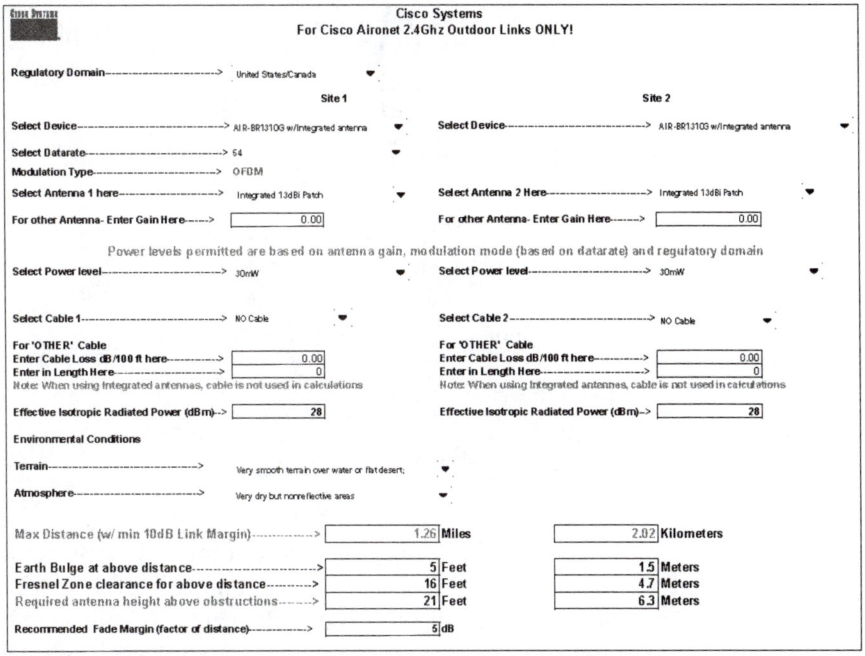

Fade Margin

In reality, the strength of an 802.11 signal won't stay constant. This is especially true for indoor environments in which the environment is constantly changing and multipath is a major factor. This is also true to some degree for long-distance outdoor links. When planning a WLAN installation, it is common to include a few extra dB of signal strength to the link budget. This extra signal strength is known as a *fade margin.* For example, if you were designing an 802.11 bridge link with bridges whose receive sensitivity was –82 dBm, you might base your link budget calculations on a receive sensitivity of –72 dBm—this would give you a 10 dB fade margin. Fade margins of between 10 and 20 dB are common for both indoor and outdoor installations.

FIGURE 4.23   Link Budget – Will the Link Work?

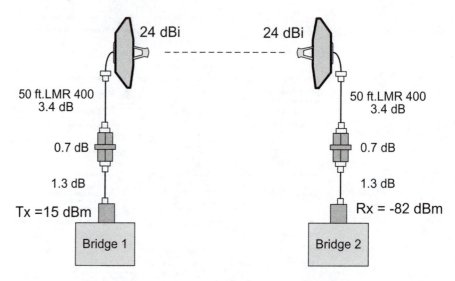

In Figure 4.23, bridge 1 is transmitting at 15 dBm, and bridge 2's receive sensitivity is –82 dBm. The loss and gain of the various components is shown. Generally 10 dB of fade margin is considered the minimum to allow for various changes in the network, such as antenna misalignment, weather, interference, etc. When a high amount of interference is expected, 15 dB of fade margin might be appropriate. When adverse weather is expected, 20 dB of fade margin might be appropriate. For the example in Figure 4.23, the network should be designed so that the received signal strength is above –72, –77, or –62 dBm, respectively, depending on weather conditions. Figure 4.24 shows how the link budget (using a 10 dB fade margin) was calculated.

FIGURE 4.24   Link Budget – The Link Will Work.

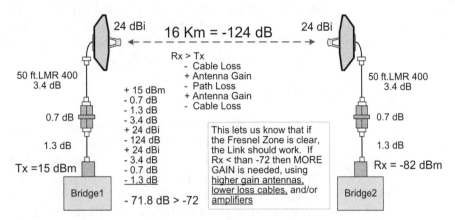

Antenna Installation

It is very important to have proper installation of the antennas in a wireless LAN. An improper installation can lead to damage or destruction of your equipment and also can lead to personal injury. Somewhat less important, but still significant, is good performance of the wireless LAN system, which is achieved through proper placement, mounting, orientation, and alignment. In this section we will cover:

- Placement
- Mounting
- Appropriate Use
- Orientation
- Alignment
- Safety
- Maintenance

Placement

Dipole

Mount omnidirectional (dipole) antennas attached to access points near the middle of the desired coverage area whenever possible. Place the antenna as high as possible to increase coverage area, being careful that users located somewhat below the antenna still have reception, particularly when using high-gain omni antennas. Outdoor antennas should be mounted above obstructions such as trees and buildings, so no objects encroach on the Fresnel Zone.

Patch / Panel

Since patch/panel antennas typically have 180 degrees or less of coverage, they should usually be mounted at the outside of the desired coverage area, pointing in. For example, patch antennas might be mounted on the walls of a warehouse, facing in. If the warehouse is large enough that the patch antennas couldn't provide adequate signal strength in the middle, a ceiling-mounted omni might fill in coverage.

Compared to using only an omnidirectional antenna, this configuration minimizes the amount of bleed that occurs outside the coverage area and maximizes signal strength at the edges of the coverage area. If an omni antenna is placed at the edge of the coverage, a large amount of signal would bleed outside the coverage area, making the network easier for attackers to locate. On the other hand, if an omni antenna is placed so its coverage ended at the walls of the building, coverage near the walls would be weak.

Patch and panel antennas are sometimes designed to be mounted on a ceiling, facing down. Depending on the antenna's coverage, it might not be ideal to use this type of antenna in a wall-based mounting, and vice versa. For example, some patch antennas have a very flat coverage area. This is fine if the antenna is mounted on a wall, but if the antenna were ceiling-mounted, it would only provide coverage in a narrow corridor.

Yagi

Mount yagi antennas at the end of a long, narrow area of desired coverage, such as shooting down a long hallway. Yagis typically have a wide enough beam to cover an entire hallway or a row of cubicles, as opposed to high-gain antennas, whose narrow beams are more suited to point-to-point application. Unlike patch and omni antennas, yagi antennae are usually too big to be installed discretely. Therefore they may be slightly less appropriate for indoor use unless they can be mounted in some out-of-the-way place. Lower-gain yagis have a wide enough beam to be useful when pointed down at the ground from the ceiling, but the higher the yagi's gain, the longer and narrower its beam will be, meaning that its coverage circle at the ground will be smaller.

Dish / Grid

Dish and grid antennas are typically mounted on outdoor masts or dedicated tripods. Specialized mounts are usually required due to this type of antenna's larger size. Mounts for dish and grid antennas must be easily adjustable since these types of antennas must be precisely aligned. In addition, they must be sturdy enough to resist weather, such as wind and snow.

Mounting

Once you have calculated the necessary output power, gain, and distance that you need to transmit your RF signal, and have chosen the appropriate antenna for the job, you must mount the antenna. There are several options for mounting antennas both indoors and outdoors, some of which are shown in Figures 4.25–4.36. Figure 4.25 shows a set of dipole antennas of different lengths. Each has an N-type female connector that can screw into a mounting plate. The middle picture shows a flange plate with dual "U" bolts mounted to a mast. The right picture shows a ceiling mounting bracket that also allows the antenna to screw in.

FIGURE 4.25 Mounting Antennas – Dipole - Screw-in

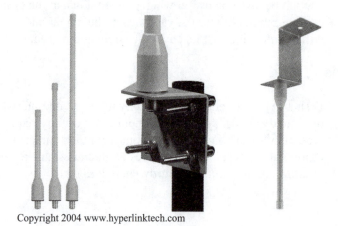

Copyright 2004 www.hyperlinktech.com

Figure 4.26 illustrates a mast-mounted dipole antenna using mounting clamps or U-bolts. A large variety of mounting clamps and U-bolt brackets is available. Most antenna manufacturers have types appropriate for mounting their antennas. A typical single U-bolt mounting bracket is shown on the right.

FIGURE 4.26 Mounting Antennas – Dipole - Mast Mount with Clamps or U bolts

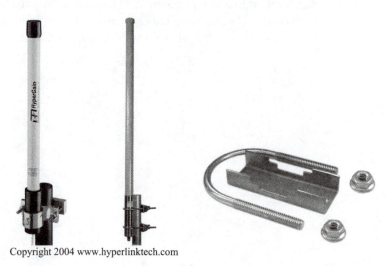

Copyright 2004 www.hyperlinktech.com

Figure 4.27 shows a dipole antenna with an N-type male connector. The magnetic mount on the right has an N-type female connector to which the antenna can connect. The base has a strong magnet underneath for mounting horizontally or vertically to any metal surface.

FIGURE 4.27   Mounting Antennas – Dipole: Magnetic Mount and Ceiling Mount

Copyright 2004 www.hyperlinktech.com

Figure 4.28 shows a "universal mount" bracket. This type of bracket can be used to mount a patch/panel antenna either to a wall or to a mast. The mount's flange plates can be screwed directly into walls, ceilings, or other flat surfaces; if the antenna is to be mounted to a mast, an additional u-bolt kit is required. This mount is made of galvanized steel for weatherproofing, so it would be appropriate for outdoor installations. Note that the base of the universal mount has a swivel attachment to allow some flexibility in aiming the antenna.

FIGURE 4.28   Mounting Antennas – Patch / Panel: Universal Mount

Copyright 2004 www.hyperlinktech.com

Figure 4.29 shows some examples of tilt-and-swivel mounts for patch and panel antennas. This type of mount is similar to the universal mount, except that it adds more flexibility in aiming the antenna. The upper-left mount uses a ball-joint with a tightening screw to allow complete aiming flexibility within the mount's movement limits. The other two mounts use dual joints—one for tilt and one for swivel. These three mounts are designed to hold small, medium, and large antennas, respectively.

FIGURE 4.29   Mounting Antennas – Patch / Panel: Tilt-and-Swivel Mounting Kits

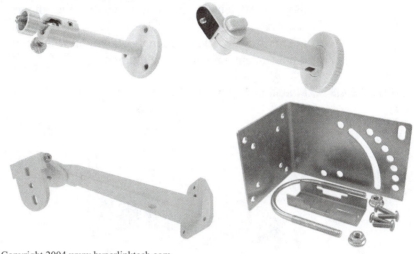

Figure 4.30 shows another example of a tilt-and-swivel mount. This mount is built into the panel antenna itself. Note that this type of mount is ideally suited for mast-mounting, while the mounts in Figure 4.29 are more appropriate for wall or ceiling-mounting.

FIGURE 4.30   Mounting Antennas – Patch / Panel: Tilt-and-Swivel Mounts

Figure 4.31 shows two specialized types of mounts. The left-hand mount is designed for installation on the outside corner of a structure. The mount is attached to the corner, and then the antenna is attached to the two plates that stick out at 90 degrees from the wall. The right-hand mount is designed for ceiling installation, where an omnidirectional dipole antenna points straight down.

FIGURE 4.31   Mounting Antennas – Patch / Panel: Ceiling / Wall Mount

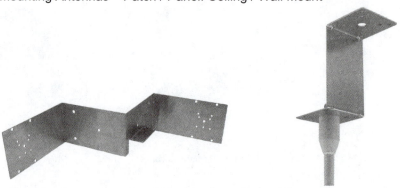

Copyright 2004 www.hyperlinktech.com

Figure 4.32 shows an example of a window mount. The suction cups attach to the window, anchoring the antenna.

FIGURE 4.32   Mounting Antennas – Patch / Panel: Window Mount

Copyright 2004 www.hyperlinktech.com

Yagi antennas come in all shapes, sizes, and gains. Many are enclosed in a radome so that moisture does not affect signal transmission. Figures 4.33–4.34 illustrate a Yagi antenna mounted on a mast using a U-bolt mounting clamp and a tilt-and-swivel bracket.

FIGURE 4.33   Mounting Antennas – Yagi: U-bolt Mount

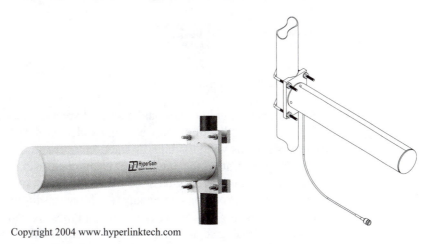

Copyright 2004 www.hyperlinktech.com

This installation may not provide enough flexibility if the users are above or below the antenna (or in the case of a point-to-point link, if the other end of the link is above or below this end). In that case, a tilt-and-swivel mount, as pictured in Figure 4.34, is appropriate. This type of mount is more mechanically complex and might not be as stable as mounting directly to the mast.

FIGURE 4.34   Mounting Antennas – Yagi: Tilt-and-Swivel Mount

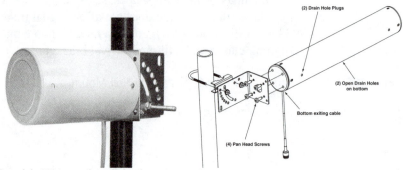

Alignment of highly directional dish/grid antennas is much more important than that of omnidirectional and semi-directional antennas. Factors such as wind loading, diffraction, reflection, and refraction mean that simply pointing the antennas at each other, using visual LOS, will usually not maximize signal strength. In addition, over long distances a few degrees of rotation can equate to a large misalignment. Therefore, while mounts for the former two antenna types are sometimes fixed, mounts for dish/grid antennas are always adjustable. More easily adjustable mounts will make installation faster.

FIGURE 4.35   Mounting Antennas – Dish / Grid – U-bolt and Tilt-and-Swivel

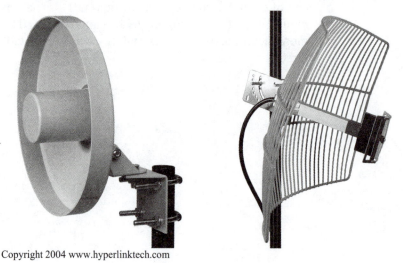

FIGURE 4.36   Mounting Antennas – Grid: U-bolt with Bracket

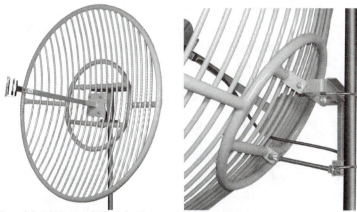

Copyright 2004 www.hyperlinktech.com

A sector antenna is a type of antenna that produces a flat, wide radiation pattern in a specific direction. Its coverage pattern is similar to a patch or panel antenna, but is usually flatter and propagates much less to the rear of the antenna. Sector antennas typically have relatively high gain—10 dBi or more. Their horizontal beamwidths range from 180 degrees to about 60 degrees. For example, a 14 dBi sector antenna might have a horizontal half-power beamwidth of 60 degrees and a vertical half-power beamwidth of 14 degrees.

As we mentioned previously, one defining characteristic of sector antennas is that they radiate relatively little power (compared to other antenna types) behind the antenna. This means that they can be placed back-to-back without interfering with each other. This has the advantage that two antennas can transmit at the same time in different directions without interfering with each other. This increases the potential throughput of the system compared to a single omnidirectional antenna. In addition this means that they can be mounted on, for example, a cell tower or high mast, and then mechanically angled down towards the ground without shooting the back half of their signal up into the sky, as a dipole would. In this configuration, the total range of the system is increased compared to a single omnidirectional antenna, since each sector antenna puts most of its power in a smaller arc. This is opposed to the omnidirectional antenna which spreads its power over a 360 degree arc.

It is common to use two to four sector antennas (depending on the antennas' horizontal beamwidth) to cover a full circle around a tower or mast.

Figure 4.37 shows a sector antenna's mounting bracket. Note that the top bracket is jointed to allow the antenna to be tilted down by a certain number of degrees.

FIGURE 4.37   Mounting Antennas – Sector: Adjustable Clamp

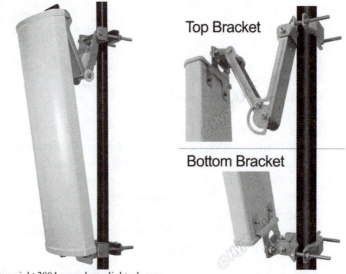

Copyright 2004 www.hyperlinktech.com

There is no single answer for where or how to mount your particular antenna. The antennas and brackets shown here are not intended to be a comprehensive list, but rather a sample of some of the available mounting options. You will learn in Chapter 13 that the recommended placement and mounting of antennas will be part of a site survey. There is no substitute for on-the-job training, which is where you are likely to learn how to mount wireless LAN antennas using various types of mounting hardware. Each type of mount will come with instructions from the manufacturer on how to install and secure it. There are many different variations of each mount type because manufacturers each have their own way of designing the mounting kit.

Some things to keep in mind when mounting antennas are:

- Many times the brackets shipped with the antenna may not work for a particular situation. Modifying brackets or building custom brackets may be necessary.
- Do not hang an antenna by its cable, and make sure the mounting is solid and secure. The cable can break and cable sway can produce a moving cell.
- Exactly how the antenna is to be mounted should be specified for each antenna in the site survey report.

Mounting Aesthetics

Antennas are usually unsightly and should be hidden when possible. Some manufacturers make ceiling panel antennas. When aesthetics are important, patch or panel antennas might be used rather than omni antennas. If possible, antennas should be hidden and secured to avoid damage by children and by adults who purposely seek to damage the gear. Figure 4.38 illustrates lockable ceiling enclosures that can house an access point with attached antennas.

FIGURE 4.38   Mounting Aesthetics – Lockable Ceiling Enclosures

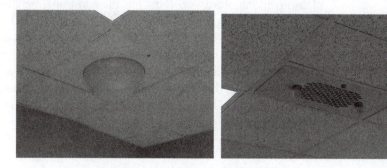

Figure 4.39 illustrates a ceiling tile with integrated antenna. The image shows the top side of the ceiling tile that would be in the dropped ceiling; from the bottom the tile looks just like any other. Antennas are integrated into the material of the tile itself, and the connectors for the antennas are visible in the image. The tile contains antennas for cellular (850/1900 MHz) and 802.11 (2.4 GHz) applications. This product represents the

ultimate in unobtrusive WLAN installation, since all cables could be routed through the ceiling, and no antenna would be visible at all.

FIGURE 4.39   Mounting Aesthetics – Ceiling Tile Antenna

Many vendors have taken steps to make their products more aesthetically pleasing and unobtrusive. This has the additional benefit of increasing security, since making APs and antennas harder to find makes it harder to steal them or hack into them. As an example, the item on the left is an access point with integrated diversity dipole antennas. It is shaped something like a smoke alarm, and is generally mistaken for one. The WLAN switch in the picture on the right is the flat panel against the wall behind the man. This unit uses a phased array of antennas on an inconspicuous flat panel.

FIGURE 4.40 Mounting Aesthetics – Various Methods of Disguising Antennas

Appropriate Use

Use indoor antennas inside of buildings and outdoor antennas outside of buildings unless the indoor area is significantly large to warrant use of an outdoor antenna. Outdoor antennas are most often sealed to prevent water from entering the antenna element area and made of plastics able to withstand extreme heat and cold. This weather protection raises the cost of the antenna. Indoor antennas that don't need to withstand the elements are not made to withstand outdoor use.

Orientation

Antenna orientation determines polarization, which was discussed previously as having a significant impact on signal reception. If an antenna is oriented with the electrical field parallel to the Earth's surface, then the clients (if the antenna is mounted to an access point) should also have this same orientation for maximum reception. The reverse is also true, with both having the electrical field oriented perpendicular to the Earth's surface. The throughput of a bridge link will be drastically reduced if both ends of the link do not have the same antenna orientation.

Alignment

Antenna alignment is sometimes critical and other times not. Some antennas have very wide horizontal and vertical beamwidths, allowing the administrator to aim two antennas in a building-to-building bridging environment in each other's general direction and get almost perfect reception. Alignment is more important when implementing long-distance bridging links using highly-directional antennas. Wireless bridges come with alignment software that aids the administrator in optimizing antenna alignment for best reception. This software helps to reduce lost packets and high retry counts while maximizing signal strength. Alternatively, some bridges have a BNC connector that can be attached to a voltmeter to aid in alignment, as seen in Figure 4.41. The bridges are properly aligned when the voltage on the meter is maximized. When using access points with omnidirectional or semi-directional antennas, proper alignment usually is a matter of covering the appropriate area so wireless clients can connect in places where connectivity is required.

FIGURE 4.41   Antenna Alignment Using a Voltmeter

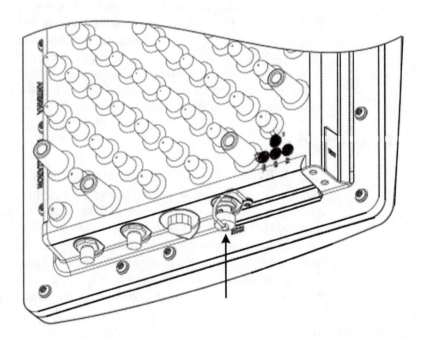

Safety

RF antennas, like other electrical devices, can be dangerous to implement and operate. The following guidelines should be observed whenever you or one of your associates is installing or otherwise working with RF antennas.

Follow the Manual

Carefully follow instructions provided with all antennas. Following all provided instructions will prevent damage to the antenna and personal injury. Most of the safety precautions found in antenna manufacturers' manuals are common sense.

Do not touch when power is applied

Never touch a high-gain antenna to any part of your body or point it toward your body while it is transmitting. The FCC allows very high amounts of RF power to be transmitted in the license-free bands when configuring a point-to-point link. Putting any part of your body in front of a 2.4 GHz highly-directional antenna that is transmitting at high power would be equivalent to putting your body in a microwave oven.

Professional Installers

For most elevated antenna installations, consider using a professional installer. Professional climbers and installers are trained in proper climbing safety, and will be able to better install and secure your wireless LAN antenna if it is to be mounted on a pole, tower, or other type of elevated construction.

Metal Obstructions

Keep antennas away from metal obstructions such as heating and air-conditioning ducts, large ceiling trusses, building superstructures, and major power cabling runs. These types of metal obstructions create a significant amount of multipath. Since these types of metal obstructions reflect a large portion of the RF signal, if the signal is being broadcast at high power, the reflected signal could be dangerous to bystanders.

Power Lines

Antenna towers should be a safe distance from overhead power lines. The recommended safe distance is twice the antenna height. Since wireless LAN antennas are generally small, this recommended practice does not usually apply. It is not a good idea to have wireless LAN antennas near significant power sources because an electrical short between the power source and the wireless LAN could be dangerous to personnel working on the wireless LAN, and would likely destroy the wireless LAN equipment.

Grounding Blocks

Use grounding blocks and follow the national electrical code and local electrical codes for proper outdoor antenna and tower grounding. WLAN systems generally should have less than 5 ohms to Earth ground. The recommended resistance is 2 ohms or less. Grounding rods placed correctly into the soil can prevent damage to the wireless LAN equipment and might even save the life of anyone climbing on the tower if the tower is struck by lightning.

FIGURE 4.42   Grounding Block

Ground Testing

You should check Earth ground at least every 12 months once a proper ground is installed and initially verified to be acceptable. You can make these measurements with an Earth Ground Resistance Tester as shown in Figure 4.43.

FIGURE 4.43   Earth Ground Resistance Testers

Safety Course

Consider taking an RF health and safety course, such as those offered by SiteSafe (http://www.sitesafe.com). These courses cover issues such as FCC and OSHA compliance that may be of importance to 802.11 installers.

Maintenance

Prevention

To prevent moisture entry into antenna cable, seal all external cable connectors using commercial products such as coax compatible electrical tape or Coax-Seal, as shown in Figure 4.44. Moisture that has entered connectors and cabling is very difficult, if not impossible, to remove. It is usually more economical to replace the cable and connectors than to remove the moisture.

FIGURE 4.44   Coax Seal

Connectors and cables with any amount of water will likely make the RF signal erratic and can cause significant signal degradation, because the presence of water will change the cable's impedance and hence the VSWR.

When installing outdoor RF cabling, make sure to mount connectors facing downward and use drip loops in the cabling so that water will be directed away from points where moisture is likely to enter connections. Check seals periodically. Sealant materials can sometimes dry rot when exposed to the sun for long periods of time, and may need replacing from time to time.

FIGURE 4.45   Drip Loop

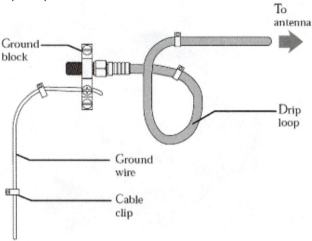

Diagnostics

In installations that use external antennas and amplifiers, bad cables can cause poor WLAN performance. In these situations a cable test kit can identify faults such as cables with water in them, crimped or damaged cables, corroded or improperly installed connectors, and so forth. Cable testing works by transmitting a fixed-power signal from a signal source (shown in Figure 4.46) into one end of the cable, putting a watt meter (pictured in Figure 4.47) in series with the RF signal, and then terminating the other end of the cable into a load device or an antenna.. The watt meter will show the power flowing through it, and when the cable or connectors are moved or jiggled, the power meter's measurement value should remain unchanged. If there is a change in the measurement displayed by the power meter, the cable or connectors are likely bad, possibly due to bad manufacturing or water damage.

FIGURE 4.46   Signal Generator

Copyright 2004 www.ydi.com

FIGURE 4.47   Watt Meter

Copyright 2004 www.ydi.com

FCC Rules Regarding Antennas

The FCC's CFR 15.203 says that antennas may be made so they can be repaired by the user, but use of a standard antenna jack or electrical connector is prohibited.

FIGURE 4.48   FCC CFR 15.203

```
[Code of Federal Regulations]
[Title 47, Volume 1, Parts 0 to 19]
[Revised as of October 1, 2000]
From the U.S. Government Printing Office via GPO Access
[CITE: 47CFR15.203]

[Page 726-727]
                   TITLE 47--TELECOMMUNICATION

              CHAPTER I--FEDERAL COMMUNICATIONS COMMISSION

PART 15--RADIO FREQUENCY DEVICES--Table of Contents

                  Subpart C--Intentional Radiators

Sec. 15.203  Antenna requirement.

     An intentional radiator shall be designed to ensure that no antenna
other than that furnished by the responsible party shall be used with
the device. The use of a permanently attached antenna or of an antenna
that uses a unique coupling to the intentional radiator shall be
considered sufficient to comply with the provisions of this section. The
manufacturer may design the unit so that a broken antenna can be
replaced by the user, but the use of a standard antenna jack or
electrical connector is prohibited. This requirement does not apply to
carrier current devices or to devices operated under the provisions of
Sec. 15.211, Sec. 15.213, Sec. 15.217, Sec. 15.219, or Sec. 15.221.
Further, this

[[Page 727]]

requirement does not apply to intentional radiators that must be
professionally installed, such as perimeter protection systems and some
field disturbance sensors, or to other intentional radiators which, in
accordance with Sec. 15.31(d), must be measured at the installation
site. However, the installer shall be responsible for ensuring that the
proper antenna is employed so that the limits in this part are not
exceeded.

[54 FR 17714, Apr. 25, 1989, as amended at 55 FR 28762, July 13, 1990]
```

Integral Antennas No Longer Required In UNII-1

In FCC Report & Order 04-165, released July 12, 2004, the FCC made some specific rule changes to CFR 15.203 and CFR 15.407. Previously, CFR 15.407(d) required that devices transmitting in the UNII-1 band (5.15-5.25 GHz) have an integral antenna (this is why 802.11a devices have always had non-removable antennas). That requirement has been removed, and now UNII-1 devices may have a detachable antenna so long as the antenna connector is unique. This requirement mirrors that of the 2.4 GHz ISM and other UNII band requirements.

Unique Connectors Still Required

Section 15.203 requires that intentional radiators use a "unique" connector to attach to the antenna. This rule is intended to prevent both intentional and unintentional circumvention of the Part 15 transmission power limits by replacing a device's authorized antenna with an unauthorized antenna having higher gain. At least in the realm of 802.11 (and possibly in other areas), this rule has not had its desired effect. The "unique" connectors used by manufacturers are widely available through mail-order and the Internet. Adapter cables, called "pigtails," can be easily purchased to convert a proprietary connector to a standard one. From the manufacturer's perspective, the "unique" connector rule creates significant costs, as the manufacturer is forced to periodically invent a new "unique" connector.

Recognizing that the current situation was not ideal, the FCC requested suggestions from vendors for changes to CFR section 15. Cisco Systems' writers commented that, "Once a 'unique' connector is put on the market, it is purchased by many companies and soon is not 'unique.' This leads to a never-ending circle, like a dog chasing its tail: as manufacturers buy a 'unique' connector, it becomes common in the market, and is no longer 'unique' – leading to a search for a new 'unique' connector." This shows that manufacturers are not required to have *their own* connector, but whatever connector they use should be non-standard. The FCC did not agree with this assessment, and thus the 15.203 requirement has remained, vague though it may be.

More Flexibility in Antenna Choice

The FCC did respond to the vendors' concerns. Instead of modifying section 15.203, the FCC thought it best to modify section 15.204 instead. Whereas before, *each combination* of intentional radiator (such as an AP) and antenna had to be certified by the FCC, section 15.204 was modified and now permits intentional radiators to be authorized with multiple antennas of similar in-band and out-of-band radiation patterns.

Compliance testing for the intentional radiator must be performed using the highest gain antenna that will be used with the device, and with the intentional radiator set to its maximum power output. Lower-gain antennae with similar in-band and out-of-band radiation patterns can be substituted for the higher-gain antenna without violating FCC regulations. This means that, for example, a manufacturer can certify an AP and antenna system with a 12 dBi dipole, and a customer could legally substitute a similar 10 dBi dipole, even if that specific combination of AP and antenna had not been certified. The FCC requires that the manufacturer must supply a list of other acceptable antennas in the literature delivered to the customer. The customer can use any antenna on the list without having to certify the system.

One common question that we would like to address regarding CFR 15.204 is that not just any antenna may be used with just any intentional radiator (bridge, PC Card, or access point, for example). This ruling directly affects those individuals who would connect a homemade (Pringles can or coffee-can-waveguide) antenna to a PC card for the purpose of war driving.

Under the pre-July 12 rules, the entire system (intentional radiator and antenna) had to be certified by the FCC. Since the homemade antenna was certainly not certified as a system with the AP, the system violated FCC rules.

Even under the post-July 12 rules, it is still not advisable to combine uncertified homemade antennas with certified intentional radiators (APs, bridges, and so on). The gain and radiation pattern of the homemade antenna is likely unknown, so it can't be determined whether use of the antenna falls under the Post-July 12 restrictions or not.

Advanced "Smart" Antennas

A "phased array" antenna consists of a number of antennas hooked up to a signal processor. By adjusting the relative strength of the signal put out by each antenna, and by adjusting the phase of the signals relative to each other, a phased array can create individual beams of signal, each pointing in a different direction. In more sophisticated arrays, such as those used most commonly by cellular phone networks, the array can even steer the beam to follow a mobile user. Because the phased array puts out a relatively narrow beam, it can transmit to more than one user simultaneously. For example, if the array consisted of four sector antennas, each with 90 degrees of coverage, pointing north, south, west, and east, the array could theoretically talk to four separate users simultaneously—one at each of the four compass points. Arrays can be far more sophisticated than this.

Phased arrays require special treatment under section 15. The goal of section 15 is to minimize interference with licensed transmitters. Because a phased array focuses its energy in specific areas, it is able to put out more total power (over the whole array) without increasing the risk of interference in those areas. For example, if a phased array were putting out three beams of 2 watts each, the total output of the array would be over the maximum power output allowed by section 15. But unless the beams overlapped, the output power in any given area would never be greater than 2 watts, which is below the maximum output allowed by section 15.

Prior to R&O 04-165, phased arrays were not addressed by section 15, although the FCC had "allowed a few phased array systems to operate … by individual interpretation of [the section 15] rules." The July 12 R&O provides guidelines for operation of phased array antennas under section 15. Specifically it addresses the maximum total width of the beams that a phased array may put out, the maximum power to each beam, and what to do if two beams are going to overlap (which might cause the power in the overlapping area to exceed section 15 maximums). Details on these requirements are provided in Chapter 8.

Key Terms

Before taking the exam, you should be familiar with the following terms:

azimuth and elevation chart

beamwidth

dipole antenna

Free Space Path Loss

Fresnel Zone

highly-directional antenna

line of sight

omnidirectional antenna

parabolic dish antenna

phased array antenna

sector antenna

semi-directional antenna

yagi antenna

Review Questions

1. Is it possible to have a clear line of sight, but not have a clear enough Fresnel zone to have a successful wireless link? Why or why not?

2. Explain how the physical attributes – dimensions and structure – affect the RF behavior of the antenna, and why both are important when choosing antenna types to implement a wireless LAN system.

3. Name and describe a real world application for each of the following antenna types:

   A. Omnidirectional

   B. Semi-directional

   C. Highly-directional

4. What is the formula for calculating the Fresnel zone, and what physical consideration is inherent in this formula?

5. Explain the need for calculating a link budget, and what items must be considered in this calculation.

Antenna Accessories

CWNA Exam Objectives Covered:

❖ Identify the use of the following wireless LAN accessories and explain how to select and install them for optimal performance within FCC regulations

- Amplifiers
- Attenuators
- Lightning Arrestors
- Grounding Rods/Wires
- RF Cables
- RF Connectors
- RF Signal Splitters

In This Chapter

Antenna Accessories

FCC Regulations

In the previous chapter, we discussed the different types of antennas that are available for use in wireless LANs. Many 802.11b and 802.11g access points come with detachable antennas, enabling the user to add antenna accessories between the antenna and the AP. Knowledge of these devices' uses, specifications, and effects on RF signal strength is essential to building a useful and legal wireless LAN.

In simple installations, such as providing wireless access to a single classroom, an 802.11 radio and an antenna are usually sufficient. For more complex installations, especially outdoor and medium to long-distance point-to-point links, antenna accessories might be required. The following types of accessories are discussed in this section:

- RF Amplifiers
- RF Attenuators
- Lightning Arrestors
- Grounding Rods/Wires
- RF Connectors
- RF Cables
- RF Splitters (also called Power Dividers)

Each of these devices is important to building a successful wireless LAN. Some items are used more than others, and some items are mandatory, whereas others are optional.

RF Amplifiers

As its name suggests, an RF amplifier is used to amplify, or increase, the amplitude of an RF signal. This increase in power is called *gain* and is measured in positive decibels. Amplifiers are used when the signal that is sent from the transmitting antenna is too weak at the receiver to be reliably interpreted. Referring back to the "link budget" or "system operating margin" calculations of chapter 4: if the link budget indicates that the received signal strength will be too weak, the use of an amplifier should be considered.

An amplifier adds *active gain*, as opposed to the *passive gain* that is added by an antenna. Whereas the antenna increases the power of the signal by focusing its energy more in one direction than another, an amplifier actually adds electrical energy to the signal. The advantage of active gain is that it increases the energy everywhere in the antenna's propagation pattern, whereas with passive gain every increase in range comes with a penalty of decreased beamwidth. The disadvantage of active gain is that it requires an external power source – the amplifier – to add the energy to the signal. The amplifier also must be powered by a power source, such as that provided by a standard electrical outlet (AC) or DC power after conversion by an AC-to-DC converter.

Most RF amplifiers used with wireless LANs are powered using DC voltage fed onto the RF cable with a DC injector. The injector is located close to a power source, such as in a wiring closet. The amplifier inserts DC voltage onto the same coaxial cable that will carry the RF data signal (the DC voltage does not interfere with the RF data signal). The amplifier, which is typically located near the antenna, uses the DC power to run the circuits that amplify the RF data signal. Sometimes the DC power that's used to power the amplifier is referred to as *phantom voltage* or *phantom power*. Figure 5.1 shows an example of an RF amplifier and a DC power injector.

FIGURE 5.1   RF Amplifier and DC Voltage Injector

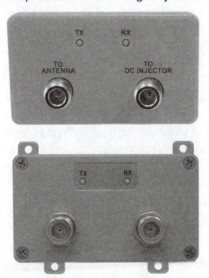

Copyright 2004 www.hyperlinktech.com

RF amplifiers come in two types: unidirectional and bidirectional. Unidirectional amplifiers only amplify the signal in one direction: transmit or receive. Bidirectional amplifiers amplify the signal in both directions: transmit and receive. Bidirectional amplifiers are most useful for applications involving small, mobile clients, such as laptops. In this case, adding an amplifier to the client would compromise the client's mobility. A bidirectional amplifier effectively amplifies both the AP's signals and the client's signals, since they amplify during both transmit and receive. For example if a unidirectional amplifier were used with an access point that was mounted on a flagpole or cell tower, it might result in a situation in which the clients could hear the AP's amplified transmissions, but the AP was too far away to hear the clients' non-amplified responses. On the other hand, a unidirectional amplifier may be more effective when both sides are capable of using an amplifier. For example, in a point-to-point bridge link, both ends could be equipped with a unidirectional, transmit-only amplifier. Since both sides are transmitting strong signals, there may not be a need to use an amplifier on the receive side.

Bidirectional amplifiers should be placed as close to the antenna as possible. The further the amplifier is placed from the antenna, the more loss will be introduced by the cable between the amplifier and the antenna. If the cable introduces too much loss, the signal might be so weak that the amplifier can't understand it. Placing the amplifier as close to the antenna as possible provides the strongest signal possible, and maximizes its ability to pull in weak signals and boost them on their way to the AP or bridge.

Another variation in amplifier type is *fixed-gain* vs. *fixed output*. A fixed-gain amplifier adds a preconfigured amount of gain (such as 6 dB or 500 mW) to the signal, while a fixed output amplifier has a preconfigured amount of output power so long as the input power and frequency are within a certain range (such as 5–50 mW at 2.4–2.5 GHz). Variable gain amplifiers are not typically used in wireless LANs due to the FCC rule on certified systems.

Common Options

Before you ever get to a point of deciding which amplifier to purchase, you should already know your amplifier specification requirements. Once you know the input and output impedance (ohms), gain (dB) or output (mW or dBm), frequency response (range in GHz), VSWR (X:1), and maximum input power (mW or dBm) specifications, you are ready to select an RF amplifier.

Frequency response is likely the first specification you will decide upon. If a wireless LAN uses the 5 GHz frequency spectrum, an amplifier that works only in the 2.4 GHz frequency spectrum will not work. Fortunately, 802.11 products are so popular now that amplifiers marketed specifically for WLAN application are available (although a generic 2.5 GHz or 5 GHz amplifier with appropriate specifications will work just as well).

Performing the link budget calculations that were described in chapter 4 will enable you to determine how much gain, input power, and output power are required for your particular solution. You should choose an amplifier that gives at least 20 dB of signal strength above the receiver's sensitivity. This is because 20 dB is generally the minimum recommended signal strength required to provide an excellent quality link in all situations. More signal strength is better, as long as you don't exceed your monetary budget (more powerful amplifiers are generally more expensive) and the FCC's power output restrictions (discussed later).

The amplifier should match impedances with all of the other wireless LAN hardware between the transmitter and the antenna. Generally, wireless LAN components have an impedance of 50 ohms; however, it is always a good idea to check the impedance of every component on a wireless LAN.

Finally, the amplifier must be connected in series with the transmitter and antenna. An amplifier should be chosen with the same kinds of connectors as the cables and/or antennas to which the amplifier will be connected. Typically, RF amplifiers will have either SMA or N-Type connectors. SMA and N-Type connectors perform well and are widely used.

Make sure that the amplifier you purchase comes with a calibration report and certificate. Although it is not feasible to disassemble your wireless LAN and send amplifiers in for calibration, an initial calibration report will at least let you know whether or not it started out working within the manufacturer's specifications.

Configuration & Management

RF amplifiers used with wireless LANs are installed in series with the main signal path as seen in Figure 5.2. Amplifiers are typically mounted to a solid surface or a mast near the antenna, using screws through the amplifier's flange plates or U-bolts. As mentioned earlier, it is usually desirable to mount the amplifier as close to the antenna as possible. If the antenna is mounted up a mast, the amplifier should probably be mounted there, too.

FIGURE 5.2 Suggested RF amplifier placement in the wireless LAN system

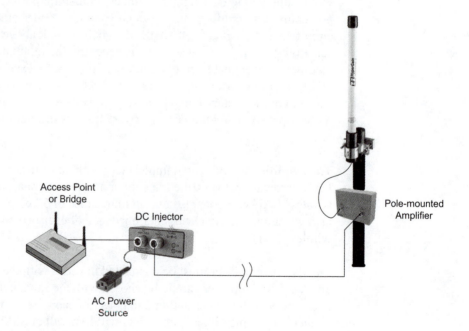

Special Stipulations on Amplifiers

The FCC's CFR 15.204 states that *every* system used in the ISM and UNII bands must be certified as a complete system.

FIGURE 5.3   FCC CFR 15.204

```
[Code of Federal Regulations]
[Title 47, Volume 1, Parts 0 to 19]
[Revised as of October 1, 2000]
From the U.S. Government Printing Office via GPO Access
[CITE: 47CFR15.204]

[Page 727]

                    TITLE 47--TELECOMMUNICATION

            CHAPTER I--FEDERAL COMMUNICATIONS COMMISSION

PART 15--RADIO FREQUENCY DEVICES--Table of Contents

                 Subpart C--Intentional Radiators

Sec. 15.204  External radio frequency power amplifiers and antenna modifications.

    (a) Except as otherwise described in paragraph (b) of this section,
no person shall use, manufacture, sell or lease, offer for sale or lease
(including advertising for sale or lease), or import, ship, or
distribute for the purpose of selling or leasing, any external radio
frequency power amplifier or amplifier kit intended for use with a Part
15 intentional radiator.
    (b) A transmission system consisting of an intentional radiator, an
external radio frequency power amplifier, and an antenna, may be
authorized, marketed and used under this part. However, when a
transmission system is authorized as a system, it must always be
marketed as a complete system and must always be used in the
configuration in which it was authorized. An external radio frequency
power amplifier shall be marketed only in the system configuration with
which the amplifier is authorized and shall not be marketed as a
separate product.
    (c) Only the antenna with which an intentional radiator is
authorized may be used with the intentional radiator.

[62 FR 26242, May 13, 1997]
```

Systems are submitted to the FCC for certification. When the system is certified, the organization submitting the system will receive a certificate that will list the pieces of equipment contained in the system. For example, a system might include a wireless bridge, one 10-foot LMR-400 cable, an amplifier, one 50-foot LMR-400 cable, a 1-foot pigtail cable, and a 14 dBi Yagi antenna. A system also could be as simple as a wireless LAN PC card, which includes all of the same basic components as the system listed above, except that everything is much smaller. A PC card still contains a transmitter, an amplifier, cables, and an antenna. A "system" is defined as the transmitting device, the antenna, and all items in between. These items may include cabling, connectors, amplifiers, attenuators, splitters, and a variety of other equipment.

Manufacturers obtain FCC approval or "certification" of their systems so an end-user may purchase any of the pieces of their systems and connect them to make an operable system without contacting the FCC for testing and certification. When additional devices from other vendors, such as amplifiers, are added into the system, the manufacturer's certification no longer applies and you must obtain your own certification for your system. This might cost thousands of dollars per system. An answer to this problem might be to purchase an FCC-certified system from a reputable vendor that meets the requirements of the wireless network.

Many manufacturers do not produce amplifiers to be used with their systems. For this reason, some companies produce amplifiers (but not wireless LAN hardware) that obtain FCC certification of an entire wireless LAN system using their amplifiers and another vendor's wireless LAN hardware together. Be careful what type of amplifiers you purchase. Some amplifiers cause the FCC to only certify systems as being able to use DSSS channels 2–10 or 3–9 instead of 1–11 like an un-amplified system. The reason for this stipulation is that the RF signal is amplified and bleeds over into licensed RF frequency spectra outside of the ISM or UNII bands. In order to avoid getting stuck in this situation, consider checking the FCC certificate of the system to see if channel restrictions exist.

Prior to July 2004, CFR 15.204 did not allow an amplifier to be marketed or sold when not part of a certified system. In FCC Report & Order 04-165, released July 12, 2004, the FCC adopted new rules to allow external amplifiers to be marketed separately if they are designed in such a way that they can only be used with a specific system that is covered by an equipment authorization, such as through use of a unique connector or via an electronic handshake with a host device. The amplifiers must have proprietary connections both into the amplifier and the associated routers and access points with which they are FCC approved to work, so consumers with any other routers or access points cannot use them. The output power of such an amplifier must not exceed the maximum permitted output power of the system with which it is authorized. In addition, the FCC required that the amplifiers must be sold with a notice that they are to be used only in conjunction with the routers and access points for which they have been approved. A description or listing of the devices with which the amplifier can be used must appear on the outside packaging as well as in the user manual for the amplifier. The amplifiers must not be used to circumvent regulations regarding output power. For example, an amplifier may not be used to increase the output power of a system that is otherwise limited to 125 mW. The party responsible for ensuring compliance with commission regulations must illustrate, during the equipment authorization process, the method used to prohibit unauthorized power increases. The marketing of RF amplifiers that are not FCC certified to be used as part of a specific system is still prohibited.

FIGURE 5.4   FCC CFR 15.204 Change

§ 15.204 External radio frequency power amplifiers and antenna modifications

(a) Except as otherwise described in paragraph (b) and (d) of this section, no person shall use, manufacture, sell or lease, offer for sale or lease (including advertising for sale or lease), or import, ship, or distribute for the purpose of selling or leasing, any external radio frequency power amplifier or amplifier kit intended for use with a Part 15 intentional radiator.

(b) A transmission system consisting of an intentional radiator, an external radio frequency power amplifier, and an antenna, may be authorized, marketed and used under this part. Except as described otherwise in this section, when a transmission system is authorized as a system, it must always be marketed as a complete system and must always be used in the configuration in which it was authorized.

(c) An intentional radiator may be operated only with the antenna with which it is authorized. If an antenna is marketed with the intentional radiator, it shall be of a type which is authorized with the intentional radiator. An intentional radiator may be authorized with multiple antenna types.

(1) The antenna type, as used in this paragraph, refers to antennas that have similar in-band and out-of-band radiation patterns.

(2) Compliance testing shall be performed using the highest gain antenna for each type of antenna to be certified with the intentional radiator. During this testing, the intentional radiator shall be operated at its maximum available output power level.

(3) Manufacturers shall supply a list of acceptable antenna types with the application for equipment authorization of the intentional radiator.

(4) Any antenna that is of the same type and of equal or less directional gain as an antenna that is authorized with the intentional radiator may be marketed with, and used with, that intentional radiator. No retesting of this system configuration is required. The marketing or use of a system configuration that employs an antenna of a different type, or that operates at a higher gain, than the antenna authorized with the intentional radiator is not permitted unless the procedures specified in Section 2.1043 of this chapter are followed.

(d) Except as described in this paragraph, an external radio frequency power amplifier or amplifier kit shall be marketed only with the system configuration with which it was approved and not as a separate product.

(1) An external radio frequency power amplifier may be marketed for individual sale provided it is intended for use in conjunction with a transmitter that operates in the 902 - 928 MHz, 2400 - 2483.5 MHz, and 5725 - 5850 MHz bands pursuant to § 15.247 of this part or a transmitter that operates in the 5.725 - 5.825 GHz band pursuant to § 15.407 of this part. The amplifier must be of a design such that it can only be connected as part of a system in which it has been previously authorized. (The use of a non-standard connector or a form of electronic system identification is acceptable.) The output power of such an amplifier must not exceed the maximum permitted output power of its associated transmitter.

(2) The outside packaging and user manual for external radio frequency power amplifiers sold in accordance with paragraph (d)(1) must include notification that the amplifier can be used only in a system which it has obtained authorization. Such a notice must identify the authorized system by FCC Identifier.

The FCC maintains a database of certified systems and companies holding these certificates. This database can be searched at the following web address:

https://gullfoss2.fcc.gov/cgi-bin/ws.exe/prod/oet/forms/reports/Search_Form.hts

A typical system certificate is shown in Figure 5.5.

FIGURE 5.5   FCC Grant of Equipment Authorization certificate

This web site is meticulously maintained by the FCC and is usually updated weekly. The end-users are liable for violations of FCC rules while they use the equipment. FCC violations may result in significant fines per violation[1]. The FCC usually allows a violator a brief (e.g., 10 days) time to correct the problem and report to the FCC how the violation was repaired. It is not uncommon for the FCC to audit a Wireless ISP looking for certified system infractions.

There are likely many WLANs today that are in violation of the FCC CFR 15.204 regulation. Some of these WLANs have combined components in such a way as to violate FCC power restrictions, while others are within FCC power restrictions, but are in violation because the

---

1. www.fcc.gov

specific system that they are using was never certified. The success of 802.11 has resulted in a proliferation of inexpensive 2.4 GHz amplifiers and antennas, but it's impossible, due to cost and time constraints, for a vendor to certify a certain antenna with every amplifier or access point on the market. Since the FCC usually gives a warning period to bring a violating system into compliance, the risk of actually paying a fine is minimal. For SOHO or home WLANs the risk of violation might not outweigh the convenience of being able to mix and match equipment at a whim.

Anyone installing an enterprise-class WLAN system should be absolutely certain that the equipment is an FCC-certified system. Imagine the cost in time and money of having to change the antenna on 1,000 access points because the antennas you bought were not certified with the access points you bought. Or consider having to shut down your statewide Wireless Internet Service Provider (WISP) service because you installed amplifiers that were not certified as part of the system you are using.

All vendors of 802.11 equipment certify their equipment as a system in and of itself. In other words, if you're using an AP with its built-in antenna, you don't need to worry about CFR 15.204. CFR 15.204 only applies for the end-user if you're mixing and matching radios, antennas, and amplifiers. Since CFR 15.204 only applies to transmission systems, you *can* safely mix and match equipment if you're using a receive-only (also known as "raw mode" or "RF monitor mode") protocol analyzer, such as AiroPeek, AirMagnet, or Network Instruments Observer. Protocol analyzers such as Ethereal are not always receive-only and may violate CFR 15.204.

RF Attenuators

An RF attenuator is a device that causes precisely measured loss (in –dB) in an RF signal. While an amplifier increases the RF signal strength, an attenuator decreases it. Why would you need or want to *decrease* the strength of your RF signal? In rare cases, the available equipment might exceed the FCC's power output restrictions and substituting less powerful equipment might not be possible. In this case, an attenuator could be used to reduce the power output of the system to within allowable limits. A more common scenario involves the desire to restrict the propagation of an 802.11 signal—e.g., for interference or security reasons. If a site survey reveals that the signal from the AP propagates too far outside the building or too far off the property, and the AP does not have adjustable output power, an attenuator could be used to reduce the power into the antenna, reducing the coverage area of the AP.

RF attenuators are available as either fixed-loss or variable-loss. Variable attenuators allow the administrator to configure the amount of loss that is caused in the RF signal with precision. Variable RF attenuators are not used in wireless LAN systems due to the FCC's regulations on certified systems. Variable RF attenuators are typically used in site surveys in order to determine antenna gain, cable length, necessity of amplifiers, etc. For example, a variable RF attenuator could be placed between an AP and an antenna to simulate the loss that would be caused by a certain length of coaxial cable.

FIGURE 5.6   An example of fixed-loss RF attenuator

FIGURE 5.7   An example of a variable-loss RF attenuator

Common Options

In choosing what kind of attenuator is required, consider similar specifications as when choosing an RF amplifier: impedance, input power maximum, fixed or variable attenuation, frequency response, connector types, etc.

All attenuators should come with a calibration report and certificate. It may not be feasible to disassemble your wireless LAN in order to calibrate an attenuator annually, so making sure that the attenuator meets the manufacturer's specifications prior to installation is a good idea.

Placement

Unlike amplifiers, which should be placed as close to the antenna as possible, it doesn't matter where you place an attenuator. Like amplifiers, attenuators are placed in series with the RF signal path. Fixed, coaxial attenuators are connected directly between any two connection points between the transmitter and the antenna. For example, a fixed, coaxial attenuator might be connected directly on the output of an access point, at the input to the antenna, or anywhere between these two points if multiple RF cables are used.

Grounding Rods/Wires

A grounding system has two main purposes. The first is to provide a safe path for lightning's current to travel to ground (the earth). When lightning strikes it takes the path of least resistance—or, more correctly, the path of least impedance. When electricity travels through an object with high impedance (such as RF equipment), it can generate an enormous amount of heat—sufficient to set buildings on fire and burn through steel. This heat, known as "Ohmic heating," is a primary (but far from the only) way that lightning causes damage. A grounding system provides a low-impedance path to ground so that the lightning current can, first, not travel through the RF equipment, and second, not generate destructive levels of heat as it travels.

The second purpose of a grounding system is to ensure that all connected electrical systems have a common ground. This is sometimes referred to as "bonding" the systems. Lightning doesn't have to travel through an object to damage it. When lightning strikes the earth it creates a voltage gradient around the strike point that can be visualized as a series of concentric circles. Voltage is highest near the strike point and weaker farther from the strike point. Consider what would happen if an RF antenna were grounded near the strike point, but the access point to which it was attached was grounded (through the office's AC wires) to a point farther from the strike point. The momentary difference in voltage between the antenna's "ground" and the AP's "ground" (which could be as high as hundreds of thousands of volts) could induce sufficient current flow to damage the AP or even the office wiring. On the other hand, if all devices were bonded to a common ground, the voltage of all the devices would go up equally and no current could flow.

Grounding is accomplished by driving a copper rod (a *grounding rod*) into the earth and then connecting equipment to that rod via low-impedance wires or straps (*grounding wires*). The National Electronics Council (NEC) requires a minimum depth of eight feet for electrical installations. This standard is commonly followed for RF antennas as well. Grounding and lightning safety is a complex topic with many potential pitfalls that could compromise the safety of your system in the event of a lightning strike. Grounding of RF systems can be different than grounding of A/C electrical systems.   If you are installing outdoor antennas, and *especially* if you are installing antennas on a cell tower or mast, we recommend that you enlist the aid of a professional antenna installer.

For more information about grounding and lightning safety, try a web search on the phrase "RF ground systems" (search for the terms, not the phrase). Here are two sites that we found via this method that are current as of the time of this publication:

http://www.radioworks.com/nbgnd.html

http://members.cox.net/pc-usa/station/ground2.htm

Lightning Arrestors

A lightning arrestor is used to shunt into the ground transient current that is caused by a nearby lightning strike. Lightning arrestors are used for protecting wireless LAN hardware such as access points, bridges, and workgroup bridges that are attached to a coaxial transmission line. Coaxial transmission lines are susceptible to surges from nearby lightning strikes. Lightning arrestors are only needed for outdoor antennas that are susceptible to lightning strikes in the vicinity. They're not necessary for indoor antennas because of the existing building ground.

One common misconception about lightning arrestors is that they are installed to protect against a direct lightning strike. No WLAN equipment can withstand a direct lightning strike. If a bolt of lightning strikes your wireless LAN antenna with the best lightning arrestor on the market installed, your antenna will be destroyed and your wireless LAN will probably be damaged as well. A lightning arrestor is not meant to withstand a direct lightning strike nor protect your network from such a strike. In addition a lightning arrestor can only protect equipment that is on the network side of the arrestor. Therefore, it cannot protect the antenna.

A lightning arrestor can generally shunt (redirect to ground) surges of up to 5000 amperes at up to 50 volts. Lightning arrestors (depending on type) function as follows:

1. Lightning strikes a nearby object
2. Transient currents are induced into the antenna or the RF transmission line
3. The lightning arrestor senses these currents and immediately ionizes the gases held internally to cause a short (a path of almost no resistance) directly to earth ground

Figure 5.8 shows an example of a lightning arrestor. Figure 5.9 illustrates the physical design of common lightning arrestor types.

FIGURE 5.8   Examples of lightning arrestors

Copyright 2004 www.hyperlinktech.com

FIGURE 5.9   Lightning Arrestor Physical Design

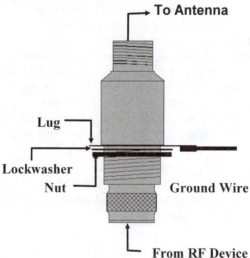

Figure 5.10 illustrates how a lightning arrestor is installed on a wireless LAN. When objects are struck by lightning, an electric field is built around that object for just an instant. When the lightning ceases to induce electricity into the object, the field collapses. When the field collapses, it induces high amounts of current into nearby objects, which in this case would be your wireless LAN antenna or coaxial transmission line. Lightning is discharged as a direct current (DC) pulse, but then causes an alternating current (AC) component to be formed, resonating as high as 1 GHz. However most of the power is dissipated from DC to 10 MHz.

FIGURE 5.10   A lightning arrestor installed on a network

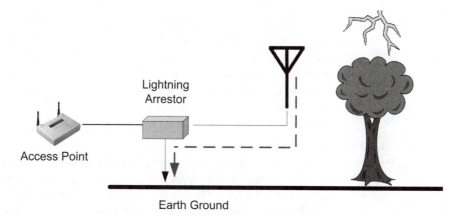

Common Options

There are few options on a lightning arrestor, and the cost will usually be $50–$150 for most brands. Some attributes should be considered for any lightning arrestor that is purchased, including:

- It should meet the IEEE standard of <8 μS
- Reusability
- Gas tube breakdown voltage
- Connector types
- Frequency response
- Impedance

- Insertion loss
- VSWR rating
- Warranty

IEEE Standards

Most lightning arrestors are able to trigger a short to earth ground in under 2 microseconds (μS), but the IEEE specifies that this process should happen in no more than 8 μS. It is very important that the lightning arrestor you choose at least meet the IEEE standard.

Reusable Units

Some lightning arrestors are reusable after a lightning strike and some are not. It is more cost effective to own an arrestor that can be used a number of times, although these units are more expensive up-front. Some reusable models have replaceable gas discharge tube elements that are cheaper to replace than the entire lightning arrestor. Other models may have physical characteristics that allow the lightning arrestor to do its job properly multiple times with no replaceable parts.

 A single-use lightning arrestor is like a fuse, in that it destroys itself to protect the equipment. When a single-use lightning arrestor takes a hit, it will stop passing the RF signal. That is the indicator that the arrestor needs replacement. From a troubleshooting perspective, if you completely lose signal in a system that contains a lightning arrestor, the arrestor should be one of the first things you check.

Voltage Breakdown

Since lightning arrestors only protect components that are on the network side of the arrestor, it is strongly suggested that you place lightning arrestors as the last component on the RF transmission line before the antenna. This placement will allow the lightning arrestor to protect amplifiers and attenuators along with your bridge or access point. Since the arrestor will introduce some loss, there is a conflict between this recommendation and the recommendation that the amplifier be as close to the antenna as possible. If the incoming signal is very weak and the loss of the arrestor is too high, the lightning arrestor might be just enough to push the signal from "weak but intelligible" to "too weak to be received."

In this case it may be necessary to put the amplifier on the antenna side of the lightning arrestor or to rethink your system operating margin.

Some lightning arrestors support the passing of DC voltage for use in powering RF amplifiers, and others do not. A lightning arrestor should be able to pass the amplifier's DC voltage if you plan to place the amplifier closer to the antenna than the lightning arrestor. In this case, the breakdown voltage (the voltage at which the arrestor begins shorting current to ground) should be higher than the amplifier's phantom voltage.

Connector Types

Make sure the connector types of the lightning arrestor you choose match those on the cable you are planning to use on your wireless LAN. If they do not match, then adapter connectors will have to be used, inserting more loss into the RF circuit than is necessary.

Frequency Response

The frequency response specification of the lightning arrestor should be at least as high as the highest frequency used in a wireless LAN. For example, if you are using only a 2.4 GHz wireless LAN, a lightning arrestor that is specified for use at up to 3 GHz is best.

Impedance

The impedance of the arrestor should match all of the other devices in the circuit between the transmitter and the antenna. Impedance is usually 50 ohms in most wireless LANs. Using an arrestor with the wrong impedance will cause a high VSWR and significant return loss.

Insertion Loss

The insertion loss should be very low (perhaps around 0.1 dB) so as not to cause high RF signal amplitude loss as the signal passes through the arrestor. Don't forget about the arrestors on each end of the link when you calculate your system operating margin.

VSWR Rating

The VSWR rating of a good quality lightning arrestor will be around 1.1:1, but some may be as high as 1.5:1. The lower the VSWR ratio of the device the better, because reflected voltage degrades the main RF signal.

Warranty

Regardless of the quality of a lightning arrestor, the unit can malfunction. Seek out a manufacturer that offers a good warranty on its lightning arrestors. Some manufacturers offer a highly desirable "no matter what happens" type of warranty.

Installation

No configuration is necessary for a lightning arrestor. Lightning arrestors are installed in series with the main RF signal path. The grounding connection should be attached to an earth ground with a measurable resistance of 5 ohms or less. It is recommended that you test an earth ground connection with an appropriate earth ground resistance tester before deciding that the installation of the lightning arrestor is satisfactory. Make it a point, along with other periodic maintenance tasks, to check the earth ground resistance and the gas discharge tube regularly.

Fiber Optic Cable

As a supplement to a lightning arrestor, some network designers insert a short run of fiber optic cable into the network somewhere between the wireless equipment (bridge or AP) and the rest of the Ethernet equipment. Use of fiber requires transceivers that can convert the Ethernet signal to optical and back. This approach provides complete protection for the network equipment against even a direct lightning strike since the voltage cannot travel through the optical cable.

In Figure 5.11, fiber optic cable is used as a supplement to a lightning arrestor. The antenna is vulnerable to lightning strikes. The bridge is protected by the lightning arrestor but would probably still be damaged in a direct strike. The switch and other wired equipment are completely protected by the fiber. In a direct strike, you could expect to lose the antenna, lightning arrestor, bridge, and one of the fiber optic transceivers; however, this is *much* better than losing the entire wireless LAN.

FIGURE 5.11   Optical cable used to protect against lightning strikes

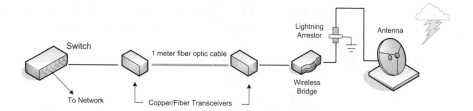

RF Splitters

An RF splitter is a device that has a single input connector and multiple output connectors. There are several names by which the RF splitter is called, such as "signal splitter," "power splitter," "RF splitter," "RF divider," "power divider," and just plain old "splitter." An RF splitter is used for the purpose of splitting a single signal into multiple independent RF signals. Use of splitters in everyday implementations of wireless LANs is not recommended except in special circumstances, such as combining two or more antennas into one "super-antenna." For example, sometimes two 120-degree sector antennas or two 90-degree panel antennas may be combined with a splitter and equal-length cables when the antennas are pointing in opposite directions. This configuration will produce a bidirectional coverage area which may be ideal along a river or major highway. Back-to-back 90 degree panels may be separated by as little as 10 inches or as much as 40 inches on either side of the mast or tower.

You should be aware that these configurations can introduce unpredictable results. For example, the rear lobe of an antenna in a back-to-back configuration can overlap with the main lobe of the other antenna, causing the signal to essentially interfere with itself. Because of this type of complication, multi-antenna configurations with a splitter are generally discouraged. In most cases, it would be better to choose a single antenna with an appropriate coverage area, or to choose a smart antenna type like a phased array or sectorized antenna. If you decide to use a splitter to create a multi-antenna configuration, you can reduce complications by minimizing the overlap of the two antennas' coverage areas.

When installing an RF splitter, the input connector should always face the source of the RF signal. The output connectors (sometimes called "taps") are connected facing the destination of the RF signal (the antenna). Figure 5.12 shows some examples of RF splitters.

FIGURE 5.12   RF Signal Splitters

2-way, RP-TNC   2-way, N-Type

3-way, N-Type   4-way, N-Type

Copyright 2004 www.hyperlinktech.com

Figure 5.13 illustrates how an RF splitter would be used in a wireless LAN installation.

FIGURE 5.13   An RF Splitter installed on a network

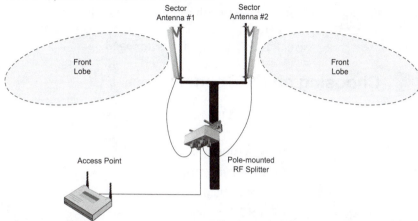

Splitters may be used to keep track of power output on a wireless LAN link. By hooking a power meter to one output of the splitter and the RF antenna to the other, you can actively monitor the output at any given time. In this scenario, the power meter, the antenna, and the splitter must all have equal impedance. Although not a common practice, removing the power meter from one output of the splitter and replacing it with a 50 ohm dummy load would allow you to move the power meter from one connection point to another throughout the wireless LAN while making output power measurements. Be very careful not to leave a tap unterminated.

FIGURE 5.14   Monitoring Power with a Power Meter

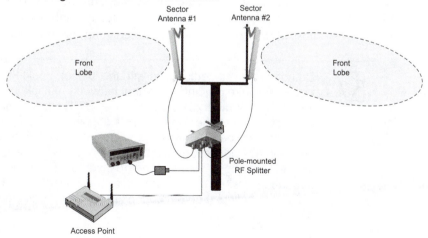

Keep in mind that the splitter must be part of a certified system if used in your wireless LAN. This requirement is yet another reason why the casual use of splitters is discouraged.

Choosing an RF Splitter

Here is a checklist of things to consider when choosing an RF splitter.

- Insertion loss
- Frequency response
- Impedance
- VSWR rating
- High isolation impedance
- Power ratings
- Connector types
- Calibration report
- Mounting options
- DC voltage passing

Insertion Loss

Low insertion loss (loss incurred by just introducing the item into the circuit) must be considered because simply putting the splitter in the RF circuit can cause a significant RF signal amplitude decrease. Insertion loss of 0.5 dB or less is considered good for an RF splitter.

Do not confuse insertion loss with the loss of amplitude incurred simply because you're dividing the signal between multiple paths (called "through loss"). The number of connectors on an RF splitter will determine the number of ways (speaking in terms of power division) that the RF amplitude will be split. A two-way splitter should have 3–4 dB loss between the input connector and either output connector. Loss higher than this can be attributed either to insertion loss (which is added to through loss when measured), inaccuracies in the splitter's ability to divide the power between output connectors, or a mismatched load on each output port.

Frequency Response

The frequency response specification of the splitter should be at least as high as the highest frequency used in the wireless LAN. For example, if you were using only a 2.4 GHz wireless LAN, a splitter specified for use at up to 3 GHz would be best. Additionally, the frequency response should be flat, meaning that the amount of loss experienced at one frequency should be the amount of loss experienced at other frequencies within the frequency range of the splitter. A calibration report will show whether the splitter is within the manufacturer's tolerances.

Impedance

The impedance of the splitter (which is usually 50 ohms in most wireless LANs) should match all of the other devices in the circuit between the transmitter and the antenna. Each port should be within 1 percent of the nominal impedance specified by the manufacturer. For example, if the manufacturer says 50 ohms, the port should be from 49.5–50.5 ohms across its supported frequency range.

VSWR Rating

As with many other RF devices, VSWR ratings should be as close to 1:1 as possible. Typical VSWR ratings on RF splitters are < 1.5:1. Low VSWR ratings on splitters are much more critical than on many other devices in an RF system because reflected RF power in a splitter may be reflected in multiple directions inside the splitter. This affects both the splitter input signal and all splitter output signals.

High Isolation Impedance

Isolation impedance is the impedance between the output ports of the splitter. High isolation impedance in an RF splitter is important for several reasons. First, a load on one output port should not affect the output power on another output port of the splitter. Second, a signal arriving into the output port of a splitter (such as the received RF signal) should be directed to the input port rather than to another output port. Typical isolation (resistance causing separation) is 20 dB or more between ports.

Power Ratings

Splitters are rated for power input maximums. This means that you are limited in the amount of power you can feed into your splitter. Exceeding the manufacturer's power rating will result in damage to the RF splitter.

Connector Types

RF splitters will generally have N-type or SMA connectors. It is very important to purchase a splitter with the same connector types as the cable being used. Doing so cuts down on couplings, reducing RF signal amplitude. This knowledge is especially important when using splitters, since splitters already cut the signal amplitude in an RF system significantly.

Calibration Report

All RF splitters should come with a calibration report that shows insertion loss, frequency response, through loss at each connector, etc. Having splitters calibrated once per year is not feasible when they're used in a production WLAN, so it is essential that the administrator know before initial installation whether the splitter meets the manufacturer's specifications. Continued calibration requires taking the wireless LAN off line for an extended period of time and may not be practical in many situations.

Mounting

Mounting an RF splitter is usually a matter of putting screws through the flange plates into whatever surface to which the splitter will be mounted. Some models come with pole-mounting hardware such as U-bolts. Depending on the manufacturer, the splitter might be weatherproof, meaning it can be mounted outside on a pole without fear of water causing problems. When this is the case, be sure to seal cable connections, use drip loops, and mount the connectors on the bottom side, as shown in Figure 5.14 above.

DC Voltage Passing

Some RF splitters have the option of passing DC voltage to all output ports in parallel. This feature is helpful when there are RF amplifiers closer to the antenna than the splitter. Amplifiers may be powered with DC voltage originating from an injector in a wiring closet.

RF Connectors

RF connectors are specific types of coupling devices used to connect cables to devices or devices to devices. Common RF connector types include N, F, SMA, BNC, and TNC connectors. FCC CFR 15.203 gave rise to the need for unique connectors; thus many variations on each connector type were made. The following shows how a standard connector is altered to make it unique.

- Standard connector type: N-type
- Alteration #1: Reverse polarity N-type
- Alteration #2: Reverse threaded N-type

Figures 5.15–5.17 illustrate common connector types.

FIGURE 5.15   N-type Male and Female Connector Examples

N-type Male Clamp   N-type Female Clamp

Copyright 2004 www.hyperlinktech.com

FIGURE 5.16   TNC Male and Female Connector Examples

TNC Male Crimp   TNC Female Crimp
Copyright 2004 www.hyperlinktech.com

FIGURE 5.17   SMA Male and Female Connector Examples

SMA Male Right-Angle Crimp   SMA Female Panel Mount
Copyright 2004 www.hyperlinktech.com

Choosing an RF Connector

You probably won't have much choice of which type of connector to use, since you'll have to match the connectors that are already on the equipment. In the past, access points, bridges, and PC cards have had a "variant" connector, such as an RP-TNC, or a proprietary connector, while amplifiers, attenuators, lightning arrestors, and antennas have had standard connectors – almost always an N-connector or SMA. Since the release of FCC R&O 04–165, amplifiers must use either an electronic identification system (such as an electronic handshake) or have a unique connector.

Five things should be considered when purchasing and installing any RF connector, and they are similar in nature to the criteria for choosing RF amplifiers and attenuators.

- The RF connector should match the impedance of all other wireless LAN components (generally 50 ohms). This is normally not a problem since similar connectors with different impedances will not properly fit together because of center-pin sizing.

- Know how much insertion loss each connector inserted into the signal path causes. The amount of loss caused will factor into your link budget and system operating margin calculations.

- Know the upper frequency limit (frequency response) specified for the particular connectors. This point is especially important when dealing with 5 GHz WLANs. Some connectors are rated only as high as 3 GHz, which is fine for use with 2.4 GHz wireless LANs, but will not work for 5 GHz wireless LANs. Some connectors are rated only up to 1 GHz and will not work with wireless LANs at all, except legacy 900 MHz wireless LANs.

- Beware of bad quality connectors. First, always consider purchasing from a reputable company. Second, purchase only high-quality connectors made by name-brand manufacturers. This kind of purchasing will help eliminate many problems with sporadic RF signals, VSWR, and bad connections. There are many low-quality generic connectors on the market today.

- Make sure you know the type of connector (N, TNC, SMA, etc.) that you need, the sex of the connector, the thread direction, and the connector's polarity. Connectors come in male and female. Male connectors have a center pin, and female connectors have a center receptacle. Thread direction refers to the direction of the threads (clockwise vs. counter-clockwise). Always be 100 percent sure that the connectors on your cables will match the connectors on your equipment (access points, antennas, etc.) in all of these qualities.

RF Cables

In the same manner that you must choose the proper cables for your 10 Gbps wired infrastructure backbone, you must choose the proper cables for connecting an antenna to an access point or wireless bridge. Below are some criteria to be considered in choosing the proper cables for your wireless network.

- Cables introduce loss into a wireless LAN, so make sure the shortest cable length necessary is used to minimize loss.
- Plan to purchase pre-cut lengths of cable with pre-installed connectors. Doing so minimizes the possibility of bad connections between the connector and the cable. Although you might save money by buying in bulk and making your own cables, professional manufacturing practices are almost always superior to cables made by untrained individuals.
- Look for the lowest-loss cable available at your particular price point (the lower the loss, the more expensive the cable). Cables are typically rated for loss in dB/100-feet. The table in Figure 5.18 illustrates the loss that is introduced by adding cables to a wireless LAN.
- Lower-loss cables are usually thicker and stiffer than higher-loss cables. In some cases, even if you can afford a lower-loss cable, you might want to choose a higher-loss cable for easier installation. As always, your link budget calculations should serve as a guide for how much loss your system can tolerate.
- Purchase cable that has the same impedance as all of your other wireless LAN components (generally 50 ohms).
- The frequency response of the cable should be considered as a primary decision factor in your purchase. With 2.4 GHz wireless LANs, a cable with a rating of at least 2.5 GHz should be used. With 5 GHz wireless LANs, a cable with a rating of at least 6 GHz should be used.
- You might have to use an extension cable when an access point and its remote antenna are far apart (such as in an outdoor installation). In this case, be aware that connectors drop ~0.25 dB and cable loss can be very significant (depending on cable type used). Use of longer Cat5 cable can sometimes remedy the

situation by allowing the access point to be moved closer to the antenna. RG-58 cable should never be used for extension cables due to bad frequency response. LMR, Heliax, or other appropriate high-frequency cable should be used for extensions.

If the FCC performs an inspection on your wireless LAN (which it is authorized to do at any time), it will make note of the manufacturer, model number, length, and type of connectors on your RF cable. This information should be documented in your system's FCC certificate.

FIGURE 5.18   Example Coaxial cable attenuation ratings (in dB/100 feet at **X** MHz)

LMR CABLE	30	50	150	220	450	900	1500	1800	2000	2500
100A	3.9	5.1	8.9	10.9	15.8	22.8	30.1	33.2	35.2	39.8
195	2.0	2.6	4.4	5.4	7.8	11.1	14.5	16.0	16.9	19.0
200	1.8	2.3	4.0	4.8	7.0	9.9	12.9	14.2	15.0	16.9
240	1.3	1.7	3.0	3.7	5.3	7.6	9.9	10.9	11.5	12.9
300	1.1	1.4	2.4	2.9	4.2	6.1	7.9	8.7	9.2	10.4
400	0.7	0.9	1.5	1.9	2.7	3.9	5.1	5.7	6.0	6.8
400UF	0.8	1.1	1.7	2.2	3.1	4.5	5.9	6.6	6.9	7.8
500	0.54	.70	1.2	1.5	2.2	3.1	4.1	4.6	4.8	5.5
600	0.42	.55	1.0	1.2	1.7	2.5	3.3	3.7	3.9	4.4
600UF	0.48	.63	1.15	1.4	2.0	2.9	3.8	4.3	4.5	5.1
900	0.29	0.37	0.66	0.80	1.17	1.70	2.24	2.48	2.63	2.98
1200	0.21	0.27	0.48	0.59	0.89	1.3	1.7	1.9	2.0	2.3
1700	0.15	0.19	0.35	0.43	0.63	0.94	1.3	1.4	1.5	1.7

Notice that attenuation increases as the frequency increases for a given cable type. For 802.11b/g signals, the right-most column (highest attenuation) should be used. Although 802.11a's 5 GHz frequency range is not listed, you can imagine how much higher the loss would be at these frequencies. This factor is one of the disadvantages of 802.11a.

Figure 5.19 illustrates a freely available calculation tool that will help you figure cable loss.

FIGURE 5.19 Cable Loss Calculation Utility

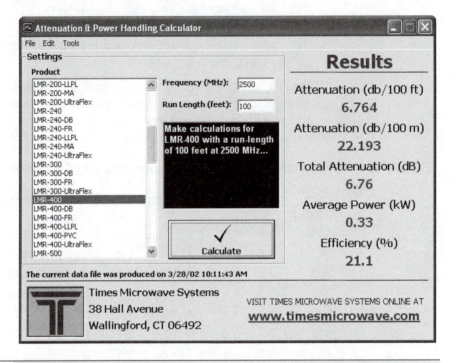

 Three major manufacturers of RF cable are used with wireless LANs: Andrew, Times Microwave, and Belden. Andrew's Heliax cable, Times Microwave's LMR, and Belden's RF-series are all popular in the wireless LAN industry. LMR cable has become somewhat of an industry standard in the same way Xerox became known for copiers. Sometimes the term "LMR" is used in place of "RF cable" in the same way "Xerox" is used in place of "copy."

RF "Pigtail" Adapter Cable

Pigtail adapter cables are used to connect cables that have industry-standard connectors like N-type and SMA connectors to wireless LAN equipment with unique (non-standard) connectors. One end of the pigtail cable is the unique connector, while the other end is the industry-standard connector. Figure 5.20 shows an example of a pigtail cable.

FIGURE 5.20   Example of RF Pigtail adapters

N-type Male to SMA Male   N-type Female to RP-TNC Male

Copyright 2004 www.hyperlinktech.com

Third party manufacturers have begun making custom "pigtail" cables and selling them inexpensively on the open market. The selling and marketing of these cables is not against FCC rules, but using a transmission system that incorporates a pigtail cable without the pigtail cable being part of a certified system violates FCC rules. Pigtails are made with the intention of circumventing the inefficiencies caused by the FCC rules on unique connectors.

Individuals using security utilities such as NetStumbler with a Pringles can (or similar) home-brew antennas are in violation of this FCC regulation, because the software transmits frames onto the wireless medium. This is mentioned both to answer the commonly asked question and as an example of how this regulation is interpreted by the FCC. Any pigtails or antennas used with a wireless LAN falling under the CFR 15.247 rules must be part of a certified system and documented as such by the FCC.

Frequency Converter

Frequency converters are used to convert one frequency range to another for the purpose of decongesting a frequency band. Suppose many companies located in the same multi-tenant office building had wireless LANs (which is common). Each of these companies wants building-to-building wireless connectivity with a building next door because each of these companies has an office in the adjacent building. Only three companies will be able to use wireless LAN building-to-building bridging due to a limited number of non-overlapping channels (channels will be explained in chapter 6). In this case, a frequency converter may be deployed that will use existing 2.4 GHz wireless equipment, but will convert the frequencies to a less congested band (such as the 5.8 GHz UNII-3 band) for this wireless bridge segment.

FIGURE 5.21   Example of a WLAN Frequency Converter

Copyright 2004 www.ydi.com

Proper antennas and cables must be used when using a frequency converter because both antennas and cables have limited frequency response, but it can be a very economical solution in a congested area. The alternative would be to replace all wireless LAN hardware with new 5 GHz hardware. Figure 5.22 shows how a frequency converter would be installed in a wireless LAN configuration.

FIGURE 5.22   Using a WLAN Frequency Converter

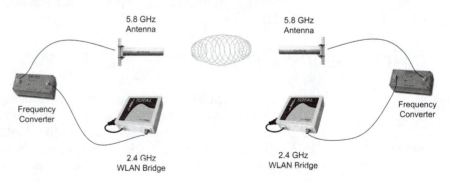

Test Kits

Many types of test kits are on the market. One of the most valuable test kits in the wireless LAN industry is used to test cables and connectors. The kit might consist of an RF signal generator and a through-line power meter. The signal generator can be hooked directly to the power meter and subsequently to a load, such as an antenna or 50 ohm load device to get a baseline measurement. When putting cables and connectors between the signal generator and the power meter, it can be determined if they meet the manufacturer's specifications and if they have intermittent connectivity. The connectors on cables can become worn and loose, making a bad or intermittently bad connection. They also can take on water, which would be highly detrimental to their RF characteristics. It is important to test cables and connectors before deployment and periodically as possible thereafter. By connecting the signal generator to the power meter and then to an antenna, if any of the devices have suffered damage and have intermittent connectivity, it can be seen on the power meter when items are wiggled in the configuration. Figure 5.23 shows both a signal generator and a through-line power meter used for cable, connector, and accessory diagnostics.

FIGURE 5.23   Sample Test Kit

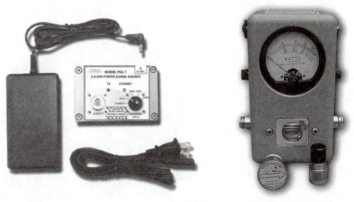

Copyright 2004 www.ydi.com

The transmitter from this type of test kit is also useful for WLAN diagnostics with roaming and security testing. When connected to an antenna, the transmitter can be used to create noise on a particular 802.11 channel, causing clients to lose their connection. This tool can be useful to force clients to roam between access points to see if they drop their TCP conversations in the process. This same setup could be used by an attacker to disrupt your network or hijack connections, but this is highly discouraged. These devices are relatively expensive (approximately $600 in some cases), which puts them out of the reach of casual mischief-makers.

Key Terms

Before taking the exam, you should be familiar with the following terms:

active gain

bidirectional amplifier

certified system

fixed attenuator

fixed-gain amplifier

fixed-output amplifier

frequency response

frequency converter

grounding rod/wire

insertion loss

lightning arrestor

LMR cable

N connector

passive gain

pigtail

SMA connector

splitter

thread direction

TNC connector

transient current

unidirectional amplifier

variable attenuator

voltage injector

Review Questions

1.   Explain the difference between active gain and passive gain. Which one is created by an amplifier, and which is created by an antenna?

2.   Explain what happens when lightning strikes close to a properly installed lightning arrestor. What happens when a properly installed lightning arrestor is struck directly by lightning?

3.   In a long distance, outdoor wireless LAN link, why is it important to know the lengths of cable that connect the antenna to the bridge or access point on either end of the link? Why does the length of connecting wired cable affect the wireless signal?

4.   Variable attenuators are commonly used in what capacity in wireless LANs?

5.   Wireless LAN test kits serve what specific purposes and may contain what specific components?

Spread Spectrum Technology

CWNA Exam Objectives Covered:

❖ Identify some of the uses for spread spectrum technologies

- Wireless LANs
- Wireless PANs
- Wireless MANs
- Wireless WANs

❖ Explain the differences between, and apply the different types of spread spectrum technologies

- FHSS
- DSSS
- OFDM

❖ Explain the underlying concepts of how spread spectrum technology works

- Modulation
- Coding

❖ Identify and apply the concepts which make up the functionality of spread spectrum technology:

- Co-location
- Channels
- Carrier Frequencies
- Dwell time and Hop time
- Throughput vs. Bandwidth
- Communication Resilience

In This Chapter

Frequency Hopping (FHSS)

Direct Sequence (DSSS)

Orthogonal Frequency Domain Multiplexing (OFDM)

Packet Binary Convolutional Code (PBCC)

Comparing 802.11 Technologies

❖ Identify the regulations set forth by the FCC that govern spread spectrum technology, including:

  ▪ Hop and Dwell Times

❖ Define and explain the basic concepts of RF behavior

  ▪ Delay Spread

In order to administer and troubleshoot wireless LANs effectively, a good understanding of spread spectrum technology and its implementation is required. In this section we will cover what spread spectrum technology is and how it is used according to FCC guidelines. We will differentiate and compare the three main spread spectrum technologies—FHSS, DSSS, and OFDM—and discuss in depth how spread spectrum technology is implemented in wireless LANs.

Introducing Spread Spectrum

Spread spectrum can be defined as "a communication technique that spreads a narrowband communication signal over a wide range of frequencies for transmission, and then de-spreads it into the original data bandwidth at the receiver." Spread spectrum communication possesses many advantages over its alternative: narrowband communication. Spread spectrum signals are less likely to interfere with non-spread-spectrum signals in the same area and, in some configurations, are less likely to interfere with other spread spectrum signals in the area. Spread spectrum signals are difficult to intercept or demodulate without the proper equipment, although this is a dubious advantage, since today "proper equipment" is readily available. Finally, spread spectrum communications are more resistant to jamming and interference than non-spread-spectrum communications. In order to discuss what spread spectrum is we must first establish a reference by discussing the alternative to spread spectrum, narrowband transmission.

Narrowband Transmission

A narrowband transmission is a communications technology that uses only enough of the frequency spectrum to carry the data signal, and no more. It has long been the FCC's mission to conserve frequency usage as much as possible, handing out only enough frequency spectrum to get the job done. Spread spectrum is in opposition to that mission since it uses much wider frequency bands than are necessary to transmit the information. This brings us to the first requirement for a signal to be considered spread spectrum. A signal is a spread spectrum signal when *the bandwidth is much wider than what is required to send the information.*

Figure 6.1 illustrates the difference between narrowband and spread spectrum transmissions.

FIGURE 6.1   Narrowband vs. spread spectrum on a frequency domain

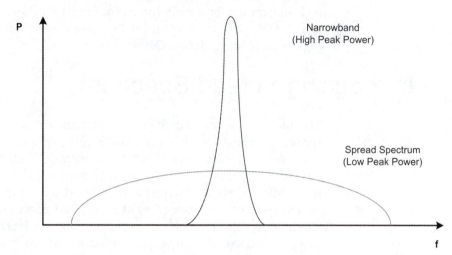

In order for narrowband signals to be received, they must stand out above the background level of RF noise, called the *noise floor*, by a significant amount. The power level of the narrowband signal relative to the power level of the noise floor is called the *signal-to-noise ratio*, which is expressed in dB. With narrowband signals, a relatively high peak power is required to achieve a sufficiently high signal-to-noise ratio to ensure error-free reception of the signal. For example, a CB radio is a narrowband transmitter. To achieve a range of about five to eight miles, a CB radio uses a transmit power of around 5 watts. By comparison, a spread spectrum transmitter can achieve a higher *effective* signal-to-noise ratio at much lower power levels. For example, an 802.11b transmitter might achieve a range of about 20–30 miles with an output signal of 4 watts (assuming the RF line-of-sight is clear), or a range of about 300– 900 meters with an output signal of 15–30 mW.

Figure 6.1 illustrates another compelling argument against narrowband transmission, other than the high peak power requirement. Because narrowband signals use such a small frequency range, they can be jammed or experience interference very easily. *Jamming* is the intentional overpowering of an intended transmission by transmitting unwanted signals in the same frequency range. Interference is the same as jamming, except that the source of the interference is not intended specifically to overpower the data transmission, but rather overpowers or diffuses it unintentionally. For example, if an attacker were using a 2.4 GHz signal generator to overpower your WLAN, that would be jamming; if a cordless phone was accidentally doing the same thing, that would be interference. Because a narrowband signal's frequency band is so focused, other narrowband signals do not have to take up much bandwidth to corrupt your intended transmission.

The FCC requires licenses for all narrowband transmitters. This governmental requirement is necessary to ensure that no two narrowband transmitters (which typically operate at very high power) use the same frequency range and interfere with one another. Because spread spectrum signals use significantly lower power than narrowband transmitters, they are less likely to cause interference. The FCC permits the unlicensed use of spread spectrum signals under certain conditions which is another argument *for* spread spectrum and *against* the use of narrowband transmission for wireless LAN technology. Among the biggest advantages of wireless LAN technology are its convenience and easy configuration. If every WLAN administrator were required to get a license from the FCC, very few would bother.

Spread Spectrum Technology

Spread spectrum technology allows us to take the same amount of information that we would previously have sent using a narrowband signal, and spread it out over a much larger frequency range at a much lower power level. For example, we might use 1 MHz at 10 watts with narrowband, but 20 MHz at 100 mW with spread spectrum. By using a wider frequency spectrum, we reduce the probability that the data will be corrupted or jammed by a narrowband transmitter. A narrowband transmitter would be less likely to interfere with (or jam) a spread spectrum signal because only a small part of the spread spectrum signal would fall into the narrowband signal's frequency range. Spread spectrum systems are designed so that if even part of the signal is corrupted, the uncorrupted part of the data can often still be received and properly decoded. Narrowband interference can reduce the performance (throughput) of a spread spectrum system, but it has a hard time jamming a spread spectrum system completely.

A spread spectrum signal uses a wide frequency range at low power levels. These two characteristics make a spread spectrum signal appear to most non-spread-spectrum receivers as if it were part of the background noise. The narrowband transmitter's high peak power level creates a high enough ratio of signal-to-noise between the spread spectrum signal and the narrowband signal that the narrowband signal is not corrupted by the spread spectrum signal. Since narrowband radio receivers will view the spread spectrum signal as noise, these receivers will not attempt to demodulate or interpret it. Some people argue that this means that spread spectrum is more secure than narrowband. To a certain degree, that is true. But today, any advantage in security due to the use of spread spectrum is minimal since you can buy spread-spectrum receiving equipment off the shelf. Although spread spectrum's security when compared to narrowband transmission was originally its greatest strength (hence its military origins), today spread spectrum's greatest strength is its noise resistance in environments with multipath properties.

Multipath and Inter-Symbol Interference

Spread spectrum signals are somewhat resistant to multipath interference, which is arguably the most common type of interference in 802.11 WLANs. Although 802.11 WLANs are often used outdoors for building-to-building bridge configurations, they are more often used indoors. Recall that multipath occurs when there are two (or more) paths from the transmitter to the receiver: a direct (LOS) path and one (or more) reflected path(s). A reflected path is longer than the direct path, so the reflected signal is delayed by some amount of time relative to the direct signal. The reflected signal interferes with the direct signal and can in some cases corrupt it. In indoor environments, there may be many different reflective paths between the transmitter and the receiver; in fact, a direct path may not even exist.

In multipath environments the main cause of interference is *inter-symbol interference* (ISI), which occurs when the difference in time between the arrival of the direct and reflected signal(s) at the receiver (called the *delay spread*) is long enough that a certain data bit overlaps with the data bit that came before or after it. When a bit overlaps with itself, the receiver can often recover the original data, but when a bit overlaps with the bit that follows it, corruption of the data is more likely. Therefore, the length of a single symbol (a data bit in our example) is directly proportional to the amount of delay spread that the system can tolerate. For example, if the system uses a signaling rate of 1 MHz, (1,000 cycles per second) then a single symbol is 1 millisecond long. If the reflected signal is delayed less than approximately 1 millisecond, ISI will not occur. If the reflected signal is delayed more than approximately 1 millisecond, ISI is likely to occur. A system with a signaling rate of 1 GHz (1,000,000 cycles per second) could tolerate a delay of approximately 1 microsecond. As an example, 802.11b systems can tolerate delay spread of up to 500 nanoseconds, but performance is much better when it is lower. Several vendors state that a 65 nanosecond or lower delay spread is required for 11 Mbps 802.11b.

802.11b systems can tolerate delay spread of up to 500 nanoseconds, but performance is much better when it is lower. As delay spread increases, the 802.11b transmitter will drop to a lower data rate. Lower data rates use longer symbols, allowing for longer delay before ISI occurs. Several vendors state that a 65 nanosecond or lower delay spread is required for 11 Mbps 802.11b.

For 802.11g, a delay spread of less than about 150 nanoseconds is required to maintain 54 Mbps speeds. This number differs per chipset: 150 nanoseconds is the longest delay spread we've found in a chipset report. In other words, other chipsets are less tolerant of multipath and would drop to a lower data rate at a shorter delay spread.

It might seem contradictory that an 802.11g system at a data rate of 54 Mbps could tolerate a higher delay spread than an 802.11b system at a data rate of 11 Mbps, since higher data rates are generally less tolerant of delay spread. This is because 802.11g uses OFDM while 802.11b uses DSSS. One of OFDM's advantages is its greater tolerance of delay spread.

Since a faster signaling rate and shorter symbols result in a higher data rate, ISI creates a conflict: higher data rates are desirable, but the faster the signaling rate the less tolerant to multipath the signal becomes. Because the spread spectrum system spreads its signal out over many different frequencies, the signal exists at many different wavelengths. If some of the wavelengths are experiencing multipath such that the signal is corrupted at those wavelengths, it is likely that other wavelengths will not be affected, or will even be strengthened by that same multipath. Although this description is somewhat oversimplified, the complete description requires more electrical engineering and calculus background than is appropriate for this text. It is sufficient to say within the confines of this text that spread spectrum systems allow higher data rates than ISI would allow in a narrowband system.

Common Uses of Spread Spectrum

Because of the advantages described previously, spread spectrum is by far the most popular method of RF signal transmission today. It is used in wireless LANs like 802.11, Wireless Personal Area Networks (WPANs) like Bluetooth, and Wireless Metropolitan Area Networks (WMANs) like 802.16 and 802.20. An 802.11 network being used to carry data long distances over rural areas might be an example of spread spectrum being used in a Wireless Wide Area Network (WWAN). It is also used in numerous other areas, such as cordless phones and wireless video cameras.

FCC Specifications

Though today there are many different implementations of spread spectrum technology used for license-free wireless LANs, only two types (DSSS and FHSS) were originally allowed in the ISM bands by the FCC. The FCC specifies regulations concerning spread spectrum devices in Title 47, Chapter 1, Part 15, a collection of regulations under the general heading of, "Telegraphs, Telephones, and Radiotelegraphs" that covers radio frequency devices. These regulations are generally referred to as the, "Code of Federal Regulations (CFR)."

 The FCC regulations concerning CFR 47, Part 15 can be found on the web at http://www.access.gpo.gov/nara/cfr/waisidx_00/47cfr15_00.html. Wireless LAN devices described in these regulations are sometimes called "part 15 devices."

CFR 47, Part 15 regulations originally described two spread spectrum technologies: *direct sequence spread spectrum (DSSS)* and *frequency hopping spread spectrum (FHSS)*. Part 15 allows DSSS and FHSS devices operating below a certain power level to transmit in the ISM bands without licensing. The third type of spread spectrum used in 802.11, *Orthogonal Frequency Division Multiplexing (OFDM)*, was originally not allowed in the ISM bands by FCC Part 15, partially explaining why 802.11 and 802.11b didn't use OFDM in the first place. OFDM is in many ways superior to DSSS and FHSS, but since OFDM wasn't covered by FCC Part 15, it would have required licensing, which would have been inconvenient and expensive for WLAN manufacturers and administrators.

802.11a was the first 802.11 standard to use OFDM. 802.11a operates in the 5 GHz UNII band (not the 5 GHz ISM band), which allows for unlicensed use of OFDM. 802.11 device manufacturers, including those in the 802.11g task group, recognized the advantage of OFDM and wanted to be able to use it in the 2.4 GHz band. A manufacturer named Wi-Lan submitted a certification application for a 2.4 GHz device using OFDM, in which it argued that the device met the technical requirements for a spread-spectrum device even if it did not use DSSS or FHSS. In response, in May, 2001, the FCC made provisions in Part 15 to allow for alternative "digital modulation techniques," in addition to FHSS and DSSS, as long as those devices met the same power and radiation limitations as previously-approved DSSS and FHSS devices. 802.11g, which uses OFDM in the 2.4 GHz band, was the result.

The vendors' argument in favor of OFDM was that FCC Part 15 was too specific in allowing only FHSS and DSSS. Vendors proposed that any spread-spectrum system that shared the desirable qualities of FHSS and DSSS should be allowed. Since OFDM shares many desirable qualities with DSSS and FHSS, the vendors argued that OFDM should be treated as a spread spectrum technology and should be allowed. There is dissent among RF engineers as to whether OFDM should be considered a spread spectrum technology. It seems that the FCC's answer is, "OFDM is not a spread spectrum technology, but it is functionally equivalent to one."

Frequency Hopping Spread Spectrum (FHSS)

 For completeness, it's good to have a basic understanding of FHSS, but the vast majority of 802.11 networks today use either DSSS or OFDM, because of their higher data rates.

Frequency hopping spread spectrum is a spread spectrum technique that uses frequency agility to spread the data over more than 83 MHz. Frequency agility refers to the radio's ability to change transmission frequency abruptly within the usable RF frequency band. FHSS is used in 802.11 to implement data rates of 1 and 2 Mbps, using a modulation type called *Gaussian Frequency Shift Keying (GFSK)*.

In the case of frequency hopping wireless LANs, the usable portion of the 2.4 GHz ISM band is 83.5 MHz (2.400 GHz to 2.4835 GHz), per FCC regulation, but the IEEE 802.11 standard further restricts the frequency range that stations may use. For example in North America, 802.11 FHSS stations may only use between 2.402 and 2.480 GHz. It is not necessary for you to memorize exactly which frequencies are used, but you should know that the IEEE usually specifies slightly more conservative frequency ranges than the FCC allows, ensuring that its stations stay within regulations. You also should realize that different countries often specify slightly different frequency ranges, depending on their local regulations. WLAN vendors design their cards to operate within the requirements of the country in which the card is intended to be used.

How FHSS Works

In frequency hopping spread spectrum (FHSS) systems, the carrier changes frequency, or *hops*, according to a predefined pseudorandom sequence. The pseudorandom sequence is a list of frequencies to which the carrier will hop at specified time intervals.

Dwell Time

Frequency hopping systems must transmit on a specified frequency for a time and then hop to a different frequency to continue transmitting. The specific amount of time that an FHSS system transmits on a certain frequency is called the *dwell time*. Once the configured dwell time has expired, the system switches to a different frequency and may transmit again if the media access rules (CSMA/CA in the case of 802.11) permit.

Suppose a frequency hopping system transmits on only two frequencies: 2.401 GHz and 2.402 GHz. The system will transmit on the 2.401 GHz frequency for the duration of the dwell time—100 milliseconds (ms), for example. After 100 ms, the radio must change its transmitter frequency to 2.402 GHz and send information at that frequency for 100 ms. Since, in our example, the radio is only using 2.401 and 2.402 GHz, the radio will then hop back to 2.401 GHz and begin the process over again.

Hop Time

When a frequency hopping radio jumps from frequency A to frequency B, it must change the transmit frequency in one of two ways. It must either switch to a different circuit tuned to the new frequency, or change some element of the current circuit in order to tune to the new frequency. In either case, the process of changing to the new frequency must be complete before transmission can resume, and this change takes time due to electrical latencies inherent in the circuitry. The small amount of time during this frequency change in which the radio is not transmitting is called the *hop time*. The hop time is measured in microseconds (μs) and with relatively long *dwell* times of around 100–200 ms, a typical hop time of 200–300 μs typically is not considered significant.

The hop time can be treated as overhead, since no station can transmit during that time period. The longer the dwell time, the less often the system needs to hop and the less often you encounter a "do not transmit" interval. Therefore, *longer dwell time = greater throughput,* and *shorter hop time = greater throughput.*

Dwell Time Limits

If you took the previous equation to an extreme, you would conclude that the highest throughput could be achieved by having an infinite dwell time and zero hop time. But an infinite dwell time is the same as using a narrowband transmitter. Not only would you have lost the noise- and interference-resistance of FHSS, but you would have the potential to interfere with other narrowband transmitters in the area. Therefore, the FCC defines the maximum dwell time of a frequency hopping spread spectrum system at 400 ms per carrier frequency in any 30-second time period. This prevents FHSS systems from acting too much like narrowband systems.

For example, if a transmitter uses a carrier frequency for 100 ms, then hops through the entire sequence of 75 hops (each hop having the same 100 ms dwell time), returning to the original frequency, it has expended slightly over 7.5 seconds in this hopping sequence. The reason it is not exactly 7.5 seconds is due to hop time. Hopping through the hop sequence four consecutive times would yield 400 ms on each of the carrier frequencies during this timeframe of just barely over 30 seconds (7.5 seconds x 4 passes through the hop sequence), which is allowable by FCC rules. Other examples of how an FHSS system might stay within the FCC rules would be a dwell time of 200 ms passing through the hop sequence only twice in 30 seconds, or a dwell time of 400 ms passing through the hop sequence only once in 30 seconds. Any of these scenarios is permitted under FCC regulations.

The major difference between each of these scenarios is how hop time affects throughput. Using a dwell time of 100 ms, four times as many hops must be made as when using a 400 ms dwell time. This additional hopping time decreases system throughput, but it has an advantage as well: the more a system hops, the more resistant it will be to narrowband noise, and the less likely it will be to interfere with narrowband transmitters in the frequency range.

Normally, frequency hopping radios will not be programmed to operate at the legal limit, but rather provide some room between the legal limit and the actual operating range in order to provide the operator with the flexibility of adjustment. By adjusting the dwell time, an administrator can optimize the FHSS network for areas where there is either considerable interference or very little interference. In an area where there is little interference, longer dwell time, and hence greater throughput, is desirable. Conversely, in an area where there is considerable interference and many retransmissions are likely due to corrupted data packets, shorter dwell times are desirable to cause the FHSS system to hop more quickly off the frequencies on which there is interference.

FHSS Hop Sequences and Channels

FHSS systems use a hopping sequence (also called a hopping set or hopping pattern) consisting of a series of carrier frequencies. The IEEE 802.11 standard specifies in section 14.6.5, 1 MHz "channels," each of which serves as the center frequency for transmission during a dwell time. Each hopping set must contain at least 75 hopping frequencies, but no more than 79 hopping frequencies, ranging from 2.402 to 2.480 GHz in 1 MHz increments. The FHSS transmitter and receiver must be on the same carrier frequency at the same time (synchronized) for successful transmissions to occur. Stations entering a basic service area (BSA) will hear the beacons (which will be discussed in chapter 9) of an AP, which includes the hop sequence information. All radios within a basic service set will synchronize to the AP and subsequently hop together. The 802.11 standard includes pre-defined hopping sets that minimize the chance that systems in the same BSA will experience collisions. Some vendors implement features in their products that allow the user to build custom hopping sets.

Figure 6.2 shows a frequency hopping system using a hop sequence of five frequencies. The stations using this hopping set will begin on frequency 2.402 GHz. After the dwell time, the stations will hop to the second frequency, and so on. Once the radios have spent one dwell time on the fifth center frequency, they will repeat the hop sequence, starting again at 2.402 GHz. The process of repeating the sequence will continue indefinitely. Note that the stations keep hopping in this pattern regardless of whether any station is transmitting data at any given point in time. Also note that a station must arrange its transmissions so that it is finished transmitting by the end of the dwell time; a station is not allowed to "overlap" transmissions between two dwell times.[1] If an FHSS station

---

1. 802.11-1999 (R2003) – section 9.2.5.1

calculates that its transmission would take it past the end of the dwell time, it must defer transmission until the next dwell time.

FIGURE 6.2   Frequency hopping system

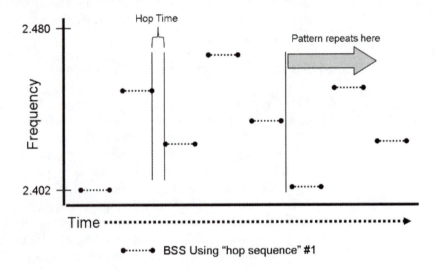

Co-Located FHSS Systems

FHSS allows for multiple systems in the same basic service area by allowing each system to use a different hopping sequence. 802.11's pre-defined hopping sequences are designed to minimize the likelihood that two stations using different hop sequences will hop to the same frequency at the same time. Therefore, two systems using different hopping sequences will probably not interfere with one another. If they do happen to hop to the same frequency at the same time, they will only interfere for a maximum of one dwell time before they hop away to a different frequency.

In Figure 6.3, note that the three systems almost never hop to the same frequency (channel) at the same time, and so do not interfere with each other even though they are in the same physical location. For illustrative purposes, we provided one instance in which channel 1 and channel 2 overlap. Though in reality this scenario is unlikely, you should realize that our example's hopping sequence, with only five hops per sequence, is much shorter than the real hopping sequences used by 802.11 WLANs.

Such hopping sequences are typically 79 hops long, which would be difficult to illustrate.

FIGURE 6.3   Co-located unsynchronized frequency hopping systems

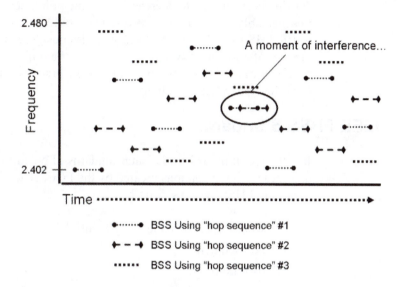

Some manufacturers build access points that can synchronize with each other over the wired distribution system, and each AP uses hopping sequences that do not conflict. Each access point assures that it instructs its stations to hop at exactly the same moment as all of the other access points. This synchronization can allow for more densely populated BSAs, where multiple FHSS systems share the same physical space. Synchronizing systems allows for more throughput in a single area, because there will be fewer collisions.

If synchronization technology is used, it is theoretically possible to have as many as 79 co-located access points in an area without ever having two systems on the same channel. This is because 802.11 FHSS divides the 2.4 GHz ISM band into 79 channels (carrier frequencies). Each frequency can support one system at a time without interference. The cost of synchronization is prohibitive, so it is generally not used. If synchronized radios are used, the expense tends to dictate 12 co-located systems as the maximum.

If non-synchronized radios are used, the maximum number of systems depends on the performance requirements and traffic loading of the system. As traffic increases due to higher load or more systems, the probability that two systems will hop to the same frequency will increase, causing performance to decrease. At some point, performance will be unacceptably low and no more systems should be added. In a medium-traffic FHSS wireless LAN, twenty-six is considered the maximum number of co-located systems. Increasing the traffic significantly, or routinely transferring large files, places the practical limit on the number of co-located systems at about 15.

IEEE FHSS Standards

It is the job of the IEEE to create standards of operation within the confines of the regulations created by the FCC. The IEEE standards regarding FHSS systems describe:

- what frequency bands may be used
- hop sequences
- dwell times
- data rates

The IEEE 802.11 standard specifies data rates of 1 Mbps and 2 Mbps. In order for a frequency hopping system to be 802.11 compliant, it must operate in the 2.4 GHz ISM band (which is defined by the FCC as being from 2.4000 GHz to 2.5000 GHz), and operate between 2.402 and 2.480 GHz (used for the FHSS channels).

FCC Rules affecting FHSS

On August 31, 2000, the FCC changed the rules governing how FHSS could be implemented. The rule changes allowed frequency hopping systems to be more flexible and more robust. The rules are typically divided into "pre-8/31/2000" rules and "post-8/31/2000" rules, but the FCC allows for some decision-making on the part of the manufacturer or the implementer.

Prior to 8/31/00, FHSS systems were mandated by the FCC (and the IEEE) to use at least 75 of the possible 79 carrier frequencies (2.402–

2.480 GHz in 1 MHz increments) in a hopping set at a maximum output power of 1 watt at the intentional radiator in point-to-multipoint systems. This rule states that the system must hop on 75 of the 79 frequencies before repeating the pattern. This rule was amended on 8/31/00 to state that only 15 hops in a set were required. If fewer than 75 hops were used, the system's maximum output power could only be 125 mW, and it could only have a maximum of 5 MHz of carrier frequency bandwidth. Keep in mind that with an increase in bandwidth, less peak power is required for the same transmission of information.

To further explain this rule change, though not in exactly the same wording used by the FCC, the number of hops multiplied by the bandwidth of the carrier frequency had to equal a total span of at least 75 MHz. For example, if 25 hops are used, a carrier frequency only 3 MHz wide is required; if 15 hops are used, a carrier frequency 5 MHz wide (the maximum) must be used.

The IEEE did not change the 802.11 standard to reflect the post 8/31/00 rules.

The IEEE 802.11 standard states that FHSS systems will have at least 6 MHz of channel separation between hops. Therefore, an FHSS system transmitting on 2.410 GHz must hop to at least 2.404 if decreasing in frequency, or 2.416 if increasing in frequency. This requirement was left unchanged by the IEEE after the FCC change on 8/31/00. The pre-8/31/00 FCC rules concerning FHSS systems allowed a maximum of 2 Mbps by today's technology. By increasing the maximum carrier bandwidth from 1 MHz to 5 MHz, the maximum data rate was increased to 10 Mbps (but since the 802.11 standard was not updated, its maximum data rate with FHSS remains 2 Mbps).

Direct Sequence Spread Spectrum (DSSS)

Direct sequence spread spectrum is one of the most widely used types of spread spectrum technology, owing its popularity to its ease of implementation and high data rates. DSSS is used in 802.11b to achieve data rates of 1, 2, 5.5, and 11 Mbps in the 2.4 GHz ISM band. 1 and 2 Mbps are specified in 802.11, while 5.5 and 11 Mbps are specified in 802.11b, which is an addendum to 802.11.

Direct Sequence Systems

In the 2.4 GHz ISM band, the IEEE specifies the use of DSSS at a data rate of 1 or 2 Mbps under the 802.11 standard. Under the 802.11b standard – sometimes called "High-Rate DSSS" or HR-DSSS – data rates of 5.5 and 11 Mbps are specified.

IEEE 802.11b devices operating at 5.5 or 11 Mbps are able to communicate with 802.11 devices operating at 1 or 2 Mbps because the 802.11b standard provides for backward compatibility. Users employing 802.11 DSSS devices do not need to upgrade their entire wireless LAN in order to use 802.11b devices on their network. The IEEE 802.11g standard uses OFDM instead of DSSS, but since 802.11g requires backwards compatibility with 802.11b, 802.11g devices can also use DSSS when they communicate with 802.11b devices.

Channels

Each DSSS channel is a contiguous band of frequencies based around a center frequency that uses 1 MHz carrier frequencies, just as with FHSS. Figure 6.4 shows the channel and frequency assignments in the U.S. (FCC) and Europe (ETSI). In the other countries, 802.11's frequencies extend slightly higher than they do in the U.S., so 802.11 defines 14 total channels, although only 11 of those can be used in the U.S. Figure 6.4 lists the channels used in certain countries, but this table is not exhaustive.

FIGURE 6.4   DSSS channel frequency assignments

Channel ID	Channel Frequencies (GHz)	US and Canada	Europe (ETSI)	Spain	Japan	France
1	2.412	Yes	Yes		Yes	
2	2.417	Yes	Yes		Yes	
3	2.422	Yes	Yes		Yes	
4	2.427	Yes	Yes		Yes	
5	2.432	Yes	Yes		Yes	
6	2.437	Yes	Yes		Yes	
7	2.442	Yes	Yes		Yes	
8	2.447	Yes	Yes		Yes	
9	2.452	Yes	Yes		Yes	
10	2.457	Yes	Yes	Yes	Yes	Yes
11	2.462	Yes	Yes	Yes	Yes	Yes
12	2.467		Yes		Yes	Yes
13	2.472		Yes		Yes	Yes
14	2.484					

Channel 14 was previously the only channel available for use by WLANs in Japan, but the regulations were changed to allow more channels to be used. This table reflects that change.

Figure 6.5 shows the *spectrum mask* of a DSSS channel. A spectrum mask represents the maximum power output for the channel at various frequencies. Although Figure 6.5 shows channel 3 specifically, the same mask applies whatever DSSS channel is in use.

An 802.11b channel is centered on a certain frequency (2.422 GHz in figure 6.5) and extends outwards from that frequency. In order to limit the overlap of two channels that are near each other (e.g., the overlap between channels 1 and 6), 802.11 requires that the signal be attenuated by at least 30 dB below the center frequency's peak power, between ±11 MHz and ± 22 MHz, and that the signal be attenuated by at least 50 dB below the center frequency's peak power outside of ±22 MHz.

For example, if Figure 6.5 represented a 100 mW transmission (20 dBm) on channel 3 (centered at 2.422 GHz), then the signal would have to be no higher than –10 dBm in the ranges 2.402–2.412 and 2.432–2.442. The signal would have to be no higher than –30 dBm above 2.442 and below 2.402 GHz.

FIGURE 6.5   DSSS Channel

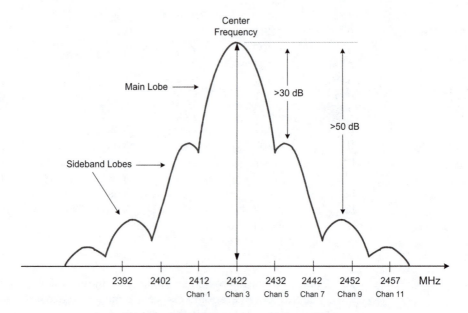

The 802.11 series of standards never directly mentions the width of a channel in MHz, but instead speaks in terms of the center frequencies used and the required distance between center frequencies for "non-overlapping" status. Non-overlapping channels are defined as follows:

- 802.11 DSSS – 30 MHz spacing (6 channels)
- 802.11b HR-DSSS – 25 MHz spacing (5 channels)
- 802.11a OFDM – 20 MHz spacing (4 channels)
- 802.11g ERP-OFDM – 25 MHz spacing (5 channels)

FIGURE 6.6   HR-DSSS non-overlapping channel allocation

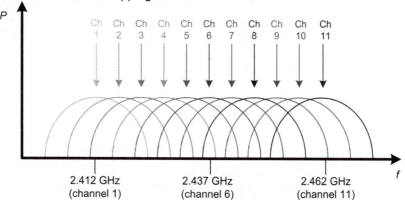

To use DSSS systems with overlapping channels (e.g., channels 1 and 2 or 10 and 11) in the same physical space would cause interference between the systems. DSSS systems using overlapping channels should not be co-located because there will almost always be a drastic or complete reduction in throughput. Because the center frequencies are 5 MHz apart, and the center frequencies for non-overlapping channels must be at least 25 MHz apart (HR-DSSS), channels should be co-located only if the *channel numbers* are at least five apart: channels 1 and 6 do not overlap, channels 2 and 7 do not overlap, etc. With this method, there is a maximum of three co-located HR-DSSS systems possible in the 2.4 GHz ISM band because channels 1, 6, and 11 are the only non-overlapping channels.

FIGURE 6.7   HR-DSSS non-overlapping channels

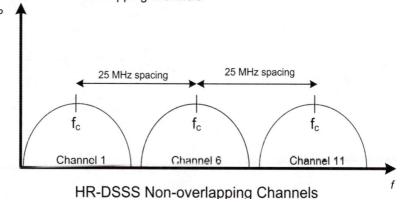

HR-DSSS Non-overlapping Channels

Channel 6 can in fact overlap (depending on the antenna used, output power, and distance between systems) with channels 1 and 11, causing degradation of the wireless LAN connection and speed.

Figure 6.8 shows a spectrum diagram for the entire 802.11b frequency range when channels 1, 6, and 11 are in use. Notice that the channels can overlap even though they have the minimum separation to be considered "non-overlapping."

Remember that 802.11 only requires that the signal be attenuated by −50 dB below the peak power at greater than ±22Mhz from the center frequency. The signal is not required to fall below any absolute power level. Therefore, it is possible for a powerful transmitter to have strong enough side-lobes that it can interfere with another transmitter on a "non-overlapping" channel. The more powerful the transmitters, the more likely that they will interfere and the more channel separation they require.

The proximity of the devices is an important factor as well. If the devices are closer to each other, their signals will have less space to attenuate and they will be more likely to interfere with each other.

FIGURE 6.8   Overlapping channels

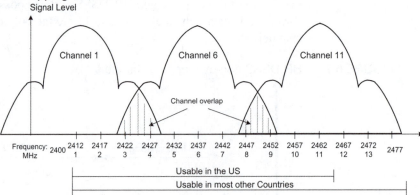

DSSS Encoding

All spread spectrum technologies increase the bandwidth of the signal compared to a narrowband transmitter carrying the same amount of information. FHSS increases the bandwidth by hopping a narrowband signal around within a much larger frequency range. In DSSS, the carrier frequency doesn't change; instead, redundant information is added to the signal prior to transmission (causing the signal to take up more bandwidth) and removed from the signal upon reception (recovering the original data).

The process of "adding redundant information" to the data is referred to as *processing gain*. Each bit in the data stream is XOR'ed (a mathematical function) with a fixed-length bit sequence called a *PN (pseudorandom number) code*. In 802.11, the PN code is '10110111000.' This specific PN code is known as the *Barker Sequence*. Figure 6.9 shows an example of how processing gain would apply to the bit sequence '10' in DSSS.

FIGURE 6.9   Processing Gain example

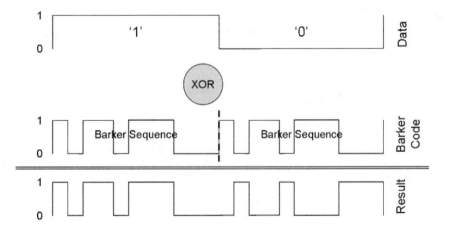

The "result" is what would actually be transmitted onto the network. Although the result, the Barker Code, and the data all contain binary information (represented by 1s and 0s), it is convenient to be able to differentiate between the 1's and 0's of the data and the 1's and 0's of the Barker Code and the "result." Therefore, the data is referred to as "bits," while the Barker Code and the "result" are referred to as *chips*. This distinction is purely semantic. Bits and chips are in many ways exactly the same: binary pieces of information—1's and 0's. But when we say "bit," we're always referring to the data; when we say "chip," we're referring to the Barker Code or the "result."

Processing gain adds corruption resistance in two ways. First, because the receiver knows that each bit has been XOR'ed with a specific pattern of chips, the receiver can look for that pattern in the signal. If a signal is received that is close to that pattern, the receiver can infer what the pattern must have been. For example, the '1' in the data above would be transmitted (after processing gain) as '10110111000.' If the receiver were to see "101101??000" (where the underlined chips have been corrupted), the receiver could infer that the original data was a '1' because that is the only value that makes the other nine chips correct. What this scenario means is that the signal can be transmitted at a lower power level since it can tolerate some corruption without losing data.

The second way in which processing gain adds corruption resistance was discussed previously when we covered inter-symbol interference. After processing gain, the signal contains eleven times as much information as it did before processing gain; each one bit of data is now represented by eleven chips. This signal will require more bandwidth to transmit. Since the signal is spread out over more bandwidth, it is more resistant to inter-symbol interference, as explained previously.

Processing Gain

In DSSS, each one bit of data is XOR'ed with an eleven-bit PN code, but there's nothing special about this ratio. Other DSSS systems might use a shorter or longer PN code. A shorter PN code will result in:

1. Less "spreading" of the signal. The resultant signal will take up less bandwidth relative to the original signal.

2. Less corruption resistance, since the signal will contain less redundant information.

3. Less overhead and higher relative data rate. If the communications channel is capable of transmitting 11 Mega-chips-per-second of information, but we are using 11 chips to represent 1 bit, then the effective throughput is 1 Mbps, only 1/11th the theoretical maximum. By contrast, if we did not spread at all (a PN code length of 1), we could achieve the full 11 Mbps.

A longer PN code has the exact opposite effects: more spreading, more corruption resistance, and more overhead.

The ratio between the number of chips in the resultant (post-processing gain) and the number of bits in the data (pre-processing gain) is referred to as the amount of processing gain. In the past, the FCC had specified a minimum processing gain of 10 (10 chips per 1 bit), while most commercial products actually operated under 20. The FCC made an important change on May 16, 2002, that removed all processing gain requirements. The IEEE 802.11 working group has set its minimum processing gain requirements at 11.

Phase Shift Keying

After processing gain, the transmitter has a sequence of chips that represent the data to be transmitted. The final step in transmission is to encode those chips in the RF signal. Wireless networks don't use *amplitude modulation*—a method in which the amplitude of the signal represents the information. Amplitude Modulation is undesirable in wireless networks because amplitude is the quality of the signal that is most likely to be changed by interference. Meanwhile the frequency and phase of the signal is unlikely to be changed by interference. Therefore, wireless networks usually represent information by manipulating the *phase* of the signal in a scheme called *Phase Shift Keying* (PSK).

Phase Shift Keying represents information by modifying the phase of the signal. Remember that the phase difference between two sine waves of the same frequency can be represented by some number of degrees. Two sine waves that peak at exactly the same moment are said to be 0 degrees out of phase, or in-phase. If one sine wave reaches its trough at the same moment that the other one is peaking, they are said to be 180 degrees out-of-phase. Every possible relationship between those extremes is represented by some number of degrees between 0 and 180.

FIGURE 6.10   In-Phase (left) and Out-of-Phase (right) sine waves

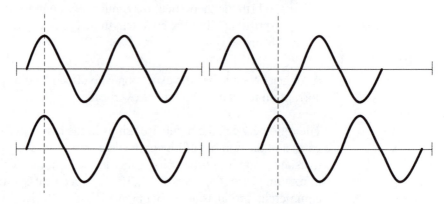

Differential Phase Shift Keying (DPSK) is a specific type of PSK and is used in 802.11 devices. It encodes information by advancing the phase of the signal by some number of degrees. The number of degrees by which the phase is advanced represents the data that is being transmitted. For example, a simple DPSK system might define that an advance of 180 degrees represents a '1,' an advance of 0 degrees represents a '0,' and each symbol is three hertz long. Figure 6.11 shows how the string '101' would be encoded in that system:

FIGURE 6.11   Representing '101' with DPSK

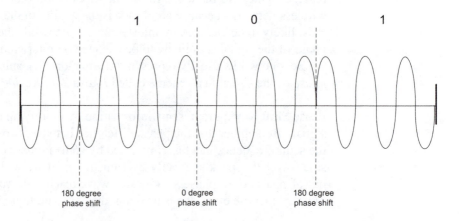

One of the parameters in a DPSK system is the number of discrete degrees of phase shift that the system will recognize. The system above recognizes two discrete phase shifts: 180 degrees and 0 degrees. Since there are only two phase shifts, each shift can represent at most one bit. This scheme is called *Differential Binary Phase Shift Keying (DBPSK)*, and is used to transmit the resultant stream of chips in 802.11 or 802.11b at 1 Mbps.

Consider a system that recognizes four discrete phase shifts: 0 degrees, 90 degrees, 180 degrees, and 270 degrees. This system is known as *Differential Quaternary Phase Shift Keying (DQPSK)* and is used in 2 Mbps 802.11b. Four phase shifts are capable of representing the four different unique two-bit combinations: 11, 10, 01, and 00. Since each phase shift represents two chips instead of one, DQPSK has twice the data rate of DBPSK at the same signaling rate (hence the 2 Mbps data rate for DQPSK vs. 1 Mbps for DBPSK).

CCK Encoding

The methods described above are used in 1 and 2 Mbps 802.11b. To achieve data rates of 5.5 and 11 Mbps, a more complex scheme called *Complementary Code Keying (CCK)* is used. While a basic understanding of how DSSS works is important, memorization of the full details of DSSS transmission is not necessary for you to pass your CWNA exam; therefore CCK is not covered in depth in this book.

In summary, CCK differs from the previous description in the following respects:

- CCK uses an 8-chip PN code instead of an 11-chip PN code. The 8-chip sequence still runs at a rate of 11 Mega-chips-per-second, just as in 1 and 2 Mbps 802.11b. At 1 and 2 Mbps, the PN code is 11 chips, resulting in a rate of 11,000,000 / 11 = 1 million PN codes per second; with CCK, the PN code is 8 chips, resulting in a rate of 11,000,000 / 8 = 1,375,000 PN codes per second. In this way, more data is squeezed into the transmission channel while keeping the basic chipping rate the same.
- CCK does not use the same PN code for every bit sequence. Instead it calculates a spreading code based on the incoming data. Each eight bits (at 11 Mbps) or 4 bits (at 5.5 Mbps) of data maps

to a unique eight-chip spreading code. The resulting chips are transmitted using DQPSK. This mapping of data to spreading code is the most complex difference between CCK and Barker Coding.

'Encoding' vs. 'Modulation'

As you may have gathered in the previous chapters of this book, the terms "encoding" and "modulation" are sometimes used interchangeably when discussing RF signal transmission. Although the correct usage of these terms might be obvious to an experienced RF engineer, it is easy for even an expert WLAN administrator to mix them up.

In our experience, "modulation" most often refers to a characteristic of the RF signal that is manipulated in order to represent data. Types of modulation include *amplitude modulation*, *frequency modulation*, and *phase shift keying* (including specific types of PSK like DBPSK and DQPSK). "Encoding," on the other hand, most often refers to the way in which the changes in the signal are translated into ones and zeros. Types of encoding include Barker Coding and CCK.

For example, using amplitude modulation we might define an encoding method that says that +5 volts is a '1' and –5 volts is a '0.' Using phase shift keying as the modulation method, we might define an encoding that uses 180 degrees phase shift as a '1' and 0 degrees phase shift as a '0' (which would be an example of DBPSK).

Summary of DSSS Encoding

FIGURE 6.12   Summary of 802.11b DSSS encoding methods

Data Rate	Encoding
1	Barker Coding (11 chip fixed PN code) with 11 chips encoding 1 bit, transmitted using DBPSK
2	Barker Coding (11 chip fixed PN code) with 11 chips encoding 1 bit, transmitted using DQPSK
5.5	CCK Coding (8 chip variable PN code) with 8 chips encoding 8 bits, transmitted using DQPSK
11	CCK Coding (8 chip variable PN code) with 8 chips encoding 4 bits, transmitted using DQPSK

This table is provided for your reference. You will not be tested on the material in this table on the CWNA exam.

Orthogonal Frequency Division Multiplexing

Orthogonal Frequency Division Multiplexing (OFDM) offers the highest data rates and maximum resistance to interference and corruption of all the signal manipulation techniques in use in 802.11 today. Although it is not considered a spread spectrum technique by the FCC, OFDM shares many qualities with spread spectrum communicators, including using a low transmit power and wider-than-necessary bandwidth. OFDM is used to provide data rates up to 54 Mbps in 802.11a and 802.11g.

How OFDM Works

OFDM achieves high data rates by squeezing a large number of communication channels into a given frequency band. Normally, two communication channels must be separated by a certain amount of bandwidth or they overlap and interfere. Specifically, each channel has *harmonics* that extend up and down the frequency space, decreasing in amplitude as they get farther from the channel's fundamental signal. Even if two channels are non-overlapping, their harmonics may overlap and the signal can be corrupted.

An OFDM communicator can place adjacent communication channels very precisely in the frequency space in such a way that the channels' harmonics exactly cancel each other out, effectively leaving only the fundamental signals. Although the theory and mathematics behind OFDM have been around for years, only recently has it been possible to market an OFDM system. Consumer-grade analog RF systems are not capable of manipulating the signals precisely enough to cancel out the harmonics exactly, but by using *digital signal processing (DSP)* to place the communications channels and sum them to get a resulting wave, extreme precision can be achieved cheaply. The only analog step in the process is the final transmission of the digitally-calculated RF waveform.

OFDM achieves high data rates by dividing a single communications channel into a large number of closely-spaced, small-bandwidth *sub-carriers*. Each sub-carrier individually has a relatively low data rate, but by transmitting data in parallel on all sub-carriers simultaneously, high data rates can be achieved.

FIGURE 6.13   OFDM Frequency Plot

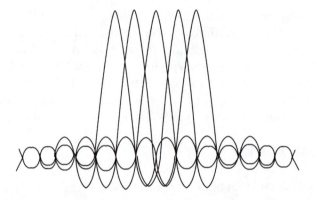

Figure 6.13 shows an example of a frequency spectrum for an OFDM transmitter. Each of the peaks represents a single sub-carrier, and the sub-carriers together make up the communications channel. Note that the sub-carriers are precisely aligned so that the zero-points of their harmonics overlap exactly. The majority of the harmonic energy will cancel out, leaving just the sub-carriers.

Convolution Coding

Imagine if narrowband interference wiped out sub-carriers 1–20 of an OFDM channel. The entire channel would be useless, since OFDM does not have the ability to "hop away" from noise. In order to increase OFDM's resistance to narrowband interference, OFDM is often implemented with a mathematical technique called *convolution coding*. Convolution coding is not technically part of OFDM, but it is used together in 802.11a and 802.11g.

Convolution coding is a form of error correction in which redundant information analogous to a parity bit in a file system is added to the data. The error correction is calculated across all of the sub-carriers, so if narrowband interference corrupts data on one sub-carrier, the receiver can reconstruct that data using the convolution coding on another sub-carrier. The net effect is as if the transmitter were transmitting the same data on multiple sub-carriers (although that is not literally what is happening).

Similar to processing gain in DSSS, convolution coding has a ratio of "bits transmitted" vs. "bits encoded." As this ratio goes up, the signal's resistance to corruption increases, but the data rate decreases due to increased overhead. Manipulating the ratio of the convolution coding is one method that 802.11a uses to achieve its different data rates. Lower data rates have a higher convolution coding ratio; higher data rates have a lower one.

OFDM in 802.11a

802.11a uses OFDM to transmit in the 5 GHz UNII bands. There are three 5 GHz UNII bands: high (UNII-3), middle (UNII-2) and low (UNII-1).

FIGURE 6.14   802.11a OFDM Frequency Plot

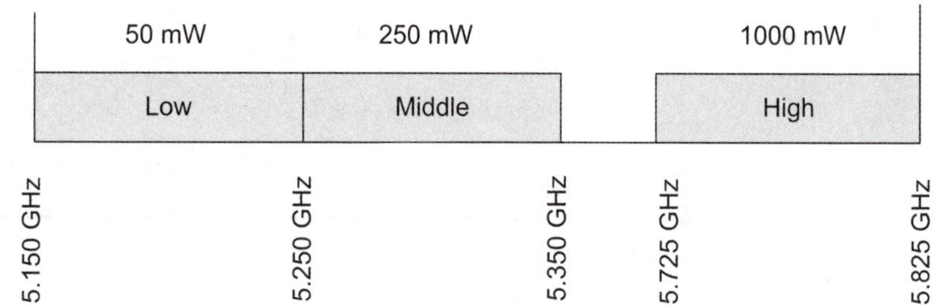

802.11a divides each of these bands into four non-overlapping channels. Consumer equipment typically uses the middle and low bands, allowing a total of eight channels for most indoor 802.11a equipment. Each channel consists of 52 sub-carriers, as shown in Figure 6.15.

FIGURE 6.15   802.11a OFDM Frequency Plot

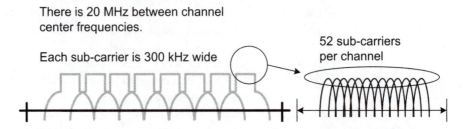

There is 20 MHz between channel center frequencies.

Each sub-carrier is 300 kHz wide

52 sub-carriers per channel

Figure 6.16 shows a summary of the previous figures. The low and middle UNII bands are broken into a total of eight channels of 20 MHz each. Each channel is broken out into 52 sub-carriers of 300 kHz each.

FIGURE 6.16   802.11a OFDM Frequency Plot

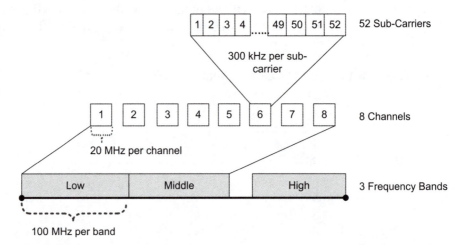

Four of 802.11a's sub-carriers are used as *pilot carriers* for monitoring the channel, while the other 48 are used to transmit data. An 802.11a station transmits in parallel across all available data sub-carriers simultaneously. The OFDM physical layers of 802.11a and 802.11g do *not allow* more than one station to use a channel at a time (e.g., "I'll use sub-carriers 1–25 and you use 26–52"). Specifically, a station will simultaneously transmit one "chip" per sub-carrier to create a "symbol" equal in length to the number of available sub-carriers ("chip" is not technically correct since we've left the realm of DSSS, but it's close enough).

For example, if we assume that DBPSK encoding is being used, then each sub-carrier can encode one bit per transition (two discrete phase shifts = one bit per transition). With 48 sub-carriers available, the total length of a symbol would be 48 bits. The overall data rate would depend on the signaling rate (symbols / second), and would be given by the formula:

$$48 \text{ bits / symbol} * N \text{ symbols / second} = X \text{ bits / second}$$

If DQPSK were used, then each transition would encode two bits (four discrete phase shifts = two bits per transition) and the length of a symbol would be 96 bits. The overall data rate would depend on the signaling rate (symbols / second) and would be given by the formula:

$$96 \text{ bits / symbol} * N \text{ symbols / second} = X \text{ bits / second}$$

In reality, the math is slightly more complex than this, since some of the sub-carriers are used to carry the convolution coding information. For example, when 802.11a uses DBPSK, depending on the data rate, either one-half or one-quarter of the bits are used for error correction (convolution coding). Therefore, only 24 or 36 of the 48 channels are actually available to carry data "chips."

OFDM in 802.11g

The 802.11g standard specifies using OFDM to transmit in the 2.4 GHz ISM band. For backwards compatibility, 802.11g radios are essentially both an ERP-OFDM radio and a DSSS radio. 802.11g radios, when operating in ERP-OFDM mode, use the same channel numbers and same spacing between center frequencies as 802.11b HR-DSSS. The data rates, modulation, and coding used by 802.11g and 802.11a systems are the same, but their non-overlapping channel spacing is different (four channels for 802.11a versus five channels for 802.11g).

802.11g Operating Modes

802.11g specifies several different signal transmission and encoding methods, each offering different compatibility and performance characteristics. For example, ERP-OFDM mode uses OFDM to transmit the entire frame in environments where only 802.11g stations are present.

DSSS-OFDM mode uses DBPSK or DQPSK modulation for two low-level headers (preamble and PLCP, specifically), and OFDM for the rest of the frame. DSSS-OFDM is a type of hybrid frame that exists somewhere between DSSS and OFDM in its frame structure. 802.11g stations also can act as purely 802.11b stations, using only DSSS technology.

802.11b stations can't "hear" OFDM transmissions, so they might believe that the network is idle. In believing that the medium is idle, they may begin transmitting in the middle of an OFDM frame. This may inadvertently cause a collision. The idea behind 802.11g modes like DSSS-OFDM is that 802.11b stations can hear the low-level headers. These headers contain enough information to let the 802.11b stations know that a frame is being transmitted and how long the frame will be on the RF medium. This prevents them from transmitting until the frame is finished. Once the 802.11g station has transmitted the low-level frame headers, it can switch up to the faster data rates made possible by OFDM for transmission of the data payload of the frame.

The operating modes and protection mechanisms specified by the 802.11g standard are covered in the CWAP wireless LAN analysis objectives and curriculum.

Summary of OFDM Encoding

FIGURE 6.17   Summary of 802.11a/g OFDM encoding methods

Data Rate (Mbps)	Modulation	Bits / Transi tion	R	Length of 1 Symbol	Data bits encoded by 1 symbol
6	DBPSK	1	1/2	48	24
9	DBPSK	1	3/4	48	36
12	DQPSK	2	1/2	96	48
18	DQPSK	2	3/4	96	72
24	16-QAM	4	1/2	192	96
36	16-QAM	4	3/4	192	144
48	64-QAM	6	2/3	288	192
54	64-QAM	6	3/4	288	216

This table is provided for your reference. You will not be tested on the material in this table on the CWNA exam.

Figure 6.17 shows a summary of data rates and encoding methods used in 802.11a and 802.11g. The table is somewhat complex and deserves an explanation. The Modulation column shows the type of modulation to encode data at the given data rate. DBPSK and DQPSK have been discussed previously. *Quadrature Amplitude Modulation ("QAM")* is a generalized form of DBPSK and DQPSK. DBPSK has two possible phase shifts and encodes 1 bit per shift; DQPSK has four possible phase shifts and encodes 2 bits per shift. But there is no need to limit ourselves to two or four possible phase shifts. Sufficiently accurate hardware exists that can recognize as many as 256 different degrees of phase shift. As the encoding method adds more possible phase shifts, more bits can be encoded per shift according the formula:

$$\text{bits per shift} = \log_2(\text{number of phase shifts})$$

The syntax used for QAM is to precede "QAM" with the number of possible phase shifts in the encoding method. Therefore, 16-QAM defines 16 possible phase shifts encoding 4 bits per shift; 64-QAM defines 64 possible phase shifts encoding 6 bits per shift. Higher levels of

QAM give higher data rates. More bits per shift results in higher throughput, assuming the shifting rate, signaling rate, or baud rate remains the same. The tradeoff with more possible shifts is that the signal is more susceptible to corruption.

The bits / transition column shows the number of bits that can be encoded by a single phase transition using the encoding method in the Modulation column.

"R" refers to the fraction of sub-carriers that are being used for data vs. convolution coding (error correction). More sub-carriers being used for convolution coding results in a more robust signal but a lower data rate, since those sub-carriers can't be used to encode data. For example, a data rate with an R of ¼ would use ¼ * 48 = 12 sub-carriers for convolution coding and 48 − 12 = 36 sub-carriers for data.

"Length of 1 Symbol" refers to the total length of a single symbol at the given data rate. This value is always equal to the number of sub-carriers (48) times the number of bits / transition. "Data bits encoded / symbol" refers to the amount of data that can be encoded by a single symbol once the overhead of convolution coding is subtracted out.

The final piece of the puzzle to relate the bits / symbol to the data rate is the signaling rate, which is 250,000 symbols / second for all data rates.

Packet Binary Convolutional Code (PBCC)

PBCC is a modulation technique that was developed by a small company later purchased by Texas Instruments. If you have ever seen a 22 Mbps "Turbo-mode" 802.11b card, chances are that it was a TI chipset using PBCC modulation. Neither Intersil (which backed OFDM) nor TI (which backed PBCC) could achieve the required supermajority in the IEEE 802.11g committee to exclude the other technology. To avoid a deadlock which would have delayed ratification of the 802.11g standard, it was decided to allow both PBCC and OFDM into the standard. It is possible that you will find 802.11g cards using PBCC instead of OFDM, but OFDM is by far the dominant technology. Therefore, PBCC is not covered in-depth in this study guide or at all on the CWNA exam. PBCC supports data rates of 11, 22, and 33 Mbps, and must be supported on both the transmitting and receiving radios.

Comparing 802.11 Technologies

802.11, 802.11b, 802.11a, and 802.11g technologies all have their advantages and disadvantages, and it is incumbent on you to give each its due weight when deciding how to implement your wireless LAN. This section will cover some of the factors that should be considered when determining which technology is most appropriate for your WLAN, including:

- Narrowband interference
- System cost
- Co-location
- Equipment compatibility and availability
- Data rate and throughput
- Range
- Security

Narrowband Interference

FHSS (802.11)

As is the case with all spread spectrum technologies, frequency hopping systems are resistant but not immune to narrowband interference. If a signal were to interfere with the frequency hopping signal on a small part of the 2.4 GHz spectrum, only the hops that occurred within that part of the spectrum would be wasted. During those dwell times, data would be corrupted, but when the stations hopped to non-obstructed frequencies, they would transmit without corruption.

FIGURE 6.18   Effect of interference on an FHSS device

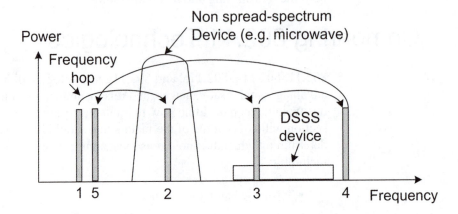

In reality, an interfering narrowband signal may occupy several megahertz of bandwidth. Since a frequency hopping band is typically 79 MHz wide, even such an interfering signal will cause little degradation of the spread spectrum signal. Interference must exist over a large portion of the ISM band before the FHSS system experiences significant performance degradation.

Some of today's newest frequency hopping systems are actually *adaptive*, which means that they will detect which frequencies have a lot of interference and use hopping patterns that avoid those frequencies. This adaptability is a relatively new technology and is not implemented in 802.11, but it has been proposed as one of the methods of minimizing interference between Bluetooth (which uses frequency hopping) and 802.11b/g (which use DSSS and OFDM). The Bluetooth communicator could detect which frequencies are in use by 802.11b/g access points and choose its hopping pattern to avoid those frequencies.

DSSS (802.11, 802.11b)

Like frequency hopping systems, direct sequence systems are resistant to narrowband interference due to their spread spectrum characteristics. A DSSS signal is more susceptible to narrowband interference than FHSS because a DSSS channel uses less bandwidth overall than a FHSS system. With FHSS, frequency agility and a wide frequency band ensures that the interference is only influential for a small amount of time, corrupting only a small portion of the data.

Nevertheless, processing gain does add some redundancy to the DSSS signal so the DSSS communicator can drop to a lower data rate if it experiences some narrowband interference. Since DSSS offers higher data rates than FHSS, it might prove just as capable in terms of throughput even in the presence of narrowband interference. Also, you should have some flexibility in which channel the DSSS system uses, allowing the system to be moved away from the interference. Ultimately, however, FHSS is more capable of avoiding narrowband interference than DSSS, since it hops across a much wider array of frequencies in the 2.4 GHZ ISM band.

OFDM (802.11a, 802.11g)

In 802.11g, a channel occupies the same bandwidth as an 802.11b channel and is similarly incapable of moving to a different channel in the presence of narrowband interference. 802.11g's more sophisticated encoding and error correction allows it to achieve much higher data rates than 802.11b (DSSS) or 802.11 (FHSS), even in the presence of narrowband interference. In terms of noise resistance, OFDM is always preferable to DSSS.

In some cases an entire width of the frequency space used for a channel might be affected by noise, completely knocking out an 802.11g transmitter. In this circumstance, theoretically, an FHSS transmitter might be preferable since it could hop out of that frequency range, but, practically speaking, few people would recommend an 802.11 FHSS access point over an 802.11g access point due to the much lower throughput of the FHSS access point. If wideband noise were present, it would probably be better to move an 802.11g access point to a different channel than to buy an 802.11 FHSS access point.

System Cost

Given the dynamic nature of the WLAN marketplace, it is difficult to cover cost in a book. At the time of this writing, 802.11 FHSS equipment is almost unobtainable except on the aftermarket, such as eBay, and from a few vendors who still sell FHSS access points for specialized applications and legacy systems. Meanwhile 802.11b, 802.11a, and 802.11g access points are available off the shelf from your local electronics or office equipment retailer.

At the time of this writing, 802.11b equipment is still available but is being substantially reduced in price. 802.11b is still appropriate for cases where cost is a major factor and high bandwidth is not needed. For example, a home user who wants to provide wireless access only to his 1.5 Mbps DSL connection would not benefit from 802.11g's higher data rates, and so might decide to save some money by buying cut-rate 802.11b equipment (but that same user might benefit from 802.11g's increased range and interference-resistance).

802.11g equipment is currently the most popular and offers the best price/performance balance, especially for cases where higher bandwidth is needed (e.g., VoIP over 802.11). In addition 802.11g equipment usually comes with the latest features and offers some degree of future-proofing, whereas 802.11b equipment sometimes lags behind in features. Equipment meeting 802.11g specifications is also backwards-compatible to 802.11b equipment, which allows the user to upgrade the network gradually.

802.11a equipment is slightly more expensive than 802.11g equipment. Multimode (a/b/g) client cards (PCMCIA, PCI, or MiniPCI) are relatively inexpensive, although multimode access points still draw a premium. Given that 802.11g offers the same data rates as 802.11a, many WLAN administrators choose not to pay the premium for the 802.11a equipment. The exceptions are cases where the 2.4 GHz band is known to be crowded with other 802.11b/g or non-802.11 equipment, such as industrial, scientific, or medical equipment. In cases where the 2.4 GHz ISM band is crowded, the relatively quiet 5 GHz UNII bands are likely to offer better performance.

Co-location

802.11 FHSS vs. 802.11/802.11b DSSS

Since frequency hopping systems are "frequency agile" and make use of 79 discrete channels, they have a co-location advantage over DSSS and OFDM systems which have a maximum co-location of three access points in the 2.4 GHz ISM band. Figure 6.19 shows a co-location and data rate comparison. DSSS and OFDM systems make up the difference with data rates what they lack in frequency agility.

FIGURE 6.19 Co-location vs. Data Rate Comparison

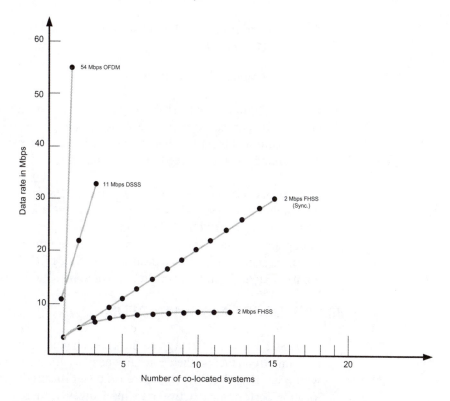

When calculating the hardware costs of an FHSS system to get the same throughput as a DSSS system, the advantage of FHSS quickly disappears. Because DSSS can have three co-located access points, the maximum throughput for this configuration would be:

3 access points x 11 Mbps = 33 Mbps

At roughly 50 percent of rated bandwidth, the DSSS system throughput would be approximately:

33 Mbps / 2 = 16.5 Mbps

To achieve roughly the same rated system bandwidth using an IEEE 802.11 compliant FHSS system would require:

16 access points x 2 Mbps = 32 Mbps

At roughly 50 percent of rated bandwidth, the FHSS system throughput would be approximately:

32 Mbps / 2 = 16 Mbps

In this configuration an FHSS system would require 13 additional access points to be purchased to get the same throughput as the DSSS system. Also, additional installation services for these units, cables, connectors, and antennas would all need to be purchased.

In summary, although FHSS enjoys a theoretical co-location advantage, the number of access points required to achieve adequate throughput is prohibitive. Nevertheless FHSS might be a viable alternative if throughput was not a major design goal and minimizing the number of users per access point was a design goal. Since FHSS allows more access points in an area without conflict, it would be ideal for such a situation.

802.11b DSSS vs. 802.11g OFDM

Since 802.11b and 802.11g use the same channel numbers and roughly the same frequencies (the center frequencies are the same, but the channel widths are slightly different) there is no significant difference in co-location performance between them. However, there is a significant difference when 802.11b access points are co-located with 802.11g access points. Because the 802.11b stations (this term is generic for both access points and client stations) can't hear OFDM signals, the 802.11g stations must enact special behaviors called *protection mechanisms* to prevent DSSS transmissions from colliding with the OFDM transmissions. These protection mechanisms result in a significant performance decrease in the 802.11g stations (from a typical real throughput of 36Mbps in an 802.11g-only environment down to a typical real throughput of about 12 Mbps in a mixed environment, for example).

A good rule of thumb, assuming maximum throughput is a goal of the system's design, is that 802.11g and 802.11b stations should never be located where they can hear each other. They should be separated onto different channels and physically located as far apart as is possible. Realistically, it may be impossible to completely separate 802.11b and 802.11g stations. In this case, an alternative might be to configure a "pure-G" BSS, in which the AP rejects associations from any 802.11b stations.

802.11a OFDM vs. 802.11g OFDM

In terms of throughput, 802.11a wins this comparison easily, since 802.11a's channels are non-overlapping. Given eight channels in the low and middle bands, an 802.11a system could have eight co-located systems with no interference, theoretically achieving a maximum throughput of 54 Mbps * 8 = 432 Mbps. 802.11g, with only three non-overlapping channels, would top out at 162 Mbps. On the other hand, 802.11g systems, which use the lower 2.4 GHz frequencies, usually have longer range than 802.11a systems at the same data rate, since higher frequencies are more susceptible to attenuation.

Equipment compatibility and availability

802.11b, 802.11g, and 802.11a devices are readily available today. In addition, the Wi-Fi Alliance certifies this equipment for interoperability. While such certification doesn't guarantee complete interoperability, it does provide some measure of confidence that, for example, vendor X's PCMCIA card will be able to talk to vendor Y's access point. By comparison, 802.11 FHSS equipment is difficult to find and no interoperability certification exists for it.

Data rate & throughput

802.11 frequency hopping systems are slower than the 802.11b DSSS systems because their data rate tops out at 2 Mbps. Currently the highest 802.11 system throughput is achieved with OFDM technologies: 802.11g and 802.11a. When considering co-located systems, 802.11a has the highest system throughput as discussed previously. In addition, 802.11a is not subject to the performance hit that 802.11g takes when an 802.11b station is in the area. Although 802.11a wins the throughput comparison on paper, 802.11g's convenience and backwards-compatibility, combined with data rates equivalent to 802.11a on a single channel, make it the most common choice.

Range

All other things being equal, the range of an 802.11 system decreases as the data rate increases. This is because higher data rates use more sophisticated encoding techniques that are more susceptible to corruption. As the signal propagates further from the transmitter, it attenuates, making it more likely to be corrupted. Higher data rate signals become corrupted sooner than lower data rate signals.

However in 802.11, not all things are equal. Specifically FHSS, DSSS, and OFDM use dramatically different encoding and modulation techniques. Therefore, it is possible for a technology like OFDM to offer *both* increased range and throughput compared to a technology like DSSS.

802.11b DSSS and 802.11 FHSS have comparable ranges at 1 and 2 Mbps, while the range of an 802.11b DSSS system might actually be lower than the range of an 802.11 FHSS system at 5.5 and 11 Mbps (but the FHSS system couldn't achieve those data rates at all).

802.11g OFDM has a longer data range than 802.11b DSSS at comparable data rates, e.g., 802.11b at 11 Mbps and 802.11g at 12 Mbps; 802.11b at 5.5 Mbps and 802.11g at 6 Mbps. Research suggests that 802.11g at 36 Mbps has approximately the same range as 802.11b at 11 Mbps. 802.11g at 54 Mbps has less range than 802.11b at 11 Mbps.

802.11a OFDM has approximately half the range of 802.11g OFDM due to the higher frequency used by 802.11a. As frequency increases, attenuation caused by certain objects and open air increases proportionally. This fact is a major limitation of 802.11a—although it offers the same data rates as 802.11g, in practice you have to be much closer to an 802.11a access point in order to actually achieve the higher data rates.

Security

It is sometimes said – but it is a myth – that frequency hopping systems are inherently more secure than direct sequence systems. The first fact that disproves this myth is that FHSS radios are only produced by a small number of manufacturers. Of this list of manufacturers, most adhere to publicly-available standards such as 802.11 in order to sell their products effectively. Second, each of these manufacturers uses a standard set of hop sequences which generally comply with a predetermined list produced by the standards body (IEEE). These two items together make breaking the code of hop sequences relatively simple.

Other reasons that make finding the hop sequence quite simple is that the channel number is broadcast in the clear with each beacon. Also, the MAC address of the transmitting access point can be seen with each beacon (which indicates the manufacturer of the radio). Some manufacturers allow the administrator the flexibility of defining custom hopping patterns. However, even this custom capability is no level of security, since fairly unsophisticated devices such as spectrum analyzers and a standard laptop computer can be used to track the hopping pattern of an FHSS radio in a matter of seconds.

Key Terms

Before taking the exam, you should be familiar with the following terms:

channel

chipping code

co-location

direct sequence

dwell time

frequency hopping

hop time

interoperability

narrowband

noise floor

processing gain

throughput

Review Questions

1. Explain the advantages that spread spectrum has over narrow band RF transmissions as they apply to wireless data systems.

2. Explain why, in a DSSS wireless LAN system, even though channels 1, 6, and 11 are considered by IEEE 802.11b as "non-overlapping" channels, there could be significant interference when these channels are used within the same physical space at high power using high-gain antennas. How can this problem be overcome?

3. Explain which modulation technologies are used in each of the following standards. Which are compatible, and which are not? Why?

    A. 802.11

    B. 802.11b

    C. 802.11a

    D. 802.11g

4. Why has the wireless LAN marketplace moved decisively toward DSSS and OFDM technology after many years of FHSS being a more popular, if not the most popular, technology? What advantages do DSSS and OFDM technologies have over FHSS systems?

5. What happens when 802.11b devices are co-located with 802.11g devices? How does it affect the network?

Wireless LAN Infrastructure Devices

CWNA Exam Objectives Covered:

❖ Identify the purpose of the following infrastructure devices and explain how to install, configure, secure, and manage them:

- Access Points
- Wireless LAN Bridges
- Wireless Workgroup Bridges
- Wireless LAN Switches
- PoE Injectors and PoE-enabled Switches
- Wireless Residential Gateways
- Enterprise Wireless Gateways
- Enterprise Encryption Gateways
- Wireless LAN Routers
- WLAN Mesh Routers

❖ Identify the purpose of the following wireless LAN client devices and explain how to install, configure, and manage them:

- PCMCIA, Compact Flash, and Secure Digital Cards
- PCI and Mini-PCI Cards
- USB Devices
- PCMCIA-to-PCI Adapters
- Serial and Ethernet Converters

❖ Describe, explain, and illustrate the appropriate applications for the following client-related wireless security solutions

- Role-based Access Control

In This Chapter

Access Points

Bridges

Workgroup Bridges

Wireless Routers

Client Devices

Wireless Residential Gateways

Enterprise Wireless Gateways

Enterprise Encryption Gateways

Wireless LAN Switches

Wireless LAN Switches with Phased Array Antennas

Wireless LAN Mesh Routers

Power-over-Ethernet Devices

This chapter of the book may be the chapter for which it is most necessary for you, the CWNA candidate, to have access to at least some wireless LAN hardware. You probably already have at least some wireless equipment either in your home or office, but if not you can purchase a basic home or SOHO wireless network for less than $400, including an access point and wireless client cards. Although with this type of equipment you won't get hands-on experience with every piece of hardware covered in this chapter, you will have a good idea of how the devices communicate and behave using RF technology.

This chapter covers the different categories of wireless network infrastructure equipment and some of the variations within each category. From reading this chapter alone you should be noticeably more versed in the actual implementation of wireless LANs, simply by being aware of all the different kinds of wireless LAN equipment that you have at your disposal when you begin to create or add to a wireless network. These hardware items are the physical building blocks for any wireless LAN.

In general we will cover each type of hardware in this section in a similar manner, according to the following topics:

- Definition and role of the hardware on the network
- Common options that might be included with the hardware
- How to install and configure the hardware

The goal of this section of the book is to make you aware of all the types of infrastructure and client hardware that are available for the many varying wireless LAN architectures that you will encounter as a wireless LAN administrator.

Here are some guidelines to help you maximize your budget if you are purchasing equipment to help you study for the CWNA exam:

Multi-mode a/b/g client cards are not much more expensive than b/g or b-only cards. Buying a multi-mode card will provide maximum flexibility for study. These cards can often be configured to use b, g, or a only if you want to simulate a single-mode card. The card you decide on should be supported by WLAN protocol analyzers within your budget. If you decide to go further with your studies or certification, both security and protocol analysis areas of expertise necessitate protocol analyzer software. There are good analyzers available for those with limited budgets.

A multi-mode access point can help to illustrate the differences in throughput and coverage between 802.11a, b, and g. These APs demand somewhat of a price premium, but several inexpensive models can be found. At the time of this printing, we found bargain models as cheap as $140, while a more typical price was in the $200–$300 range.

A single AP with clients is limited in its ability to illustrate the complex interactions that can occur between 802.11 devices. If your budget permits, you should buy two APs (preferably of the same type) to allow you to explore these interactions. For example: what happens to throughput when two APs are on the same channel? What happens when a device roams between two APs? What happens to throughput when two APs are on nearby channels?

If possible, buy APs that are capable of acting in both bridge mode and access point mode (these modes are described fully in this chapter). Some consumer-grade APs are not capable of acting in bridge mode but there are a few out there that can. Buying an AP that can perform in both of these modes will allow you to explore both types of devices (bridges and APs) while only buying one piece of equipment. Some APs are actually capable of acting in bridge mode and AP mode simultaneously, although this is even more rare (in consumer-grade APs, at least).

Access Points

Second only to the basic wireless PC card, the access point, or "AP," is probably the most common wireless LAN device you will encounter as a wireless LAN administrator. As its name suggests, the access point provides wireless clients with a wireless point of access into a network. Stations are grouped according to their access point, and each group, or basic service set (BSS), has one access point. Although an access point usually links wireless clients to a wired LAN, this doesn't have to be the case. Figure 7.1 shows an example of an access point, while Figure 7.2 illustrates where an access point is used on a wireless LAN.

FIGURE 7.1   A sample access point (Proxim AP-700)

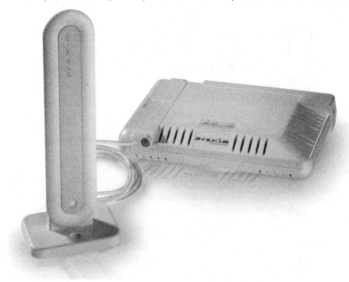

FIGURE 7.2   An access point connected to a wired network

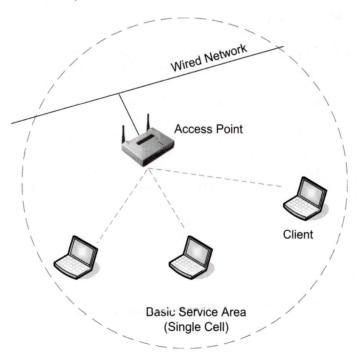

Access Point Modes

Access points communicate with their wireless clients, with devices on the wired network, and with other access points. There are three modes in which an access point typically can be configured:

- Root Mode
- Repeater Mode
- Bridge Mode

The IEEE has defined none of these modes, although the standard operation of an AP could be said to match "Root Mode." The other two modes are extensions of an AP's functionality that vendors have added. These extensions are undeniably useful, but, like any proprietary technology, there's no guarantee that two different vendors' equipment will work together when using the proprietary modes. Also, when two different vendors say "repeater mode" or "bridge mode," there is no guarantee that they are referring to exactly the same type of functionality.

Root Mode

Root Mode is used when the access point is connected to a distribution system through its wired (usually Ethernet) interface, or when the AP is not connected to any wired interface and is just providing access between the wireless clients attached to that AP. Most access points that support modes *other* than root mode come configured in root mode by default. When in root mode, access points that are connected to the same wired network can talk to each other over the wired segment, allowing stations on one access point to talk to stations on another access point, as shown in Figure 7.3. One such application of APs communicating with each other is when coordinating client roaming, which is when a station moves from one access point to another.

FIGURE 7.3   Two access points in root mode

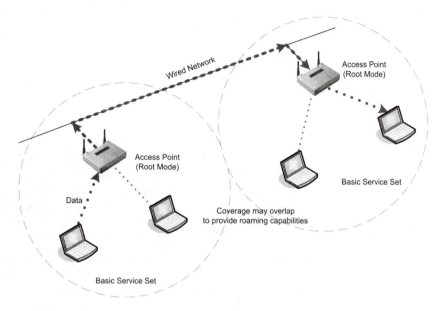

Bridge Mode

Bridge mode creates a wireless distribution link between two (point-to-point) or more (point-to-multipoint) access points. "Bridge mode" access points "associate" only with each other and typically do not allow associations from wireless stations, although *some* vendors give the end-user both feature sets simultaneously. The point of bridge mode connectivity is to offer a wireless link between two wired LAN segments. Essentially, access points that are configured for bridge mode are wireless bridges performing identical functions through additional firmware/software features. Bridge mode is commonly used with semi-directional or highly-directional antennas to make mid- and long-range connections.

FIGURE 7.4   Access points in bridge mode, connecting two wired LAN segments

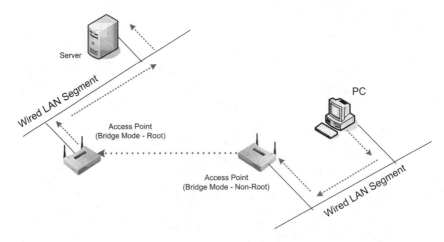

Consider a scenario in which you want to provide network access to clients in a remote building, but wired connectivity to the building is not possible. If bridge mode didn't exist, one solution would be to put a strong antenna on an AP and aim the antenna at the building. With appropriate output power and antenna gain, the access point's signal could probably reach the building just fine, but the much weaker output of the clients' PCMCIA cards would have a difficult time getting a signal back to the AP. In addition, you could not optimize the location of the antenna to provide maximum coverage to the building. For example, if a sheet metal fence were between the AP and the remote building, creating a "shadow" in the coverage, there would be nothing you could do about it.

On the other hand, with bridge mode, you can beam a point-to-point link between the APs. Because both APs can take an external antenna (most enterprise APs have removable antennas), you would have the option of adding amplifiers and higher-gain antennas to maximize the signal between the APs. Because the APs are stationary, you can optimize their placement for best signal reception. You can provide wired network access within the remote building or add a second AP with a low-gain omni-directional antenna (on a different channel from the bridge) to provide wireless access to the clients within the building. Instead of the clients having to associate to a distant AP, they can associate to a nearby AP and then have their signal forwarded over the much-stronger bridge link.

It is quite common to use bridge mode to beam wireless access to a remote location. Since a "bridge mode" AP only associates with other bridges, this configuration usually requires two access points at the remote site: one to receive the bridge link and a second to provide wireless access to clients within the remote site building. Some vendors, such as Buffalo, Cisco, and D-Link, make access points that are capable of acting in both bridge mode and root AP mode simultaneously, allowing a single AP to receive the bridge link and provide access to clients at the same time. When used in this capacity, bandwidth of the bridge link and the local wireless clients is shared.

Repeater Mode

In repeater mode, access points provide intermediate connectivity between a root AP and clients that are out of range of the root AP. As shown in Figure 7.5, one access point serves as the "root" access point and the other serves as a "wireless repeater." The "wireless repeater" acts as an access point to its associated clients while simultaneously acting as a client to the "root" access point. Both the "repeater" and the "root" access points can have other clients.

FIGURE 7.5   An access point in repeater mode

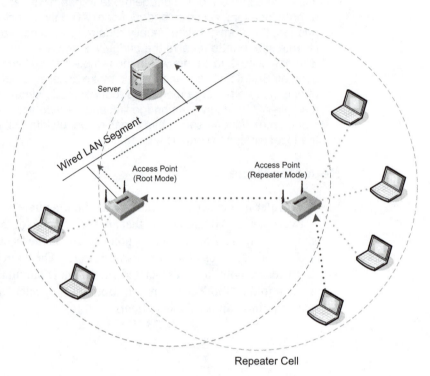

Unlike "bridge mode," in which the name is fairly descriptive of the AP's function, "repeater mode" is not descriptively named. In reality, a "repeater mode" AP is simply doing a different form of bridging and is not acting in any way like an Ethernet repeater. In a pure "bridge mode," the APs have a point-to-point or point-to-multipoint link with no associated client devices. In "repeater mode," the AP acts as a client to the "root mode" AP, which can have still other clients of its own. Other than that, these two methods of forwarding packets are equivalent. Some vendors may provide both repeater mode and bridge mode functionality in an AP.

Using an access point in repeater mode is not suggested unless absolutely necessary because Basic Service Areas around each access point in this scenario must overlap by a minimum of 50 percent. This configuration drastically reduces the range at which clients can connect to the repeater access point. Additionally, the repeater access point is communicating with the clients as well as the upstream access point on the same channel, reducing system throughput dramatically. Users attached to the repeater access point will likely experience low throughput and high latencies in this scenario. Another limitation of repeater mode is that the "repeating" AP must use an omnidirectional antenna in order to provide coverage to clients all around it. This same antenna must provide the uplink capability to the "root mode" access point. This means that the "repeater mode" AP must be even closer to the "root mode" AP than it would have to be if it were using a directional antenna, further reducing the coverage of the AP.

Common Options

Understanding what features to expect on a SOHO, SMB (small-to-medium business), and enterprise-grade access points is an important part of being a wireless network administrator. Below are some common features to look for in SOHO, SMB, and enterprise categories. This listing is by no means comprehensive because manufacturers release new features frequently at each level. This list is meant to provide an idea of where to start looking for an appropriate access point. Some features we will discuss in the following paragraphs are:

- Fixed or Detachable Antennas
- Filtering
- Removable Radio Cards
- Variable Output Power
- Varied Types of Wired Connectivity
- Security Features
- Management Features
- IEEE Standards Support
- Connectivity Modes
- Mounting Options

Fixed or Detachable Antennas

Depending on your organization's or client's needs you will need to choose between having an access point with fixed (meaning non-removable) antennas or detachable antennas. An access point with detachable antennas gives you the ability to attach a different set of antennas to the access point, using whatever length of cable you require. For example, if you needed to mount the access point inside and give outdoor users access to the network, you could attach a cable and an outdoor antenna directly to the access point and mount only the antenna outside. Remember however, that if the antenna and access point have not been certified *together* as an FCC system, connecting them together will violate FCC Part 15 rules.

Access points may be shipped with or without diversity antennas. Wireless LAN antenna diversity is the use of multiple antennas with multiple inputs on a single receiver in order to sample signals arriving through each antenna. The point of sampling two antennas is to pick the input signal of whichever antenna has the best reception. The two antennas might have different signal reception because of a phenomenon called multipath, which will be discussed in detail in Chapter 11.

Filtering

MAC or protocol filtering functionality may be included on an access point. Filtering is typically used to screen out intruders on your wireless LAN. As a basic security provision, an access point can be configured to filter out devices that are not listed in the access point's MAC filter list, which the administrator controls.

Protocol filtering allows the administrator to control which protocols should be used across a wireless link. For example, if an administrator only wishes to provide HTTP access across the wireless link so that users can browse the web and check their web-based e-mail, then setting an HTTP protocol filter would prevent all other types of protocol access to that segment of the network.

Removable Radio Cards

Some access points allow the user to add and remove radios to and from built-in PCMCIA slots on the access point. Some access points may have two PCMCIA slots for more advanced functionality. Having two radio slots in an access point allows one radio card to act as an access point while the other radio card is acting as a wireless bridge (in most cases a wireless backbone). Another somewhat dissimilar use is to use each radio card as an independent access point. Having each card act as an independent access point allows an administrator to accommodate twice as many users in the same physical space without the purchase of a second access point, further reducing costs. When the access point is configured in this manner, each radio card should be configured on a non-overlapping channel (such as 1 and 11) or band (such as ISM and UNII).

Variable Output Power

Variable output power allows the administrator to control the power (in milliwatts) that the access point uses to transmit data. Increasing and decreasing the AP's power allows the administrator to control the size of the coverage area of the AP. As the power output is increased on the access point, the coverage area increases and clients are able to move further away from the access point without losing connectivity. At the same time, the AP is more likely to interfere with nearby APs on the same channel, and in extreme cases even APs on different channels. Adjusting cell size through power output also aids in security by preventing intruders from connecting to the network from outside the building's walls.

In older hardware, many radios did not support variable output power, so whatever device that was using them was limited in its functionality. Today, most enterprise-class access points and client devices provide variable output power support while most SOHO-class equipment provides only fixed output power support. Because properly adjusting the coverage area is so important to wireless network performance, variable power output should be given high priority when choosing an AP. Some vendors advertise the fact that their equipment's power output is adjustable in minute increments for more accurate configuration of the network.

Varied Types of Wired Connectivity

Connectivity options for an access point can include a link for 10 Mbps Ethernet, 10/100 Ethernet, Token Ring, or others. Because an access point is typically the device through which clients communicate with the wired network backbone, you must understand how to properly connect the access point into the wired network. Proper network design and connectivity will help prevent the access point from being a bottleneck and will result in far fewer problems due to malfunctioning equipment.

Consider a situation where you might be using an off-the-shelf access point in an enterprise wireless LAN. In this case, the access point is located 150 meters from the nearest wiring closet. Running a category 5 (Cat5) Ethernet cable to the access point will not provide data connectivity. This scenario is a problem because Ethernet over Cat5 cable is only specified to 100 meters. In this case, purchasing an access point that has a 100Base-FX connector and running fiber from the wiring closet to the access point mounting location ahead of time will allow this configuration to function properly. Practically speaking, this solution will be more expensive than Cat5 to implement, due to wiring costs and the fact that the vast majority of APs come configured with only 10/100 Ethernet LAN interfaces. Fortunately, Ethernet-to-fiber converters are available.

Power over Ethernet Support

Power over Ethernet (PoE) is a means of providing electrical power to the access point through the Ethernet cable. An AP that is powered via PoE doesn't need to be plugged into a standard AC outlet. The major advantage of PoE is the ability to install APs in areas where AC power is not available, such as in dropped ceilings. Enterprise access points typically support PoE while SOHO and residential access points typically do not. PoE is discussed later in this chapter.

Security Features

Security has been one of the fastest-developing areas of 802.11. All access points will support WEP, but, due to its well-documented weaknesses, you should consider WEP only as a last resort, especially if your network is anything more than a home installation.

WPA (Wi-Fi Protected Access) is currently supported by nearly all access points, including those aimed at the consumer market. WPA includes two modes: PSK (pre-shared key) and RADIUS. In PSK mode, a shared password is configured into the access point and all of the clients. Clients that are not configured with the correct password cannot authenticate with the AP and cannot decrypt the packets on the BSS. In RADIUS mode, the clients authenticate with a RADIUS server. Although RADIUS mode is more secure than PSK mode, SOHO installations probably will not have a RADIUS server, so WPA-PSK may provide the best balance between security and convenience. Enterprise and SMB installations should use RADIUS mode if at all possible.

WPA was based on a pre-release version of the 802.11i standard. When 802.11i was ratified, the Wi-Fi alliance released the WPA2 certification, which certifies that equipment is compliant with a subset of the final 802.11i standard. Like WPA, WPA2 has both PSK and RADIUS modes; however, whereas WPA only supported the RC4 encryption that was used in WEP, WPA2 also supports the AES encryption required by 802.11i. At the time of this printing, 802.11i has only recently been ratified; therefore, almost no equipment currently supports 802.11i or has received WPA2 certification. In the future, WPA2/802.11i will probably become the most common means of securing 802.11 networks. WPA, WPA2, and 802.11i are covered in more detail in Chapter 12.

Another security feature that some enterprise-level access points support is the ability for the AP to act as a wireless intrusion detection sensor. The AP runs integrated code that communicates with a management console to report intrusion attempts and unauthorized stations. If you buy an AP that includes this functionality make sure that the AP can act as a sensor and an AP *at the same time*. Some APs can only act *either* as an AP *or* as a sensor, requiring you to manually configure the unit as one or the other. Others may be configured to be automatically switched between sensor and AP, but require kicking the users off the AP to change to sensor mode.

Management Features

The methods used to configure and manage access points will vary with each manufacturer. The choices include console (serial), telnet, SSH, SNMP, custom software application, or a built-in web server for browser access via HTTP or HTTPS. Custom applications typically work at the MAC layer for discovery and configuration. Access points that support SNMP may support a wide variety of versions such as v1, v2c, and v3, depending on the vendor. SSH access is typically found only on enterprise-grade access points, and serial and telnet access is beginning to show up in some SOHO-grade units. Most SOHO-grade units are configured via an integrated web server supporting only HTTP.

Managing access points becomes more complicated as the number of access points grows. The ability to manage and configure many access points simultaneously from a central location is critical to an enterprise installation (SOHO and residential installations can probably get away with managing APs individually). Most enterprise vendors provide some sort of software utility for managing and configuring multiple access points.

Some access points come pre-configured with a static IP address from the manufacturer, and others are pre-configured for DHCP. Still others try first to obtain an IP via DHCP, and then when no response is heard from a DHCP server, they invoke a pre-configured static IP address. Private IP subnets such as 10.x.x.x, 172.16.x.x, and 192.168.x.x are almost always used in these cases.

If the administrator needs to reset the device to factory defaults, there will usually be a hardware reset button on the outside of the unit for this purpose. Hard reset procedures differ by access point and you should practice this procedure in the lab before deploying the APs to the field. This recommendation might sound like a waste of time, but hanging from the top of a tower is not the place to find out that the "reset" button reboots the AP and the "reboot" button resets the AP to defaults (a real example). Also, make sure to document the AP's default configuration, especially its manufacturer's IP addressing rules. If you reset the AP and then don't know its IP address, serial configuration may be your only option (assuming the AP even has a serial port). If you don't know an AP's IP address, many vendors make auto discovery applications that can find the AP on the subnet.

IEEE Standards Support

When purchasing an access point, you should consider which 802.11 standards the AP supports. Most of the 802.11 standards are described in Chapter 8 but we will list some specific considerations here. One of the most basic choices to make is whether the AP will support 802.11b, 802.11b/g, or 802.11a/b/g. 802.11b access points are quickly being phased out and can be bought very cheaply, but should be avoided unless cost is a large factor and only the bare minimum of functionality is necessary. Not only do they offer the lowest throughput, but they often don't support newer authentication and security mechanisms, such as 802.11i/WPA2 or WPA. Chapter 6 contains a detailed comparison of 802.11b (DSSS), 802.11g (OFDM), and 802.11a (OFDM) to help you decide which of these standards is best for your needs.

An access point that supports 802.11i will have stronger authentication and encryption capabilities available than an access point that does not. If an 802.11i access point is not available, WPA support is the next best thing.

If multimedia streaming or VoIP are intended uses of your network, an access point that supports 802.11e may improve performance. 802.11e describes a set of QoS extensions to 802.11. Although the 802.11e standard has not been finalized at the time of this printing, the Wi-Fi alliance has released the WMM certification which is based on a subset of the pre-release 802.11e standard. WMM-compliant access points are currently available (see the Wi-Fi alliance website, http://www.wi-fi-org, where you can search its database for certified equipment).

If you are buying an AP for use in Europe, make sure that it is compliant with 802.11h; in Japan, make sure that the AP is compliant with 802.11j. These standards address specific requirements for the regulatory domains of those countries.

Connectivity Modes

Consider whether you need an AP that supports root mode only, root and bridge mode, or repeater mode (which is equivalent to simultaneous root/bridge mode). Most consumer grade APs support root mode only, although some can act in bridge mode as well. Enterprise-grade APs commonly can act in either bridge or root mode. Some enterprise-grade access points use the term "wireless distribution system (WDS)," which is another way of saying repeater mode or bridge mode.

Mounting Options

The most attractive and secure options for mounting APs are usually the vendor's mounting kits. Nearly all enterprise AP vendors sell custom mounting kits for their wireless infrastructure devices, such as APs, wireless bridges, and antennas. These devices are often designed for mounting on common surface types, such as walls, cubicles, drop ceilings, and masts (poles). You should make sure that the mounting kit you buy will work in the location where you plan to use the infrastructure equipment. Figures 7.6a–7.6h below illustrate a step-by-step illustration of using the manufacturer's components to mount an access point to a suspended ceiling.

FIGURE 7.6a   Mounting an Access Point to a Suspended Ceiling – Components

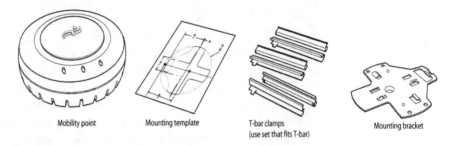

Mobility point   Mounting template   T-bar clamps
(use set that fits T-bar)   Mounting bracket

Copyright Trapeze Networks® 2004

FIGURE 7.6b   Mounting an Access Point to a Suspended Ceiling – Installing the T-bar clamp that fits the T-bar

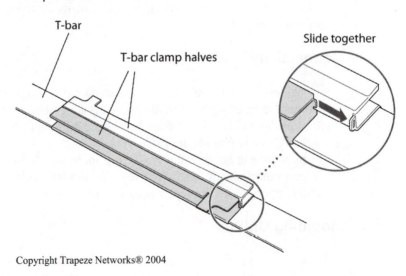

T-bar

T-bar clamp halves

Slide together

Copyright Trapeze Networks® 2004

FIGURE 7.6c   Mounting an Access Point to a Suspended Ceiling – Removing the Mounting Bracket

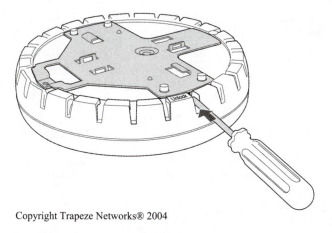

Copyright Trapeze Networks® 2004

FIGURE 7.6d   Mounting an Access Point to a Suspended Ceiling – Removing the Mounting Bracket

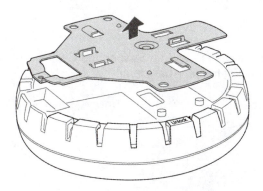

Copyright Trapeze Networks® 2004

FIGURE 7.6e Mounting an Access Point to a Suspended Ceiling – Attaching the Mounting Bracket to the T-bar clamp

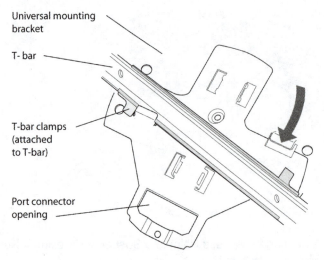

Universal mounting bracket

T- bar

T-bar clamps (attached to T-bar)

Port connector opening

(Viewed from above ceiling tiles, looking down.)

Copyright Trapeze Networks® 2004

FIGURE 7.6f Mounting an Access Point to a Suspended Ceiling – Attaching the Mounting Bracket to the T-bar clamp

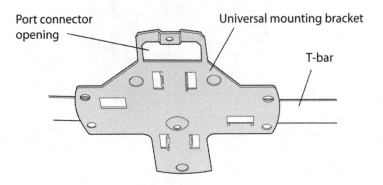

Port connector opening

Universal mounting bracket

T-bar

Copyright Trapeze Networks® 2004

FIGURE 7.6g   Mounting an Access Point to a Suspended Ceiling – Plugging the Cat5 cable into the Access Point through the port connector opening

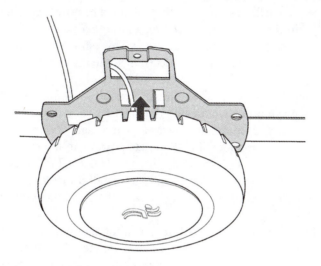

Copyright Trapeze Networks® 2004

FIGURE 7.6h   Mounting an Access Point to a Suspended Ceiling – Attaching the access point to the Mounting Bracket

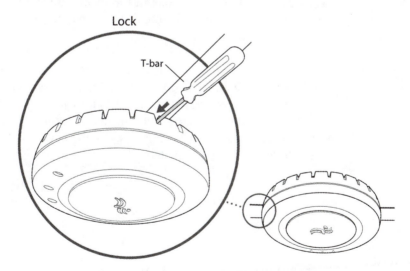

Copyright Trapeze Networks® 2004

If you decide not to use your vendor's mounting kit or a mounting kit is not available, industrial-strength zip ties might be a viable option. Zip ties can affix the AP directly to a beam or post. Alternatively, the AP can be zip-tied to a 2x4, a metal plate, or other mounting surface that can be secured to a convenient location. This isn't the best looking option but aesthetics may not be a concern in some installations.

Consider the location of the AP carefully. Before installation, a site survey should have located the ideal position of the AP and its antenna. If necessary, ensure that power and wired data connectivity is available at the installation location. Separate power cabling may not be necessary if you are using PoE to power the AP. If the AP is not plenum-rated, it may be a violation of building codes to install it inside the wall or ceiling, including a dropped ceiling. Check the building codes for your locality.

If possible, mount the AP in a location that will not attract the attention of network attackers and thieves. Secure the AP so that it can't be stolen or replaced with a device that compromises network security (one method of doing this is to use a lockable ceiling enclosure, such as those pictured in Figure 7.7). Ensure that the AP's status lights are visible from a convenient location. You don't want to be digging around in the dropped ceiling or climbing up a ladder just to make sure that the AP is powered up. You might decide to ignore this advice if aesthetics dictate that the APs are hidden from view.

If possible allow yourself convenient access to the AP's power and reset buttons in case you have to reboot the device. You must balance this concern with the concern that an attacker (or just a prankster) will use that same convenient access to reboot the device. PoE devices can make this choice easier, since you can power-cycle the device simply by unplugging the Ethernet cable at the switch.

FIGURE 7.7a   Lockable Ceiling Enclosure

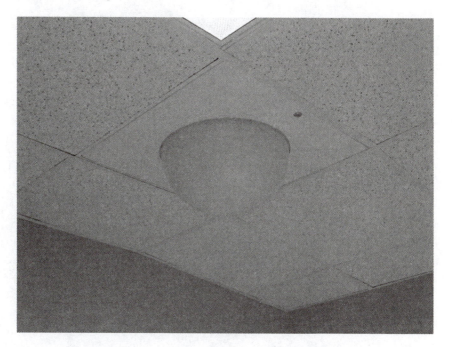

FIGURE 7.7b   Lockable Ceiling Enclosure

Special considerations must be taken when mounting an access point
outdoors. Rain, snow, temperature changes, and other environmental
effects may damage or destroy access points, and might additionally
create a health hazard, such as a risk of electric shock. Fortunately, the
National Electrical Manufacturers Association (NEMA) has established a
range of standards for electrical equipment enclosures, and many vendors
make NEMA-compliant enclosures for 802.11 access points. NEMA
standards for electrical enclosures are defined in NEMA Standards
Publication 250, which is available from NEMA's home page at
http://www.nema.org.

FIGURE 7.8   Mounting Access Points in NEMA Enclosures

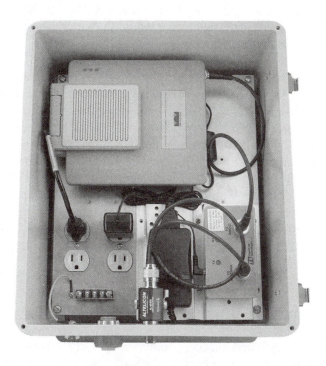

Figure 7.8 shows a NEMA-standard enclosure. The enclosure has standard 120-volt AC outlets on the inside, which provide power to any devices mounted in the enclosure (in this case, a Cisco 1200 access point (upper left), an RF amplifier (lower-right), and a lighting arrestor (lower center, front). This enclosure brings AC power in through the hole in the bottom plate (to the left of the lighting arrestor). The wires screw into the power receptacles in the lower-left (below the AC power outlets).

The enclosure also has a standard N-type RF connector that brings the RF signal from the internal device to an external antenna. This connector can be seen on the bottom panel in the middle of the enclosure with coaxial cable running to it from the amplifier. This connector is necessary because the metal walls of the enclosure block RF signals, so the antenna must be mounted on the outside. When mounting an access point in a NEMA enclosure, it is important to position the antenna so the enclosure doesn't block the signal from reaching the users. For example, if the antenna were mounted on a mast above the users, it might be better to mount the enclosure above the antenna so users would always have a clear line of sight to the antenna. On the other hand, if the antenna was a 180-degree patch antenna, it wouldn't matter where the enclosure was as long as it wasn't directly in front of the antenna.

There are many different types of NEMA enclosure, and each type is rated for different environmental conditions. For example, NEMA type 4 enclosures are intended for indoor or outdoor use and primarily to provide a degree of protection against windblown dust and rain, splashing water, and so forth. They are also intended to be undamaged by the formation of ice on the enclosure. But they are not intended to protect against conditions such as internal condensation or internal icing. On the other hand, NEMA type 13 enclosures are intended for indoor use only and primarily to protect against lint, dust, sprayed water, oil, and non-corrosive coolant. Some vendors may add features to NEMA enclosures, such as fan-based cooling or solar power. If possible, you should verify which environmental conditions an enclosure is designed to protect against before purchase to make sure that it meets your needs.

Summary

Features found in access points vary widely; however, one thing is constant: the more features the access point has, the more the access point will cost. SOHO access points will usually have WEP, WPA-PSK, MAC filters, and even a built-in web server. If features such as viewing the association table, WPA/WPA2, VPN support, routing functionality, fast roaming support, and RADIUS support are required, expect to pay several times as much for an enterprise-level access point.

Even features that are standard on Wi-Fi compliant access points sometimes vary in their implementation. For example, two different brands of a SOHO access point may offer MAC filters, but only one of them might offer MAC filtering where you can explicitly permit *and* explicitly deny stations, rather than only one or the other.

As a wireless LAN administrator, you should know your environment, then look for products that fit your deployment and security needs, and then compare features among three or four vendors that make products for that particular market segment. This evaluation process will undoubtedly take a substantial amount of time, but time spent learning about the different products on the market is useful. The best possible resource for learning about each of the competing brands in a particular market is each manufacturer's web site. When choosing an access point, be sure to take into account manufacturer support, in addition to features and price.

Wireless Bridges

Some confusion in the marketplace has resulted from vendors' choice to sell both "access points" and "wireless bridges." As discussed above, "wireless bridging" is merely a special application of an access point's normal functionality. Therefore, it should come as no surprise that most "wireless bridges" can also be configured to act as access points.

For example, a certain vendor makes an "access point" that can optionally be configured to act in bridge mode and a "wireless bridge" that can optionally be configured to act in access point mode. What is the difference? Functionally, there might be no difference whatsoever. When considering whether to buy a "bridge" or an "access point," you should focus on the service that the devices provide and how they provide them. Some questions to consider include:

- Does the device allow clients to associate with it? (AP)
- Does it create a dedicated point-to-point connection with one or more peer devices? (bridge)
- Does it do both at the same time? (AP/bridge)
- What standards does the device support?

The main differences between bridges and access points are likely to come from their different intended uses. An AP is intended to allow connections from many clients, so it might include, for example, advanced authentication methods for those clients. A bridge might not make advanced authentication methods available unless it is acting in access point mode. Bridges often come with weatherproof cases since they are intended for outdoor applications more often than access points. An access point might have a more attractive but less rugged case for use indoors, in plain view of customers.

Modes

When you configure a wireless bridge link, one bridge must be a root and all others must be non-root. If two bridges are both configured as a root or no bridge is configured as the root, the bridges won't associate with each other. In a point-to-point link, it doesn't matter which bridge is the root. All bridges in a point-to-multipoint link must have RF line-of-sight to the root, so, in a point-to-multipoint link, the central bridge should be the root.

FIGURE 7.9   Root and Non-Root Modes

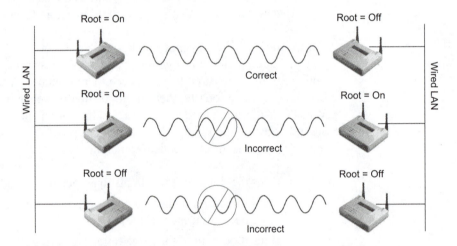

When access points were covered, we defined three modes that an AP could use: root, bridge, and repeater. It's important that you not confuse an AP in "root mode" with the "root bridge" of a root link. An AP that is configured to act in bridge mode may or may not be configured to be the "root bridge" for its bridge link. This double-usage of the term "root" can be a source of confusion. It is also important that you not confuse an 802.11 bridge in "root mode" with the "root bridge" that you might have heard of in the context of the Spanning Tree algorithm. Those two terms are not equivalent.

Aligning Bridges

Whereas access points usually serve many clients close to the AP, bridges create links between peers (whether point-to-point or point-to-multipoint) and may be separated by a long distance (sometimes as much as several miles). Therefore, properly aligning bridge antennas is more critical than with access points. A difference in alignment of just a few millimeters could add up to tens or hundreds of feet at the other end of a long link.

Aligning bridge antennas correctly maximizes signal strength and thus system operating margin. Simply aiming the antennas at each other visually isn't the best way of aligning them, since visual LOS and RF LOS are not always the same. Remember that RF signals may experience reflection, refraction, and diffraction in circumstances where visible light does not. In addition objects may intrude on the Fresnel Zone of a point-to-point link without blocking visual LOS. Finally, the polarization of the antennas affects signal strength, so the antennas' rotation is a factor.

Three main methods of aligning a bridge antenna are:

1. Through a software utility that reads signal strength (or RSSI value) information directly from the bridge's radio.

2. Through LEDs or other indicator on the bridge. For example, Cisco's Aironet 1400 series bridge has LEDs that blink in certain patterns to indicate RSSI. More LEDs blink faster.

3. Through a voltmeter that attaches to a connector on the bridge. In this case, the voltage on the connector indicates the signal strength. Higher voltages are associated with higher RSSI, and the vendor will probably provide a table that maps specific RSSI values to specific voltages.

FIGURE 7.10 Antenna Alignment Using a Voltmeter and/or LEDs

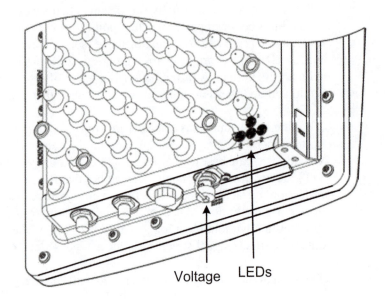

Voltage   LEDs

Common Options

Just as with access points, wireless bridges come in enterprise-grade and consumer-grade models. Consumer-grade models are usually a consumer-grade access point with optional bridging functionality that can be enabled in software. Enterprise-grade bridges are designed first and foremost to act as bridges, but they can usually be configured to act as access points also. If an AP can become a bridge and a bridge can become an AP, then you might wonder what the real difference is between them. The main difference seems to be in the way in which the device is *primarily* intended to be used. Bridges and access points have a great deal of functionality in common.

FIGURE 7.11   A sample enterprise-grade wireless bridge (Cisco 1400)

FIGURE 7.12   A sample consumer-grade wireless bridge (Linksys WET54GS5)

"Wireless game adapters" are another common example of consumer-grade 802.11 bridges, although they are not always called that on the packaging. A common problem is that a game console such as a Playstation® or Xbox® doesn't have the drivers for a USB adapter and doesn't have the physical port for a PCMCIA card or a PCI card. But the game console does have an Ethernet port! How can a user connect this device to the Internet via a wireless network? The answer is a wireless bridge, which will forward packets from the Ethernet port over the wireless network without requiring any driver installation on the game console.

FIGURE 7.13   Game Console Wireless Workgroup Bridge (Linksys WGA54G)

These game adapters should only be considered wireless bridges if they come with two devices that create a peer-to-peer wireless connection between themselves. If the game adapter associates with a root-mode access point, then it would be considered a "wireless workgroup bridge" (WGB), which is discussed in the next section of this chapter.

You should be aware that some wireless game adapters use proprietary protocols in the 2.4 GHz range and not 802.11! These adapters are often advertised as "zero configuration." The two adapters are configured to pair with each other at the factory. When they are powered up, they form a dedicated point-to-point link between themselves and cannot communicate with 802.11-compliant devices at all. An example of this type of device is the Logitech® Play Link™. This type of device may interfere with 802.11 networks in the area, depending on the frequency range that it uses. For example, the Logitech Play Link uses 900 MHz frequencies, so it wouldn't interfere with an 802.11 network. For compatibility, you should choose a game adapter that either uses a different frequency range from your Wi-Fi network, or is Wi-Fi compliant.

Because bridges and access points have so much functionality in common, in many cases these options will be the same as those described in the "access points" section. In those cases we will refer back to the "access points" section.

Alignment and Path Calculation Utilities

Consumer-grade bridges probably won't include any method of optimizing the antennas' alignment. Remember that these devices are often primarily designed as APs, with the "bonus" that they can also act as bridges, if needed. Even in cases where consumer-grade devices are specifically advertised as bridges, they are usually not intended to be used in long-distance links where precise alignment is critical. Enterprise bridges, on the other hand, should include a precise method of optimizing alignment. This method could be through a software utility or through some hardware feature such as voltage ports, whereby a multimeter can be used to optimize alignment.

The process of aligning bridges typically depends on the nature of the link. If it's a short point-to-point link the procedure is relatively simple. You must first align the bridges visually and then use the method provided by the manufacturer (whether through software, through multimeter connectivity, or other) combined with a simple trial-and-error method to optimize the alignment. If moving the antenna one way increases the strength of the link, then move it a little further in that direction and see if it gets stronger or weaker. Once the aim of the antennas is optimized, you should rotate one antenna around the axis of the link to find the polarization that maximizes signal strength. The strongest signal is likely to be when the antennas are rotated to exactly the same orientation, but not always.

With long distance point-to-point links or point-to-multipoint links, the process becomes exponentially more complex. Tools such as range calculation utility software, a GPS device, and GPS-enabled topographical maps and software will be needed. *Many* factors must be taken into account when performing point-to-multipoint or long distance point-to-point links, such as terrain and obstacle height at any point between two bridge devices, beamwidth and gain of antennas to which the bridges are connected, output power of the bridges, and antenna height at each end of the link.

FIGURE 7.14   Topographical Software and GPS Receiver

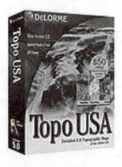

It is highly recommended that professional wireless bridge installers attend a course specifically designed for this line of work. Many important details can be learned in such a course that are commonly missed in self-study.

Long-distance bridge links require more extensive calculation than short-distance and omnidirectional links. Calculating fade margin and the minimum height of the antennas to clear earth bulge is especially important. Some vendors give away path calculation utilities, such as the one in Figure 7.15 that simplify these calculations. Some vendors have free online calculation utilities such as one found at http://www.connect802.com/fspl.php.

FIGURE 7.15   Path Calculation Utility (Copyright Cisco Systems® 2004)

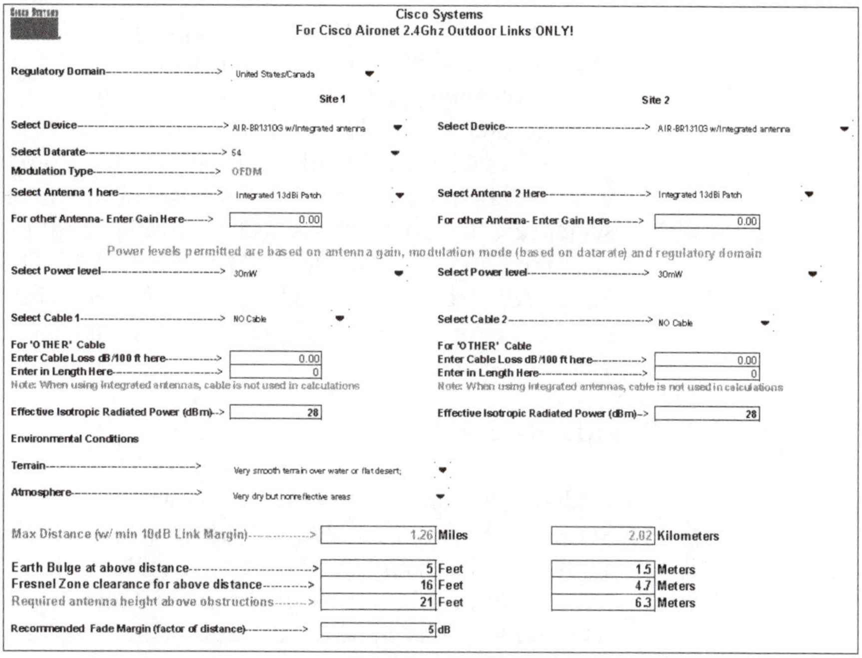

Fixed vs. Detachable Antennas

Enterprise-grade bridges will usually have detachable antennas, while consumer-grade bridges will likely have fixed antennas as a cost-saving measure. The requirements of the link should dictate whether this is a consideration in your purchase. If the bridge is intended for a long-distance point-to-point link, then detachable antennas are required, but if you are connecting a game console to the Internet, fixed antennas are likely acceptable.

Security Features

In some ways, bridges are even more susceptible to attacks than access points. Bridges may be configured to have client associations or not, and may even allow clients to associate by default. This is access point functionality and can lead to insecurity of the wireless network. When acting *purely* as bridges, bridges disallow client associations, which rules out an entire class of attacks, but bridge links are often so long that it's impossible to secure the entire path along the link. Although the bridges themselves might be physically secure, depending on the path that the link takes, an attacker might be able to position himself in the RF line-of-sight (in the Fresnel Zone) in order to capture traffic from the link. Encryption is just as important with bridge links as it is with access points, but seldom are the same security features available. While a wireless bridge acting in access point mode might provide EAP-TTLS, PEAP-MSCHAPv2, and EAP-FAST, the same bridge in bridge mode might only provide LEAP. This is a serious security weakness presently inherent to wireless bridges.

Standards Support

Bridges are similar to access points in which standards they support. Some standards such as 802.11f, which deals with client roaming, do not apply to bridges and so will not be available on them. But a bridge that can be configured to act as an access point may support exactly the same set of standards as a dedicated access point. The bottom line is that you should confirm which standards the bridge supports, and if the bridge can be configured to act as an access point, you should confirm standards support for both modes separately. Just because a bridge says it supports 802.11i, for example, doesn't mean that it supports 802.11i in both bridge and access point mode.

We have recently seen support for Wi-Fi Multimedia (WMM) certification in bridges, as with access points. This certification will increase the performance of multimedia applications, such as streaming video and VoIP, when used with WMM-aware applications. WMM is covered more fully in Chapter 8.

Management Utilities

Consumer-grade bridges will usually be managed via an HTTP web interface. Enterprise-grade bridges will also have an HTTP web interface, but will likely also support SNMP, HTTPS, custom management applications and appliances, SSH, Telnet, and Serial (console). Keep in mind that the more management interfaces that a bridge has, the more security holes exist by default.

Mounting Options

Because bridges are more likely to be used in outdoor links, they are more likely to be mounted outdoors. Likely placement would be on top of buildings, on the side of towers, and on high masts. These specialized circumstances might require a custom mounting kit and possibly a weatherproof enclosure from the manufacturer. Getting AC power to these locations can be difficult, so enterprise-class bridges almost always support PoE.

Wireless Workgroup Bridges

Similar to and often confused with wireless bridges are wireless *workgroup* bridges (WGB). A WGB is a bridge in that it provides wireless access to a group of wired stations "behind" the bridge. The difference between a "wireless bridge" and a "wireless workgroup bridge" is that the wireless bridge always forms a link with another bridge, while a WGB associates with an access point as a client. A WGB is useful when one or more wired Ethernet clients need access to the wireless network and you already have an access point installed and within range of those devices.

FIGURE 7.16 Wireless workgroup bridge (Cisco 350 series)

Notice that the same architecture in Figure 7.17 could be created using two bridges instead of a WGB and an AP. The only difference would be that in the architecture in Figure 7.17, wireless clients can associate with the AP. If you used two bridges (acting strictly as bridges), wireless clients could not associate with either bridge.

FIGURE 7.17 A wireless workgroup bridge installed on a network

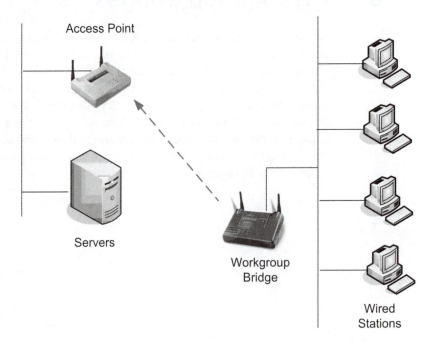

Workgroup bridges are especially useful in environments such as classrooms, cube farms, or even remote campus buildings where a small, wired group of users need access into the main network, and wireless is the easiest method of providing that access. Bridges can be used for this type of functionality; however, if an access point, rather than a bridge, is in place at the central site, then using a workgroup bridge saves the administrator from having to buy an additional bridge for the central site.

Common Options

Because the wireless workgroup bridge is a type of bridge, many of the options that you will find in a bridge – MAC and protocol filtering, fixed or detachable antennas, variable power output, and varied types of wired connectivity – are also found in a workgroup bridge. The primary factor that differentiates workgroup bridges is that there is a limit to the number of stations that may access the network through the WGB from the wired segment. Some "wireless game adapters," which are really just specialized 802.11 workgroup bridges, have a limit of only one client behind the bridge, whereas some WGBs can support up to 16 wired clients. As we stated in the previous section, if the "game adapter" only talks to another "game adapter," then it is most likely acting as a bridge; if it talks to a regular 802.11 access point, then it is most likely acting as a WGB.

Fixed vs. Detachable Antennas

Like access points and bridges, wireless workgroup bridges can come with fixed or detachable antennas.

Security Features

Workgroup bridges typically support a minimal complement of security features. They are basically a client device running firmware and usually offer no more than static WEP, WPA-PSK, and WPA.

Management Utilities

Workgroup bridges are usually configured manually on the device via a web browser, serial (console) interface, or through a custom software application. They are usually even simpler to configure than client software that would be installed on a client PC.

Filtering Options

Workgroup bridges support similar MAC address and protocol filtering options to access points and bridges in the same price range.

Connectivity Modes

Workgroup bridges tend to work only in "workgroup bridge" mode. They are less likely to work in multiple modes as bridges and access points do. It has recently been seen that access points and bridges are configurable as WGBs, but not vice versa.

Number of Clients

Wireless workgroup bridges have some maximum number of clients that can be on the wired side of the bridge. Consumer-grade bridges might support up to eight or sixteen clients, while enterprise-grade bridges might support up to 255. Ensure that your WGB will support the number of wired clients that you require.

Summary

Workgroup bridges associate to an AP like a client, but forward frames and filter like a bridge. Their limitations (only a few clients behind the WGB, for example) mean that they will not be effective in every situation. In many cases, an AP or a wireless bridge will be more effective. Nevertheless, the fact that vendors continue to produce WGBs indicates that there is still demand for a device that fills their specialized niche.

Wireless Routers

Most access points bridge frames between the wired and their wireless interfaces. The administrator should think of the wireless network as merely an extension (through a medium change) of the wired network. When using an access point, both sides of the access point (wireless and wired) share the same IP subnet. A *wireless router* is an access point that routes packets between the wireless and the wired interfaces, instead of bridging frames. With a wireless router, the wireless interface on the AP has its own IP subnet and IP address, which is separate from the IP subnet on the wired interface(s).

Wireless routers present a challenge with clients that roam, since roaming between roaming between APs means roaming across subnets as well. This situation may break many applications. Each wireless router may need to be configured to handle DHCP requests in a specific manner to enable seamless roaming. An advantage of a WLAN router is that it is easier to implement a VPN endpoint in a WLAN router than in an access point. This means that clients can create a VPN to the WLAN router itself, which then forwards those packets unencrypted onto the wired network. With an access point, the encrypted tunnel typically goes through the AP to a VPN endpoint on the wired network.

Wireless LAN Client Devices

The term "client devices" will, for purposes of this discussion, cover several wireless LAN devices that an access point recognizes as a client on a network. These devices include:

- PCMCIA (PC),Compact Flash (CF), and Secure Digital (SD) Cards
- PCI and Mini-PCI Cards
- USB Devices
- PCMCIA-to-PCI Adapters
- Serial and Ethernet Converters

Wireless LAN clients are end-user nodes such as desktop, laptop, or PDA computers, sensors, handheld scanners, and many other devices that need wireless connectivity into the network infrastructure and that may use any number of wireless LAN radio devices, such as those in the list above.

PC, CF, and SD Cards

The PCMCIA card is the most common 802.11 client device. Also known as "PC cards," these devices are commonly used in laptop computers and PDAs. The PC card used to serve as a modular radios in access points, bridges, workgroup bridges, USB adapters, and PCI adapters, but are being replaced by Mini-PCI (discussed later) in this role. Figure 7.18 shows an example of a PCMCIA card.

FIGURE 7.18 PCMCIA Radio Card (Linksys WPC55AG)

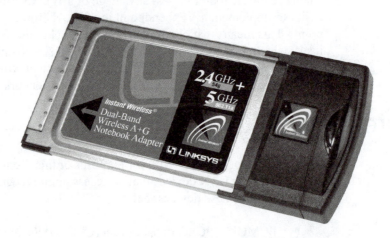

Antennas on PC cards vary with each manufacturer. The majority are integrated into the card itself, as in Figure 7.18. Some integrated antennas have the ability to fold, with the intention of increasing their coverage. Some PCMCIA cards also have the availability of an external antenna connector.

 Relatively few manufacturers make radio chipsets, which are the core of 802.11 radio cards. These manufacturers sell their chipsets to the PC, CF, USB, SD, and other radio card manufacturers (the wireless LAN hardware manufacturing companies) that use the radios in their product lines. It is common to see many different vendors using the same chipset in their radio cards. In this case, the primary differentiator between these vendors is the performance and capabilities of their drivers and client utilities.

Compact Flash Cards, more commonly known as "CF cards," are very similar to wireless PC cards in that they have the same functionality, but CF cards are smaller and are typically used in handheld devices, not laptops. This is not to say that they are not used in laptops, because some new laptops have CF slots, but it is currently uncommon. Wireless CF cards draw very little power and are about the size of a matchbook. Many end-users purchase CF cards because of their flexibility. You can use a CF-to-PCMCIA adapter card (about $10 as of this writing) to adapt them to the PC Card format. This gives the end-user both formats with a single purchase.

FIGURE 7.19   Compact Flash Radio Card (Symbol Mobile Networker)

Recently, vendors have released 802.11b cards in the Secure Digital form factor. Even smaller and thinner than CF cards, for many years SD cards could not provide enough power to the 802.11 radio to provide adequate performance. SD cards are also made in combination units that provide Wi-Fi connectivity and flash storage.

FIGURE 7.20   Secure Digital Radio Card (SanDisk SD Wi-Fi Card)

PCI and Mini-PCI Adapters

Wireless PCI adapters are installed inside desktop computers. Early 802.11 PCI cards were often simply PCMCIA-to-PCI adapters with an 802.11 PCMCIA card inserted. Today PCI cards are usually manufactured with integrated radio devices. One advantage of this is that a dedicated PCI card uses a larger, external antenna, which offers better signal reception than the smaller, internal antenna usually found on PCMCIA cards. PCI cards have the disadvantage that the antenna is almost always behind the computer's metal case, potentially causing significant loss of signal strength, depending on the access point's location relative to the PC. Unless you are running out of USB slots, a wireless USB adapter with a cable is usually preferable to a PCI adapter that sits inside the PC. Since PCI cards usually have a detachable antenna, you could optionally use a pigtail cable to place the antenna in a better place than behind the computer.

FIGURE 7.21   PCI Radio Card (Linksys WMP55AG)

Laptops commonly use 802.11 cards in a form factor known as "Mini-PCI." Mini-PCI is similar to the version of PCI that is used in desktop machines but optimized for the requirements of mobile devices—specifically, small size. A laptop with a Mini-PCI port can accept any type of mini-PCI accessory, of which 802.11 cards are only one. One advantage of a Mini-PCI port compared to integrated wireless is that a Mini-PCI adapter can be upgraded as technology evolves.

FIGURE 7.22 Mini-PCI Radio Card

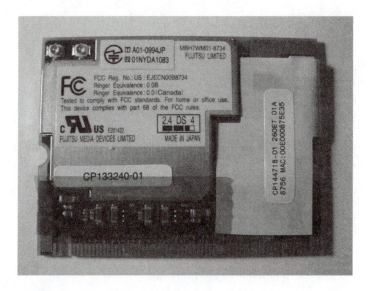

USB Adapters

USB clients are popular due to their simple connectivity. USB client devices support plug-n-play and require no additional power other than what is delivered through the USB port on the computer. USB clients can be moved between laptop and desktop computers easily (which can't be said for PCMCIA, CF, Mini-PCI, and SD, since most desktops don't have any of these slots).

USB adapters come in two major form factors, "wired" and "dongle." A wired USB adapter attaches to the computer via a standard USB cable. The advantage of this form factor is that the adapter can be moved to the position that maximizes signal strength. The dongle form factor is a small, one-piece device that looks something like a USB "pen-drive." The advantage of this form factor is its small size and convenient portability. Figure 7.23 shows examples of USB clients.

FIGURE 7.23   USB Radio Devices (Linksys WUSB12 & WUSB54GP)

PCMCIA-to-PCI Adapters

A PCMCIA-to-PCI adapter is a generic device that allows PCMCIA cards to be plugged into a desktop computer. A PCI card plugs into the desktop computer like any other, and provides one or more PCMCIA slots into which standard PCMCIA cards, including wireless cards, can be inserted.

In the early days of 802.11, manufacturers made 802.11 cards almost exclusively in the PCMCIA form factor. PCI cards were implemented by inserting a PCMCIA card into a generic PCMCIA-to-PCI adapter and adding the vendor's sticker on the outside. With some of these cards, you could actually remove the PCMCIA wireless card and insert any other PCMCIA card that you wanted. Today, manufacturers are more likely to make dedicated PCI cards.

Ethernet & Serial Converters

Ethernet and serial converters are used to provide wireless access to devices that don't have PCMCIA, Mini-PCI, PCI, CF, SD, or USB ports, but do have Ethernet or 9-pin serial ports. The converter plugs into the Ethernet or serial port and converts the data to wireless frames. These devices are typically used on legacy devices, such as cash registers and serial printers, on which the newer interfaces were not yet available when they were manufactured.

Common Options

There are two distinct steps to installing wireless LAN client radio devices after they are connected to the computer:

- Install the drivers
- Install and configure the manufacturer's wireless utilities (if available)

Driver Installation

Drivers for wireless LAN cards are installed in the same way as their wired counterparts. Most devices are plug-n-play compatible, which means that when the client device is first installed, the user will be prompted to insert the CD or disks containing the driver software into the machine. In many cases, basic drivers for wireless adapters are included with modern operating systems (O/S) like Windows 2000 and Windows XP. The manufacturer's drivers (on the installation CD or downloaded from the manufacturer's web site) are often more recent than the basic O/S drivers and may contain bug fixes or enhanced functionality. Specific steps for device installation will vary by manufacturer. Be sure to follow the instruction manuals for your specific brand of hardware.

Manufacturer Utilities

In the early days of 802.11, some manufacturers offered a full suite of utilities, considered advanced for that time period, while others simply provided the user with the most basic means of connectivity. Today, a robust set of utilities might include:

- Basic site survey tools
- Power and speed monitoring tools
- Profile configuration utilities
- Link status monitor with link testing functionality
- Manual protection mechanism and frame fragmentation adjustments
- Robust set of security protocols

Basic site survey tools can include many different items that allow the user to find networks, identify MAC addresses of APs, quantify signal strengths and signal-to-noise ratios of APs' beacons, see interfering access points, and identify which APs are using which types of security, all at the same time.

FIGURE 7.24   NetGear client utility showing basic site survey tools

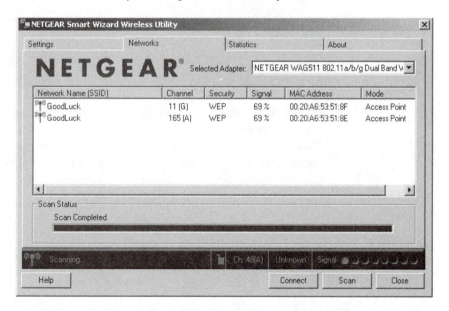

Power output and speed configuration utilities and monitors are useful for setting and knowing what a wireless link is capable of doing at any particular time. For example, if a user were planning to transfer a large amount of data from a server to a laptop, the user may not want to start

the transfer until the wireless connection to the network is 11 Mbps, instead of 1 Mbps. Knowing the location of the point at which throughput increases/decreases is valuable for increasing user productivity.

FIGURE 7.25   Cisco client utility showing data rate and power output configuration

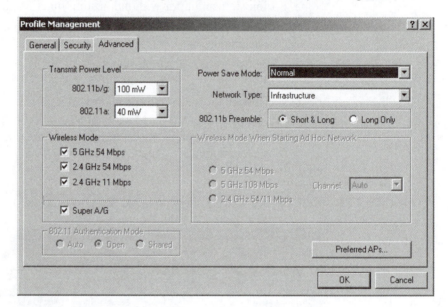

Profile configuration utilities ease administrative tasks considerably when changing from one wireless network to another. Instead of manually having to reconfigure all of a wireless client's settings each time you change networks, you may configure profiles for each wireless network during the initial configuration of the client device to save time later.

FIGURE 7.26   Proxim client utility showing profile management screen

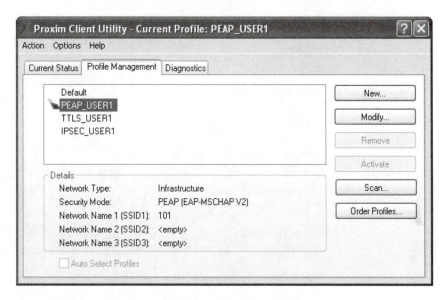

Link status monitor utilities allow the user to view packet errors, successful transmissions, connection speed, link viability, and many other valuable parameters. There is usually a utility for doing real-time link connectivity tests so that, for example, an administrator would be able to see how stable a wireless link is while in the presence of heavy RF interference or signal blockage.

FIGURE 7.27   Cisco link status utilities showing signal strength and quality

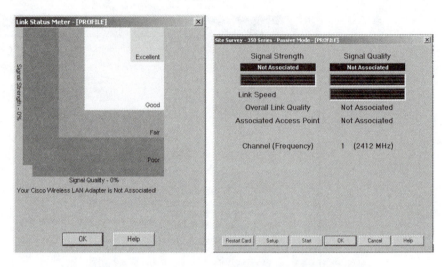

Performance of the card can sometimes be improved by manually configuring certain advanced parameters. For example, an 802.11 card can break a large frame into smaller fragments. This can improve throughput on networks with lots of frame corruption. By default, cards do not fragment at all, but you can override this behavior if you think it will increase performance (if you're not sure, try setting the fragmentation threshold to a value like 500 or 1000 bytes and see if throughput increases).

Manual "protection mechanisms" is another type of advanced configuration that can affect network performance. In a mixed 802.11b/g BSS, the 802.11b DSSS stations cannot detect the OFDM transmissions of the 802.11g stations. Therefore, the 802.11g stations will invoke certain behaviors, called "protection mechanisms," to make sure that the 802.11b stations are aware of the 802.1g stations' OFDM transmissions. These protection mechanisms degrade performance compared to a network comprised purely of 802.11g stations, but it is a necessary tradeoff to prevent the 802.11b stations in the mixed BSS from corrupting the 802.11g stations' OFDM transmissions. 802.11g stations automatically choose the type of protection mechanism that they think is best, but you can force them to use a certain kind if you think it will improve performance. Protection mechanisms are covered fully in the CWAP materials.

FIGURE 7.28   Threshold configuration values for the NetGear WAG511 card

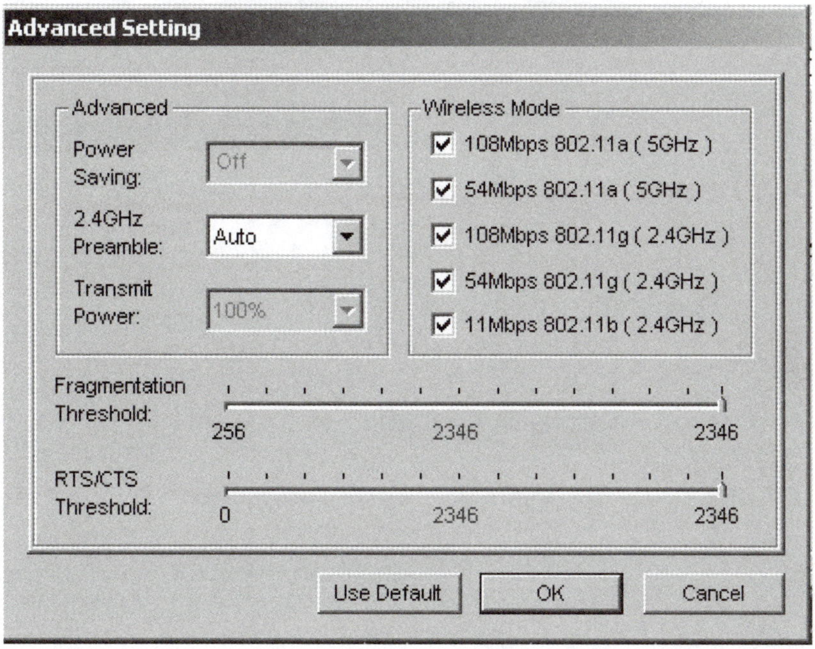

Finally, it will be necessary to configure the necessary authentication credentials that the card will use to join the network. If WEP is used, you will need to configure the WEP key. If WPA-PSK is used, you will need to configure the "pre-shared key." One example each of configuring SOHO-class (WPA-PSK) and enterprise-class (PEAP-EAP-MSCHAPv2) security will be given here, but others will be left to the security chapter (chapter 12), and the CWSP class.

FIGURE 7.29 WPA-PSK Configuration

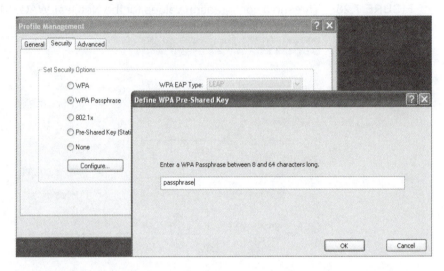

FIGURE 7.30 PEAP-EAP-MSCHAPv2 Configuration

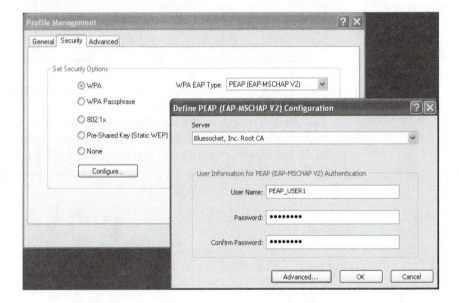

Windows XP – Wireless Zero Config

With Windows XP, Microsoft introduced "Wireless Zero Config," which is the idea that the operating system should take care of configuring the wireless card with minimal user intervention. While this had the advantage of standardizing configuration for all vendors' cards, it had the unfortunate disadvantage that vendors no longer had the incentive to make their own utilities. As a result, more and more vendors have dropped their site survey tools from their client utility package, leaving users and administrators with only the very rudimentary tools included in Windows XP. Fortunately, third-party vendors have picked up where WLAN manufacturers left off and have started providing (for a fee, of course) very in-depth wireless site survey software.

Wireless Residential Gateways

Manufacturers have taken residential routers (gateways) to the next level by adding wireless functionality. Wireless residential gateways usually include a NAT (network address translation) router, an integrated switch, and a fully configurable Wi-Fi compliant access point. The WAN port on a wireless residential gateway is an Internet-facing Ethernet port. It may be connected to the Internet through one of the following:

- Cable modem
- xDSL modem
- Analog modem
- Satellite modem

The same functions could be performed by having both an access point and a residential gateway in the network, but for cost-cutting measures, manufacturers are integrating all of the features of both into a single unit. Figure 7.31 gives an example of a wireless residential gateway, while Figure 7.32 illustrates where a wireless residential gateway is used on a wireless LAN.

FIGURE 7.31   A wireless residential gateway

FIGURE 7.32   A wireless residential gateway installed on a network

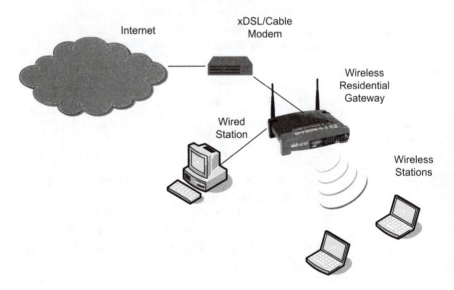

Common Options

Because wireless residential gateways are becoming increasingly popular in homes of telecommuters and in small businesses, manufacturers have begun adding more features to these devices to aid in productivity and security. Common options that most wireless residential gateways include are:

- Port Address Translation (PAT)
- Integrated, multi-port Ethernet switches
- Port Forwarding
- Virtual Private Network (VPN) Endpoint
- Dynamic Host Configuration Protocol (DHCP) Server and Client
- Configurable Firewall
- Configurable Wi-Fi Access Point

Some gateways even bundle the cable or DSL "modem" into the device. This diverse array of functionality allows home and small office users to have an all-in-one solution that is easily configurable and meets most business needs. Wireless residential gateways have all of the expected SOHO-class access point configuration selections such as WPA, MAC filters, channel selection, and SSID.

Configuration and Management

Configuring and installing wireless residential gateways generally consists of browsing to the built-in HTTP server via one of the built-in Ethernet ports and changing the user-configurable settings to meet your particular needs. This configuration may include changing ISP, LAN, VPN, or wireless settings. Configuration and monitoring are done in similar fashion through the browser interface. Some wireless residential gateways units support console, telnet, and SNMP connectivity for management and configuration. The text-based menus typically provided by the console port and telnet sessions are less user-friendly than the browser interface, but adequate for configuration. Statistics that can be monitored may include items such as up-time, dynamic IP addresses, VPN connectivity, and associated clients. These settings are usually well marked or explained for the non-technical home or home office user.

When you choose to install a wireless residential gateway at your home or business, be aware that your ISP will not provide technical support for getting your unit connected to the Internet unless it specifically states that it will. ISPs usually will only support the hardware that you have purchased from them or that they have installed. This lack of service can be especially frustrating to the non-technical user who must configure the correct IP addresses and settings in the gateway unit to get Internet access. Your best sources of support for installing these devices are the manual provided with the device or someone who has already successfully installed similar units and can provide free guidance. Wireless residential gateways are so common now that many individuals who consider themselves non-technical have gained significant experience installing and configuring them.

Enterprise Wireless Gateways (EWGs)

An enterprise wireless gateway (EWG) is a device that can provide specialized authentication and connectivity for wireless clients. EWGs are appropriate for medium- and large-scale wireless LAN environments providing a multitude of manageable wireless LAN services, such as client role-based access control, quality of service, encrypted VPN tunneling, infrastructure management, and support for a variety of back-end authentication systems. EWGs should have either Fast Ethernet or Gigabit Ethernet wired interfaces, due to the large number of high-speed access point they support. The more access points the EWG is supporting, the higher speed the uplink interface speed should be. Figure 7.33 shows an example of an enterprise wireless gateway, while Figure 7.34 illustrates where it is used on a wireless LAN.

FIGURE 7.33   A sample enterprise wireless gateway (Vernier IS-6500p)

FIGURE 7.34 How an Enterprise Encryption Gateway fits into the network

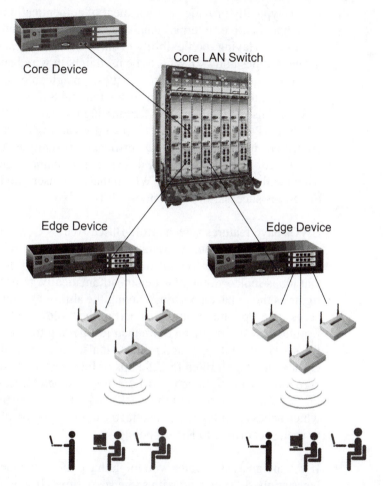

Some EWGs may provide PoE to downstream APs through multiple downlink ports, and others may not. Some have a client/server architecture (as shown in Figure 7.34 above), some have a peer-to-peer architecture, and some have the ability to collapse all functionality into a single platform for SMB operations.

Configuration and Management

EWGs typically provide an assortment of authentication mechanisms, including a native (internal) database, RADIUS, internal 802.1X, LDAP, and more. Having the flexibility to authenticate a client against many database types allows EWGs to be used in both wired and wireless networks and to meet the largest requests imaginable. One of the newest available authentication options is the internal 802.1X authentication server. This feature works by terminating the outer TLS tunnel of EAP-TTLS, EAP-FAST, or PEAP, and then forwarding the inner user credentials to a database for ID verification (usually to a RADIUS server). This function allows the EWG to see the user name inside the TLS tunnel, which will in turn allow the EWG to place the user into the proper role if the user is successfully authenticated.

EWGs have features such as Role-Based Access Control (RBAC) that allows an administrator to assign a certain level of wireless network access to a particular job position in the company. If the person doing that job is replaced, the new person automatically gains the same network rights as the replaced person. Having the ability to limit a wireless user's access to corporate resources as part of the "role" can be a useful security feature. RBAC can mean more than just getting to a resource, such as a file server, the Internet, or a printer. It also can mean rate limiting. Guests might be limited to 128 kbps of Internet bandwidth while corporate users might be up to 1.5 Mbps. "When" (meaning what time of the day and which days of the week) and "where" (meaning through which access points) might also factor in the equation of providing access to users, according to RBAC policy.

If you are an avid traveler, you might have found yourself in an airport, bus station, or truck stop with some spare time. If you turned on your wireless laptop in any of these places you might have noticed wireless networks that looked "wide open." If you chose to connect to them you could easily do so, get an IP address, and when you opened your browser, you immediately were greeted by a welcome screen asking for your name and credit card information. This is a captive portal. This is yet another beneficial feature found in many EWGs. The EWG can handle the DNS requests a number of ways (such as handing out its own IP or allowing DNS requests to pass through for unregistered users), and HTTP GET requests are immediately redirected to either an internal or protected external HTTP (or HTTPS) page for collecting billing information.

Most EWGs support directional layer 3-7 filtering. For example, you might only want to allow TCP port 21 inbound or you might only want to deny SMTP outbound. This type of filtering also could be tied to a role so that, for example, the ACCOUNTING role cannot send SMTP outbound, but everyone else can.

Some EWGs are software-only implementations built around license-free operating systems, such as Free-BSD or Linux. In these cases the manufacturer will usually give you a list of known-working hardware, but will try to help you support what hardware you have to some degree. Some EWGs are appliance implementations built around pre-fabricated hardware platforms running proprietary and/or license-free operating systems, such as Free-BSD, Linux, etc. When comparing the cost of software-only and appliance solutions, don't forget to factor in the cost of the hardware you will have to add to the software-only solution to be able to compare prices.

Many EWGs terminate PPTP, L2TP, SSH, and IPSec VPN tunnels. They also support a variety of encryption algorithms, such as RC4, DES, 3DES, AES-128, AES-192, and AES-256. What the manufacturer advertises in throughput for the box may be without any encryption enabled. There is a *huge* difference in the maximum throughput of an EWG when the traffic is encrypted versus unencrypted. Termination of VPN tunnels brings up another interesting issue: roaming. Since most VPN technologies exist at or above layer 3, roaming with tunnels built presents a problem for EWG designers. Most EWGs present a unique (proprietary) approach for fixing this problem. It is worth your time as an administrator to read the manufacturer's manual to see how layer 3 roaming is handled before you purchase the equipment, if roaming is a business requirement.

Enterprise wireless gateways are so comprehensive that we highly recommend that you take the manufacturer's training class before making a purchase so that the deployment of the enterprise wireless gateway will go more smoothly. Consultants finding themselves in a situation of having to provide a security solution for a wireless LAN deployment with many access points that do not support advanced security features might find enterprise wireless gateways a good solution. Enterprise wireless gateways are not priced for SOHO implementation, but, considering the number of management and security solutions they provide, they are usually worth the expense to any SMB or large enterprise.

Enterprise wireless gateways are usually configured through console (serial) ports (using the CLI), Telnet, SSH, or internal HTTP/S servers. Enterprise wireless gateways are normally upgraded through use of TFTP or HTTP in the same fashion as many switches and routers on the market today. Configuration backups and operating system code upgrades can often be automated so that the administrator will not have to spend additional management time doing it manually. Enterprise wireless gateways are typically rack-mountable 1U or 2U devices that can fit into your existing data center design.

Enterprise Encryption Gateways (EEGs)

WEP, WPA, and WPA2/802.11i are all examples of layer 2 encryption. The payload of the layer 2 frames are encrypted, and a bit in the frame header is set to indicate when encryption has been used on the frame payload. This is good except for the fact that encryption techniques traditionally used with wireless have been very weak. WPA2/802.11i was only recently introduced to give the market standards-based strong authentication and encryption. Some vendors previously had taken it upon themselves to build stronger solutions based on the Advanced Encryption Standard (AES), which uses the Rijndael encryption algorithm. These solutions also encrypt data at layer 2 of the OSI model, and are considered very strong measures of protecting data.

Now the comparison discussion becomes whether proprietary or standards-based solutions are better. Before strong standards-based solutions were available, there was no choice. Now that 802.11i has been ratified, there is a choice, but hackers undoubtedly will target standards-compliant software and hardware prior to going after proprietary gear, simply because they make easier targets. Additional gains that you might see in some of these EEGs are that they implement high compression in order to offset the latencies experienced by extreme encryption.

VPN technologies such as IPSec, SSH, and SSL all encrypt data at layer 3 and above. While offering strong data encryption in their own right, they each introduce other design problems that could be avoided if layer 2 encryption were used. For that reason, use of a very strong layer 2 encryption mechanism (like AES), along with strong authentication, makes sense in a wireless environment.

FIGURE 7.35   An Enterprise Encryption Gateway

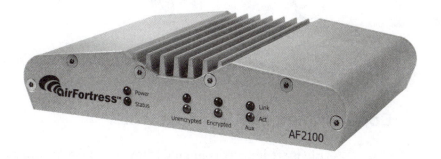

EEGs have an "encrypted" side an "unencrypted" side. The unencrypted side is the "upstream" backbone side where all of the network resources reside. Access points and client devices reside downstream on the encrypted side. Everything on the encrypted side of the EEG is encrypted unless you, as the administrator, specifically configure it not to be. For example, you might configure AP management traffic to pass unencrypted only to the IP addresses of known APs on specific management ports (like port 80, 443, 21, or 22). Clients must use special software that communicates with the gateway to build a secure tunnel. Users authenticate so they can gain access to upstream network resources. In this solution, like any other where the APs themselves are not specifically involved in the security protocol, the APs are left open to attack and should be secured as tightly as possible.

FIGURE 7.36 How an Enterprise Encryption Gateway fits into the network

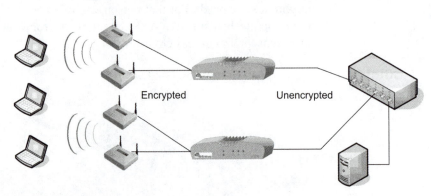

Encrypted   Unencrypted

Configuration and Management

EEGs are initially configured through a console port, and then through a secure web interface (port 443) or a secure shell interface (SSH, port 22). EEGs are designed to be some of the most secure devices in wireless networking, even if manageability is not maximized.

Wireless LAN Switches

The traditional architecture of an 802.11 wireless LAN maps a single physical device to the logical function of an access point. This model may have scalability issues unless specific planning measures are taken. As the number of access points grows, the difficulty of configuring and maintaining them outweighs their usefulness. In addition, roaming between independent access points is often unreliable, mainly because the IEEE didn't standardize roaming behavior in 802.11 (a subsequent recommended practice defining the Inter-Access-Point Protocol addresses this). Therefore, some vendors have taken the access point's functionality and moved it from the edge of the network into a central device known as a wireless LAN switch. Don't let the "switch" term mislead you: this device is much more than an Ethernet switch.

A wireless LAN switch contains all of the functionality of one or more "virtual" access points. Wireless LAN switches look like any other Ethernet switch, but contain much different code. Each Ethernet port connects to a proprietary access point provided by the same vendor, often called a "thin" access point. Many vendors like to differentiate their thin access points by giving them non-standard names like Access Port or Mobility Point. All of the APs in a WLAN switching system are logical and reside in the WLAN switch itself, which aids in management, since all APs can be managed (configured and monitored) from the same interface.

Since everything in WLAN switching is "logical" instead of "physical," it is simple to configure VLANs to reside wherever in the network you would like. It is also simple to give users access to the wireless network based on location, time, and resource type because the entire wireless network is treated as a living entity instead of lots of individual parts.

Thin access points vary greatly in implementation. One might be simply an antenna in a plastic case, and the next might house dual radios and an encryption/decryption accelerator. Though the connection between the thin access point and the WLAN switch uses Cat5 cable, it might use Ethernet and it might use a different protocol for data transfer. Some use 802.11 even on the wired medium, and others convert 802.11 frames to 802.3 and then encapsulate 802.3 inside GRE tunnels or proprietary protocols for transport back to the switch. You must check with the vendor to see what they do in this area. Most WLAN switch vendors provide Power-over-Ethernet (discussed in the next section) to every port for powering up the thin APs.

Each wireless LAN switch vendor has its own pitch on how things "should" be done in wireless networking. You will hear everything from "You should set all devices on a single DSSS or OFDM channel for maximizing fast roaming" to "You should let the network auto-survey and auto-configure for channels 1, 6, and 11 since the environment changes over time anyway." There is no such thing as a perfect answer for all occasions. Understanding how the technology works and how the solution might fit your environment, and then performing verification testing, is the best way to get optimum results.

Some switch vendors get more involved with the RF site survey portion of wireless networking than others, providing advanced tools that allow the administrator to import data into the switch for network planning and switch configuration. Keep in mind that these tools are never 100 percent accurate, and walking around an area to check coverage may still be required to validate the site survey information. EWGs and WLAN switches are certainly competitors in the market, and rightly so, since WLAN switches are an expansion on what EWGs originally brought to the market in the first place. You can think of a WLAN switch as an EWG with many additional features below (in the OSI model) that of an EWG (such as access points). It also means that EWGs may be able to do some of the same functions for wired users as they can for wireless users, which is impossible for WLAN switches, since they can do wireless only.

FIGURE 7.37   A Wireless LAN Switch

Network switches began with everyone thinking the switch could only exist at the network edge in the wiring closet. That philosophy quickly changed when designers introduced switches and thin APs that could communicate over GRE and proprietary tunnels across the existing Ethernet network infrastructure. Existing 802.3af PoE edge switches could power the thin APs and then they could "call home" to build a logical tunnel back to their switch. Soon after this new technique was introduced, vendors whose products were "edge-only" suddenly changed. Today, you have the choice of putting the WLAN switch either at the core or at the edge of the network. Why would you want to put the WLAN switch at the edge? There's a simple answer: when there's no existing PoE and you are going to need a very high-density of access points. Figure 7.38 illustrates how a WLAN switch fits into a network.

Although WLAN switches started out as high-end enterprise devices that were only affordable to those with large budgets and the need to install many access points, WLAN switch technology has trickled down to the

SOHO level. Vendors are currently producing affordable WLAN switches that support just a few thin access points. These are intended either as a stand-alone solution for a small office or as a remotely-managed solution for a remote office.

FIGURE 7.38 How a Wireless LAN Switch fits into the network

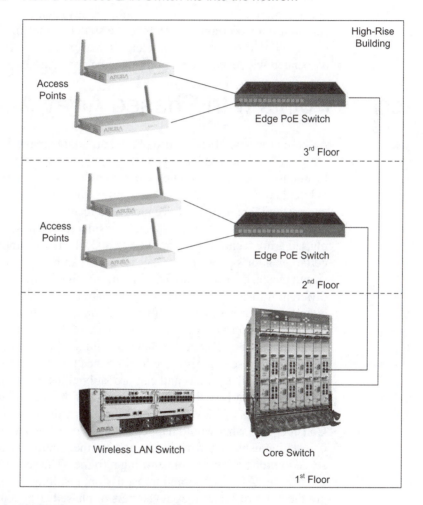

Configuration and Management

Wireless switches are configured through a variety of interfaces, including HTTP/HTTPS and TELNET/SSH (command line).

Configuration of a wireless switch is more complex than configuration of a single access point since you are essentially configuring many access points all at once, but it is much simpler than configuring many access points individually. Configuration of a wireless switch differs somewhat from vendor to vendor. Typically you first configure which thin access point should connect to which switch. This step might include configuration of the type of encryption (if any) that the access points should use to communicate back to the switch. Once the access points are connected to the switch, parameters such as which VLANs and SSIDs are associated with each access point must be configured.

Access Points with Phased Array Antennas

APs are now available that use phased array antenna technology to deliver "directed" or "steered" beams of RF energy to individual clients' physical locations. The reality is much more complex than the marketing suggests. While there is no doubt that phased array antennas can steer beams of energy, and that they can have increased receive sensitivity compared to non-phased-array antennas, special considerations must be taken when phased array technology is applied to 802.11. For example, consider if a certain vendor's phased array access point can have up to six simultaneous beams of traffic. This means that it could transmit six different frames to six different clients simultaneously, as long as the clients were far enough apart from each other that their frames didn't overlap. This phased array could produce six times the performance of a standard antenna. But performance would not be as good when the clients tried to send a response back. Since the clients probably have omnidirectional antennas and can probably all hear each others' transmissions, it is probable that only one of them could transmit at a time due to the rules of CSMA/CA, the wireless medium arbitration protocol. Consider also what would happen if the AP was transmitting a frame to one station using a narrow beam, and another station performed carrier-sense in preparation for transmitting a frame. The second station might not hear the AP's directional transmission, resulting in a collision. These are the types of issues that developers of phased array antennas for 802.11 access points have had to confront. Unfortunately, the details of the answers to any of these questions are not available because the technical details of any particular phased array 802.11 technology are kept secret by its developers.

FIGURE 7.39   Access Point with Phased Array Antenna Technology (Front / Back)

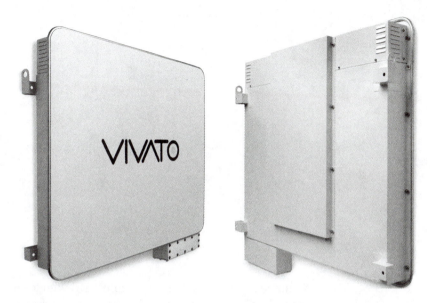

Phased array antennas fit into the network similar to the way that regular antennas do; they just have much larger coverage areas and can support more throughput. They are usually directional in their coverage – similar to a 180-degree panel antenna – so vendors usually suggest mounting them on a wall facing into the coverage area (for inside installations).

FIGURE 7.40   Example of how a Switching Antenna fits into the network (outdoor installation)

College Campus

Copyright Vivato™ 2004

A phased array antenna must be combined with a specialized radio that knows how to manipulate the beams for best performance. Since that functionality is not part of the 802.11 standard, you always have to buy the AP and the phased array antenna together as a unit. These "AP/antenna" combinations are typically more expensive than a non-phased-array access point, but manufacturers claim that, since they have much greater coverage than a standard access point, the cost difference is reduced since you can buy fewer of them.

WLAN Mesh Routers

WLAN mesh routers are the antithesis of traditional wireless networking. Until mesh routers were introduced, WLANs were used only at the edge and distribution layers of the WLAN. Mesh routers introduce WLAN technology at the core of the network with the hope of giving certain types of networks a much needed component: reliability. These network types are specific, such as (but not limited to) across cities, within historic buildings where cabling isn't allowed, and for quickly constructed networks such as disaster relief sites. Reliability is achieved through high availability, and high availability is achieved through instant failover within a network mesh. If one unit fails, another unit takes over its responsibilities. Figure 7.41 illustrates a wireless mesh router.

FIGURE 7.41   A Wireless Mesh Router

WLAN mesh routers use proprietary routing protocols to route data traffic between the mesh routers. Manufacturers do not make information available about these protocols because it is part of their trade secrets. This closed information loop means that the customer is relying on the vendor to provide the necessary tools for monitoring, troubleshooting, and configuring the WLAN mesh network. Without those tools, you would be operating in the dark as with any proprietary hardware/software solution. For example, if traffic were re-routed away from mesh router 409A due to power supply failure, you might want to know the following:

- What router(s) picked up the additional workload that was previously on router 409A?
- What are those routers' current workloads?
- What are the data rates of those routers currently?

- What was the data rate of router 409A when it failed?
- What was the average throughput over the last 24 hours of router 409A when it failed?

Some application has to be able to retrieve this information from the mesh units and put it in front of you quickly. Without it, troubleshooting would be almost impossible. Can you imagine walking around a building or even a city with a wireless LAN protocol analyzer trying to capture frames from a dynamically re-routing wireless LAN?

It is important to understand that while wireless mesh routers use wireless technology to communicate with each other, they may not be designed to communicate with wireless LAN client devices at all. Mesh wireless routers form a core network into which you can plug wired Ethernet devices ranging from a print server to an access point. It is these edge devices that will allow you to have wireless client access. Many brands of mesh routers have multiple fast Ethernet ports on the back of the unit for plugging in multiple devices. If mesh routers are used to extend a wireless network, the administrator should make sure that the edge and core wireless devices are using different WLAN channels so they do not interfere.

FIGURE 7.42   How a Wireless Mesh Router fits into the network

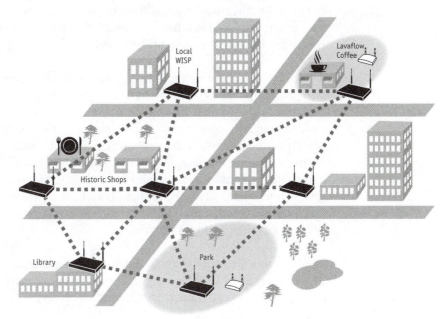

Figure 7.42 depicts one example of how mesh routers might be used. The buildings in the town are wired for Ethernet but do not have any network connection between each other. In the past, the administrator might have used ISDN or some other type of WAN line to link the buildings back to the ISP and to each other. Instead, you can place a mesh router on top of each building and link the building's wired Ethernet network to the router. The routers provide connectivity between all buildings, including forwarding frames from one building to another, if necessary. In locations where wireless access is needed, such as the park and the coffee shop, an access point is plugged into the mesh router. This is necessary since this particular brand of mesh router does not support connections to 802.11 clients, only other mesh routers.

Configuration and Management

Access points, bridges, and WGBs are usually configured by an administrator. Automatic configuration of those devices is difficult because each AP must communicate with a variety of types of devices from a variety of vendors. By comparison, mesh routers from one vendor only talk to other mesh routers from the same vendor. This means that the vendor can build in a higher degree of automatic configuration than is possible with access points, bridges, and WGBs.

Typically, mesh routers are delivered in a zero-configuration mode: they will power up and form an unsecured mesh with any other mesh routers that they find. If you want to add security to the mesh, you will probably need to manually configure some form of secret key (such as a pre-shared secret) on the routers. Mesh routers also might include the ability to segment meshes, meaning to prevent routers in one building from connecting to routers in a neighboring building, but they typically don't give you too much control over the flow of traffic within the mesh since that would contradict the simplicity and ease of deployment that is the primary advantage of mesh routers.

Mesh routers are usually configured via a custom application running on a PC, as opposed to HTTP configuration. The entire mesh is typically configured en masse, rather than individual routers.

Power over Ethernet (PoE) Devices

Power over Ethernet (PoE) is a method of delivering DC voltage to an access point or wireless bridge over Cat5 cable for the purpose of powering the unit over the same cable that carries data to the unit. Standard Cat5 cables have four pairs of wires. It always takes two pairs to carry the data, but the DC voltage may or may not be carried on the same pairs that carry the data, depending on the implementation.

PoE is primarily used when AC power receptacles are not available where wireless LAN infrastructure devices are to be installed. PoE also has secondary advantages in terms of convenience and administration that will be discussed in a moment. Consider a warehouse where the access points need to be installed in the ceiling of the building. The labor costs that would be incurred to install electrical outlets throughout the ceiling of the building to power the access points would be considerable. On the other hand, since Cat5 cable is low-voltage, it is not necessary to hire a professional electrician to run it and building codes are usually not involved. A LAN engineer could run the Cat5 cable through the ceiling and then use PoE to power the APs. Figure 7.43 illustrates how a PoE injector would provide power to an access point.

FIGURE 7.43 PoE Configuration with DC Voltage Injector

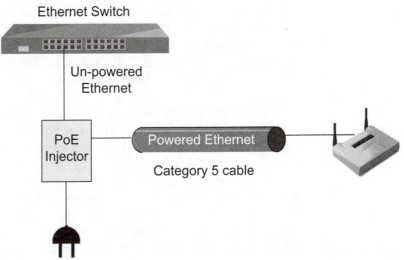

Even in cases in which AC power is available, PoE has some advantages. First, running power over the Cat5 cable simplifies the installation: there's one less cable to run, adapter to plug in, etc. Second, some PoE devices allow the administrator to turn power to a given port on or off from a central management console, which means that you can power-cycle a malfunctioning device without climbing into the ceiling to get to the unit.

Common Options

Several types of devices are capable of putting voltage onto a Cat5 cable to power a PoE-enabled device:

- Single-port DC voltage injectors
- Multi-port DC voltage injectors
- "Active" or "PoE" Ethernet switches designed to inject DC voltage on each port on a given pair of pins

Although configuration and management generally means only "off" or "on" for a given switch port or device, there are some caveats to be aware of if and when you begin to implement PoE. These caveats come in the form of mismatched pin usage and mismatched voltage and current ratings. When one manufacturer uses one voltage and another manufacturer uses another voltage on the same set of pins, damage to equipment can occur. Also, some manufacturers may use different pins to power equipment. In this case, damage to the equipment is unlikely since the unused pins are not electrically connected, but the device won't receive power through the Ethernet cable.

There is an industry standard on implementation of PoE (802.3af amendment to 802.3-2002: Data Terminal Equipment (DTE) Power via Media Dependent Interface (MDI)). Not all equipment complies with this standard, especially equipment that was sold before 802.3af was ratified in 2003. If you are using a wireless device such as an access point, and will be powering it using PoE, it is recommended that you confirm that all equipment is 802.3af-compliant. If for some reason 802.3af-compliant equipment is not available, the safest bet is to buy all equipment from the same manufacturer. This recommendation holds true for any device when considering powering with PoE.

The details of the 802.3af specification (voltages, amperages, which pins it uses, and so on) are beyond the scope of this text. All you really need to know is that devices that are 802.3af-compliant should work together. This insurance of compatibility is 802.3af's primary advantage over the proprietary PoE solutions that vendors invented before 802.3af. In addition, you should recognize the terms that 802.3af uses to refer to PoE devices. 802.3af defines two types of devices: *end-span* and *mid-span*. End-span refers to an active Ethernet switch, as described previously. Mid-span refers to a multi-port injector that sits between a non-PoE switch and one or more PoE devices.

Single-port DC Voltage Injectors

PoE is so useful that some APs and bridges don't offer any other method of powering the device. These devices come standard with a single-port DC voltage injector (See Figure 7.44) for the purpose of powering the unit. These single-port injectors are acceptable when used with a small number of wireless infrastructure devices, but quickly clutter wiring closets when building medium or large wireless networks.

A single-port injector takes the unpowered Ethernet cable (carrying data) and a DC plug in one side and outputs powered Ethernet (data + power) on the other side. The DC plug plugs into the wall like any other power converter.

FIGURE 7.44   A Single-Port PoE Injector

Multi-port DC Voltage Injectors

Several manufacturers offer multi-port injectors. These models may be economical or convenient for installations where many PoE devices are being added to a network with existing switches that are not PoE capable. See Figure 7.45 for an example of a multi-port PoE injector. A multi-port DC voltage injector looks like an Ethernet switch with twice as many ports as would be needed for the number of devices to be powered. A multi-port DC voltage injector is a pass-through device that sits in-line between the hub or switch and the PoE device (access point, bridge, etc.). Unpowered Cat5 patch cables connect from the network's data switch ports into the input ports of the injector. The injector adds power to each line, and each injector output port carries both data and voltage to power PoE devices. These multi-port injectors are appropriate for medium-sized wireless network installations; however, in large enterprise rollouts, even the densest multi-port DC voltage injectors, combined with Ethernet switches, can become cluttered when installed in a wiring closet.

FIGURE 7.45   A multi-port PoE injector

PoE Capable Ethernet Switches

The next step up for large enterprise installations of access points is PoE capable Ethernet switches. These devices incorporate DC voltage injection into the Ethernet switch itself, allowing for large numbers of PoE devices without any additional hardware in the network. See Figure 7.46 for an example of a PoE capable Ethernet switch.

The advantage of PoE switches over power injectors is two-fold. First, no additional hardware is installed in the wiring closet other than the Ethernet switches that would already be there for a non-PoE network. Second, the switch will often give the ability to enable and disable power to individual ports through a management console, allowing you to remotely power-cycle devices or even to turn off all PoE devices at once. This feature also provides an interesting Denial of Service possibility for an attacker, if he or she were able to compromise a PoE switch.

PoE switches that are compliant with 802.3af can auto-sense PoE client devices on the network. If the switch does not detect a PoE device on the line, the DC voltage is switched off for that port. Some proprietary implementations of PoE also can do this. Remember that even if PoE voltage is applied to a non-PoE device, it is unlikely that the device will be damaged because the voltage is on pins that non-PoE devices do not use anyway.

FIGURE 7.46   A Power-over-Ethernet Capable Switch (Cisco 3550-24PWR)

As you can see from Figure 7.46, a PoE Ethernet switch looks no different than an ordinary Ethernet switch. The only difference is the added internal functionality of supplying DC voltage to each port. PoE Ethernet switches are clearly the best choice for medium to large-scale PoE installations. The switch in Figure 7.46 is a stackable, 24-port model. Much larger, modular PoE switches are available for higher port densities.

A PoE switch will typically be supporting some mixture of PoE and non-PoE devices. The majority of the devices plugged into a PoE-capable switch will probably be standard Ethernet devices and will not be drawing power from the switch. Therefore, vendors sometimes design PoE switches with a power supply that is not capable of supplying power to all Ethernet ports on the switch. You should confirm that the switch supports the maximum number of simultaneously-powered ports that you expect to use. When buying a modular switch, buy the largest power supply you can afford.

PoE-capable Ethernet switches have significant advantages over single- and multi-port injectors, and will greatly enhance the simplicity of installation and management of a medium- to large-sized wireless network. PoE Ethernet switches should be preferred over single or multi-port injectors if at all possible.

Fault Protection

The primary purpose of fault protection is to protect the cable, the equipment, and the power supply in the event of a fault or short-circuit. There are many ways a fault might be introduced into the Cat5 cable, including the following examples.

- The attached device may be totally incompatible with PoE and may have some non-standard or defective connection that short-circuits the PoE conductors. At present, most non-PoE devices have no connection on the PoE pins, but if a device looped two PoE pins together, a short circuit would result, possible damaging the device.

- Incorrectly wired Cat5 cabling. Cut or crushed Cat5 cable in which the insulation is damaged, allowing one or more of the conductors to come in contact with each other or another conducting material.

During any fault condition, the fault-protection circuit shuts off the DC voltage injected onto the cable. Fault protection circuit operation varies from model to model. Some models continuously monitor the cable and restore power automatically once the fault is removed. Some models must be manually reset by pressing a reset button or cycling power.

Key Terms

Before taking the exam, you should be familiar with the following terms:

bridge mode

Compact Flash

dongle

Dynamic Host Configuration Protocol (DHCP)

firewall

mesh router

modular cards (in an AP)

Port Address Translation (PAT)

PCI card

PCMCIA card (PC card)

PoE Injector (Single-port & Multi-port)

repeater mode

root mode

Secure Digital card

serial-to-802.11 converter

Simple Network Management Protocol (SNMP)

Universal Serial Bus (USB)

variable output power

Virtual Private Networks (VPNs)

virtual servers

wireless router

Review Questions

1. Explain in basic terms the purpose of using a wireless LAN switch instead of using access points connected to a traditional wired switch. How do the access points of a wireless LAN switch differ from traditional access points in functionality, features, and management?

2. Where on the network should you install an enterprise wireless gateway? What is the purpose of an EWG?

3. Describe a common real world enterprise scenario in which you would use both a wireless bridge and a wireless workgroup bridge.

4. How could access points, enterprise wireless gateways, PoE injectors, and wireless bridges all be used together within the same network?

5. Describe the differences in applications and functionality between wireless routers and wireless mesh routers.

Wireless LAN Organizations And Standards

CWNA Exam Objectives Covered:

❖ Identify, explain, and apply the concepts covered by the IEEE 802.11 standard and the differences between the following 802.11 clauses

- 802.11
- 802.11a
- 802.11b
- 802.11d
- 802.11e
- 802.11F
- 802.11g
- 802.11h
- 802.11i
- 802.11j
- 802.11n
- 802.11s

❖ Define the roles of the following organizations in providing direction, cohesion, and accountability within the wireless LAN industry

- FCC
- IEEE
- The Wi-Fi Alliance

In This Chapter

Major IEEE 802.11 standards and amendments

Power output and other regulations for Part 15 FCC systems

FCC

IEEE

Wi-Fi Alliance

- ❖ Identify the regulations set forth by the FCC that govern spread spectrum technology, including:
  - ▪ Power output
  - ▪ Frequency band use
- ❖ Understand the differences between licensed bands and unlicensed bands and what it means for a frequency band to be unlicensed
- ❖ Identify the differences between FCC regulations for the license-free ISM and UNII bands
- ❖ Identify and summarize the differences between the power output regulations for Point-to-Point and Point-to-Multipoint outdoor links

Like most computer-related hardware and technologies, wireless LANs are based on standards. In this chapter we will discuss the FCC's role in defining and enforcing the regulations governing wireless communication and the IEEE's role in creating standards that allow wireless devices to interoperate. We will discuss the frequency bands on which wireless LANs operate and examine the 802.11 family of standards. We will discuss a new kind of organization introduced into the IT market along with wireless LANs: The Wi-Fi Alliance. The Wi-Fi Alliance certifies 802.11b and later WLAN equipment for interoperability. This is an important new role in the IT arena, especially for WLANs. Familiarity with regulations, standards, and certifications that govern and guide wireless LAN technology is a key component of becoming a wireless administrator and enhances your ability to implement cost-effective, efficient WLANs within regulatory requirements.

Federal Communications Commission

The Federal Communications Commission (FCC) is an independent United States government agency, directly responsible to Congress. The FCC was established by the Communications Act of 1934 and is charged with regulating interstate and international communications by radio, television, wire, satellite, and cable. The FCC's jurisdiction covers not only the 50 states and the District of Columbia, but also all U.S. possessions such as Puerto Rico, Guam, and The Virgin Islands.

The FCC creates regulations within which wireless LAN devices must operate. The FCC mandates where on the radio frequency spectrum wireless LANs can operate, at what power, using which transmission technologies, and how and where various pieces of wireless LAN hardware may be used.

 The website for the FCC is www.fcc.gov

License-free Bands

The FCC establishes rules limiting which frequencies wireless LANs can use and the output power on each of those frequency bands. The FCC has specified that wireless LANs can use the Industrial, Scientific, and Medical (ISM) bands, which allow end-users to transmit without applying for an FCC system certificate (however, a manufacturer will have applied for a certificate for the system before selling it.) The ISM bands are centered at 915 MHz, 2.45 GHz, and 5.8 GHz, and vary in width from about 26 MHz to 150 MHz. Devices complying with the 802.11 series of standards do not currently use the 915 MHz and 5.8 GHz ISM bands.

In addition to the ISM bands, the FCC specifies three Unlicensed National Information Infrastructure (UNII) bands. Each one of these UNII bands is in the 5 GHz range and is 100 MHz wide. Figure 8.1 illustrates the ISM and UNII bands available for license-free operation of WLAN equipment.

FIGURE 8.1   ISM and UNII Spectra

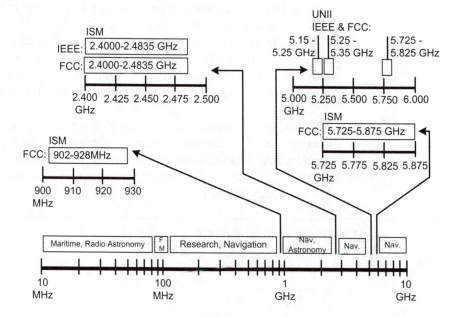

Advantages and Disadvantages of License-Free Bands

License-free bands have the advantage of allowing users to set up transmission equipment without the delay and expense of applying for an FCC license. The license-free nature of the ISM and UNII bands is very important because it allows entities like small businesses and households to implement wireless systems and fosters the growth of the wireless LAN market.

This freedom from licensing also has a major disadvantage. The same license-free band you use (or intend to use) is also license-free to others. Suppose you install a wireless LAN system on your home network. If your neighbor installs a wireless LAN, a cordless 2.4 GHz phone system, or some other device that uses the 2.4 GHz band in his home, his system may interfere with yours and vise versa. If he uses a higher-power system, his wireless LAN may disable your wireless LAN entirely. The two competing systems don't necessarily have to be on the same channel, or even be using the same spread spectrum technology. The ISM and UNII bands are truly the "wild west" of RF.

Industrial Scientific Medical (ISM) Bands

There are three license-free ISM bands: the 915 MHz, 2.4 GHz, and 5.8 GHz bands.

915 MHz ISM Band

The 915 MHz ISM band is defined as the range of frequencies from 902 MHz to 928 MHz. This band may be additionally (and correctly) defined as 915 MHz ± 13 MHz. Though the 915 MHz ISM band was once used by wireless LANs, it has been largely abandoned in favor of the higher frequency bands which have wider bandwidths and allow more throughput. Some of the wireless devices that still use the 915 MHz band are wireless home phones, game systems, and camera systems. Organizations that use obsolete 915 MHz WLANs find out the hard way that obsolete equipment is expensive to replace should any piece of their hardware malfunction. A single 915 MHz radio card may cost as much as $800 and might only be able to transmit at speeds up to 1 Mbps. In comparison, an 802.11g compliant wireless card will support speeds up to

54 Mbps and sell for roughly $60. Finding support or replacements for these older 915 MHz units is almost impossible.

2.4 GHz ISM Band

This band is used by all 802.11, 802.11b, and 802.11g compliant devices and is by far the most populated (with WLAN devices) space of the three ISM bands presented in this chapter. The FCC specifies that the 2.4 GHz ISM band runs from 2.4000 GHz to 2.4835 GHz.

5.8 GHz ISM Band

This band is also frequently called the "5 GHz ISM Band." The 5.8 GHz ISM band is bounded by 5.725 GHz and 5.875 GHz, which yields a 150 MHz bandwidth. Although 802.11a uses frequencies that fall in the range of the 5.8 GHz ISM band, the 802.11a standard specifies use of the UNII-3 band, not use of the 5.8 GHZ ISM band. There is often confusion over whether 802.11a uses ISM or UNII, since the upper UNII band overlaps with a portion of the 5.8 GHZ ISM band.

Unlicensed National Information Infrastructure Bands

The 5 GHz UNII bands are made up of three separate 100 MHz-wide bands which are used by 802.11a compliant devices, among others. The three bands are known as the lower (UNII-1), middle (UNII-2), and upper (UNII-3) bands. Unlike the ISM bands, which can be used for whatever the user wants, the FCC places additional restrictions (discussed below) on the UNII bands.

Lower Band (UNII-1)

The lower UNII band, also known as UNII-1, runs from 5.15 GHz to 5.25 GHz and is specified by the FCC and IEEE to have a maximum output power of 40 mW. Devices used in the UNII-1 band are restricted to indoor use only (FCC 15.407, page 755, paragraph e).

When 802.11a was originally specified, the FCC required that transmitters in the low UNII band have fixed antennas even if those transmitters also used the middle and high UNII bands where detachable antennas were allowed. This meant that 802.11a cards and access points always had fixed antennas, along with multi-mode cards and access points that used the same antenna for 2.4 GHz and 5.8 GHz transmission. In 2004, the FCC changed that requirement and transmitters in all three UNII bands can now use detachable antennas.

Middle Band (UNII-2)

The middle UNII band, also known as UNII-2, runs from 5.25 GHz to 5.35 GHz and is specified at 200 mW of output power by the FCC and IEEE. The middle band can be used indoors or outdoors. Early access points and client cards sometimes supported only the low and middle bands. The reason for this type of support was that the upper band is intended for long-distance outdoor and point-to-point use, and most APs are installed indoors (coverage of outdoor areas is still less prevalent than coverage of indoor areas). Today most 802.11a cards and access points support all three UNII bands, allowing for up to 12 non-overlapping channels of 802.11a coverage in a coverage area.

Upper Band (UNII-3)

The upper UNII band, also known as UNII-3, is limited by the FCC and IEEE to 800 mW of output power at the intentional radiator. This band occupies the range of frequencies between 5.725 GHz and 5.825 GHz and is typically used for outdoor, long-distance links.

Power Output Rules

The FCC enforces certain rules regarding the power radiated by the transmitter and by the antenna element, depending on whether the implementation is a point-to-multipoint or a point-to-point implementation, and also depending on what frequencies are used. Remember that the term used for the power radiated by the antenna is *Equivalent Isotropically Radiated Power* (EIRP).

Point-to-Multipoint (PtMP) – 2.4 GHz ISM

PtMP links have a central point of connection and two or more non-central connection points. PtMP links are typically configured in a star topology and the central connection point may or may not have an omnidirectional antenna. It is important to note that when an omnidirectional antenna is used, the FCC automatically considers the link a PtMP link.

For a PtMP link, the FCC limits the intentional radiator power to 1 watt (+30 dBm), and the EIRP to 4 watts (+36 dBm) in the 2.4 GHz ISM band. Performing the math reveals that, with a 1-watt intentional radiator, the maximum antenna gain is 6 dBi, since 1 watt plus 6 dBi equals 4 watts (refer back to Chapter 3 on RF Math). It is important to remember that the FCC limits both power output at the intentional radiator and the EIRP of the antenna. The FCC stipulates that for every 3 dBi above the initial 6 dBi of antenna gain, the maximum power at the intentional radiator (the transmitter) must be reduced by 3 dB below the initial maximum of +30 dBm.

Suppose a radio transmitting at 1 watt (+30 dBm), which is the FCC's maximum for an intentional radiator used in the 2.4 GHz ISM band, was connected to a 12 dBi omnidirectional antenna. The EIRP of the antenna would be about 16 watts, which is well above the FCC's 4 watt limit. Since the antenna has 12 dBi of gain, which is 6 dBi greater than the "free" 6 dBi granted by the FCC, the power at the intentional radiator must be reduced by 6 dB. This reduction will result in an intentional radiator power of +24 dBm (+30 dBm – 6 dB), or 250 mW and an EIRP of +36 dBm (+24 dBm + 12 dBi antenna gain), or 4 watts, which is the maximum EIRP allowed by the FCC.

To summarize, in the 2.4 GHz band the FCC restrictions allow for a maximum of 6 dBi of antenna gain if the intentional radiator is transmitting at maximum power (1 watt). EIRP must never go above 4 watts, so, for each additional 3 dBi of antenna gain, the power at the intentional radiator is reduced by 3 dB. The result is that the maximum EIRP in a point-to-multipoint configuration is always exactly 4 watts. Since the power at the intentional radiator is reduced in exact proportion to the increase in antenna gain, this is sometimes referred to as the "one-to-one rule" or the "1:1 rule."

FIGURE 8.2   Point-to-Multipoint Power Limit Table

Max Power from the Intentional Radiator (dBm)	Max Antenna Gain (dBi)	EIRP (dBm)	EIRP (watts)
30	6	36	4
27	9	36	4
24	12	36	4
21	15	36	4
18	18	36	4
15	21	36	4
12	24	36	4

When using an omnidirectional antenna, the rules for point-to-multipoint links must be followed regardless of whether the actual implementation is point-to-point or point-to-multipoint.

Point-to-Multipoint (PtMP) – 5.8 GHz UNII

For a PtMP link in the three UNII bands, the maximum power from the intentional radiator is 40 mW, 200 mW, and 800 mW for the low, middle, and high bands respectively, with a maximum antenna gain of 6 dBi. If a PtMP transmitter desires to use an antenna with a gain of greater than 6 dBi, then the 1:1 rule applies: for each 1 dB of gain above 6 dB the power from the intentional radiator must be reduced by 1 dB. From these rules, we can derive the maximum EIRP allowable for a PtMP link under FCC regulations:

- Maximum power from the IR (UNII-1) = 40 mW = 16 dBm
- 16 dBm maximum power from the IR + 6 dBi maximum antenna gain = 22 dBm = 160 mW maximum EIRP in the UNII-1 band.
- Maximum power from the IR (UNII-2) = 200 mW = 23 dBm
- 23 dBm maximum power from the IR + 6 dBi maximum antenna gain = 29 dBm = 800 mW maximum EIRP in the UNII-2 band.
- Maximum power from the IR (UNII-3) = 800 mW = 29 dBm
- 29 dBm maximum power from the IR + 6 dBi maximum antenna gain = 35 dBm = 3200 mW maximum EIRP in the UNII-3 band.

Note that since the 1:1 rule applies to PtMP links in this band, these EIRP maximums cannot be exceeded, as Figure 8.2 demonstrated for the 2.4 GHz ISM band. Every increase in antenna gain must be accompanied by an equivalent decrease in power from the intentional radiator.

Point-to-Point (PtP) – 2.4 GHz ISM

PtP links include a single directional transmitting antenna and a single directional receiving antenna. These connections will typically include building-to-building or similar links and have slightly different power output rules than PtMP links. For a PtP link using the 2.4 GHz ISM band, the FCC mandates that for every 3 dBi above the initial 6 dBi of antenna gain, the power at the intentional radiator must be reduced by 1 dB from the initial maximum of +30 dBm.

Consider our previous example using the same values: 1 watt (+30 dBm) at the intentional radiator and a 12 dBi antenna, but in this case the antenna will be a directional antenna and the link is PtP. The EIRP is still 16 watts. In this example, since the antenna gain is 12 dBi, the power at the intentional radiator must be reduced by only 2 dB, as opposed to a 6 dB reduction in the previous example. This reduction will result in an intentional radiator power of +28 dBm (+30 dBm – 2 dB), or about 630 mW and an EIRP of +40 dBm (+28 dBm + 12 dBi), or 10 watts.

In the case of PtP links, the power at the intentional radiator is still limited to 1 watt but the limit of the EIRP *increases* with the gain of the antenna (Figure 8.3). This regulation makes sense since a directional antenna focuses its energy much more tightly than an omnidirectional antenna, and is therefore less likely to interfere with other transmitters. It is important to clearly distinguish between the rules that govern PtP and PtMP wireless links. Since the power at the intentional radiator is reduced 1 dB for every 3dB increase in antenna gain, this is sometimes referred to as the "three-to-one rule" or the "3:1 rule."

FIGURE 8.3   Point-to-Point Power Limit Table

Max Power from the Intentional Radiator (dBm)	Max Antenna Gain (dBi)	EIRP (dBm)	EIRP (watts)
30	6	36	4
29	9	38	6.3
28	12	40	10
27	15	42	16
26	18	44	25
25	21	46	39.8
24	24	48	63
23	27	50	100
22	30	52	158

Point-to-Point (PtP) – 5.8 GHz UNII

Point-to-point links in the UNII-1 and UNII-2 bands follow exactly the same rules as point-to-multipoint links. The FCC has a separate rule for PtP links in the UNII-3 band. Fixed PtP UNII devices operating in the UNII-3 band may employ transmitting antennas with directional gain up to 23 dBi without any corresponding reduction in the output power from the intentional radiator. For fixed point-to-point UNII transmitters that employ a directional antenna gain greater than 23 dBi, the 1:1 rule applies: a 1 dB reduction in power from the intentional radiator for each 1 dBi of antenna gain in excess of 23 dBi is required. Note that by having an output power maximum of +30 dBm at the intentional radiator, and having a maximum of 23 dBi antenna gain before any reduction in transmitter output power is required, PtP UNII-3 systems are allowed to have an output of 200 watts EIRP. Two hundred watts is an enormous amount of power for a WLAN application.

Sector and Phased-Array antennas

As described in Chapter 4, a phased array antenna consists of a number of antennas hooked up to a signal processor. By adjusting the relative strength of the signal transmitted by each antenna and by adjusting the phase of the signals relative to each other, a phased array can create individual beams of signal, each pointing in a different direction.

Phased arrays require special treatment under FCC Part 15 rules. The goal of Part 15 rules is to minimize interference with licensed transmitters. Because a phased array focuses its energy in specific areas, it is able to put out more total power (over the whole array) without increasing the risk of interference in those areas.

Prior to the FCC Report & Order 04-165, released July 12, 2004, sectorized and phased-array antennas were not specifically covered under Part 15 rules. The July R&O defines new regulations, including power output stipulations that allow these antennas to operate under section 15 rules without impeding growth of these technologies.

Under R&O 04-165, Part 15 allows a sectorized or phased array antenna system to "…operate at the same power levels permitted for point-to-point directional antennas by limiting the total power that may be applied to each individual beam." This means that each individual beam of the array may be treated as a single point-to-point link for the purposes of determining maximum power output and antenna gain.

This configuration could result in very high power output from a single array. In order to limit the total power output of an array, the FCC also requires that the aggregate power transmitted simultaneously on all beams be no more than 8 dB above the limit for an individual beam. This means that at most six individual beams can operate simultaneously at maximum transmission power. If more beams are needed, then the power of the beams must be reduced so that the aggregate power falls below the 8dB limit.

Consider also a situation in which two beams of a phased array system are using the maximum allowable power for a point-to-point connection, and the beams cross or overlap. In this case, the power at the point of overlap would be too great. Therefore, the FCC specified that the antenna system must detect when two beams would overlap and adjust the power of the beams so that the power at the point of overlap does not exceed the maximum power for any single beam.

IEEE

The Institute of Electrical and Electronics Engineers (IEEE) is the key standards maker for most things related to information technology in the United States and even the world at large. The IEEE creates its standards within regulatory guidelines of the countries in which the standards will be applied. Within the U.S., the IEEE specifies wireless LANs that meet the requirements for RF devices as defined by the Federal Communications Commission (FCC). In Europe, RF requirements are defined by the European Telecommunications Standards Institute (ETSI). In Canada, the regulatory body is Industry Canada (IC). In Japan, it is the Association of Radio Industries and Businesses (ARIB). There are similar regulatory bodies in each country. Fortunately, these bodies usually work together to ensure that their regulations are compatible and that RF devices that work in one country won't violate regulations in another country. For example, when 802.11 was first released, Japan's frequency allocation only allowed DSSS channel 14 to be used. Later, the ARIB changed the allocation to allow channels 1 through 13 to be used, making Japan's frequency allocation more consistent with that used in Europe and the United States.

The IEEE specifies many technology standards, such as Public Key Cryptography (IEEE 1363), FireWire (IEEE 1394), Ethernet (IEEE 802.3), and wireless LANs (IEEE 802.11).

 The website for the IEEE is www.ieee.org

It is part of the mission of the IEEE, through its 802.11 committee, to develop standards for wireless LAN operation within the framework of regulatory guidelines. The base IEEE standard for wireless LANs currently in use is the 802.11–1999 edition (reaffirmed in 2003). The original 802.11 standard was ratified in 1997 and later updated in 1999. Each document that amends the base standard is identified by a lower case letter. Amendments will be absorbed by later editions of the base 802.11 standard, and at that time the amendments will no longer exist as separate authorities. In addition to amendments to the 802.11 standard, the 802.11 committee has published recommendations. These are each identified by an upper case letter. Some examples of amendments (also called "clauses") and recommendations follow.

- 802.11b
- 802.11a
- 802.11d
- 802.11h
- 802.11g
- 802.11e
- 802.11F
- 802.11i
- 802.11j
- 802.11s

IEEE 802.11 Base Standard

The 802.11 base standard was the first 802.11 standard. It describes Direct Sequence Spread Spectrum (DSSS), Frequency Hopping Spread Spectrum (FHSS), and infrared physical layers.

 Infrared's wireless LAN market share is quite small and the technology is very limited by its functionality. Due to the lack of popularity of infrared technology in the wireless LAN marketplace, IR will not be covered in this book.

The IEEE 802.11 base standard describes DSSS system stations that operate at 1 Mbps and 2 Mbps only. These systems are known as clause 15 systems because of the clause of the 802.11 standard that refers to them. If a DSSS system operates at other data rates as well, such as 1 Mbps, 2 Mbps, and 11 Mbps, it can still be an 802.11-compliant system. If, however, the system is operating at any rate other than 1 or 2 Mbps, then even though the system is 802.11-compliant because of its ability to work at 1 and 2 Mbps, it is not operating in an 802.11-compliant mode and cannot be expected to communicate with other 802.11-compliant devices.

IEEE 802.11 is one of many standards that describe the operation of frequency hopping wireless LAN systems. The 802.11 standard describes use of FHSS systems at 1 and 2 Mbps only. These systems are known as clause 14 systems because of the clause of the 802.11 standard that refers to them. There are FHSS systems on the market that extend this functionality by offering proprietary modes that operate at 3–10 Mbps. Just as with DSSS, if the proprietary FHSS system is operating at speeds other than 1 and 2 Mbps, it cannot be expected to automatically communicate with 802.11 devices.

802.11 FHSS and DSSS products operate strictly in the 2.4 GHz ISM band between 2.4000 and 2.4835 GHz. Infrared, covered by 802.11, is light-based technology and does not fall into the 2.4 GHz ISM band.

802.11b Supplement

Though the 802.11 base standard was successful in allowing DSSS, as well as FHSS, systems to interoperate with other stations with the same PHY, the technology quickly outgrew that standard. Soon after the approval and implementation of the original 802.11–1997 edition, proprietary DSSS wireless LANs were exchanging data at up to 11 Mbps. Without a standard to guide the operation of such devices, problems developed with interoperability and implementation. The manufacturers ironed out most of the implementation problems, so the job of IEEE was relatively easy: create a new 802.11 standard PHY to comply with the general operation of wireless LANs then on the market. It is not uncommon for the standards to follow the technology in this way, particularly when the technology evolves quickly.

The 802.11b supplement specifies DSSS systems that operate at 1, 2, 5.5, and 11 Mbps, and calls them "High-Rate DSSS." The 802.11b supplement does *not* describe any FHSS systems. 802.11b devices, known as clause 18 devices, will interoperate with 802.11 DSSS (clause 15) devices by default, meaning they are backward compatible and support both 2 and 1 Mbps data rates. Backward compatibility is very important because it allows a wireless LAN to be upgraded without the cost of replacing the existing hardware. This low-cost feature, together with the higher data rate, made the 802.11b hardware very popular and contributed greatly to 802.11's success.

The higher data rate of 802.11b is the result of using a different coding technique. Though the system is still a direct sequencing system, the way the chips are coded (CCK rather than Barker Code), along with the way the information is modulated (DQPSK at 2, 5.5, and 11 Mbps, and DBPSK at 1 Mbps) allows for a greater amount of data to be transferred in the same time frame. 802.11b compliant products operate only in the 2.4 GHz ISM band between 2.4000 and 2.4835 GHz.

802.11a Supplement

The IEEE 802.11a Supplement describes wireless LAN device operation in the UNII bands using OFDM technology to boost data rates to 54 Mbps. Operation in the UNII bands automatically makes 802.11a devices incompatible with all devices complying with previous (and subsequent) 802.11 clauses. The reason for this incompatibility is simple: systems using 5 GHz frequencies will not communicate with systems using 2.4 GHz frequencies. WLAN devices operating in compliance with the 802.11a supplement are known as clause 17 devices.

Using non-overlapping channels in the UNII bands, 802.11a devices are able to achieve data rates of 6, 9, 12, 18, 24, 36, 48, and 54 Mbps using OFDM technology. Some of the devices employing the UNII bands have achieved data rates of 108 Mbps by using proprietary technology. The highest rates of some of these devices are the result of newer technologies not specified by 802.11a. IEEE 802.11a *requires* data rates of only 6, 12, and 24 Mbps and specifies a maximum of 54 Mbps. Though most "802.11a" equipment implements all of the data rates specified in the 802.11a supplement, it is not required that they do so.

802.11g Supplement

802.11g provides the same maximum speed as 802.11a. 802.11g also uses OFDM technology in the same manner as 802.11a. Additionally 802.11g devices provide backwards compatibility for 802.11b devices through use of DSSS technology. This backwards compatibility makes upgrading wireless LANs simple and inexpensive.

IEEE 802.11g specifies operation in the 2.4 GHz ISM band. This specification allows a single access point to serve both 802.11g and 802.11b stations, but also creates potential for interference between these stations. Because the 802.11b stations cannot receive OFDM signals, they may perceive the transmissions of the 802.11g stations as non-802.11 background noise and transmit over them.

If an 802.11g access point detects the presence of 802.11b stations, it will indicate that 802.11g stations should activate "protection mechanisms," which are behavior modifications that prevent 802.11b stations from interfering with 802.11g transmissions. These protection mechanisms reduce the throughput of the BSS compared to a purely 802.11g BSS, but they raise throughput on mixed 802.11b/g BSS's by preventing frame collisions between the 802.11b and 802.11g stations.

802.11e Supplement

802.11 wireless LANs were designed with LAN-style data transmission in mind. Only recently have multimedia applications been introduced onto the LAN, and wireless soon followed. The natural progression was to see multimedia applications move onto the wireless infrastructure, making mobile voice and video possible. 802.11 WLANs require careful design to provide support for these real-time applications.

The IEEE 802.11e amendment to the 802.11 base standard defines a set of Quality of Service (QoS) extensions to the 802.11 MAC layer that are designed to provide higher-quality and more consistent voice and video transmission. 802.11e is covered in more detail in Chapter 10.

802.11F Recommended Practice

The 802.11 base standard defines the management frame that stations use to request reassociation with a second access point, and the management frame that access points use to grant or deny the reassociation. However, the standard does not define the mechanisms that the access points should use to hand the station off. This omission by the IEEE was intentional. Knowing that many different types of networks could be used to connect access points, the IEEE left it up to the vendors to create protocols that the access points could use to talk to each other over whatever particular wired medium might be in use. As might be expected, proprietary protocols resulted, meaning that stations would not roam seamlessly between different vendors' access points even if everything in the AP's configuration suggested that they could.

The 802.11F recommended practice addresses this situation by defining the *inter-access-point protocol (IAPP)*. By using a suggested method of (1) allowing access points to discover each other, and (2) allowing access points to "hand off" stations to each other, clients will be able to roam seamlessly between 802.11F-compliant access points.

802.11F was ratified in 2003 and, though there are access points on the market today that support this recommended practice, it has seen less than popular acceptance. 802.11F does not address roaming in a time-efficient manner, which is likely the most important reason behind roaming to begin with. Time-sensitive applications, such as voice over wireless LAN (VoWLAN), require very fast handoff times (typically <150ms). For this reason, most vendors have their own mechanisms for supporting fast handoff of clients, creating a vendor interoperability problem. This situation is further exacerbated by the time-intensive security mechanisms that are typically in use by client devices today.

802.11i Supplement

The 802.11i supplement addresses the relative weakness of 802.11's built-in security mechanism: WEP. The 802.11i supplement includes the use of 802.1X for port-based authentication and use of the thought-to-be-unbreakable AES encryption algorithm, instead of WEP's RC4 encryption algorithm. While 802.11i significantly increases the strength of 802.11's security, legacy equipment is not upgradeable to 802.11i compliance, due to the extreme processor requirements imposed by the complex AES algorithm. AES-upgradeable and 802.11i compliant equipment has recently been introduced into the market.

802.11i introduces two new cipher suites beyond what is specified in 802.11: TKIP and CCMP. TKIP is intended to be a field upgradeable software patch to legacy RC4-based hardware, while CCMP is expected to be implemented on newer AES based hardware.

802.11h Supplement

The 802.11h amendment allows an 802.11a device to conform to regulatory requirements of the 5 GHz band in Europe. Specifically, it describes mechanisms for dynamic frequency selection (DFS) and transmission power control (TPC), which are mandated by European regulations.

The DFS requirement is to avoid interference between 802.11a transmitters and radar systems that might be in use in the area. 802.11h defines services that allow for the following:

- A station can associate with an AP based on the channels that the AP supports. If the AP and station do not have compatible channel sets the station will not attempt to associate with the AP.
- The AP can test for the presence of radar on the channel. If the AP detects radar, it may move to a different channel to avoid interfering with the radar.
- The AP can quiet the channel so that it can test for the presence of radar without the added noise of stations' transmissions.
- The AP can select a new channel and announce that channel to the stations on the BSS, so the BSS can be gracefully moved to the new channel when interference is detected.

The TPC requirement essentially allows the AP to mandate maximum power output requirements to the stations. In that way, an AP can be configured with the appropriate power output rules for the regulatory domain, and 802.11h-compliant stations that associate with the AP will automatically comply with those rules.

Dynamic frequency selection and transmission power control are implemented through additions to existing management frames, such as beacons, probe requests, association requests, and so on. Non-802.11h-compliant stations should simply ignore the 802.11h portions of these frames. However, a non-802.11h-compliant station may be rejected by an 802.11h-compliant access point, since it may not be able to comply with the frequency and power output requirements of the access point.

802.11j Supplement

The 802.11j amendment, approved in November, 2004, allows an 802.11 network to conform to the frequency rules for the 4.9 GHz (not available in the U.S.) and 5 GHz bands in Japan. In 2002, the Japanese government published new rules opening up frequency ranges in these bands that had not been available at the time of 802.11's original ratification. This amendment has little effect on 802.11 networks outside of Japan since those regulatory domains are already covered under 802.11 standards that existed prior to 802.11j.

802.11d Supplement

The 802.11d amendment modifies the 802.11 MAC layer to allow FHSS stations to fine-tune their physical-layer parameters to comply with the rules of the country in which the network is being used. The original 802.11 standard was written with FCC regulations in mind, but many countries around the world have different requirements for FHSS transmitters. 802.11d defines a field that an FHSS AP can optionally add to its beacons. That field tells the stations associated with the AP what channels (frequency ranges), hopping patterns, and power output they are allowed to use.

The intent of 802.11d is that FHSS stations can dynamically choose parameters that comply with the regulatory domain in which the station is being used, instead of forcing manufacturers to sell different cards and access points for each regulatory domain. Given the general decline in the use of 802.11 FHSS transmitters since 801.11b and 802.11g's release, 802.11d is not considered one of the major 802.11 standards.

802.11s Supplement

When it is ratified, the 802.11s amendment will define standards for automatically forming mesh networks with 802.11 access points. A mesh is a network in which each node has direct connections to many other nodes in the network. Mesh networks offer high reliability since there may be many paths through the network from one node to another. If one node becomes unavailable, packets can just take a path through a different node. As this statement implies, dynamic routing is one of the characteristics of a wireless mesh network.

Currently 802.11 networks are not mesh networks, since a single AP usually connects either to a shared wired LAN or to other APs in a point-to-point link. APs in "repeater mode" could be used to create a pseudo-mesh network in which packets are forwarded wirelessly from AP to AP, but this network would not truly be a mesh network since each repeater-mode AP would link to just one root-mode AP. Additionally, the network would not have the ability to dynamically find the best route through the network.

The 802.11s committee first met in September 2004, and its first call for proposals was in January 2005. At the time of this printing, 802.11s is in very preliminary stages.

Clause Summary

Since it is common to refer to both the 802.11 supplement number (802.11a, 802.11b, etc.) and the clause number of the 802.11 standard that defines the PHY, here is a summary table to help you remember these.

FIGURE 8.4   Summary of IEEE 802.11 Standard Clauses

Clause 14	Defines an FHSS PHY in the 2.4 GHz ISM band using data rates of 1 and 2 Mbps. Clause 14 was part of the original 802.11–1999 standard.
Clause 15	Defines a DSSS PHY in the 2.4 GHz ISM band using data rates of 1 and 2 Mbps. This PHY is essentially obsolete today, having been superseded by Clause 18. Clause 15 was part of the original 802.11–1999 standard.
Clause 16	Defines an Infrared PHY using data rates of 1 and 2 Mbps. This PHY is essentially obsolete. Clause 16 was part of the original 802.11–1999 standard.
Clause 17	Defines an OFDM PHY in the 5 GHz UNII bands, at data rates of 6, 9, 12, 18, 24, 36, 48, and 54 Mbps. Clause 17 is defined in the 802.11a supplement.
Clause 18	Defines a DSSS PHY in the 2.4 GHz ISM band using data rates of 1, 2, 5.5, and 11 Mbps. Interoperates with clause 15 and clause 19 PHYs. Clause 18 is defined in the 802.11b supplement.
Clause 19	Defines several PHYs, including an OFDM PHY in the 2.4 GHz ISM band using data rates of 6, 9, 12, 18, 24, 36, 48, and 54 Mbps. Other PHYs defined in Clause 19 are intended to provide interoperability with Clause 15, 17, and 18 stations. Clause 19 is defined in the 802.11g supplement.

Wi-Fi® Alliance

The Wi-Fi Alliance promotes and tests for wireless LAN interoperability of 802.11b, 802.11a, and 802.11g devices. The Wi-Fi Alliance's mission is to certify interoperability of Wi-Fi (IEEE 802.11) products and to promote Wi-Fi as the global wireless LAN standard across all market segments. The Wi-Fi Alliance's primary task is to certify that devices compatibly implement the 802.11 standards released by the IEEE.

When a product meets the interoperability requirements as described in the Wi-Fi Alliance's test matrix, the Wi-Fi Alliance grants the product a certification of interoperability which allows the vendor to use the Wi-Fi logo on advertising and packaging for the certified product. Wi-Fi certification assures the end-user of a certain basic level of interoperability with other wireless LAN devices from other vendors that also bear the Wi-Fi logo. The Wi-Fi Interoperability Certificate, shown in Figure 8.5 indicates which technologies (802.11b, g, and/or a) the device is certified to work with, and which security and multimedia standards it complies with.

FIGURE 8.5   Wi-Fi, WPA, WPA2, & WMM Certification

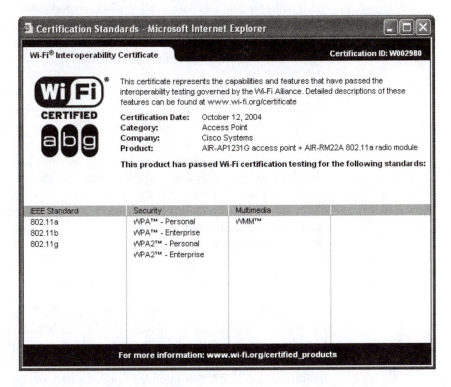

Wi-Fi Protected Access (WPA™)

In October 2002, the Wi-Fi Alliance announced that a new solution to counteract the weaknesses in WEP would be included in all Wi-Fi branded products starting in early 2003. The IEEE was working on an answer to WEP's weakness – 802.11i – but the Wi-Fi Alliance felt that the IEEE solution would take too long to be released. The Wi-Fi Alliance's solution was WPA.

WPA can be thought of as a "snapshot" of the incomplete 802.11i standard. Usually when vendors release products based on incomplete versions of standards, the products are not compatible with each other. WPA provided a touchstone that vendors could use to ensure that their pre-802.11i products would work together.

WPA (Wi-Fi Protected Access) included both TKIP and 802.1X with EAP authentication as part of all Wi-Fi certified devices starting in early 2003. WPA was and is a valuable solution that immediately brings increased security to home and business wireless networks by protecting against the vulnerabilities inherent with WEP.

WPA has two distinct modes: WPA and WPA-PSK. WPA mode requires a RADIUS server for user authentication, such as might be found in an enterprise environment. Realizing that SOHO installations probably wouldn't have a RADIUS server (they can be expensive, and their complexity may be unnecessary in a small network), the Wi-Fi Alliance also defined "pre-shared key" (PSK) mode. In PSK mode, a text string known as a "key" is configured in all stations. This key is similar to a WEP key in that it is static and manually configured, but the WPA key is used as the seed for a much more robust encryption mechanism than WEP. This offers WPA users a compromise between WEP's simple configuration and WPA's security. WPA and WPA-PSK mode are based upon equivalent modes in the 802.11i standard.

After the 802.11i amendment was ratified, the Wi-Fi Alliance introduced the WPA2™ certification. Whereas WPA was based on a pre-release version of 802.11i, WPA2 certifies that devices are compatible with the final version of 802.11i. Although WPA devices are still being manufactured, WPA was intended only as a temporary solution, and it should eventually be made obsolete by WPA2. At the time of this printing, devices that support 802.11i are relatively rare, and devices that have been certified as WPA2 compliant are rarer still. Therefore, there is currently no real guarantee of cross-vendor interoperability for 802.11i devices. This will change as time passes and 802.11i becomes more established in the marketplace.

Wi-Fi Multimedia (WMM)

Wi-Fi Multimedia™ is a certification based on a subset of the features described in the 802.11e draft standard, similar to the way that WPA was based on a preliminary version of 802.11i. 802.11i described QoS (quality of service) extensions to 802.11 to allow it to better support multimedia applications like streaming video and VoIP. 802.11e and WMM are described in more detail in chapter 10, "MAC and Physical Layers."

The website for the Wi-Fi Alliance is www.wi-fi.com

Key Terms

Before taking the exam, you should be familiar with the following terms:

1:1 rule

3:1 rule

802.11a

802.11b

802.11g

FCC

IEEE

ISM bands (915 MHz, 2.4 GHz, and 5.8 GHz)

license-free bands

point-to-multipoint

point-to-point

UNII bands (low, middle, and high)

Wi-Fi Alliance

WPA / WPA2 / WMM

Review Questions

1. Explain in your own words what the roles of the FCC, IEEE, and Wi-Fi Alliance are, and how these three organizations dictate the direction of the wireless LAN industry.

2. Explain the differences – both technically and in regulatory terms – between the UNII and ISM bands that are used in WLAN technologies today.

3. What are the FCC regulations for PtP and PtMP systems in UNII and ISM bands? During a wireless LAN implementation, when should these regulations come into consideration?

4. Name all the IEEE amendments (clauses) and recommended practices, and give a one sentence summary that describes the intent of each clause. For example, "802.11b – specifies DSSS systems that operate at 1, 2, 5.5, and 11 Mbps."

5. Name and explain the three different product certifications offered by the Wi-Fi Alliance, and explain why each is important to the wireless LAN industry.

802.11 Network Architecture

CWNA Exam Objectives Covered:

❖ Identify methods described in the 802.11 standard for locating, joining, and maintaining connectivity with an 802.11 wireless LAN

❖ Identify methods described in the 802.11 standard for locating, joining, and maintaining connectivity with an 802.11 wireless LAN

- Active Scanning (Probes)
- Passive Scanning (Beacons)

❖ Summarize the processes involved in authentication and association

- The 802.11 State Machine
- Open System and Shared Key Authentication
- Association, Reassociation, and Disassociation
- De-authentication

❖ Define, describe, and apply the following concepts associated with wireless LAN service sets

- BSS & BSSID
- ESS & ESSID / SSID
- IBSS
- Roaming
- Infrastructure Mode
- Ad Hoc Mode

❖ Explain and apply the following power management features of wireless LANs

- Power Saving Mode

In This Chapter

The Basic Service Set

Locating a wireless LAN

Joining a wireless LAN

The Distribution System

Roaming

Power Management Features

- Active Mode
- TIM / DTIM / ATIM

This chapter covers some of the key concepts of the 802.11 network architecture. Most of the topics in this chapter are defined directly in the 802.11–1999 base standard and are required for implementation of 802.11-compliant hardware. In this chapter, we are going to examine the process by which clients connect to an access point, the terms used for organizing wireless LANs, and how power management is accomplished in wireless LAN client devices.

Without a solid understanding of the principles covered in this chapter, it would be quite difficult to design, administer, or troubleshoot a wireless LAN. This chapter holds some of the most elementary steps of both wireless LAN design and administration. As you administer wireless LANs, the understanding of these concepts will allow you to more intelligently manage your day-to-day operations.

The Basic Service Set

The Basic Service Set (BSS) is the fundamental building block of an 802.11 network. The first type of BSS is an *independent* basic service set (IBSS), used to create an ad hoc network. An IBSS consists of one or more 802.11 stations that are within mutual communication range of each other. In other words, every station in the IBSS can "hear" every other station in the IBSS. This is required because an IBSS doesn't have an access point to forward frames between stations, so each station has to be capable of sending data directly to every other station in the IBSS. An IBSS is typically set up only for a short period of time and is not typically used in corporate installations.

FIGURE 9.1   An Independent Basic Service Set

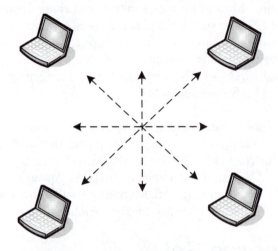

The second type of BSS, an *infrastructure* basic service set (this would also have the acronym "IBSS" except that acronym is already taken so we just say "BSS"), is more commonly used in permanent installations. An infrastructure BSS consists of one or more access points with zero or more client stations within communications range. Access points forward frames between stations in a BSS and also may forward frames between the wireless network and a wired network, though this functionality is not a requirement to be an access point.

FIGURE 9.2   An Infrastructure Basic Service Set

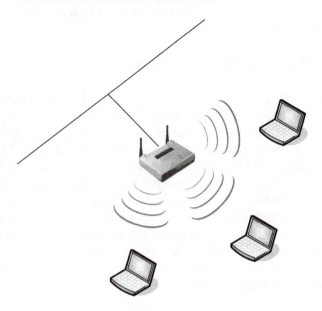

In the wired world, you must connect a Cat5 cable to a switch to become part of the Ethernet network. In wireless LANs, being *associated* to a BSS is the functional equivalent. Simply being within proximity of an access point is not enough to make a station a member of the BSS. The station must go through a process called "association," through which it formally requests to join the BSS and is accepted into the BSS. Stations can't send data within the BSS unless they are properly associated (actually they can transmit all they want but the frames will be ignored). The concept of association applies equally to both BSS and IBSS networks. Association is important because physical proximity is easy to come by in a wireless LAN. We do not want an attacker to gain access to the network just because he can get close to the AP, nor do we want a station that happens to be within range of more than one AP to be confused about which AP the station should connect to.

Basic Service Set Identifier

A BSS is identified by a 48-bit hexadecimal value called the BSS Identifier, or BSSID. An infrastructure mode BSS can only have one access point; therefore, the MAC address of the access point is a unique identifier for the BSS and is used as the BSSID. An IBSS doesn't have an access point, so the first station of an IBSS makes up a random 48-bit value to act as the BSSID.

Extended Service Set Identifier

One of the advantages of 802.11 is the ability to roam between different access points without losing your network connection as you move. Therefore, the 802.11 standard provides the ability to group basic service sets together into an *extended service set* (ESS). An ESS consists of two or more BSSs that share the same *service set identifier* (SSID). An SSID is a unique, case sensitive, alphanumeric value from 2–32 characters long. The administrator configures the SSID in each access point, and users may configure the SSID within their client device. Security mechanisms aside, when the SSID is properly configured (matching) on the client and AP, a client should be able to roam between access points within a single ESS. We use the word *should* because, as we have discussed earlier, interoperability problems may arise.

FIGURE 9.3   Two BSSs forming an ESS (both access points would be configured with the same SSID)

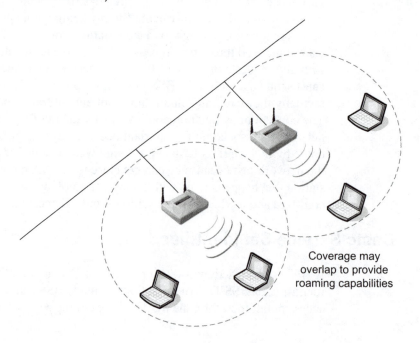

Coverage may overlap to provide roaming capabilities

The SSID is used to control the access points with which a station can associate. A station should not attempt to associate with an access point unless the station and the AP share the same SSID. Likewise, an access point should reject association attempts from stations that do not have the same SSID as the access point. Clients also may have the ability to use a special "null" SSID value known as the "any SSID," which indicates that they would like to associate with any access point within range regardless of the access point's SSID. Access points may be configured to accept clients using the "any SSID" or not. Configuring the AP to reject clients using the "any SSID" adds only a small amount of security, since the SSID is regularly transmitted onto the network in a variety of frame types. An intruder with a packet capture application can quickly learn the SSID of a wireless network. In some cases a station may be configured with multiple SSIDs. In these cases the station will associate with whichever SSID it finds first, or it may be configured to give certain SSIDs priority. Regardless, a single station can be associated with only one BSS at a time.

Do not confuse the ESSID with the BSSID. The Basic Service Set Identifier is a 6-byte hexadecimal number identifying a single BSS, whereas the ESSID denotes a group of BSSs sharing a common SSID within which a station can roam seamlessly.

Locating a Wireless LAN

When an 802.11 client such as a USB adapter or PCMCIA card starts up, the client first attempts to discover if there is a BSS within range. This process of discovery is called *scanning*. Scanning occurs before any other process, since scanning is how the client *finds* the BSS. Scanning involves three types of frames: beacons, probe requests, and probe responses.

Beacons

Beacons are frames sent from the access point to stations (in infrastructure networks) or station-to-station (in ad hoc networks) in order to organize and synchronize communication within the BSS. Beacons serve several functions, including those discussed in the sections following.

Time Synchronization

Each beacon contains a timestamp value placed there by the access point. When stations receive the beacon, they change their clock to reflect the time of the clock on the access point. Once this change is made to the client stations, the two clocks are synchronized. Synchronizing the clocks of communicating stations ensures that all time-sensitive functions, such as hopping in FHSS systems, are performed without error. The beacon also contains the beacon interval which informs stations how often to expect the beacon. Note that this time synchronization is an 802.11 function. The beacon does not reset the O/S's system clock.

FH or DS Parameter Sets

Beacons contain information specifically geared to the PHY or PHYs the service set is using. For example, in an FHSS service set, hop and dwell time parameters and hop sequence are included in the beacon. In a DSSS system, the beacon would contain channel information.

SSID Information

Beacons are one place where the SSID of the wireless network may be found. In most access points this announcement can be disabled, making it slightly more difficult for an attacker to learn the network's SSID. For example, if "SSID broadcast" is disabled, Windows XP will show that a wireless network has been found but will simply show a blank line in the "wireless networks" dialog box. Some people mistakenly believe that turning off "SSID broadcast" disables beacons entirely, which is not true. As you can see from this section, beacons do a lot more than just announce the SSID. If an access point stopped sending beacons, the stations in the BSS would assume that the access point had gone down and would lose their network connection.

Traffic Indication Map (TIM)

The TIM is used an as indicator of which stations operating in power-save mode have packets queued at the access point. This information is passed in each beacon to all non-dozing stations. While operating in power-save mode, synchronized stations power up their receivers, listen for the beacon, check the TIM to see if they are listed; then if they are not listed, they power down their receivers and resume dozing. This process is covered in more detail later in the chapter.

Supported Rates

With wireless networks, there are many supported speeds, depending on the PHY of the hardware in use. For example, an 802.11b compliant device supports 11, 5.5, 2, and 1 Mbps speeds. This rate information is passed in the beacons to inform the stations what speeds are supported on the access point. There is more information passed within beacons, but this list covers most things that could be considered important from an administrator's point of view.

Passive Scanning

Passive scanning is the process of listening for beacons on each channel for a specific period of time. These beacons are sent by access points (infrastructure networks) or client stations (ad hoc networks), and the scanning station catalogs characteristics about each BSS based on the beacons it hears. The station searching for a network listens for beacons until it hears a beacon containing the SSID of a network to which it has been configured to associate. The station then attempts to join the BSS using the access point that sent the beacon. Passive scanning is illustrated in Figure 9.4.

FIGURE 9.4 Passive Scanning

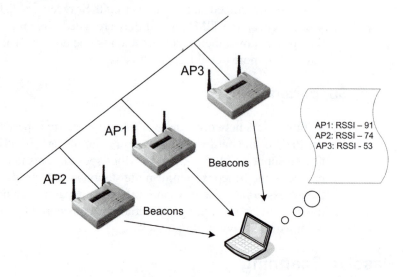

In configurations in which multiple access points form an ESS, each access point in the network will be configured for the same SSID. If the station is in a location where it can hear more than one AP broadcasting the SSID it wishes to use, it will attempt to associate with the access point with the best RSSI value (which is usually a combination value of something like highest signal strength and lowest bit error rate). Received Signal Strength Indicator (RSSI) is a combination value unique to each vendor but used in the same basic way by each of them. The RSSI value is made up of many variables such as signal strength, bit error rate, signal to noise ratio, etc. Other vendor-specific factors may determine the AP to which the station tries to associate.

Active Scanning

Active scanning involves the sending of a probe request frame from a client station to an access point. Stations send this probe frame when they are actively seeking a network to join. The probe request frame contains either the SSID of the network that the station wishes to join or the field may be null, meaning "any SSID." If a probe request is sent specifying an SSID, then only basic service sets that are servicing that specific SSID will respond with a probe response frame. If a probe request frame is sent with the "any SSID," all access points within range should respond with a probe response frame unless they have been configured to ignore the "any SSID." Ignoring the "any SSID" is contrary to the 802.11 standard, but it is common for vendors to implement this functionality as a security precaution. Once a BSS with the proper SSID is found, the station initiates authentication and association, which are the next steps of joining the BSS. Active scanning is illustrated in Figure 9.5.

FIGURE 9.5   Active Scanning

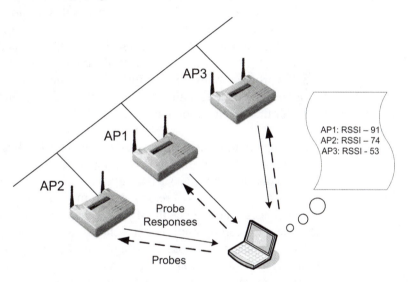

The information passed from the access point to the station in probe response frames is almost identical to that of beacons. Probe response frames differ from beacons only in that they do not include a Traffic Indication Map (TIM).

If a station receives beacons or probe responses from multiple access points, it can use various criteria to choose one with which to associate (remember that a station can be associated with only one access point at a time). Signal strength and quality are characteristics used by many manufacturers to decide which access point clients should connect to. Some vendors implement proprietary extensions that allow their stations to make more informed decisions. For example, the access point might include in its beacons or probe responses the number of stations that are currently associated to it. In that case, the station could choose the access point with the fewest stations when all other factors are equal. The

802.11 standard defines a way that vendors can implement these proprietary extensions without breaking compatibility with stations that do not understand the extensions. The non-compatible station will not be able to take advantage of the extra information in the proprietary extension, but it will still be able to use the standard parts of the beacon in standard ways.

Active scanning is much faster than passive scanning. Typically, an AP sends a beacon every 100 ms, which means that a station performing passive scanning would have to listen on each channel for a up to 100 ms to see if there was an AP on that channel. With 11 channels, it would take 1.1 seconds to scan all channels. With active scanning, the station knows that the probe response should follow very quickly after the probe request, so it does not have to wait very long at all on each channel to determine whether there's an AP on that channel.

Active scanning is the primary method that 802.11a/b/g stations use to find access points. In fact, it is common to see a station continue to send probe requests every few seconds even after it has successfully associated with an AP. Stations will reassociate from a weak access point to a stronger access point once the signal strength from the weak access point goes below a certain minimum threshold. By continuing to scan even after the station is successfully associated, the station can maintain a list of all APs that are currently in the area around it in case it has to roam. For this reason it is appropriate to have approximately 20–30 percent overlap between access point cells. This overlap allows stations to learn of a nearby AP before they completely lose connection with their current AP. Stations can then seamlessly roam between access points without the user's knowledge.

Joining a Wireless LAN

The process of joining, or connecting to, an infrastructure wireless LAN consists of two separate sub-processes. These sub-processes always occur in the same order and are called *authentication* and *association*. Keep in mind that when we speak of association, we are speaking of Layer 2 connectivity, and authentication pertains directly to the radio PC card, not to the user.

Authentication

The first step in connecting to a wireless LAN is authentication. Authentication is the process through which a station verifies that another station has permission to talk to it. In an infrastructure network, all clients authenticate with the access point, whereas in an ad-hoc network all clients authenticate individually with the station to which they are transmitting a frame. For the rest of this section, we will consider the case of authentication in an infrastructure network, since that is by far the most common case. Ad-hoc authentication uses exactly the same frames as infrastructure authentication, except that the frames go between two clients instead of between a client and an access point.

Authentication Methods

The IEEE 802.11-1999 (R2003) standard specifies two methods of authentication: *Open System authentication* and *Shared Key authentication.* In the following sections we will discuss each authentication process specified by the 802.11 standard, how they work, and why each is used.

Open System Authentication

The 802.11 standard requires that authentication occur before the station can successfully send data through the access point, but not every administrator wants to require users to have a password in order to access the network. What about a hotspot operator? What about a person who wants to share his or her broadband connection? For these types of situations, the 802.11 standard specifies Open System authentication. Open System authentication is a method of "authenticating without really authenticating." A station using Open System authentication can go through the (required) motions of authentication without needing the user to enter any kind of key or password. If an access point uses Open System authentication, a station can associate with that access point based only on knowing the access point's SSID. A client should not attempt to authenticate with an access point that has a different SSID than the client.

Open System Authentication Process

The Open System authentication process occurs as follows:

1. The client sends an authentication frame to the access point, indicating that the client seeks Open System authentication. The AP sends an acknowledgement (ACK).

2. The access point sends an authentication frame to the client indicating a positive response, and the client becomes authenticated. The client sends an ACK.

FIGURE 9.6   Open System Authentication

No	M	Time	Delta	CH	Len	S	🔴	Source	Dest	Summary
10		5/5 20:53:51.449511	3.540251	1	30	48	1	Netgear:66:E5:F1	00:0D:ED:A5:4F:70	802.11 authentication
11		5/5 20:53:51.449822	3.540562	1	10	73	1		Netgear:66:E5:F1	802.11 acknowledgement
12		5/5 20:53:51.450089	3.540829	1	30	73	11	00:0D:ED:A5:4F:70	Netgear:66:E5:F1	802.11 authentication
13		5/5 20:53:51.450297	3.541037	1	10	81	11		00:0D:ED:A5:4F:70	802.11 acknowledgement
14		5/5 20:53:51.451488	3.542228	1	69	51	1	Netgear:66:E5:F1	00:0D:ED:A5:4F:70	802.11 association request
15		5/5 20:53:51.451798	3.542538	1	10	71	1		Netgear:66:E5:F1	802.11 acknowledgement
16		5/5 20:53:51.452242	3.542982	1	80	76	11	00:0D:ED:A5:4F:70	Netgear:66:E5:F1	802.11 association response
17		5/5 20:53:51.452352	3.543092	1	10	81	11		00:0D:ED:A5:4F:70	802.11 acknowledgement

This process is considered a null authentication and no identity check occurs. An AP configured to use Open System authentication will always respond positively to authentication requests. Open System authentication is a very simple process. You have the option of using encryption, also known as frame protection, with Open System authentication. If frame protection is used with the Open System authentication process, there is still no verification of the client's identity during the authentication phase. Rather, the WEP key is used only for encrypting data once the client is connected (associated).

Open System authentication allows anyone to access an 802.11 system for cases where that is desired (such as a hotspot). Most 802.11-compliant wireless LAN hardware is configured to use Open System authentication by default, making it easy to get started building and connecting your wireless LAN right out of the box (this is a choice of manufacturers, not a requirement of the 802.11 standard).

Open System authentication is also used when the administrator has decided to use 802.1X/EAP, WPA, or WPA/802.11i authentication, instead of WEP. The WPA or 802.1X frames are simply "data" to the 802.11 MAC layer. This means that when WPA or 802.1X is used, the station will need to get through the 802.11 authentication and association before it can proceed with the WPA or 802.1X authentication. Therefore, stations using WPA or 802.1X authentication always use Open System authentication so that they can commence with the network authentication as soon as possible.

Shared Key Authentication

Shared Key authentication uses the WEP key to authenticate the station; therefore, Shared Key authentication requires that a WEP key be configured in both the client and the AP. These keys must match on both sides for WEP to work properly. Shared Key authentication uses WEP keys in two fashions as we will describe here.

The authentication process using Shared Key authentication occurs as follows:

1. A client requests authentication to an access point: this step is the same as that of Open System authentication except that the authentication frame indicates that the station will use Shared Key authentication instead of Open System. The AP sends an ACK.

2. The access point issues a challenge to the client: this challenge is randomly generated plain text which is sent in a second authentication frame from the access point to the client. The client sends an ACK.

3. The client responds to the challenge: the client responds by copying the challenge text into a third authentication frame and sending it back to the access point, but encrypting the frame with its WEP key. The AP sends an ACK.

4. The access point responds to the client's response: the access point decrypts the third authentication frame and compares the challenge text found there to the original challenge text. If they match, then the client must possess the same WEP key as the AP. If the client encrypted the text properly, the access point will respond positively in a fourth authentication frame and authenticate the client. If the text is not correctly encrypted, the access point will respond negatively and not authenticate the client. The client sends an ACK.

FIGURE 9.7   Shared Key Authentication

No	M	Time	Delta	CH	Len	S	🌼	Source	Dest	Summary
87		6/24 23:54:43.512430	6.512430	1	30	83	1	00:0C:30:52:93:6A	00:0D:ED:A5:4F:70	802.11 authentication
88		6/24 23:54:43.512730	6.512730	1	10	71	1		00:0C:30:52:93:6A	802.11 acknowledgement
89		6/24 23:54:43.513395	6.513395	1	160	61	11	00:0D:ED:A5:4F:70	00:0C:30:52:93:6A	802.11 authentication
90		6/24 23:54:43.513601	6.513601	1	10	83	11		00:0D:ED:A5:4F:70	802.11 acknowledgement
91		6/24 23:54:43.515249	6.515249	1	168	81	1	00:0C:30:52:93:6A	00:0D:ED:A5:4F:70	802.11 authentication
92		6/24 23:54:43.515555	6.515555	1	10	60	1		00:0C:30:52:93:6A	802.11 acknowledgement
93		6/24 23:54:43.515829	6.515829	1	30	61	11	00:0D:ED:A5:4F:70	00:0C:30:52:93:6A	802.11 authentication
94		6/24 23:54:43.516037	6.516037	1	10	81	11		00:0D:ED:A5:4F:70	802.11 acknowledgement
95		6/24 23:54:43.517081	6.517081	1	83	83	1	00:0C:30:52:93:6A	00:0D:ED:A5:4F:70	802.11 association request
96		6/24 23:54:43.517390	6.517390	1	10	60	1		00:0C:30:52:93:6A	802.11 acknowledgement
97		6/24 23:54:43.517834	6.517834	1	80	60	11	00:0D:ED:A5:4F:70	00:0C:30:52:93:6A	802.11 association response
98		6/24 23:54:43.517948	6.517948	1	10	83	11		00:0D:ED:A5:4F:70	802.11 acknowledgement

The authentication behaviors described in this chapter are the basic behaviors defined in the original 802.11 standard. Today Shared Key authentication and WEP encryption are considered to be inadequate for even small networks, given that WEP is easily crackable and that much stronger and equally simple alternatives are available, such as 802.1X/EAP, WPA, and WPA2/802.11i. These and other advanced security methods are covered in chapter 12.

Association

Once a wireless client has been authenticated the client may then attempt to *associate* with the access point. *Associated* is the state at which a client is a member of a particular infrastructure BSS. The process of association involves only four frames. The client sends an association request frame to the access point, which replies to the client with an association response frame, either allowing or disallowing association. Each of these two frames is followed by an ACK. Association request and association response are two types of 802.11 management frames.

If a station authenticates successfully, the station will usually associate successfully as well. Although there are some compatibility issues that could prevent a station from successfully associating, the station will usually be able to figure out from the access point's beacons whether any of those issues exist and will not attempt to associate with an AP unless the station believes that the association will be successful.

802.11 State Machine

The 802.11 state machine has three distinct states:

- Unauthenticated and Unassociated
- Authenticated and Unassociated
- Authenticated and Associated

Unauthenticated and Unassociated

In this initial state, the client is completely disconnected from the network and unable to pass frames through the access point. Access points keep a table of client connection statuses known as the association table. It is important to note that different vendors refer to the unauthenticated and unassociated state in their access points' association tables differently. This table may show "unauthenticated" for any client that has not completed the authentication process or has attempted authentication and failed. A client that has not completed authentication may not be shown in the authentication table at all.

Authenticated and Unassociated

In this second state, the client has passed the authentication process but is not yet associated with (connected to) the access point. The client is not yet allowed to send or receive data through the access point. The access point's association table will typically show "authenticated." Because clients pass the authentication stage and immediately proceed into the association stage very quickly (milliseconds), rarely do you see the "authenticated" step on the access point. It is far more likely that you will see "unauthenticated" or "associated."

However there is one situation in which a station may be authenticated without being associated. Stations can only be associated with a single AP but they can authenticate with as many APs as they like. If a station is within range of several APs, the station might choose to authenticate with more than one of the APs so that, if necessary, it could roam to another AP with minimal delay. In this case, the client would be authenticated (sometimes called "pre-authenticated") and yet still unassociated with those APs.

Authenticated and Associated

In this final state, the wireless node is completely connected to the network and able to send and receive data through the access point to which the node is associated. Figure 9.8 illustrates a client associating with an access point. You will likely see "Associated" in the access point's association table, denoting that this client is fully connected and authorized to pass traffic through the access point.

FIGURE 9.8   Association Table

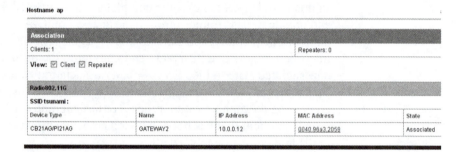

Hostname ap				
Association				
Clients: 1			Repeaters: 0	
View: ☑ Client ☑ Repeater				
Radio802.11G				
SSID tsunami :				
Device Type	Name	IP Address	MAC Address	State
CB21AG/PI21AG	GATEWAY2	10.0.0.12	0040.96a3.2058	Associated

The Distribution System

The Distribution System (DS) is the architectural component that connects individual BSSs into an ESS. The DS includes Distribution System Services (DSS) typically implemented as software in access points and a logical Distribution System Medium (DSM) across which access points communicate with each other. As such, the distribution system is critical to roaming (discussed in the next section). The 802.11 standard does not define the details of the distribution system, only that it must provide certain services, such as tracking which stations are associated with which access points, and which access points are on the network. This somewhat vague specification leaves you with significant flexibility in implementing the distribution system in the manner that best fits the network.

Ethernet as a Distribution System Medium

Ethernet is by far the most common network used as a distribution system. Nearly all access points come with Ethernet uplink ports and no other. When implementing an Ethernet distribution system medium, it is important to make sure that the uplink speed of the Ethernet port is greater than the maximum throughput of the wireless network. In other words, make sure that the switch port is in 100 Mbps full-duplex mode, not 10 Mbps mode. Given the speed of the Ethernet network, it is also possible for data from the distribution system to overwhelm an 802.11a, b, or g access point. If this situation occurs, the AP will buffer the frames, but once the AP's buffer is full, frames will be dropped. If this is the case, it may be helpful to implement traffic shaping or flow control in the switch or an enterprise gateway.

Powerline Networking as a Distribution System Medium

Powerline networking is a standard that allows for the transmission of network data over standard home power lines. Powerline-to-Ethernet bridges can connect an 802.11 access point to a remote Ethernet network in cases where AC power to the remote site *is* available, but Ethernet cabling *is not* available. Powerline-to-802.11 bridges are also available with integrated access points, meaning that you plug the device directly into the wall and you instantly have an AP that connects back to the main network over the power lines. You would need a powerline-to-Ethernet bridge back at the main site to connect the powerline AP back into the main Ethernet network.

FIGURE 9.9   Wireless Networking with a Powerline Distribution System (NetGear WGXB102)

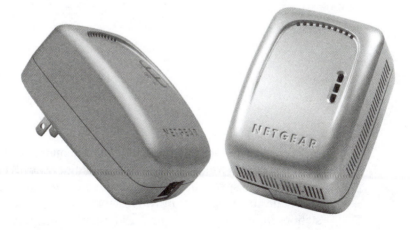

Powerline networking has data rates of approximately 14 Mbps, meaning that it is appropriate for 802.11b, but it would provide limited capacity 802.11g networking. In addition, the characteristics of the local AC lines significantly affect the throughput and frame corruption rates that can be achieved. Noisy lines and excessive distances can drop data rates from 14 Mbps to something significantly less. Nevertheless, powerline networking can provide network access in areas that would otherwise be difficult or impossible to wire.

Roaming

Roaming is the ability of a wireless client to move seamlessly from one BSS to another without losing network connectivity. Access points hand the client off from one to another in a way that is invisible to the user, ensuring continuous network connectivity. Figure 9.10 illustrates a client roaming from one BSS to another BSS.

FIGURE 9.10   Roaming in an ESS

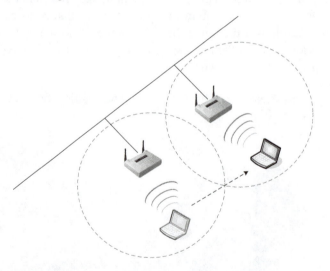

When roaming is seamless, a session can be maintained while moving from one basic service area to another. Multiple access points can provide wireless roaming coverage for an entire building or campus. When the coverage areas of two or more access points overlap, the stations in the overlapping areas can establish the best possible connection with one of the access points while continuously searching for the next-best access point. When the signal from the current access point gets below a certain threshold, the station can immediately request reassociation to the next-best access point. In order to frame retransmission during roaming, the "old" and "new" access points communicate to coordinate the handoff process.

Standards

The 802.11 standard does not define the protocol that should be used between the two access points when a client roams. The 802.11 standard does define the frames that should be sent between the client and the second access point when the client roams. This vagary in the standard has led to many different vendor-specific implementations of roaming protocols, with the effect that stations usually could not roam seamlessly between access points from two different vendors. The 802.11F recommended practice which defines the Inter-Access-Point Protocol (IAPP) addresses this issue.

It is important to distinguish between "seamless" roaming and just "roaming." Two access points that are capable of providing "seamless" roaming will hand the client off in such a way that no frames are dropped. If two access points coordinate this process and work together to hand over the client, it is likely that the client can still move between them by sending a reassociation request to the second. In this case, there is no guarantee that the first AP will immediately learn of the new association and no guarantee that the first AP will forward buffered frames by way of the second AP. In addition, the client might have a different IP address on the new access point, causing it to lose all of its active IP conversations. This type of roaming is referred to as just "roaming."

Reassociation

Reassociation is the process by which a station moves its association from one access point to another. Each vendor's drivers have unique qualities under which a station will attempt reassociation but signal strength to the current access point is one common factor. Many vendors have created proprietary extensions to 802.11 that allow the access point to report additional information, such as the number of associated stations and the average throughput through the access point, giving clients even more information from which to make their association decision. The 802.11 standard allows for these extensions and stations that do not understand the extensions will simply ignore them.

Regardless of the specific qualities that factor into the decision, at some point the client will decide that the current access point is not the "best" access point for it to be associated with, and attempt reassociation with a "better" access point. The process of reassociation works as follows:

1. The client sends a reassociation request frame to the access point to which it wants to move its association. Call this access point the "new" access point. A reassociation request is a specific type of 802.11 management frame. The reassociation request includes the BSSID to which the station is currently associated, which is the same as the MAC address of the access point to which the station is currently associated. Call this access point the "old" access point.

2. The "new" access point uses proprietary protocols (or IAPP, if it supports 802.11F) to contact the "old" access point through the distribution system medium, which is usually an Ethernet network. The "new" access point notifies the "old" access point that the client is attempting to associate to it.

3. The "old" access point acknowledges the new association again over the distribution system medium using proprietary protocols or IAPP.

4. The "new" access point sends a reassociation response frame to the client over the 802.11 network. If reassociation is successful, the station's association will have been moved to the "new" access point. The client does *not* need to send a disassociation frame to the "old" access point since reassociation moves the station's association from one AP to the other within the DS.

FIGURE 9.11   Reassociation Process

26	5/7 20:13:41.840229	3.738712	1	30	83	1	00:0C:30:52:93:6A	Aironet:3A:6A:C7	802.11 authentication
27	5/7 20:13:41.840541	3.739024	1	10	81	1		00:0C:30:52:93:6A	802.11 acknowledgement
28	5/7 20:13:42.058855	3.957338	1	30	83	11	Aironet:3A:6A:C7	00:0C:30:52:93:6A	802.11 authentication
29	5/7 20:13:42.059062	3.957545	1	10	80	11		Aironet:3A:6A:C7	802.11 acknowledgement
30	5/7 20:13:42.060165	3.958643	1	88	78	1	00:0C:30:52:93:6A	Aironet:3A:6A:C7	802.11 reassociation request
31	5/7 20:13:42.060477	3.958960	1	10	85	1		00:0C:30:52:93:6A	802.11 acknowledgement
32	5/7 20:13:42.073595	3.972078	1	92	85	11	Aironet:3A:6A:C7	00:0C:30:52:93:6A	802.11 reassociation response

There are however, several ways that reassociation can go wrong. First, the "new" access point might not allow the station to associate to it. In this case, steps 2 and 3 won't occur. The process will skip right from step 1 to step 4 and the reassociation response will indicate failure. Note that, even though reassociation failed, the station still has its existing association to the "old" access point. No data has been lost.

What if the communication between the "new" and the "old" access point fails? Such a situation might happen if the two APs are from different vendors and don't support 802.11F. This situation might also occur if the APs are in a different ESS from each other, such as if they are separated by a router. It would be possible for vendors to program access points to create a distribution system through a router, but most vendors do not. Therefore, two access points need to be on the same IP subnet if you want clients to be able to roam seamlessly between them. In this case, the "new" AP will eventually time out after step 2 and send the station back a failed reassociation response. Again, nothing has been lost since the station still has its existing association with the "old" AP.

What if, after the station has roamed to the "new" AP, the backbone Ethernet switch continues to send packets to the "old" AP? This situation will happen until the station sends frames through the "new" AP, updating the switch's CAM (content addressable memory) table. Some access points anticipate this issue and resolve it by having the "new" access point spoof a frame from the client as soon as the client roams, which forces the switch's CAM table to update.

802.11F (IAPP) Summary

802.11F defines IAPP (Inter-Access-Point Protocol), which creates a recommended method of implementing the distribution system's roaming functionality. Clients will be able to reassociate between access points that support 802.11F regardless of whether the access points are from the same vendor or not.

IAPP describes three protocol sequences:

- Adding a station's information after the station associates
- Moving a station's information after the station reassociates

- A caching action that, while technically not necessary, improves the performance of IAPP when a station reassociates

The 802.11F recommended practice defines the format and sequence of the frames that should be used during these three actions.

The "Add" sequence occurs after a station associates with an AP. First, the AP sends an IAPP "ADD-notify" message onto the distribution system. This message is carried in an IP packet that is sent to a layer 2 and layer 3 multicast address that only other IAPP stations will recognize. The ADD-notify message contains the MAC address of the station that has just associated. Any AP that receives the notification message removes the station's MAC address from its association table. Remember that a station is only allowed to be associated with one AP at a time, so if the station associates with a new AP, any leftover associations that exist in other APs must be terminated. Stations are supposed to disassociate when they leave a BSS, but sometimes this does not occur. For example, if the station roamed out of range so quickly that the disassociation packet was corrupted and the AP didn't hear it, then the station would not have properly disassociated. The 802.11 MAC layer can compensate for cases where disassociation does not occur.

The "Move" sequence occurs when a station attempts to roam to a new AP by sending a Reassociation Request to the AP. The new AP sends an IAPP "MOVE-notify" message to the old AP over the distribution system. This message contains the MAC address of the station that is roaming. The old AP sends back an IAPP "MOVE-response," which indicates whether the roaming should be successful. These messages are sent over a TCP session between the APs. To make it more difficult for an attacker to spoof a roaming event, the MAC address of each AP is mapped to its IP address, either in a static table in each AP, or via a RADIUS server.

The 802.11F recommended practice also defines security methods so that one access point can ensure that another access point is authorized to join the ESS. These security methods and the "caching" action will not be covered in this book.

Mobile Subnets

The Mobile IP protocol used to be all the rage in wireless LANs. That was the industry-standard method of handling mobile subnetting, but vendors have found faster, better ways of doing the same thing in ways that allow for handling time and latency sensitive applications, such as voice and video. The methods in which mobile subnetting is now done vary greatly from vendor to vendor and is beyond the scope of this book.

Load Balancing

Congested areas with many users and heavy traffic load per AP may require a multi-cell network structure. In a multi-cell structure, several co-located access points "illuminate" the same area, creating a common coverage area which increases aggregate throughput. Stations inside the common coverage area automatically associate with the access point that is less loaded and that provides the best signal quality.

As illustrated in Figure 9.12, the stations are equally divided between the access points in order to equally share the load between the access points. Efficiency is maximized because all access points are working at the same low-level load. Load balancing is also known as load-sharing and is configured on both the stations and the access point in most cases. Most WLAN switches today handle load balancing clients and their traffic automatically. The administrator may be able to configure some settings regarding these parameters through the switch console.

FIGURE 9.12   Load balancing

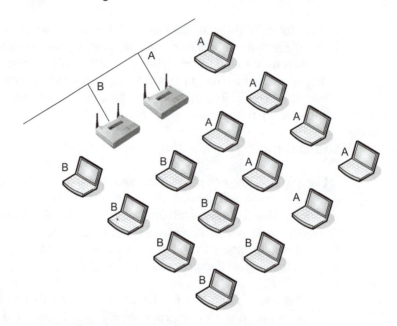

Power Management Features

Wireless clients are often battery operated, and RF transmission can drain batteries quickly. To address this issue, the IEEE specified two power management modes that clients can use, known as *active mode* and *power save mode.* These power management modes are sometimes called *continuous aware mode* (CAM) and *power save polling* (PSP) mode by vendors. We will use the standard terms throughout this section.

802.11 defines two states that a client can be in relative to power saving. If the client is *awake,* it is using full power and is capable of transmitting and receiving frames. If the client is *dozing,* it has powered down some parts of the 802.11 card. It is using minimal power, and it cannot transmit or receive frames.

Active Mode

When a station is in active mode, it stays awake 100 percent of the time. The AP (in an infrastructure network) or other stations (in an ad-hoc network) can send frames to an active mode station at any time. Active mode provides no power conservation. Because active mode provides higher throughput and lower latency than power save mode, active mode is the default mode for most wireless client devices. Computers that are plugged into an AC power outlet should be set for active mode to achieve optimum performance. Under these circumstances, there is no reason to have the client conserve power.

Power Save Mode

When a station is in power save mode, it alternates between dozing and awake, depending on its need to transmit and receive frames. Since there will be periods of time when the station cannot receive frames, the normal rules for frame transmission must be amended. This amended behavior is slightly different, depending on whether the BSS is an ad hoc BSS or an infrastructure BSS. Both sets of behavior are covered:

Power Save Mode in an Infrastructure Basic Service Set

Every 802.11 data frame contains a bit in the MAC header called the Power Save bit. A station uses this bit to indicate to its access point what power saving mode it will be in (active or power save) following the successful completion of the current frame exchange. For example, a station that was in active mode that desired to go into power save mode would send a frame with the Power Save bit set to 1. Upon reception of the ACK for that frame (assuming the frame required an ACK, the ACK would indicate successful completion of the frame exchange), the station could then enter power save mode. The station could later indicate that it was entering active mode by successfully sending a frame with the Power Save bit set to zero. 802.11 gives the station the ability to switch back and forth between active and power save mode, but not all vendors implement this functionality in their drivers. Some vendors' cards stay either in power save or active mode until the user changes the power save setting in the client's configuration utility, while other vendors' cards switch back and forth. You can verify this functionality by looking at the "Power Save" bit in the header of a stations' frames with a protocol analyzer. If the "Power Save" bit changes from a 1 to a 0 and back, the station is dynamically going into and out of power-save mode.

The AP is required to track the current power saving status of all stations in the BSS, whether the station is in power save mode or active mode. But the AP does not track the specific state (awake or dozing) of each station. Therefore, when the AP receives a frame for a station that is in power save mode, the AP cannot immediately forward the frame, since the station might be dozing and miss the frame. Instead, the AP buffers the frame.

Each client has an association identifier (AID) that it receives when it associates with the AP. Inside each beacon is a data element called the *traffic indication map* (TIM). The AP indicates to the stations in the BSS that it has frames buffered for them by setting their AIDs in the TIM. To summarize, each beacon contains a list of all of the stations for which the AP currently has frames buffered. The TIM will continue to indicate the AIDs of the stations that have traffic buffered until those queues are emptied due to frame delivery or the frames are dropped.

Since beacons are transmitted at regular intervals, a station can predict when a beacon is about to be transmitted. A station that is operating in power save mode will transition from dozing to awake shortly before it expects a beacon to be transmitted, allowing it to receive the beacon. By reading the TIM in the beacon, the station can determine whether the AP has any frames for the station. A station is not required to wake up for every beacon. To increase power savings, a station can decide to wake up only every other beacon, every third beacon, every fourth beacon, and so forth. This might be an option that you can configure in your client configuration utility.

If a station in power save mode receives a beacon with a TIM that indicates that the AP has no frames buffered for that station, the station will quickly return to dozing. If the TIM in the beacon indicates that the AP has a frame buffered for the station, the station will remain awake and send a PS-Poll Control frame to the AP. Upon receipt of the PS-Poll frame, the AP will forward the buffered frame to the station. The station must stay awake until it receives the buffered frame.

There is a bit in the MAC header called the More Data bit. If the AP has multiple frames buffered for the station, it will set the More Data bit to one in the data frame that it sends to the station. The station can then send another PS-Poll frame and receive another data frame from the AP.

This process will continue until all data frames are delivered to the station. The last data frame will have the More Data bit set to zero. There is no requirement that the station retrieve all frames from the AP, but the AP might drop frames that have been buffered too long.

Broadcasts and Multicasts

Multicast and broadcast frames must be delivered to all stations on the BSS. If the AP were to transmit a broadcast or multicast frame while a power save station was dozing, the dozing station would miss the frame. Therefore, if *any* station on the BSS is in power save mode, the AP must buffer *all* broadcasts and multicasts.

As we discussed, an AP can indicate that it has frames queued for a station by setting a value in the TIM. There is a similar structure that additionally indicates whether the AP has frames queued for a multicast or broadcast address. This type of TIM is known as a *delivery traffic indication message* (DTIM). Keep in mind that a TIM indicates for which stations the AP has frames buffered; a DTIM indicates for which stations the AP has frames buffered, and *in addition* it indicates whether the AP has frames buffered for a broadcast or multicast address.

Not every beacon contains a DTIM. The AP is configured with an integer value known as the *DTIM Interval*. Every Nth beacon contains a DTIM, while every non-Nth beacon contains a TIM. If the DTIM Interval were equal to 3 (the default value on many APs) and the AP were sending beacons every 100 ms, the AP would transmit:

> Beacon (DTIM) → 100 ms → Beacon (TIM) → 100 ms → Beacon (TIM) → Beacon (DTIM) → 100ms → Beacon (TIM) → Beacon (TIM) … and so on

Following the transmission of a beacon containing a DTIM, the AP will immediately send its buffered broadcast and multicast frames. Stations in power save mode are not expected to send a PS-Poll frame before this happens, and the AP will not wait for such a frame. This is a case of "the needs of the many outweigh the needs of the few." All stations are expected to wake up for the DTIM and be ready to receive broadcast frames. If a few stations do not make it, it is preferable to let them miss out than to keep every other station waiting. Regardless of how often a station decides to wake up and listen for TIMs, most stations will wake up for every DTIM to ensure that they don't miss broadcast frames. Fortunately, the AP announces the DTIM interval in every beacon.

FIGURE 9.13   Power Saving in an Infrastructure BSS

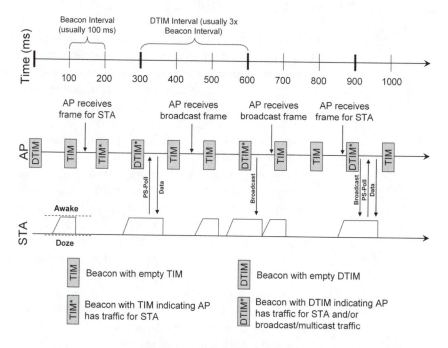

Figure 9.13 shows an example of several power management exchanges. The AP line represents the AP's activities, while the STA line represents activities of a station in power saving mode. The "DTIM" and "TIM" boxes represent a beacon sent by the AP containing either a DTIM or TIM. In this example, the AP's DTIM interval is set to 3, meaning that it sends a DTIM every three beacons. The "fins" on the STA line indicate when the station is awake or dozing. In this example, the STA is configured to wake up every two beacon intervals.

- At t=100 ms, the STA wakes up and receives a beacon. The TIM does not indicate that the AP has data for the STA, so the STA goes back to dozing.
- Between t=100 ms and t=200 ms, the AP receives a unicast frame for the STA.

- At t=200 ms, the AP sends a beacon with a TIM that indicates that it has data for the STA. Since the STA is not awake during this time, the STA does not receive the beacon. The AP continues to hold the packet.

- At t=300 ms, the AP sends a beacon. This beacon has a DTIM instead of a TIM, since this is the third beacon, and the DTIM interval is set at three. Because the AP has not yet delivered its packet for the STA, the DTIM indicates that the AP has a packet for the STA, just as the previous beacon's TIM did. For this beacon, the STA is awake, since the STA is configured to wake up every other beacon, and this is the second beacon since the STA last woke up.

- The STA indicates that it is awake by sending a PS-Poll to the AP, which allows the AP to forward the queued data frame to the station. *Both of these frames are acknowledged*, but the diagram doesn't show the acknowledgements for simplicity. At this point, if the AP had multiple frames queued, several PS-Poll and Data exchanges might occur.

- At t=400, the AP sends a beacon with a TIM indicating that it has no packets buffered for any power-saving station. The STA does not wake up for this, since it is configured to wake up every other beacon, and it woke up for the last one.

- Between t=400 and t=500, the AP receives a broadcast frame.

- At t=500, the AP sends a beacon with a TIM indicating that it has no packets buffered for any power-saving station. Although the AP does have a broadcast frame buffered, it can't forward that frame until the next DTIM, and this is just a TIM. The STA wakes up for this beacon, hears that there are no packets buffered, and goes immediately back to dozing.

- At t=600, it's time again for the AP to send a beacon with a DTIM. This DTIM will indicate that the AP has a broadcast frame buffered. The station normally would have skipped this beacon, since it only wakes up for every other beacon. But the station *does* wake up for this beacon, because it contains a DTIM, and the station doesn't ever want to miss a DTIM.

- Following the beacon containing the DTIM, the AP immediately transmits the broadcast frame. No PS-Poll is required or expected.

- Between t=600 and t=700, the AP receives a broadcast frame. This frame will be buffered until the next DTIM interval.

- At t=700, the STA continues its normal pattern of waking up every other beacon. The AP sends a beacon with a TIM indicating that it has no packets buffered for any power-saving station. The STA wakes up for this beacon, hears that there are no packets buffered, and goes immediately back to dozing.

- Between t=800 and t=900, the AP receives a frame for the STA.

- At t=900, the AP sends a beacon containing a DTIM, since this is the third beacon since the last DTIM, and the AP's beacon interval is set to three. This DTIM indicates both that the AP has a broadcast/multicast frame and that the AP has a frame for the STA.

- The STA wakes up for this beacon and stays awake because the DTIM indicates that the STA has data to receive. First, the AP sends the broadcast frame (broadcast frames always get priority in power-save transmission), then the STA sends a PS-Poll and receives its data frame.

Power Save Mode in an Independent Basic Service Set

The power saving communication process in an IBSS is very different than when power saving mode is used in a BSS. An IBSS does not contain an access point, so there is no device to track the power saving status of the stations and to buffer frames for stations in power saving mode. Coordination of sending frames to power save mode stations in an IBSS takes cooperation of all of the stations in the IBSS.

When a station wants to send a frame to another station that is in power saving mode, the transmitting station buffers the frame. The 802.11 standard defines a time period known as the *ad-hoc traffic indication message* (ATIM) *window*. The ATIM window is similar to the beacon interval in that all stations on the BSS can predict when the ATIM window will occur. During the ATIM window, all stations are required to be awake, and any station with data buffered for a power saving recipient sends a unicast frame known as an ATIM frame to the recipient. The recipient will acknowledge the ATIM frame, and then stay awake to receive the expected data frame. A station that receives an ATIM frame must stay awake until the next ATIM window. Stations that don't receive an ATIM frame within the ATIM window may go back to dozing after the ATIM window.

Once the ATIM window expires, normal data transmission commences. Stations that have frames buffered for power saving recipients now know that the recipient is awake and can transmit their frames according to the normal rules of CSMA/CA. If, for some reason, a station fails to transmit a frame, it will simply send another ATIM frame during the next ATIM window. As a wireless LAN administrator, you need to know what effect power management features will have on performance, battery life, broadcast traffic on your LAN, etc. Although power saving can increase the battery life of stations to some degree, it also lowers throughput.

Key Terms

Before taking the exam, you should be familiar with the following terms:

active mode

active scanning

announcement traffic indication message (ATIM)

association

authentication

BSSID

delivery traffic indication message (DTIM)

distribution system

ESSID

open system authentication

passive scanning

power saving mode

reassociation

shared key authentication

traffic indication map (TIM)

Review Questions

1. Describe a real world example of how an IBSS, BSS, and ESS would be utilized in the enterprise.

2. Name and describe five items contained in a Beacon Management Frame.

3. List and explain the three distinct states of the 802.11 state machine. Which comes first: association or authentication, and why?

4. Define "roaming," and explain why it is such an integral function of today's wireless LAN technology.

5. Does the 802.11 standard define the protocol that should be used between the two access points when a client roams? Why or why not?

MAC and Physical Layers

CWNA Exam Objectives Covered:

❖ Describe and apply the following concepts surrounding wireless LAN frames

- 802.11 Frame Format vs. 802.3 Frame Format

- Layer-3 Protocol Support by 802.11 Frames

❖ Identify, understand and correct or compensate for the following wireless LAN implementation challenges:

- Hidden Node

❖ Identify methods described in the 802.11 standard for locating, joining, and maintaining connectivity with an 802.11 wireless LAN

- Dynamic Rate Selection

❖ Define, describe, and apply 802.11 modes and features available for moving data traffic across the RF medium

- DCF vs. PCF modes

- CSMA/CA vs. CSMA/CD protocols

- RTS/CTS and CTS-to-Self protocols

- Fragmentation

- QoS via 802.11e and WMM

In This Chapter

802.11 Frame
Transmission

Distributed Coordination
Function

Point Coordination
Function

QoS via 802.11e and
WMM

RTS/CTS

CTS-to-Self

Fragmentation

Dynamic Rate Selection

In this chapter we will discuss some of the MAC and Physical layer characteristics of wireless LANs. We will explain the difference between Ethernet and wireless LAN frames, and how wireless LANs try to avoid the bulk of collisions instead of dealing with them after the fact. We'll walk through the ways that wireless LAN stations communicate with one another under normal circumstances, and how collision handling occurs in a wireless LAN.

Much of the information in this chapter has direct implications for your ability to administer a wireless LAN. RTS/CTS and Fragmentation are two such topics. Properly configuring the RTS/CTS and Fragmentation thresholds on your WLAN can either improve or worsen network performance significantly. Other information in this chapter will deepen your understanding of the 802.11 standard, but has less practical application. CSMA/CA is one such topic. Understanding CSMA/CA will support your knowledge of other topics, but you will probably never interact directly with the CSMA/CA process.

802.11 Frame Transmission

In order to understand how to configure and manage a wireless LAN, you must understand communication parameters that are configurable on the equipment and how to implement those parameters. In order to estimate throughput across wireless LANs, you must understand the effects of these parameters and of collision handling on system throughput. This section conveys a basic understanding of many configurable parameters and their effects on network performance.

802.11 data transmission is complex. It is difficult to discuss any one part of WLAN technology without immediately involving several other parts. This section will include references to topics covered later in this chapter.

802.11 devices communicate using frames exactly like any other 802 network. To clear up a common misconception, wireless LANs *do not* use 802.3 Ethernet frames. The term *wireless Ethernet* is something of a misnomer.

802.11 frames use a frame format that is similar to 802.3 Ethernet, just as all 802 frame formats share certain characteristics, but 802.11 frames use a different MAC header than 802.3 frames. 802.11 frames are designed so that they can be easily translated to 802.3 Ethernet frames, and vice versa. The details of the differences in structure between a wireless LAN frame and an Ethernet frame are beyond the scope of both the CWNA exam and a wireless LAN administrator's job.

Wireless Frame Types

Whereas wired LANs such as Ethernet usually only have one type of frame that carries data, 802.11 defines three types of frames: control frames, management frames, and data frames. Control frames are used to acknowledge the receipt of data frames, and for certain functions related to frame transmission (which will be discussed later). Management frames are used in the process of joining and leaving a BSS. Data frames, as the name implies, carry upper-layer data. Each of these three frame types is divided into sub-types.

Below is a list of the frame sub-types defined by 802.11. This list is comprehensive, except that the 802.11 standard defines several frame sub-types that are used in a process called Point Coordination. Point Coordination is an optional part of the 802.11 standard and is not implemented by any known vendor (as of this writing), so those frames are omitted from this list.

Management Frames:

- Association request frame
- Association response frame
- Reassociation request frame
- Reassociation response frame
- Probe request frame
- Probe response frame
- Beacon frame
- ATIM frame
- Disassociation frame
- Authentication frame
- Deauthentication frame

Control Frames:

- Request to send (RTS)
- Clear to send (CTS)
- Acknowledgement (ACK)
- Power Save Poll (PS Poll)

Data Frames (no sub-types shown)

The CWAP certification is geared toward learning each of the frame types' purpose and structure. That information will not be presented as part of the CWNA curriculum or exam objectives.

Maximum Frame Size

Wireless LAN frames can carry a maximum of 2304 bytes of "upper-layer" data payload. Ethernet is only capable of carrying frames up to 1518 bytes (or 1522 bytes if 802.1q is used). When a frame is sent from an 802.11 station to an Ethernet station, the AP must translate that frame from using 802.11 format MAC headers to using 802.3 format MAC headers. If the 802.11 frame carried more than 1500 bytes of data, the resulting Ethernet frame would be too big, since the Ethernet headers add 18 bytes to the payload, and the maximum Ethernet frame size is 1518 bytes. The AP could not forward the frame onto the Ethernet network. Even though 802.11 supports payloads of up to 2304 bytes, it wouldn't be a good idea for stations to use frames with more than 1500 bytes of data, since many wireless frames are destined for Ethernet networks.

In practice, however, the difference in maximum frame size between 802.11 and Ethernet rarely comes into play because most TCP/IP stacks in use today use an IP MTU (maximum transmission unit) of 1500 bytes. This means that the IP stack will fragment a block of data if the block, including the IP header, exceeds 1500 bytes. Since IP is the most common layer 3 protocol, layer 2 (802.11) is unlikely to get a block of data larger than 1500 bytes, even though it is capable of carrying larger blocks.

Wireless LANs support practically all Layer 3–7 protocols, including IP, IPX, NetBEUI, AppleTalk, RIP, DNS, FTP, etc. The main differences from 802.3 Ethernet frames are implemented at the Media Access Control (MAC) sub layer of the Data Link layer and the entire Physical layer. Upper layer protocols are simply considered payload by the Layer 2 wireless frames.

CSMA/CA

The process of transmitting an 802.11 frame has many steps. On some level, it is amazing that this complex process occurs at a microsecond time scale, and continuously as long as your wireless card is powered up! A complete understanding of the frame transmission process is not required for the wireless administrator. We will cover as much information as you need to know, and just enough supplementary information to provide context for the required information.

Shared media are subject to the restriction that no two stations can transmit on the medium at the same time (known as a *collision*), since the stations' signals will corrupt each other. Therefore, all LANs require an access, or arbitration, method. This method is a set of rules that determines which stations may talk when, and that prevents two stations from talking at the same time. This method also, if necessary, compensates for the circumstance when they do talk at the same time. The arbitration method for 802.11 is Carrier Sense, Multiple Access with Collision Avoidance (CSMA/CA).

Carrier Sense

Frame transmission begins with *carrier sense*. Carrier sense is the process of determining whether any other station can be heard currently transmitting on the medium. If two stations transmit at the same time, they will corrupt each others' frames. CSMA/CA's basic logic is "if no one else is transmitting, then you may transmit." The ability to determine whether another station is transmitting is critical.

The most basic form of carrier sense is physical carrier sense, also known as *clear channel assessment (CCA)*. Clear channel assessment involves simply listening to the medium and determining whether the amount of ambient RF energy exceeds a certain threshold. CCA alone does not provide sufficient collision avoidance in an 802.11 network, since 802.11 does not require that all stations in a BSS be able to hear all other stations in the BSS. The 802.11 standard requires only that all stations in a BSS be able to hear the AP in the BSS. Therefore, a situation can occur in which two stations with overlapping coverage are unable to hear each other. This situation is known in the trade as the *hidden node problem*. If one of these stations were transmitting a frame, the other station's CCA would incorrectly report that the medium was idle, and a collision might result. To address the problem of two transmitters out of range of one another colliding at a common receiver, 802.11 provides a second type of carrier sense that does not rely on the presence of RF energy near the receiving station. This type of carrier sense is known as *virtual carrier sense*. The details of virtual carrier sense will be discussed later in this chapter.

For a station to consider the medium to be idle, *both* physical and virtual carrier sense must report that the medium is idle. If a station wants to transmit a frame, and *either* physical or virtual carrier sense reports that another station is transmitting (the medium is busy), the station must enter a mode called *deferring,* in which the station waits until both physical and virtual carrier sense report an idle medium.

Interframe Spacing

After both physical and virtual carrier sense report that the medium is clear, the station must next observe *interframe spacing (IFS)*. IFS means that before a station can transmit a frame, the network has to be idle (no station is heard transmitting) for a certain minimum period of time. Interframe spacing ensures that no two frames run so close together that stations mistake them for one big frame. In addition, IFS provides a priority access mechanism whereby certain types of frames are able to preempt the transmission of certain other types of frames.

IFS provides priority access to certain frames by allowing them to be preceded by a shorter interframe spacing. To understand how IFS length corresponds to priority access, consider the example in which station A is transmitting a frame and stations B and C both have a frame queued to transmit. Station B has a higher-priority frame and Station C has a lower-priority frame. To avoid a collision, stations B and C must wait until station A finishes transmitting. Then, per the rules of CSMA/CA, they must wait the appropriate IFS for their type of frame. Since station C has a lower-priority frame, it will be required to use a longer IFS than station B, which has a higher priority frame with a shorter IFS. By the time Station C has waited the required time, station B will already be transmitting, and station C will go back into "deferring" mode. Frames using a shorter IFS will have priority access to the medium over frames using a longer IFS.

The 802.11 standard defines three main lengths of interframe spacing. They are, in order of length from shortest to longest: SIFS (*short interframe spacing*), PIFS (*point-coordination interframe spacing*), and DIFS (*distributed-coordination interframe spacing*). 802.11 defines which IFS must be used in each circumstance. For example, when a station sends a data frame, it uses the DIFS interval; the ACK to that data frame will use the SIFS interval. On the other hand, when a station transmits a frame that has been fragmented by 802.11, the first fragment uses DIFS, but all subsequent fragments and ACKs use SIFS. (Fragmentation will be covered later in the chapter.) It is not important for a CWNA to memorize which IFS value is used in every circumstance, but you should understand that the varied IFS values give certain frames prioritized access to the medium in certain situations.

Do not be misled into believing that DIFS, SIFS, and PIFS make up some sort of class-of-service for 802.11, where a station can arbitrarily choose to use a shorter IFS if it feels that its frames are particularly important. That is not the case. The 802.11 standard defines exactly what IFS *must* be used for each circumstance in which a station wants to transmit a frame. The "class-of-service" confusion sometimes arises when people learn about the 802.11e amendment that defines eight *new* IFS values that *are* intended to provide class-of-service access to the medium. These IFS values and interaction with 802.11's default IFS values is not covered by the CWNA exam.

Short Interframe Space (SIFS)

SIFS is the shortest interframe space. Frames using SIFS will preempt frames using any other IFS. Generally speaking, SIFS is used when 802.11 needs to ensure that a certain frame immediately follows the frame that preceded it. For example, 802.11 requires that each unicast data frame be followed by an 802.11 ACK frame. The ACK must be received within a certain time window after the data frame, or the data frame will be treated as lost and will be retransmitted. To ensure that the ACK is sent immediately after its corresponding data frame, ACKs use the SIFS interval.

Consider the scenario in which Station A has just transmitted a data frame to Station B and, during that transmission, Station C is waiting to transmit a data frame of its own. After Station A finished transmission, both Station B and C want to transmit, but Station B can use the SIFS to send its ACK while Station C must use the longer DIFS to send its data frame. Station B will always "win" and the ACK will preempt Station C's data frame.

The following is a list of the main times that SIFS is used.

- An ACK immediately following a data frame uses SIFS
- A CTS frame sent in response to an RTS frame uses SIFS
- The data frame following a CTS frame uses SIFS
- All fragments except the first fragment of a fragment burst use SIFS
- All frame exchanges during PCF mode (discussed later) except the first exchange and error conditions use SIFS

Point Coordination Function Interframe Space (PIFS)

A PIFS interframe space is neither the shortest nor longest fixed interframe space, so it gets more priority than DIFS and less than SIFS. Access points use PIFS to take the network from distributed coordination (DCF) to point coordination (PCF). Point coordination is a special mode in which the AP controls which stations may transmit, instead of all stations contending for network access. As previously mentioned, point coordination is an optional part of 802.11 and no known vendor implements it. Therefore, we do not cover it in detail in the CWNA curriculum.

PIFS is shorter in duration than DIFS, but longer than SIFS. Use of PIFS allows the access point to preempt stations that want to transmit data frames, but not to interrupt any of the SIFS transmissions listed above.

Distributed Coordination Function Interframe Space (DIFS)

DIFS is the longest fixed interframe space. Frames using DIFS will be preempted by frames using SIFS or PIFS. DIFS is used to transmit most data and management frames, including the RTS frame that begins an RTS/CTS/Data/ACK exchange and the first fragment of a fragment burst.

Extended Interframe Space (EIFS)

The EIFS is used by DCF stations whenever a frame reception began but the received frame was incomplete or did not have a correct Frame Check Sequence (FCS) value. Essentially, EIFS is used by a station when the last frame the station received was corrupted.

The Contention Window

Following the interframe spacing, a period of time known as the *contention window* might begin. During the contention window, all stations with a frame to transmit choose a random time period between zero and some pre-defined upper limit. This time period is known as the *backoff timer*. As long as the medium is idle (no other station is transmitting), the stations count down their backoff timer. When a station's backoff timer reaches zero, it is allowed to transmit its frame.

To understand the how contention works and why contention is necessary, consider this example:

1. Station A is transmitting the last frame of a frame exchange sequence.
2. Stations B, C, and D receive a data frame from their protocol stacks. They determine that the medium is busy and enter the deferring state.
3. Station A finishes transmission. Stations B, C, and D perceive that the medium is now idle. They begin counting off the required IFS. Since all three stations have a data frame to transmit they must use the DIFS. *(If Station A's frame required an ACK, this is where the ACK, which uses the SIFS, would preempt stations' B, C, and D frames, which would use DIFS. However, we stated in step 1 that this is the "last frame of a*

frame exchange sequence," which means that either station A's frame was an ACK to a previous frame, or station A's frame didn't require an ACK.)

If we did not have contention, what would happen next? The DIFS would expire and stations B, C, and D would begin transmitting, essentially at the same time. A collision would almost certainly result. From this example, you should see that the time immediately following a frame's transmission is the time when, without contention, collisions would be most likely. The end of a data frame acts to synchronize the transmission of any stations that were deferring during the frame, nearly guaranteeing that they will collide. Here is what happens with contention, continuing the previous numbered sequence of events:

4. Stations B, C, and D each choose a random amount of time: their backoff timer. Because the backoff timer is random, it will probably be different for each station. The stations begin counting off the backoff timer.

5. Assume that Station C happened to choose the shortest backoff timer. Station C's backoff timer expires and Station C begins transmission. Station B and C detect that the network is now busy. They pause their backoff timer and go back into deferring mode.

6. Station C finishes transmission. Station B and C detect idle medium.

7. Stations B and C wait the DIFS. (If station C's frame required an ACK, then, after a SIFS, the ACK would be sent and Stations B and C would go back to deferring until it was completed. We omit the ACK for simplicity.)

8. After the DIFS, stations B and C resume their backoff timer where they last left off. They do not have to choose a new random number.

As you can see from this example, the random length of the backoff timer serves to significantly reduce the likelihood of collisions immediately following a frame transmission, when collisions would otherwise be nearly certain to occur.

The contention window is not always used. The following examples define when contention must be used and when the station may skip over contention to frame transmission. For simplicity, we will refer to a frame that would use the SIFS as a "SIFS frame" and a frame that would use the DIFS as a "DIFS frame."

- Stations that have a SIFS frame to transmit may transmit that frame immediately following the expiration of the SIFS; they do not have to participate in contention. Remember that SIFS is used when one frame is intended to immediately follow another frame. The purpose of SIFS is to prevent any other station from preempting the SIFS frame. If stations had to count down a backoff timer before transmitting a SIFS frame, that frame might be preempted by a station using a shorter backoff timer.

- Stations that have a DIFS frame to transmit only have to participate in contention if they are deferring before transmission. In other words, if a station gets a frame, performs carrier sense, senses idle medium, and waits the DIFS without hearing any other station transmitting, the station may commence transmission immediately. It does not have to perform the backoff process.

- Any station that wants to transmit a frame that uses the DIFS *and* that was deferring to another station before transmitting must participate in contention following the expiration of the DIFS. The reason a station must participate in contention if it were deferring, but may skip contention if it did not defer, is that, as described above, collisions are much more likely immediately following a frame transmission. If a station is deferring, chances are that there are other stations also deferring, and a collision is likely to occur after the frame ends. The contention window alleviates this problem.

FIGURE 10.1 Contention Window Length

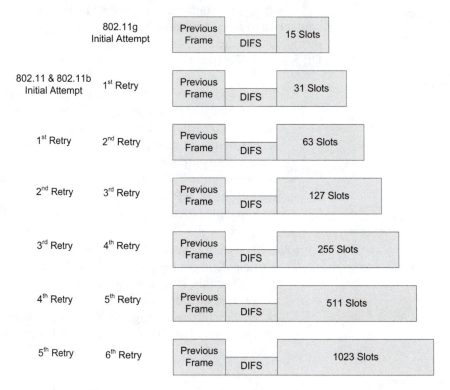

Slots

To choose the length of the backoff timer, a station chooses a random integer and then multiplies that number by a fixed-length time interval known as the *slot time*. The station counts down that timer, performing a clear channel assessment (CCA) after each slot time to see if the medium is busy. The length of a slot time is defined for each PHY (DSSS, FHSS, OFDM, etc.) by the relevant 802.11 clause. The specific value of each PHY's slot time is beyond the scope of the CWNA curriculum. The contention window, which follows the appropriate IFS, is made up of a variable number of slot times (slots) per station, depending on the number of retries that station has attempted per transmission. For example, if an 802.11g station attempts to transmit a data frame for the first time, the contention window is only 15 slots long. If the slot time is equal to 9 microseconds, then the maximum contention window for that station is 9 x 15 = 135 microseconds for that transmission.

Collision Handling (Acknowledgements)

What if a collision occurs, despite the safeguards described so far? Wireless LANs have to deal with the possibility of collisions just the same as traditional wired LANs do. The difference is that, on a wireless LAN, there is no means through which the sending station can determine that there has actually *been* a collision. In a wired network, the NIC can simply listen to the voltage on the wire to determine if a collision has occurred. What would a wireless radio hear if it "listened" at the same time it transmitted? First, it would need a second antenna. Assuming it had a second antenna, its own transmission would drown out any other transmitter with which the station was transmitting.

For this reason, 802.11 wireless LANs utilize the Carrier Sense Multiple Access / Collision *Avoidance* protocol, also known as CSMA/CA. CSMA/CA is somewhat similar to the protocol CSMA/CD, which is common on Ethernet networks. The main difference between CSMA/CA and CSMA/CD is that CSMA/CA always enters backoff after deferring to avoid a potential collision, while CSMA/CD only enters backoff when a collision actually occurs.

Distributed Coordination Function

The depth of terminology associated with 802.11 frame transmission can be confusing. The algorithm that we described above – CCA, IFS, Backoff, Transmit – is generally known as CSMA/CA. The 802.11 standard refers to its implementation of this algorithm as the *Distributed Coordination Function (DCF)*. Practically speaking, the distinction between these terms is insignificant and most WLAN administrators can assume that DCF and CSMA/CA are the same thing.

The term "Distributed Coordination Function" refers to the fact that the *coordination* of which station may transmit is *distributed* between all of the stations in a given area. There is no central station to say, "You may transmit...now you may transmit." It is a testament to the ingenuity of the 802.11 engineers that DCF works regardless of how many BSSs are in an area. Whether there is one AP with two stations or five APs with ten stations each, DCF ensures that collisions are minimized. Consider, however, the effect that CSMA/CA has on network throughput as the number of stations on the channel increases. If *any* station is transmitting, all other stations within hearing range must defer.

Point Coordination Function

One weakness of DCF is that it does not guarantee timely access to the medium. On average, all stations get somewhat equal access to the medium, but depending on the random backoff timer that they choose, over a short period of time, some stations might get to transmit much more than other stations. *Point Coordination Function (PCF)* is an arbitration algorithm that provides managed access to the medium. In Point Coordination, all stations stop transmitting and the access point selectively gives particular stations the right to transmit a frame through a process called *polling*. The intent of Point Coordination is that devices that need guaranteed regular access to the medium, such as VoIP devices, can get that access.

To participate in PCF, both the station and an access point must support it. As of this printing, no access points on the market support PCF. As VoIP over 802.11 becomes more popular, APs supporting PCF may become available.

The PCF Process

A station that supports PCF notifies the AP that it would like to participate in polling as a part of the association process. Two bits in the association request frame indicate first, whether the station is capable of participating in the PCF, and second, whether the station wants to be polled.

If the AP is configured to use PCF, then the BSS will alternate between periods of time when all stations may transmit according to the rules of CSMA/CD—the *distributed coordination function* (DCF)—and periods of time when all stations that registered as pollable must wait to be polled by the AP in order to send data, known as the *contention-free period* (CFP). If the AP is not configured to use PCF, then the network will use DCF exclusively, and no polling will occur.

An AP that is configured to use PCF will put information into its beacons that allows stations to predict when a contention-free period is about to begin. After the CFP begins, any stations that want to transmit a frame will be forced to defer. During the CFP, the AP sends CF-Poll frames to stations that have requested to participate in the PCF, one station after another. These stations are allowed to transmit one frame per poll. At the end of the CFP, the AP sends a frame called a CF-End frame, and normal DCF resumes. The CFP has a certain maximum duration that prevents the PCF stations from completely dominating the DCF stations.

Interaction of PIFS and DIFS

When an AP has PCF enabled, the BSS will alternate between periods of point coordination and periods of distributed coordination. These periods fit together to form the Contention-Free Period (CFP) Repetition Interval, which is shown in Figure 10.2

FIGURE 10.2   Contention Free Period (CFP) Repetition Interval

PIFS	Beacon	Contention-Free Period (CFP)	Contention Period (CP)

If we start from a hypothetical beginning point on a network that has the access point configured for PCF mode, and some of the clients are configured for polling, the process is as follows.

1. At the beginning of the CFP Repetition Interval, the access point broadcasts a beacon indicating the beginning of the CFP. Just prior to this broadcast, all stations realize that the CFP is about to begin and NAV to a value of 32,768, meaning *infinite*. The non-zero NAV causes the station's virtual carrier sense to indicate that the network is not idle, which means that if the station wants to transmit a frame during this time, it will have to defer.

2. During the contention-free period, the access point polls stations that have indicated that they would like to participate in polling. The access point may also use this time to forward frames to the stations from the wired network.

3. When the AP polls a station, the station is allowed to send one data frame to the AP. If the station doesn't need to send a data frame, it indicates that by setting a certain value in the frame. If a

station sends a frame to the AP, the AP may forward the frame to another wireless station or to the wired network, as necessary.

4. Polling continues throughout the contention-free period.

5. At the end of the CFP, the AP sends a CF-End frame, which ends the CFP and resets the NAV timer on all stations to 0. Any stations with frames to send perform contention (set a backoff timer, etc...), per the normal rules of DCF.

Think of the PCF as using a "controlled access policy" and the DCF as using a "random access policy." During the contention-free period, the access point is in complete control of all functions on the wireless network; outside of the contention-free period, stations arbitrate and randomly gain control over the medium.

QoS via 802.11e and WMM

802.11 WLANs generally require very careful design to provide the consistently low latency required by VoIP and other similar applications. 802.11 is increasingly being used for voice, video, and other time-sensitive applications both in the home and in the enterprise. Streaming of multimedia content over wireless networks no longer requires a technically advanced user. Appliances such as the one in Figure 10.3 make it simple to stream audio and video from a computer to any television or stereo in range of the wireless network. This type of device associates to your AP as a client, and allows the playback of audio and video files stored on a Windows Media Center PC.

FIGURE 10.3 Linksys WMCE54AG Dual-Band Wireless A/G Media Center Extender

Point coordination function mode was intended to address situations in which stations needed guaranteed regular access to the medium, such as VoIP and multimedia streaming. Since PCF mode was optional, few, if any, vendors implemented it. In addition, PCF isn't a very robust QoS mechanism: it gives priority access to certain MAC addresses, but it can't prioritize different applications coming from a single MAC address. To address these limitations, the IEEE released the 802.11e supplement. The IEEE 802.11e amendment to the 802.11 base standard defines a set of Quality of Service (QoS) extensions to the 802.11 MAC layer that are designed to provide higher-quality and more consistent voice and video transmission.

802.11e Supplement

The 802.11e supplement defines extensions to the frame transmission behavior described previously in this chapter. *Enhanced Distributed Channel Access Function* (EDCAF) modifies the DCF rules, while *Hybrid Coordination Function* (HCF) modifies the PCF rules. At the time of this publishing, 802.11e has not been ratified, so all of this information is subject to change in the final amendment.

Enhanced Distributed Channel Access Function (EDCAF)

The 802.11e supplement defines enhancements to both DCF and PCF. In 802.11e, the IEEE replaces DCF with Enhanced Distributed Channel Access Function (EDCAF). EDCAF defines eight traffic categories, or priority levels. Traffic using a lower priority level must wait for a longer period of silence compared to traffic using a higher priority level.

Consider the example in which station A is transmitting and stations B and C both have a frame queued to transmit. Station B has a higher-priority frame and Station C has a lower-priority frame. Per CSMA/CA, stations B and C must wait until station A finishes transmitting, and then they must wait the interframe spacing (IFS). Under DCF, both stations would use the DIFS, so they would have an equal chance of transmitting their data. Under EDCAF, Station C must wait longer than Station B.

Think of the process as lower-priority frames having to wait extra periods of time, and higher-priority frames getting to participate in regular DCF mode. If an additional station were also using a higher-priority level, then it would have an equal chance to station B of transmitting. Therefore, EDCAF doesn't provide any *guaranteed* bandwidth, but it does provide an increased probability that stations with high-priority traffic will transmit before stations with lower-priority traffic.

Notice that this is similar to the way in which CSMA/CA's IFS prioritizes traffic. But whereas CSMA/CA's interframe spacings (SIFS, DIFS, and PIFS) require all data transmissions to have the same priority, EDCAF extends this concept to allow individual data frames to have different priorities.

For backwards-compatibility reasons, the 802.11e interframe spacings are all longer than the default interframe spacing specified in 802.11. This specification means that a pre-802.11e station will essentially transmit as if it were always using the highest priority level. However, the network will still realize the benefit of 802.11e's QoS. Remember that in an infrastructure mode BSS, all frames must go through the AP. Therefore, a non-802.11e client will transmit using the highest-priority IFS, but the 802.11e-compliant AP can be configured to put frames coming from non-802.11e clients into a lower-quality class. This means that non-802.11e frames may be *transmitted* as if they were high-priority, but they will be *forwarded* at a lower priority than 802.11e frames. The non-802.11e station will not send another frame until it gets an ACK for its previous frame, which can not happen until the AP forwards the frame. (If the AP holds the frame too long, the station will time out and attempt to retransmit.) This allows an 802.11e access point to enforce QoS onto non-802.11e stations.

Hybrid Coordination Function (HCF)

If EDCAF is "DCF plus QoS," then HCF is "PCF plus QoS." HCF gives the access point the option of preempting non-AP stations on the network, either during the contention-free period (which it could always do) or the contention period (which PCF does not allow). This specification *does not* mean that the AP can interrupt another station's frame transmission. Rather, it means that the AP can always guarantee that it will be the *next* station to transmit a data frame, after the current frame exchange sequence is finished.

Wireless Multimedia (WMM)

In order to speed the adoption of QoS in the 802.11 marketplace, the Wi-Fi alliance released the WMM certification. The WMM certification is a "snapshot" of the draft 802.11e standard. Vendors that want to implement QoS, but don't want to wait for 802.11e to be ratified, can comply with the WMM certification instead. WMM certifies that a manufacturer's equipment is compliant with a subset of 802.11's functionality. When 802.11e is finally released, the vendor can bring its software into compliance with the final standard. Until then, WMM-compliant devices are available today.

In some respects, there is not much to add about WMM that was not covered in the discussion of 802.11e, since WMM is based on 802.11e. We will only describe the major differences between WMM and 802.11e.

Whereas 802.11e specifies eight priority levels, WMM specifies four *access categories*. They are:

- Voice Priority – Highest priority. Corresponds to 802.11e priority levels 6 or 7.
- Video Priority – Corresponds to 802.11e priority levels 4 or 5.

- Best Effort Priority – Corresponds to 802.11e priority levels 0 or 3. This is the priority level into which the AP places frames from non-802.11e (or non-WMM) stations.

- Background Priority – Lowest Priority. Corresponds to 802.11e priority levels 1 or 2.

Notice that each access category can have one of two priority levels. These would be configured by the administrator, depending on the needs of the users. In reality, the relative priority of the access categories is fixed in most cases (i.e., *voice* is always higher than *video*), except that *best effort* can be prioritized at level 0 or 3, either above or below *background*.

WMM provides priority access to the medium in two main ways. First, the stations and AP prioritize the order in which they will transmit frames, based on the access category of the traffic. Second, lower-priority traffic must use longer IFS values than higher-priority traffic. As with 802.11, the IFS is based on a multiple of a value called the *slot time*, which varies per physical layer (DSSS vs. OFDM vs. FHSS). In addition, the backoff timer for each category is different, with lower-priority categories more likely to use longer backoff timers. In WMM, the IFS and background timer for each access category is:

- *Voice* – 2 slots (IFS) plus 0 to 3 slots (random backoff).
- *Video* – 2 slots (IFS) plus 0 to 7 slots (random backoff).
- *Best Effort* – 3 slots (IFS) plus 0 to 15 slots (random backoff).
- *Background* – 7 slots (IFS) plus 0 to 15 slots (random backoff).

It's important to remember that, in order to take full advantage of 802.11e or WMM, applications must be programmed to request certain access categories or priority levels. This will require coordination between application programmers and 802.11 vendors. Given the performance gain that can be realized through WMM or 802.11e, we expect that application programmers will be eager to release compliant versions of their software.

Request to Send/Clear to Send (RTS/CTS)

As covered earlier in this chapter, there are two carrier sense mechanisms used on wireless networks: *physical carrier sense* and *virtual carrier sense*. Physical carrier sense uses clear channel assessment, which is simple, but does not provide sufficient collision avoidance in an 802.11 network. The 802.11 standard does not require that all stations in a BSS be able to hear all other stations in the BSS. It only requires that all stations in a BSS be able to hear the AP for the BSS. Therefore, two stations with overlapping coverage may be unable to hear each other, creating what is known as the *hidden node problem*. If one of these stations were transmitting a frame, the other station's CCA would incorrectly report that the medium was idle, and a collision might result. *Virtual carrier sense* addresses this situation.

Virtual carrier sense works using a timer in each station called the Network Allocation Vector (NAV). If a station's NAV is non-zero, its virtual carrier sense will indicate that the network is busy. The NAV will count down until it reaches zero. Remember that *both* physical *and* virtual carrier sense must report an idle network before the station can attempt to transmit.

Each data frame contains a Duration field that sets the NAV in all stations that hear the frame to a value that is long enough to transmit the ACK for that frame (if an ACK is required), including any required IFS. The Duration field in the data frame is said to "protect" the ACK, since any station that hears the data frame will believe that the network is busy through the end of the ACK, regardless of whether the station actually hears the ACK. (Why exactly a station would hear the data frame and not the ACK is another topic.)

If an RF coverage area is particularly prone to collisions, it might be beneficial to have stations announce their intention to transmit frames before actually transmitting them, thereby reserving the network for the required time period. The "announcement" frame might be corrupted by a collision, but since the announcement frame is much smaller than the data frame, it doesn't cost much to retransmit the announcement frame. Once the "announcement" frame is successfully transmitted, the data frame won't be corrupted by a collision. This "reservation" exchange is called RTS/CTS.

If a station has been configured to use RTS/CTS, it will transmit an RTS frame (which is a type of Control Frame) before sending a data frame. Upon receiving the RTS frame, the AP will broadcast a CTS frame. The RTS and CTS frames contain a Duration value that will "protect" the network long enough for the station to transmit its data frame and receive the ACK. Since all stations are required to be within range of the AP, all stations will hear either the RTS and/or the CTS. The stations will then set and/or reset their NAV, causing them to perceive that the network is busy until the data frame and its ACK has been transmitted, *even if they can't hear the frame itself* due to "hidden node."

As you can imagine by this brief description, RTS/CTS will cause significant network overhead. If RTS/CTS is used, it is performed before each data frame, lowering throughput noticeably for the entire network as a whole. Most vendors' configuration utilities allow you to specify an RTS/CTS threshold. Frames smaller than the threshold do not use RTS/CTS; frames longer than the threshold use RTS/CTS.

Because it increases overhead, RTS/CTS is turned OFF by default on a wireless LAN. If you are experiencing an unusual amount of collisions on your wireless LAN (as evidenced by high retransmission rates by end stations), using RTS/CTS can increase the traffic flow on the network by decreasing the retransmission overhead. Setting the RTS/CTS threshold correctly is important. If you have low throughput with a lot of corrupted frames, try decreasing the RTS/CTS threshold value on a station. If throughput increases, try lowering it more until throughput starts to decrease again. If throughput does not increase, then you should leave RTS/CTS off because collisions are not the cause of your low throughput.

Figure 10.4 shows an example of an RTS/CTS exchange when a data frame is transmitted from a wireless station to a wired station. First, the station sends an RTS frame. The AP receives the RTS frame and transmits a CTS frame back to the station. Keep in mind that all stations on the BSS hear the CTS frame, even though the arrow in the diagram only shows the frame going to station #1. Once the station receives the CTS frame, it transmits its data, and the AP acknowledges the data. Finally, the AP forwards the frame to the wired station. No RTS/CTS can happen on the wired side, since Ethernet doesn't support or require such a mechanism.

FIGURE 10.4   RTS/CTS – Infrastructure – Wireless-to-Wired

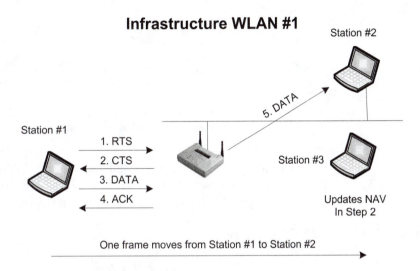

Infrastructure WLAN #1

Station #2

Station #1

5. DATA

1. RTS
2. CTS
3. DATA
4. ACK

Station #3

Updates NAV
In Step 2

One frame moves from Station #1 to Station #2

Figure 10.5 depicts RTS/CTS when a frame is transmitted from a wireless station to another wireless station. In this case, the procedure is the same as in Figure 10.4, except that the RTS/CTS exchange also happens between the AP and Station #2. This assumes that RTS/CTS is enabled in both Station #1 and the AP. In reality, there is no requirement that all stations in a BSS have RTS/CTS enabled at the same time. A station that has RTS/CTS enabled will perform the RTS/CTS exchange before transmission; a station that doesn't have RTS/CTS enabled will not.

FIGURE 10.5   RTS/CTS – Infrastructure – Wireless-to-Wireless

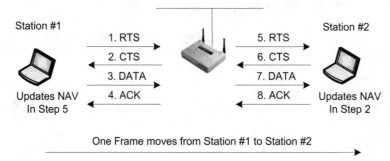

Infrastructure WLAN #2

Station #1 | 1. RTS → | 5. RTS → | Station #2

| 2. CTS ← | 6. CTS ←

| 3. DATA → | 7. DATA →

Updates NAV | 4. ACK ← | 8. ACK ← | Updates NAV
In Step 5 | | | In Step 2

One Frame moves from Station #1 to Station #2 →

Figure 10.6 depicts RTS/CTS in an ad hoc WLAN. In this environment, there is no AP to forward the frames, so the RTS/CTS exchange happens directly between the transmitting and receiving stations.

FIGURE 10.6   RTS/CTS – Ad Hoc

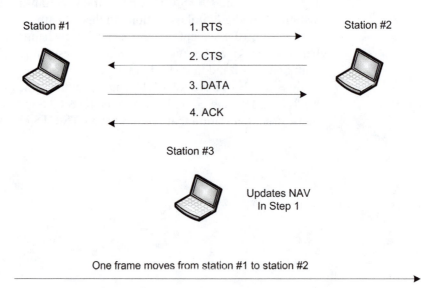

Ad Hoc WLAN

Station #1 | | Station #2

1. RTS →

2. CTS ←

3. DATA →

4. ACK ←

Station #3

Updates NAV
In Step 1

One frame moves from station #1 to station #2 →

CTS-to-Self

If a single BSS contains stations operating under both 802.11b and 802.11g, then 802.11g stations (and the AP) can send OFDM-modulated frames that the 802.11b stations cannot receive. In this case, the 802.11b stations' CCA function might determine that the network was idle when in reality an 802.11g station was transmitting a frame. Therefore, 802.11g defines a *protection mechanism* other than RTS/CTS that 802.11g stations (including the AP) can use to notify 802.11b stations when they are going to transmit.

Before it transmits a data frame, an 802.11g station using CTS-to-Self sends a CTS frame addressed to its own MAC address. This frame is not preceded by an RTS packet. The CTS frame is modulated in a way that the 802.11b stations can understand, using one of the modulation types described in the 802.11b supplement. Upon receipt of the frame, 802.11b stations set their NAV to a non-zero value (meaning that they understand the network is busy), allowing the 802.11g station to transmit its frame using entirely OFDM modulation (which produces higher data rates than DSSS modulation). It is common to see the AP using CTS-to-Self more often than the stations in a BSS.

Fragmentation

The 802.11 standard provides a standard method of fragmenting large frames into smaller pieces. Fragmentation of frames adds overhead and reduces protocol efficiency (decreases network throughput) when no errors are observed, but can reduce the time spent on retransmissions if errors are likely. If we assume that a corruption event will occur every few milliseconds on average, then the probability of a large frame being corrupted may be relatively high. If any part of the frame is corrupted, the entire frame is lost. By fragmenting the frame into smaller chunks, individual chunks may get through and only the chunks that happen to come during a corruption event need to be retransmitted.

A tradeoff must be made between the lower frame error rate that can be achieved by using smaller frames and the increased overhead of more frames on the network due to fragmentation. Each fragment requires its own headers and ACK, so the adjustment of the fragmentation level is also an adjustment to the amount of overhead associated with each frame transmitted. Stations never fragment multicast and broadcast frames, but rather only unicast frames, in order not to introduce unnecessary overhead onto the network. Finding the optimal fragmentation setting to maximize the network throughput on an 802.11 network is an important part of administering a wireless LAN.

Most wireless LAN client software utilities allow you to configure a fragmentation threshold. Frames that are smaller than the fragmentation threshold are not fragmented (no need to fragment it if it is already small), while frames larger than the fragmentation threshold are broken into fragments equal in size to the fragmentation threshold. Normally, the fragmentation threshold is set at its maximum value, meaning that the station will never fragment a frame. For most WLANs, this fragmentation threshold is the highest-performance setting. If your network is experiencing a high rate of frame corruption due to weak signal or RF interference, and increasing signal strength or removing interference sources has not solved the problem, decreasing the fragmentation threshold may increase throughput. While running a file transfer or other network-intensive activity, gradually decrease the fragmentation threshold until an improvement shows. Continue to decrease the fragmentation threshold until performance begins to decrease again.

If fragmentation is used, the network will experience a performance hit due to the overhead incurred with fragmentation. Sometimes this hit is acceptable in order to gain higher throughput due to a decrease in frame errors and subsequent retransmissions. Decreasing the fragmentation threshold should usually be a last resort solution, if for no other reason than that the fragmentation threshold is the same regardless of where the station is physically located. Decreasing the fragmentation threshold might make performance better in one interference-heavy area, but it will make performance worse everywhere else that the client goes. Different areas are likely to have different optimal fragmentation thresholds. It would be beneficial if 802.11 had provided some means for stations to automatically determine the best fragmentation threshold for a network; however, it does not and no vendor provides a proprietary version of this functionality.

Dynamic Rate Selection

Dynamic Rate Selection (DRS) is a term used to describe a method of dynamic speed adjustment on wireless LAN clients. There are many other terms for this functionality. This speed adjustment occurs as distance increases between the client and the access point, or as interference increases. It is imperative that you understand how this function works in order to plan for network throughput, cell sizes, and power outputs of access points and stations.

Modern spread spectrum systems are designed to make discrete jumps only to specified data rates, such as 1, 2, 5.5, and 11 Mbps (for 802.11b DSSS) or 6, 12, 18, 24, 36, 48, and 54 Mbps (for 802.11g OFDM). As distance increases between the access point and a station, the signal strength will decrease to a point where the current data rate cannot be maintained reliably. When this signal strength decrease occurs, the transmitting unit will drop its data rate to the next lower specified data rate, say from 11 Mbps to 5.5 Mbps or from 54 Mbps to 48 Mbps. As discussed in chapter 6, "Spread Spectrum," more complex signal encoding methods gives higher data rates, but these more complex signal encoding methods are more susceptible to corruption at a given distance from the AP. Therefore, for a given spread spectrum technology (DSSS vs. OFDM), higher data rates equate to lower range.

The RF coverage area is often visualized as a series of concentric circles around the AP, representing the coverage range of each data rate, with the highest data rates having the smallest circles. These zones of coverage will not be exact circles, but you can often find a fairly definite line where a station will drop from one data rate to a lower one. Figure 10.7 shows an example of such an illustration.

FIGURE 10.7 Dynamic Rate Selection

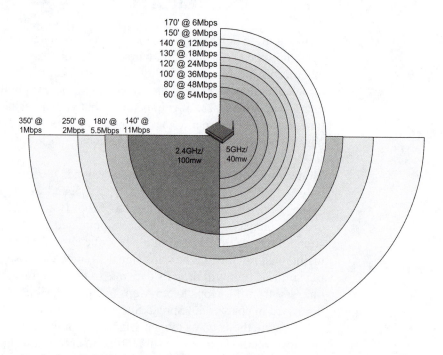

A wireless LAN system will never drop from 54 Mbps to 50 Mbps, for example, since 50 Mbps is not a specified data rate. The method of making such discrete jumps is typically called either Dynamic Rate Selection, Automatic Rate Shifting, or something similar, depending on the manufacturer. All 802.11 WLANs implement proprietary DRS, since the standard does not specify the details of how it is to be accomplished.

Key Terms

Before taking the exam, you should be familiar with the following terms:

Acknowledgement

Backoff

Clear channel assessment

Control Frame

CSMA/CA

Data Frame

DCF

DIFS

Dynamic rate selection

fragmentation

Interframe space

Management Frame

Physical carrier sense

PCF

PIFS

RTS/CTS

SIFS

Virtual carrier sense

Review Questions

1. 802.11 is often dubbed "wireless Ethernet." Explain why 802.11 is not wireless Ethernet, and the differences between an Ethernet transmission and an 802.11 transmission.

2. Which Layer 3–7 protocols do Wireless LANs support? Why is that important to the wireless LAN industry?

3. Explain the difference between CSMA/CA and CSMA/CD protocols. Which protocol do wireless LANs use? Why?

4. What is "interframe spacing" and what are the four types of interframe spaces defined in this text?

5. Explain why, in a practical everyday sense, RTS/CTS and CTS-to-Self are important to the operation of an efficient wireless LAN system.

Troubleshooting Wireless LAN Installations

CWNA Exam Objectives Covered:

❖ Identify, understand, and correct or compensate for the following wireless LAN implementation challenges:

- Multipath
- Hidden Node
- Near/Far
- Narrowband and Wideband RF Interference
- System throughput
- Co-channel and adjacent-channel interference
- Weather

❖ Identify RF signal characteristics, the applications of basic RF antenna concepts, and the implementation of solutions that require RF antennas

- Antenna Diversity

In This Chapter

Multipath

Hidden Node

Near/Far

Throughput

Interference

Range Considerations

Just as traditional wired networks have challenges during implementation, wireless LANs have their own set of challenges, mainly dealing with the behavior of RF signals. In this chapter, we will discuss the more common obstacles to successful implementation of a wireless LAN and how to troubleshoot them. There are different methods of discovering when these challenges exist, and each of the challenges discussed has its remedies and workarounds. The challenges to implementing any wireless LAN discussed herein are considered by many to be "textbook" problems that can occur within any wireless LAN installation, and, therefore, can be avoided by careful planning and simply being aware that these problems can and will occur.

Multipath

If you will recall from Chapter 2, "RF Fundamentals," there are two types of line of sight (LOS). First, there is *visual* LOS, which is what the human eye sees. Visual LOS is your first and most basic LOS test. If you can see the RF receiver from the installation point of the RF transmitter, then you have *visual* line of sight. Second, and different from visual LOS, is RF line of sight. RF LOS is what your RF device can "see."

The general behavior of an RF signal is to grow wider as it is transmitted farther. Because of this behavior, the RF signal will encounter objects in its path that will reflect, diffract, or otherwise interfere with the signal. When an RF wave is reflected off an object (a body of water, a tin roof, other metal objects, etc.) while moving towards its receiver, multiple wave fronts are created (one for each reflection point). There are now waves moving in many directions, and many of these reflected waves are still headed toward the receiver. This behavior is where we get the term *multipath,* as shown in Figure 11.1. Multipath is defined as the composition of a primary signal plus duplicate or echoed wave fronts caused by reflections of waves off objects between the transmitter and receiver. Since the reflections take a longer path to the receiver, they arrive after the direct signal. The delay between the instant that the main signal arrives and the instant that the last reflected signal arrives is known as *delay spread.*

FIGURE 11.1   Multipath Example

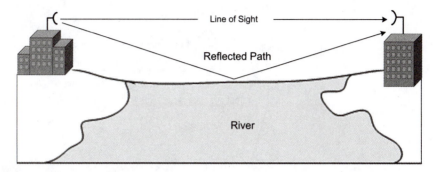

Effects of Multipath

Multipath can cause several different conditions, all of which can affect the transmission of the RF signal differently. These conditions include:

- Decreased signal amplitude
- Data corruption
- Signal nulling
- Increased signal amplitude

Decreased Signal Amplitude

When an RF wave arrives at the receiver, many reflected waves may arrive at the same time from different directions. The combination of these waves' amplitudes is additive to the direct (main) RF wave. Reflected waves, if out-of-phase with the main wave, can cause decreased signal amplitude at the receiver, as illustrated in Figure 11.2. This occurrence is commonly referred to as *downfade* and should be taken into consideration when conducting a sight survey and selecting appropriate antennas.

FIGURE 11.2 Downfade

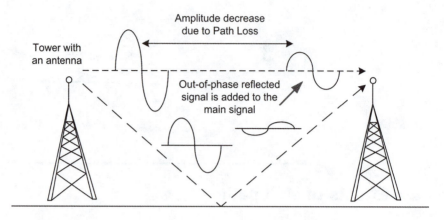

Corruption

Corrupted signals (waves) due to multipath can occur as a result of the same phenomena that cause decreased amplitude, but to a greater degree. When reflected waves arrive at the receiver out-of-phase with the main wave, as illustrated in Figure 11.3, they can cause the wave to be greatly reduced in amplitude, instead of only slightly reduced. The amplitude reduction is such that the receiver is sensitive enough to detect most of the information being carried on the wave, but not all.

FIGURE 11.3   RF Signal Corruption

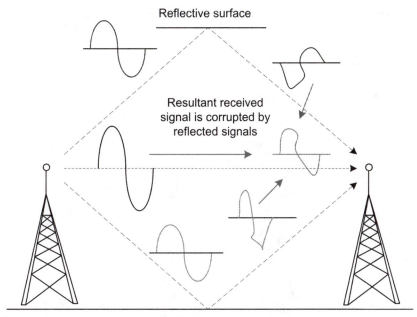

Reflective surface

In such cases, the signal to noise ratio (SNR) is generally very low, where the signal itself is very close to the noise floor. The receiver is unable to clearly decipher between the information signal and noise, causing the data that is received to be only part (if any) of the transmitted data. This corruption of data will require the transmitter to resend the data, increasing overhead and decreasing throughput in the wireless LAN.

Nulling

The condition known as nulling occurs when one or more reflected waves arrive at the receiver out-of-phase with the main wave with such amplitude that the main wave's amplitude is cancelled. As illustrated in Figure 11.4, when reflected waves arrive out-of-phase with the main wave at the receiver, the condition can cancel or "null" the entire set of RF waves, including the main wave.

FIGURE 11.4 RF Signal Nulling

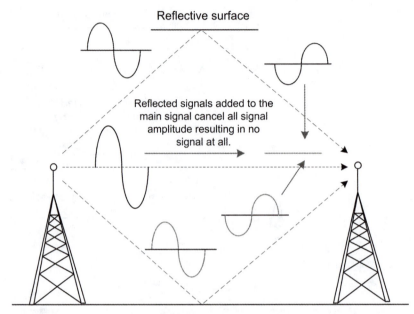

When nulling occurs, retransmission of the data will not solve the problem. The transmitter, receiver, or reflective objects must be moved. Sometimes more than one of these must be relocated to compensate for the nulling effects on the RF wave.

Increased Signal Amplitude

Multipath conditions also can cause a signal's amplitude to be increased from what it would have been without reflected waves present. *Upfade* is the term used to describe when multipath causes an RF signal to gain strength. Upfade, as illustrated in Figure 11.5, occurs due to reflected signals arriving at the receiver in-phase with the main signal. Similar to a decreased signal, all of these waves are additive to the main signal. *Under no circumstance can multipath cause the signal that reaches the receiver to be stronger than the transmitted signal that left the transmitting device.* If multipath occurs in such a way as to be additive to the main signal, the total signal that reaches the receiver will be stronger than the signal would otherwise have been without multipath present.

FIGURE 11.5 Upfade

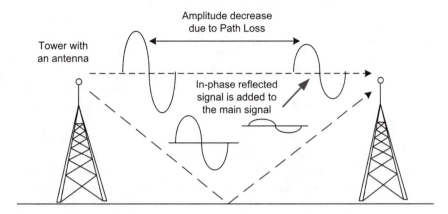

It is important to understand that a received RF signal can never be as strong as the signal that was transmitted, due to the effect of free space path loss (also called *path loss*). Path loss is the effect of a signal losing amplitude due to natural expansion as the signal travels through open space.

Think of path loss as someone blowing a bubble with bubble gum. As the gum expands, the gum at any point becomes thinner. If someone were to reach out and grab a 1-inch square piece of this bubble, the amount of gum they would actually get would be less and less as the bubble expanded. If a person grabbed a piece of the bubble while it was still small (close to the person's mouth, which is the transmitter in this analogy), the person would get a significant amount of gum. If the person waited to get that same size piece until the bubble were large (further from the transmitter), the piece would be only a very small amount of gum. This illustration shows that path loss is affected by two factors: first, the distance between transmitter and receiver, and second, the size of the receiving aperture (the size of the piece of gum that was grabbed).

Troubleshooting Multipath

An in-phase or out-of-phase RF wave cannot be seen, so you must look for the effects of multipath in order to detect its occurrence. When doing a link budget calculation, in order to find out just how much power output you will need to have a successful link between sites, you might calculate an output power level that should work, but does not. Such an occurrence is one way to determine that multipath is occurring.

Another common method of finding multipath is to look for RF coverage holes in a site survey. These holes are created both by highly-attenuating objects, such as metal-lined elevator shafts, and by multipath reflections that cancel the main signal. Understanding the sources of multipath is crucial to eliminating its effects.

Multipath is caused by reflected RF waves, so obstacles that more easily reflect RF waves, such as metal blinds, bodies of water, and metal roofs, should be removed from or avoided in the signal path, if possible. This procedure may include moving the transmitting and receiving antennas. Multipath is likely the most common "textbook" wireless LAN problem. Administrators and installers deal with multipath daily. Even wireless LAN users – because they are mobile – experience problems with multipath. Users may roam into an area with high multipath, not knowing why their RF signal has been so significantly degraded.

Solutions for Multipath

Antenna diversity was devised for the purpose of compensating for multipath. Antenna diversity means using multiple antennas, inputs, and receivers in order to compensate for the conditions that cause multipath. Diversity mitigates the effect of multipath because often, if a signal is being cancelled in one location, it may actually be reinforced in a nearby location. By placing antennas at both locations, the receiver can compensate. Diversity is used both to receive and transmit packets. When the AP detects the beginning of a frame transmission, the AP listens to one antenna, then the other, and determines which antenna has the highest signal strength. The AP then uses that antenna to receive the frame. The AP continues to listen on that antenna until it detects the beginning of the next frame, at which point it repeats this process. Although it might seem that, since the AP is stationary, one antenna will always be the "best," remember that the AP is serving many clients, and the multipath characteristics between each client and the AP differ. One client might be very weak on the "left" antenna and very strong on the "right" antenna; this situation might be reversed for a different client.

It is important to realize that, in this form of antenna diversity, the AP never receives on both antennas at the same time, nor does it switch from one antenna to another in the middle of a frame. These types of antenna diversity do exist, but they require more sophisticated (and expensive) radios. Interestingly, a form of "diversity" like this, known as Multiple-in/Multiple-out (MIMO), is planned for use in the 802.11n standard, giving data rates in excess of 100 Mbps. In a MIMO radio, two or more antennas are used simultaneously. Combined with sophisticated signal processing techniques, much greater range and throughput are possible.

Transmit diversity requires a different logic than receive diversity. Since the AP has no way of knowing what signal strength the client is seeing, there is no way for the AP to tell which antenna is best for each client. Typically, manufacturers implement transmit diversity by having the AP transmit each frame on the antenna that was last used to receive a frame. A more intelligent algorithm would be for the AP to remember the "last" antenna on a per-station basis. No vendors currently implement this algorithm.

Figure 11.6 illustrates an access point with multiple antennas to compensate for multipath.

FIGURE 11.6 Antenna Diversity

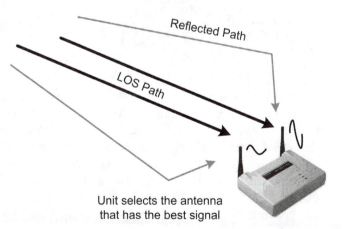

Hidden Node

Hidden node is a situation in which at least one node is unable to hear one or more of the other nodes connected to the wireless LAN. In this situation, a node can hear the access point, but cannot hear that there are other clients also connected to the same access point. This is due to some obstacle or a large amount of distance between the nodes. This situation causes collisions, which can result in significantly degraded throughput in the wireless LAN. One scenario that might cause the hidden node problem is illustrated in Figure 11.7.

FIGURE 11.7   Hidden Node Illustration

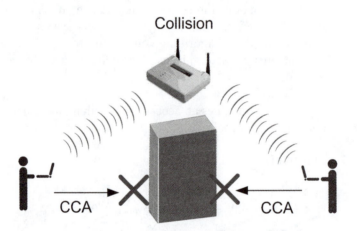

Figure 11.7 illustrates a thick block wall with an access point sitting on top. On each side of the wall is a wireless station. These wireless stations cannot hear each other's transmissions, but both can hear the transmissions of the access point. If station A is transmitting a frame to the access point, and station B cannot hear this transmission, station B assumes that the medium is clear and can begin a transmission of its own to the access point. The access point will, at this point, be receiving two different transmissions and there will be a collision. The collision will corrupt both frames and require both stations A and B to retransmit. Since they cannot hear each other, they will repeatedly transmit at will, thinking the medium is clear, and there will likely be another collision. This problem is exacerbated with many active nodes on the wireless LAN that cannot hear one another.

The hidden node problem can occur in three main ways. First, hidden node can occur when there is some obstacle between the stations, as described above. Second, hidden node can occur in a way in which the stations are on opposite sides of the AP. In this case, each station is within range of the AP, but they are far enough from each other that they can not hear each other. The stations can still communicate with each other since the AP will forward their frames, but since they cannot hear each others' transmissions, the hidden node condition exists and collisions are much more likely. A third way in which hidden node can occur is if one node is in a "null" relative to another node, due to multipath interference. Although the first type (a physical obstacle) is the most obvious, hidden nodes occur as a result of all three of these causes.

Diagnosing Hidden Node

Although we speak of hidden node as if it is a problem, you should realize that most 802.11 networks will have nodes that are hidden from each other at some point. For most 802.11 networks, hidden node is a normal state, not an exceptional state. The question with hidden nodes is not whether you have them at all, but whether they are decreasing performance enough to warrant some corrective action.

One signature of a hidden node is increased corruption near the AP and increased retransmissions from the clients *without* increased corruption near the clients. A hidden node will result in decreased throughput for that node and for all nodes that are associated with the same AP. If you perform a capture with a protocol analyzer near the AP, you will see high levels of corrupted frames (more than approximately 15 percent of data frames as a rough guideline, but you should compare current conditions to your baseline). If you capture with a protocol analyzer near an end station that is being affected by hidden node, you will *not* see excessive corrupted frames, but you *will* see lots of retransmissions (again, more than approximately 15 percent of data frames). Remember that the frames are being corrupted where the signals overlap (near the AP). Therefore, near each station, that station's signals are strong and uncorrupted. The frame is corrupted near the AP and the station must retransmit when it doesn't get its ACK.

A second method for diagnosing hidden node is to enable RTS/CTS on a station. RTS/CTS is discussed in chapter 10, "MAC and Physical Layers." Since RTS/CTS will specifically mitigate the effects of the hidden node problem, if RTS/CTS fixes the problem, then you know that the problem was hidden node. To implement RTS/CTS, you would decrease the RTS/CTS threshold on a client from its maximum value down to some smaller value – approximately 500 bytes – and then do a file transfer. If throughput improves relative to baseline, then hidden node is your problem. If throughput decreases, try again with higher values (1000 bytes, 1500 bytes, and so on). If *any* setting of RTS/CTS causes an increase in throughput, then you most likely have a hidden node. A network with no hidden nodes should *always* show a decrease in throughput when RTS/CTS is enabled. Since this method is basically trial-and-error, it may not be the fastest or most efficient way of diagnosing or correcting hidden node.

Because the nature of a wireless LAN increases mobility, you may encounter a hidden node at any time, despite a flawless design of your wireless LAN. If a user moves his or her computer to a conference room, another office, or into a data room, the new location of that node can potentially be hidden from the rest of the nodes connected to your wireless LAN.

Solutions for Hidden Node

Once you have done the troubleshooting and discovered that there is a hidden node problem, the problem node(s) must be located. Finding the node(s) will include a manual search for nodes that might be out of reach of the main cluster of nodes. This process is usually trial-and-error. Once these nodes are located, there are several remedies and workarounds for the problem.

- Use RTS/CTS
- Increase power to the nodes
- Remove obstacles
- Move the node

Use RTS/CTS

The RTS/CTS protocol is not necessarily a solution to the hidden node problem. Instead, it is a method of reducing the negative impact that hidden nodes have on the network.

Increase Power to the Nodes

Increasing the transmission power of the nodes can solve the hidden node problem by allowing the cell around each node to increase in size, encompassing all of the other nodes. This configuration might enable the hidden nodes to hear each other; however, if the nodes are far enough apart or the obstruction between them is sufficiently attenuating, it might not be possible to increase power enough to compensate.

While increasing power can solve the hidden node problem, it has disadvantages. First, most client cards have a fixed power output. Increasing transmission power on these cards will not be an option unless you want to use an external amplifier (which introduces still more issues with FCC system certification). Second, increasing transmission power increases co-channel and adjacent channel interference, which can lead to decreased system throughput. 802.11b and 802.11g channels are especially susceptible to adjacent channel interference from too much output power at too close range. Third, increasing output power will decrease the battery life of the node. Finally, it is often desirable to have a node's coverage area be as large as is needed and no larger. Increasing the node's output power to increase coverage in one direction may have the secondary effect of increasing coverage in undesired directions.

Remove Obstacles

Increasing the power on your mobile nodes may not work if, for example, the reason one node is hidden is that there is a cement or steel wall preventing communication with other nodes. It is doubtful that you would be able to remove such an obstacle, but removal of the obstacle is another remedy for the hidden node problem. Keep these types of obstacles in mind when performing a site survey.

Move the Node

Another method of solving the hidden node problem is moving the nodes so that they can all hear each other. If you have found that the hidden node problem is the result of a user moving his computer to an area that is hidden from the other wireless nodes, you may have to force that user to move again. The alternative to forcing users to move is extending your wireless LAN to add proper coverage to the hidden area, perhaps using additional access points.

Near/Far

The near/far problem in wireless LANs results from the scenario in which there exist stations that are near the access point and have high power settings, and then at least one station, using low power, that is much farther away from the access point than the aforementioned stations. The result of this type of situation is that the client(s) that are farther away from the access point, and using less power, simply cannot be heard over the traffic from the closer, high-powered clients, as illustrated in Figure 11.8.

FIGURE 11.8   Near/Far

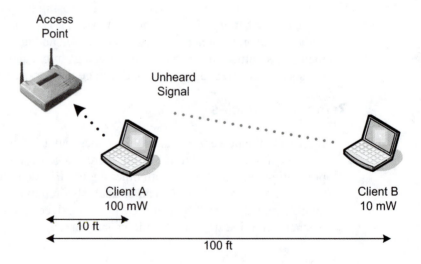

Near/far is similar in nature to a crowd of people all screaming at one time into a microphone, and one person whispering from 50 feet (15.2 meters) away from that same microphone. The voice of the person 50 feet (15.2 meters) away is not going to reach the microphone over the noise of the crowd shouting near the microphone. Even if the microphone is sensitive enough to pick up the whisper under silent conditions, the high-powered close-range conversations have effectively raised the noise floor to a point where low-amplitude inputs are not heard.

In a wireless LAN, the node that is being drowned out is well within the normal range of the access point, but it simply cannot be heard over the signals of the other clients. You must be aware of the possibility of the near/far problem during site surveys, and understand how to overcome the problem through proper wireless LAN design and troubleshooting techniques.

Troubleshooting Near/Far

Troubleshooting the near/far problem is normally as simple as taking a good look at the network design, locations of stations on the wireless network, and transmission output power of each node. These steps will give you clues as to what is likely going on with the stations having connectivity problems. Since near/far prevents a node from communicating, you should check to see if the station has drivers loaded properly for the wireless radio card, and has associated with the access point (shown in the association table of the access point).

The next step in troubleshooting near/far is use of a wireless protocol analyzer, which will pick up transmissions from all stations it hears. If a station that should be within the range of the AP can't connect, and you suspect the near/far problem as the culprit, you can confirm your diagnosis by measuring the signal strength of clients as you move from the "far" client's position toward the access point. When you are close to the "far" client, its signal strength should be high and its frames should be uncorrupted, but you will see an unusually high occurrence of retransmissions. Although the frames are not corrupted near the client, where the analyzer is located, they are being corrupted close to the access point, requiring retransmission. As you move the analyzer closer to the AP, the analyzer will see increased corruption of the frames sourced from the "far" client.

One other way to diagnose near/far is this: if a client can connect to the AP from a given position when there are no other clients near the AP, but the client cannot connect to the AP when there are other clients near the AP, then the problem is most likely near/far.

Solutions for Near/Far

Although the near/far problem can be debilitating for those clients whose RF signals get drowned out, near/far is a relatively easy problem to overcome in most situations. It is imperative to understand that the CSMA/CA protocol solves much of the near/far problem with no intervention by you. If a node can hear another node transmitting, it will stop its own transmissions, complying with shared medium access rules of CSMA/CA. However, if for any reason the near/far problem still exists in the network, the following is a list of remedies that are easily implemented and can overcome the near/far problem:

- Increase power to remote node (the one that is being drowned out)
- Decrease power of local nodes (the close, loud ones)
- Move the remote node closer to the access point
- Move the access point to a more central location
- Add another access point closer to the far node

The solution of moving the access point to a more central location should be viewed as a last resort, since moving an access point will likely disrupt more clients than it would help. Furthermore, the need to move an access point likely reveals a flawed site survey or network design, which is a much bigger problem. In this case, perhaps the network design should have included another access point closer to the "far" node.

Throughput

Throughput on a wireless LAN is based on many factors. For instance, the amount and type of interference may impact the amount of data retransmitted on the network. If security solutions such as WPA or VPN are implemented, then the additional overhead of encrypting and decrypting data may cause a decrease in throughput. Fragmentation, depending on how it is implemented, can have a severe detrimental affect on throughput. Greater distances between the transmitter and receiver will cause the throughput to decrease either because of an increase in corruption and retransmissions due to weaker signal strength, or because the transmitter drops to a lower data rate to avoid that corruption. Since WLANs are half-duplex, the number of users attempting to access the medium simultaneously will have an impact. An increase in simultaneous users will decrease the throughput each station receives from each access point.

The type of spread spectrum technology used – 802.11b, 802.11a, and/or 802.11g – will make a difference in throughput for several reasons. First, the data rates for 802.11b and 802.11g systems are quite different, with 802.11g systems extending up to 54 Mbps, while 802.11b systems max out at 11 Mbps. Second, when an area contains a mixture of 802.11b and 802.11g systems, throughput of the entire area is reduced. For example, an 802.11g system might achieve 20 Mbps of actual throughput, but if 802.11b stations are added to the area, actual throughput might be as low as 11 Mbps. This issue is discussed more completely in the CWAP class and study guide. 802.11a provides 54 Mbps data rates (~20 Mbps throughput) with no co-location issues with 802.11b or 802.11g.

The use of fragmentation (which requires the reassembly of frames) and RTS/CTS will affect throughput. Fragmentation and RTS/CTS always lower throughput below the theoretical maximum, but they might increase your actual throughput by compensating for other factors that hurt throughput, such as hidden node or interference. Fragmentation may introduce more interframe spaces, more MAC headers, and even more collisions on the medium, but can ultimately increase throughput if properly used.

Traffic patterns through the access point affect throughput. Traffic going between two wireless stations on the same AP must use the 802.11 interface twice: once going into the AP, and once coming out. Traffic going from a wireless station to a wired station only uses the 802.11 interface once. Therefore, the throughput for wireless-to-wireless communication is approximately half the maximum throughput for wireless-to-wired communication.

Co-location Throughput

Co-location is a common wireless LAN implementation technique that is used to provide more throughput to wireless users in a given area. You can reuse the same physical space, but use a different channel within that space over which to move data. Each IEEE standard has its own implementation challenges for co-location. 802.11b and 802.11g offer channels 1, 6 and 11 as "non-overlapping" channels. By "non-overlapping," we mean that channels are sufficiently spaced in the frequency spectrum so that they do not have adjacent (side-by-side) channel interference. An example of co-location is shown in Figure 11.9.

FIGURE 11.9   Access Point Co-location

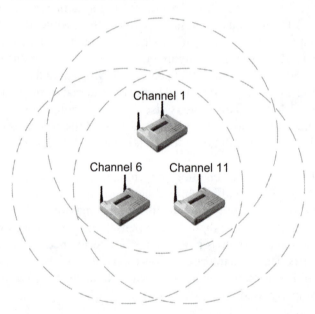

When co-locating multiple access points in the 2.4 GHz ISM band, it is highly recommended that you:

1.   Avoid mixing 802.11b and 802.11g access points if at all possible, to avoid having problems with protection mechanisms
2.   Use the same vendor for all access points (or use a WLAN switch) when possible to take advantage of load-balancing features

3. Use channels specified by 802.11b and 802.11g as non-overlapping (1, 6, and 11).

As shown in Figure 11.10, non-overlapping channels still have some amount of overlap, depending on proximity, power output, antenna gain and type, etc. We will discuss some solutions for minimizing the problems caused by this overlap in the section following.

FIGURE 11.10 2.4 GHz PHY Channel Overlap

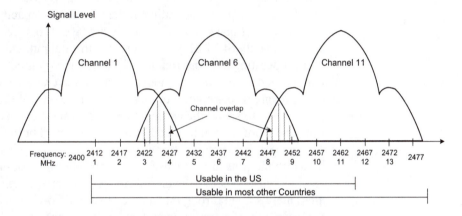

Co-location Throughput Problems and Solutions

The IEEE 802.11b and 802.11g standards call channels whose center frequencies are separated by at least 25 MHz "non-overlapping" channels. This definition is sufficient to yield good throughput results in well-designed WLANs. However, when access points are placed too close together, have too much output power, or have too much antenna gain, the 25 MHz channel separation is simply not enough to keep these "non-overlapping" channels from interfering with each other. Throughput is degraded on each channel, sometimes severely.

Many APs come configured to use their maximum output power. In many cases, this default setting provides a much larger coverage area than is useful. Clients at the edge of the AP's coverage may be able to hear the AP's strong signal, but their weak radios will not be able to send frames back on a consistent basis. By this logic, if all of your clients are PCMCIA cards with 30 mW of output power, there is no point in having a

200 mW access point, or any access point with much more than 30 mW of transmit power. There are cases that defy this logic, such as when using WLAN switches with phased array antennas, but that is another technical matter entirely that is not covered in this book.

One option, which is the easiest, is to use channels 1 and 11 with only 2 access points, as illustrated in Figure 11.11. Using only these two channels will ensure that you have minimal overlap between channels, regardless of proximity between systems, and, therefore, no detrimental effect on the throughput of each access point. By way of comparison, two 802.11b access points operating at the maximum capacity of 5.5 Mbps (about the best that you can expect by any 802.11b access point), give you a total capacity of 11 Mbps of aggregate throughput, whereas three access points operating at approximately 4 Mbps each (degraded from the maximum due to actual channel overlap) on average yields only 12 Mbps of aggregate throughput. For an additional 1 Mbps of throughput, you would have to spend the extra money to buy another access point, take the time and labor to install it, and have the continued burden of managing it. This means that if co-location is not properly accomplished, it might not be worth the time and expense. This configuration does not apply to channel reuse, where cells on different non-overlapping channels are alternately spread throughout an area to avoid co-channel interference. In that case, the APs are far enough away from each other that co-channel interference is not a factor.

FIGURE 11.11 Using two access points instead of three

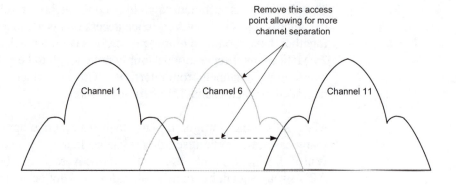

802.11a Equipment

The 802.11a standard specifies no overlapping channels, and, regardless of which channels you use, the network typically has no adjacent channel interference. We still say "typically" because at very close range, directly adjacent channels, such as 36 and 40, can still experience adjacent channel interference if the output power is high enough, proximity close enough, and antenna gain high enough on all of the units concerned. However, by design, there are no "overlapping" channels, and there are more "non-overlapping" channels in the 5GHz UNII bands than in the 2.4 GHz ISM band. This gives the potential for an incredible amount of throughput in the same physical space.

Interference

Due to the unpredictable behavioral tendencies of RF, you must take into account many kinds of RF interference during implementation and management of a wireless LAN. Narrowband, all-band, RF signal degradation, and adjacent and co-channel interference are the most common sources of RF interference that occur during implementation of a wireless LAN. In this section, we will discuss these types of interference, how they affect the wireless LAN, how to locate them, and, in some cases, how to work around them.

Narrowband

Narrowband RF is basically the opposite of spread spectrum technology. Narrowband signals, depending on output power, frequency width in the spectrum, and consistency, can intermittently interrupt or even disrupt the RF signals emitted from a spread spectrum device such as an access point. However, as the name suggests, narrowband signals do not disrupt RF signals across the entire RF band. Thus, if the narrowband signal is primarily disrupting the RF signals in channel 3, then you could, for example, use Channel 11, where you may not experience any interference at all. It is also likely that only a small portion of any given channel might be disrupted by narrowband interference. Typically, only a small amount of the entire width of a channel, perhaps a 1 MHz wide section somewhere near the center frequency of an 802.11b MHz channel, would be disrupted due to narrowband interference. Given this type of interference, spread spectrum technologies will usually work around this problem without any additional administration or configuration.

To identify narrowband interference, you will need a spectrum analyzer, shown in Figure 11.12. Spectrum analyzers can measure the amount of RF energy at various frequencies in the area.

FIGURE 11.12 Handheld digital spectrum analyzer showing a narrowband signal

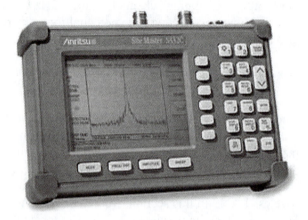

Spectrum analyzers useful for analyzing wireless LANs typically must cover a spectral range up to 6 GHz and be portable. Units from reputable vendors such as Anritsu and Rohde & Schwarz may range from $3,000– $15,000, depending on options and size.

In order to remedy a narrowband RF interference problem, you must first find where the interference originates by using the spectrum analyzer, typically with a directional antenna attached to it. As you walk closer to the source of the RF signal, the RF signal on the display of your spectrum analyzer grows in amplitude (size). When the RF signal peaks on the screen, you have located its source. At this point, you can remove the source, shield it, or use your knowledge as a wireless network administrator to configure your wireless LAN to efficiently deal with the narrowband interference. Of course, there are several options within this last category, such as changing channels, changing spread spectrum technologies (DSSS to FHSS or 802.11b to 802.11a), and others that are covered in later sections.

All-band Interference

All-band interference is any signal that interferes with the RF band from one end of the radio spectrum to the other. All-band interference does not refer to interference only across the 2.4 GHz ISM band, but rather is the term used in any case where interference covers the entire range you are trying to use, regardless of frequency. Technologies like Bluetooth (which hops across the entire 2.4 GHz ISM band many times per second) can, and at close range usually do, significantly interfere with 802.11 RF signals. Bluetooth is considered all-band interference for an 802.11 wireless network.

When all-band interference is present, the best solution is to change to a different technology, such as moving from 802.11b (which uses the 2.4 GHz ISM band) to 802.11a (which uses the 5 GHz UNII bands). If changing technologies is not feasible due to cost or implementation problems, the next best solution is to find the source of the all-band interference and remove it from service, if possible. Finding the source of all-band interference is more difficult than finding the source of narrowband interference, because you are not watching a single signal on the spectrum analyzer. Instead, you are looking at a range of signals, all with varying amplitudes.

Weather

Severely adverse weather conditions can affect the performance of a wireless LAN. In general, common weather occurrences like rain, snow, or fog do not have an adverse affect on wireless LANs. However, extreme occurrences of the elements, such as lightning, wind, hail, and perhaps even smog, can cause degradation or even downtime of your wireless LAN. Smog contains chemicals that can cause RF signals to refract. Hail can damage exposed WLAN components.

Water

Snow, when collecting on trees and obstacles normally in part of the RF path (like the Fresnel Zone), can act as a wall of water which can attenuate an RF signal to some degree; the same can hold true for leafy trees that hold lots of rain water for long periods of time.

 2.4 GHz signals may be attenuated by up to 0.05 dB/km (0.08 dB/mile) by torrential rain (4 inches/hr). Thick fog produces up to 0.02 dB/km (0.03 dB/mile) attenuation. At 5.8 GHz, torrential rain may produce up to 0.5 dB/km (0.8 dB/mile) attenuation, and thick fog up to 0.07 dB/km (0.11 dB/mile). These numbers are only provided as informational, not for test purposes.

Wind

Wind does not affect radio waves or an RF signal, but it can affect the positioning and mounting of outdoor antennas. For example, consider a wireless point-to-point link that connects two buildings that are 12 miles (20 km) apart. Taking into account the curvature of the Earth (Earth bulge), and having only a five-degree vertical and horizontal beam width on each antenna, the positioning of each antenna would have to be exact. A strong wind could easily move one or both antennas enough to completely degrade the signal between the two antennas. This effect is called "antenna wind loading," and is illustrated in Figure 11.13. Grid antennas, which are like parabolic antennas but are made of a wire mesh instead of solid metal, alleviate this problem by reducing the surface area that the antenna presents to the wind. Because of the properties of RF signals, grid antennas are no less powerful or sensitive than their solid counterparts, even though they have less surface area.

FIGURE 11.13 Antenna wind loading on point-to-point networks

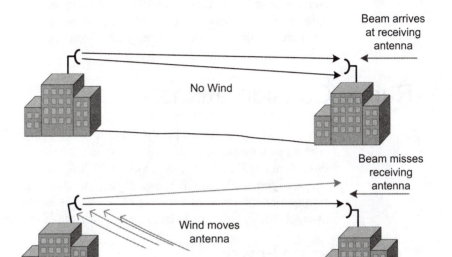

Other similarly extreme weather occurrences, like tornadoes or hurricanes, must also be considered. If you are implementing a wireless LAN in a geographic location where hurricanes or tornadoes occur frequently, you should certainly take that into account when setting up any type of outdoor wireless LAN. In such weather conditions, securing antennas, cables, and the like are all very important.

Air Stratification

Extreme altitude changes can mean extreme temperature changes. Air stratification (layering) may cause RF signals to bend. This bending may mean that long distance point-to-point links are degraded because they become misaligned.

Protective Equipment

A *radome* can be used to protect an antenna from the environmental elements. If used, radomes must have a drain hole for condensation drainage. Yagi antennas without radomes are vulnerable to rain, snow, and ice. This precipitation will accumulate on the antenna elements and detune the performance. The droplets actually make each antenna element look longer than it really is. Ice accumulation on exposed antenna elements can cause the same detuning effect as rain; however, it stays around longer. Radomes may also protect an antenna from falling objects, such as ice falling from an overhead tree.

Range Considerations

When considering how to position wireless LAN hardware, the communication range of the units must be taken into account. Generally, three things will affect the range of an RF link: transmission power, antenna type and location, and environment. The maximum communication range of a wireless LAN link is reached when, at some distance, the link begins to become unstable but is not lost.

Transmission Power

The output power of the transmitting radio will have an effect on the range of the link. A higher output power will cause the signal to be transmitted a greater distance, resulting in a greater range. Conversely, lowering the output power will reduce the range. Output power does not always mean a higher quality link. It only means that the transmission is going farther in a given environment.

Balancing the power of the client and the AP is another consideration. Increasing AP power may not increase effective range if the AP is much more powerful than the clients. For example, if the AP has a 100 mW radio and the clients have 30 mW radios, a situation can arise in which the clients can hear the AP's powerful signals, but cannot transmit a powerful enough signal to get a response back. A careless site survey might focus on what the client can hear from the AP and overlook whether the AP could hear the client. This would result in measuring the AP's coverage range as being much larger than it effectively is. Our guideline is that there is rarely a good reason for the AP to be more powerful than its most powerful client, and that site surveys should be done assuming that the AP's output power is no stronger than the weakest expected client.

Antenna Type

The type of antenna used affects the range either by focusing the RF energy into a tighter beam to transmit the beam farther (as a parabolic dish antenna does) or by transmitting the beam in all directions (as an omni-directional antenna does), reducing the range of communication. Phased-array antennas can create directed, focused beams of coverage, potentially increasing range by a great deal.

Whereas an AP with higher output power than the clients may not increase effective range, a principle of RF transmission called *antenna reciprocity* means that you *can* increase effective range by putting a higher gain antenna on the access point. Antenna reciprocity essentially means that "all other things being equal, if I can transmit to you, I can also hear your transmissions." The same principles that make a high-gain antenna a more powerful transmitter make it an equally more sensitive receiver.

Environment

A noisy or unstable environment can cause the range of a wireless LAN link to be decreased. The bit error rate of an RF link is greater at the fringes of coverage due to a small signal to noise ratio. Also, adding interference effectively raises the noise floor, lessening the likelihood of maintaining a reliable link.

The range of an RF link also can be influenced by the frequency of the transmission. Though it is not normally a concern within a wireless LAN implementation, frequency might be a consideration when planning a bridge link. For example, a 2.4 GHz system will be able to reach farther at the same output power than a 5 GHz system.

Key Terms

Before taking the exam, you should be familiar with the following terms:

all-band interference

antenna diversity

co-channel Interference

downfade

free space path loss

narrowband interference

nulling

spectrum analyzer

upfade

Review Questions

1. Explain what multipath is, and what antenna technology helps alleviate the effects of multipath on wireless LAN systems.

2. Describe a real world example of the hidden node problem. How does the hidden node problem occur? How can it be solved?

3. In a situation in which there are three co-located 802.11b access points in the same physical space, explain the proper method of implementing these access points, what problems can occur, and how to alleviate those problems when they do occur.

4. How does the co-location of 802.11b/g access points differ from that of 802.11a access points? How do the IEEE standards differ in their explanations of non-overlapping standards?

5. When should you consider RF interference during the implementation of a wireless LAN? What types of interference are there, and how can each be mitigated?

Wireless LAN Security

CWNA Exam Objectives Covered:

In This Chapter

802.11 Security Methods

Additional Security Methods

Attacks on Wireless LANs

Corporate Security Policy

❖ Identify the strengths, weaknesses, appropriate uses, and appropriate implementation of the following 802.11 security-related items

- Shared Key Authentication

- Encryption Algorithms

- Key Management Mechanisms

- Access Control and Authentication

- MAC Filters

❖ Describe the following types of wireless LAN security attacks, and explain how to identify and prevent them where possible

- Eavesdropping

- RF Jamming (Denial of Service)

- Man-in-the-Middle

- Management Interface Exploits

- Encryption Cracking

- Hijacking

❖ Describe, explain, and illustrate the appropriate applications for the following client-related wireless security solutions

- IPSec VPN

- PPTP VPN

- Profile-based Firewalls

- Captive Portal

- ❖ Describe, explain, and illustrate the appropriate applications for the following wireless LAN system security and management features
  - Rogue AP detection and/or containment
  - SNMPv3 / HTTPS / SSH
- ❖ Identify the purpose and features of the following wireless analysis systems and explain how to install, configure, integrate, and manage them as applicable
  - Distributed Wireless Intrusion Detection Systems (WIDS)
  - Remote hardware and software sensors
  - Handheld and laptop protocol analyzers
- ❖ Describe the following General Security Policy elements
  - Risk assessment
  - Impact Analysis
  - Security Auditing
- ❖ Describe the following Functional Security Policy elements
  - Baseline Practices
  - Design and Implementation Practices
  - Physical Security
  - Social Engineering
  - Monitoring, Response, and Reporting

Wireless LANs are not inherently secure; however, if you do not take any precautions or configure any defenses with *wired* LAN connections, they are not secure either. The key to making a wireless LAN secure and keeping it secure is educating those who implement and manage the wireless LAN. Education on routine and advanced security procedures for wireless LANs is essential to preventing network security breaches via your wireless LAN.

Some administrators have concluded that the right answer to wireless security is simply to outlaw wireless networks altogether. This logic fails on several fronts. First, although wireless LANs today are sometimes just an added convenience, the use of wireless LANs is likely to continue to increase. This means that eventually a "killer application" will come along that will cause users to demand wireless access. At that point, outlawing wireless equipment entirely will no longer be an option. VoWiFi has been suggested to be such a killer application. Second, in every case that we have seen where corporate policy outlawed wireless LANs, users have set up their own wireless equipment. This means that instead of having a controlled, secure wireless LAN, the administrator had an uncontrolled, hidden, and most likely insecure, wireless LAN. This is a case of, "better the devil you know than the devil you don't." It is better to have an official WLAN that you can secure than dozens of unofficial WLANs over which you have no control.

Despite the challenges of securing wireless networks, they can be made secure with proper education of users and administrators, and the application of appropriate technology. In this chapter, we will discuss the various methods that can be used to secure a wireless network. We will describe why WEP is essentially useless for security, and methods that can be used in place of WEP, including 802.1X/EAP, and WPA/WPA2/802.11i. We also will discuss methods that can be used on top of 802.11, including network layer VPN mechanisms like IPSec and PPTP, and application layer mechanisms such as SSL/TLS. We will explain the various methods that can be used to attack a wireless LAN so that, as an administrator, you will know what to expect and how to prevent it. Finally, we will offer some recommendations for maintaining wireless LAN security and discuss corporate security policy as it pertains specifically to wireless LANs.

This chapter on wireless LAN security is by no means the end of knowledge on the subject. Rather, this chapter should serve as a basic introduction to the inherent weaknesses of wireless LANs and the available solutions to compensate for these weaknesses. The most thorough and complete information about securing wireless LANs is available in the CWSP Official Study Guide.

802.11 Security Methods

Wireless security can generally be divided into two categories: solutions that are built into the 802.11 series of standards (those that are defined by 802.11 committees) and solutions that are independent of 802.11 (that either ride "on top" of 802.11 or offer a proprietary AES-based layer 2 solution). Solutions such as WEP, TKIP, 802.1X/EAP, and 802.11i are examples of the former. Solutions such as IPSec, SSL, or PPTP encryption are examples of the latter. This section of the chapter will cover solutions that are built into or defined by the 802.11 series of standards.

Wired Equivalent Privacy (WEP)

WEP is the original authentication and encryption mechanism specified by the 802.11 standard. WEP is a simple encryption algorithm that utilizes a pseudorandom number generator (PRNG) and the RC4 stream cipher. The RC4 stream cipher is fast and efficient when encrypting and decrypting, which minimizes its impact on network throughput. It is simple to implement in inexpensive hardware, which made it a good candidate when the 802.11 standard was in its infancy. On the other hand, as implemented in 802.11, RC4 is not as cryptographically strong as encryption algorithms like AES, but it was believed to be "strong enough" for 802.11.

To encrypt or decrypt data with WEP, the RC4 algorithm is used to create a pseudorandom string of bits, known as a *keystream*. The WEP key is used as the "seed" for the pseudorandom algorithm, so any two stations that have the same WEP key can generate the same keystream. The sender XORs the unencrypted data, known as the *plaintext*, with the keystream to create the encrypted data, known as the *ciphertext*. Although an XOR is a very simple mathematical algorithm, the data can nevertheless be considered encrypted since no one can generate the correct keystream, reverse the XOR, and recover the plaintext without knowing the WEP key. Upon reception of the frame, the receiver (who has the same WEP key as the sender) generates a keystream, reverses the XOR process, and recovers the plaintext.

WEP encrypts all data in the frame from the LLC layer on up the OSI stack, such as IP headers, TCP headers, application data, and so forth. Layer 2 (802.11) headers are not encrypted. In addition, management and control frames are not encrypted. Therefore, an attacker could see the MAC addresses of your wireless stations, SSID information, etc., but could not see IP addresses or other information above the MAC sublayer of the Data Link layer.

Although WEP was not intended to provide unbreakable security, it turned out to have significant and unforeseen weaknesses. It is not essential for you to know the details of WEP's cryptographic weaknesses, but we provide a summary of them here so you can understand decisions that were later made in mechanisms designed to address WEP's weaknesses.

- WEP implements the RC4 encryption algorithm in a way that allows attackers to determine which frames are encrypted, using mathematically "weak" keys. An analysis of these frames can allow an attacker to learn the encryption key for a network. Aircrack is one application that takes advantage of this weakness.

- The RC4 algorithm requires that an attacker not be able to capture two ciphertexts (encrypted data frames) that were encrypted with the same keystream. Because each frame is encrypted with a different keystream, it is possible that the number of possible keystreams will be exhausted in a short period of time, allowing this event to occur. The specific amount of time that it takes for this to happen depends on how busy the network is (more frames per second exhausts the keystreams faster) and the number of possible keystreams that are available. The number of keystreams is based on the length of a field called the Initialization Vector (IV). In WEP, the IV is 24 bits (3 bytes) long, meaning that there are 2^{24} possible keystreams.

- WEP does not protect against replay attacks. An attacker can capture a frame and then retransmit the frame onto the network at a later time. The frame would be indistinguishable from the original.

- WEP does not protect against forgeries. Even without knowing the WEP key, it is possible for an attacker to modify arbitrary bits in an encrypted frame in ways that are undetectable to receiving stations.

- 802.11 provided no means for centrally managing WEP keys. They must be manually configured on all stations. If a WEP key is compromised, changing to the new key is difficult if the network contains more than a few stations.

At this point in the development of 802.11 security, all you need to know is that, even in the best case, WEP is too cryptographically weak to be considered secure. Even in very low security settings, such as a home network, replacements for WEP (like WPA) provide much better security at zero additional cost or complexity. Unless the network contains legacy equipment that is not capable of more advanced security methods, there is no reason for an 802.11 network to use WEP. If the network contains legacy equipment, it should be migrated to more modern equipment as soon as is feasible.

Temporal Key Integrity Protocol (TKIP)

Temporal Key Integrity Protocol (TKIP) was the first attempt to fix the security holes in WEP. As with WEP, TKIP's designers realized that TKIP was not a perfect solution to 802.11 security, but it was hoped that TKIP would provide better security than WEP until more robust methods could be devised. One of the limitations in developing more robust security methods is that it takes time to develop standards. 802.11i, the current "ultimate" answer to 802.11 security, was only ratified in June 2004, approximately three years after the 802.11i committee was first formed in May of 2001. A second limitation was that any security solution had to be able to be deployed through firmware and driver updates to existing hardware. Any solution that needed more powerful hardware would have required customers to replace their equipment, which many would have been hesitant to do. This would have left too many systems vulnerable to attack.

To address the issue of hardware compatibility, TKIP continues to use RC4 encryption, just as WEP did. WEP supports both 64-bit and 128-bit encryption keys, but TKIP uses only 128-bit keys, which does not increase security over a 64-bit key as much as you might think. Most attacks on 802.11's WEP encryption are independent of the key length.

TKIP's implementation of RC4 encryption is stronger than WEP's implementation. One major problem with WEP's implementation of RC4 was that it made it too easy for an attacker to capture frames that were encrypted with the same keystream. In WEP, the keystream is a function of the WEP key and a value called the initialization vector (IV), which increments for every frame. Since the WEP key is static and is the same in all stations in a BSS, within a single BSS, the keystream is a direct function of the IV: if the IV changes, the keystream changes; if the IV stays the same, the keystream stays the same. The goal of having the IV change every frame is to prevent two frames that were encrypted with the same keystream from being captured by an attacker (a known weakness of the RC4 algorithm). Since WEP's IV is 24 bits long, that means that within a single BSS, there are only 2^{24} possible keystreams. Although this seems like a large number, a busy network can use up all possible keystreams in only a few hours at most. In addition, most stations choose the IV in a sub-optimal way; e.g., instead of starting with a random number, they start with an IV of zero each time the station reboots or the card is plugged in. This increases the likelihood of an attacker capturing two frames that were encrypted with the same keystream.

TKIP addresses this weakness through *per-packet key mixing* and *automatic rekeying*. In per-packet key mixing, each station is assigned a static WEP key that is the same for all stations (just as in WEP). This key is known as the *temporal key*. Each station then combines this key with its six-byte MAC address to create an encryption key that is unique for each station. This creates a much larger number of available keystreams for a single BSS, since each station effectively is using a different WEP key. To further increase the number of available keystreams, TKIP uses a six-byte IV instead of WEP's three-byte IV.

The combination of the temporal key with the station's MAC address is known as the *Phase 1 intermediate key*. In the second half of per-packet key mixing, the Phase 1 intermediate key is run through a simple algorithm (known as the *mixing algorithm*) to produce the encryption key for the frame. The purpose of the mixing algorithm is to make it more difficult for an attacker to determine whether a frame was encrypted with a mathematically "weak" WEP key.

Even with a longer IV and per-packet key mixing, a station would eventually exhaust the total number of available keystreams, so TKIP provides a mechanism whereby a station's temporal key can be periodically changed. This is typically performed every 10,000 frames, but the rekeying interval can be configured by the administrator.

Rekeying ensures that 1) no station has a temporal key long enough to exhaust the keystream associated with that key; 2) no station has a temporal key long enough for an attacker to crack the key; and 3) even if an attacker does crack the key, the crack is only good for the balance of the current set of 10,000 frames, at which point the temporal key changes and the attacker has to start from scratch.

TKIP addresses replay attacks by enforcing sequence number ordering on frames. Even if a frame is retransmitted by a station, it must be updated with a correct sequence number, which will require the station to update certain encrypted fields of the frame. An attacker who was replaying a previously-captured frame would not be able to correctly update those fields since the attacker would not have the required keys.

Finally, TKIP addresses frame forgery through the use of a *message integrity checksum* (MIC, also known as "Michael"). A complete description of Michael is somewhat complex, so suffice it to say that Michael is a small (eight bytes), additional encryption method that detects if the frame has been modified. Unlike the previous parts of TKIP, Michael is optional (forgery is ostensibly the least likely type of attack against an 802.11 network). Since most 802.11 cards do not have hardware support for MIC calculation, Michael must be performed in software. As a result, most machines will suffer a throughput and processor cycle loss if Michael is enabled. Michael is implemented in addition to the four-byte CRC-32 that is part of WEP.

Most hardware that supports WEP can be upgraded to use TKIP through a standard firmware update. Most APs and clients support TKIP out of the box today, since TKIP is a required part of WPA certification (discussed next). Access points running TKIP will still be able to service WEP-only clients for backwards compatibility, but supporting both WEP and TKIP clients on the same network will introduce a security flaw into the network.

TKIP was released in 2002 by Cisco. Initially, TKIP was only available with Cisco clients and access points. The devices would use TKIP to encrypt the frames and 802.1X/EAP (discussed later) to authenticate the users and distribute the encryption keys. Specifically, Cisco used a proprietary version of EAP known as *Lightweight Extensible Authentication Protocol* (LEAP). Originally, TKIP and LEAP were only available together and the terms were somewhat interchangeable. Today, TKIP has been separated from LEAP and is used in WPA and 802.11i (discussed later). The original combination of TKIP and LEAP is now referred to as CKIP, while TKIP refers to the encryption mechanism described above, regardless of where it is being used.

802.1X/EAP Framework

After TKIP, 802.1X/EAP was the next part of increasing the security of 802.11 WLANs. Whereas TKIP addressed weaknesses in 802.11's implementation of encryption, 802.1X/EAP addressed weaknesses in 802.11's authentication. As you learned in chapter 9, WEP provides rudimentary security in the form of Shared Key authentication, but the "CHAP-style" or "hashed-password" authentication used in Shared Key authentication is vulnerable to certain well-known attacks and is too easily defeated. 802.1X/EAP is combined with TKIP encryption to address both authentication and encryption security.

The 802.1X standard ties an existing security protocol called EAP (*Extensible Authentication Protocol*) to both the wired and wireless LAN media. Since EAP is a generic authentication protocol framework, it can work with many different types of authentication mechanisms. For example, depending on which type of authentication was being used, EAP might authenticate a user based on a username and password combination, an SSL certificate, a Kerberos ticket, or the information contained in a SIM chip in the user's cell phone. This flexibility is the key to EAP's power and its complexity. On the one hand, EAP can be tied into many different security architectures, but on the other hand, just saying that you are using EAP does not say much since so many different types of EAP exist. In the wireless space, EAP has largely replaced other layer 2 authentication protocols, such as PAP and CHAP.

Because EAP was not part of the original 802.11 standard, EAP frames are considered to be upper-layer data by the MAC layer of the station and the AP. An 802.11 station cannot send upper-layer data through the AP until it is in the "authenticated and associated" state (see chapter 9 for more details). Therefore, a station using 802.1X/EAP authentication must authenticate and associate to the AP (using 802.11 management frames) before it can commence with the *network* authentication and association (using 802.1X/EAP). Stations using 802.1X/EAP network authentication will use Open System authentication to complete the association with the access point before continuing on to the 802.1X/EAP network authentication process.

Typically, user authentication is accomplished using a Remote Authentication Dial-In User Service (RADIUS) server and some type of user database. The user database might be "native RADIUS," in which case it is configured directly on the RADIUS server itself, or the RADIUS server might interface with the Windows Active Directory, allowing users to log in to the wireless network with the same username and password that they log in to their desktop. In this case, users might not even have to manually enter a username and password since the client software could be configured to automatically attempt to log in with the current Windows username and password. Thus, whether or not a RADIUS server supported Active Directory integration would be a major consideration for the WLAN administrator. *Lightweight Directory Access Protocol* (LDAP) is another common authentication protocol that might be supported by a RADIUS server. Although LDAP is a generic protocol for looking up information in a database, it is commonly used to access databases containing security information, such as usernames and passwords.

The process of authentication using 802.1X/EAP is shown in Figure 12.1. A wireless network using 802.11i can support 802.1X/EAP, AAA, mutual authentication, and dynamic encryption key generation, none of which were included in the original 802.11 standard. "*AAA*" is an acronym for *authentication* (identifying who you are), *authorization* (attributes to allow you to perform certain tasks on the network), and *accounting* (shows what you have done and where you have been on the network).

In the 802.1X/EAP framework model, network authentication consists of
three pieces: the supplicant, the authenticator, and the authentication
server. The supplicant is the device that is requesting access to the
network. The authenticator is an intermediate device that passes frames
from the client to the authentication server (typically an AP). The
authentication server is the device that actually authenticates the user
(typically a RADIUS server). The general process of authentication is
shown in Figure 12.1.

FIGURE 12.1   802.1X/EAP Authentication Framework

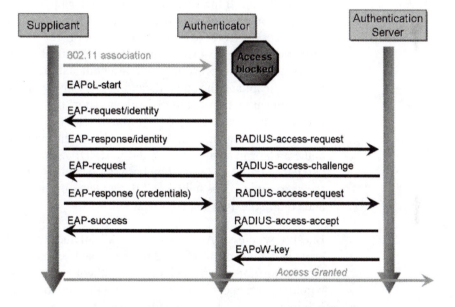

First, the supplicant indicates that it would like to perform EAP
authentication by sending an EAPoL-Start frame to the authenticator.
The authenticator sends a request/identity frame to the supplicant, asking
the supplicant to provide some piece of identifying information. The
specific information depends on what type of EAP is being used. For
example, in EAP-MD5, it would be a username, while in EAP-TLS, the
requested information would be an SSL certificate. Fortunately, the
authenticator does not care what EAP type is being used or what
information the supplicant provides, because the authenticator is simply

going to pass whatever information the supplicant provides on to the authentication server.

Following the request/identity, a series of frames is exchanged between the supplicant and the authentication server. Technically, the authenticator forwards the frames between the supplicant and the authentication server. These frames carry out the actual process of authenticating the user, and the data they carry is specific to the EAP type being used.

If the authentication is successful, an EAP-success frame is delivered to the supplicant. If the EAP type being used supports dynamic encryption key assignment (most do), the next step is for the supplicant and the authentication server to derive the encryption key. They do this based on information that was exchanged in the authentication process, or based on information that is preconfigured into both stations. After this step, both the supplicant and the authentication server know the encryption key that the supplicant will use, but the authenticator (the AP) does not. The AP needs to know the client's encryption key so it can send messages to the client. So, the authentication server delivers the encryption key to the authenticator in an attribute field of a RADIUS frame, which is encrypted using the shared secret held by both the AP and RADIUS server. Now the encryption key is held by all three pieces of the 802.1X/EAP model and communication can commence.

Because wireless LAN security is essential and EAP authentication types provide the means of securing the wireless LAN connection, vendors are rapidly developing and adding EAP authentication support to their wireless LAN access points. Knowing the type of EAP that is being used is important in understanding the characteristics of the authentication method, such as passwords, key generation, mutual authentication, and protocol. When choosing your security solution, you must make sure that the client software and RADIUS server you select all support the EAP type you plan to use. Since the AP simply passes the EAP packets through to the RADIUS server, the AP does not need to support any particular EAP type as long as it supports the 802.1X/EAP framework. Most clients and servers *do not* support all forms of EAP. Some of the commonly deployed EAP authentication types include:

EAP-MD-5 Challenge

EAP-MD-5 Challenge is the earliest EAP authentication type, and essentially duplicates CHAP password protection on a wireless LAN. In other words, EAP-MD5 uses usernames and passwords for authentication. EAP-MD5 represents a kind of base-level EAP support among 802.1X devices.

EAP-MD5 has three main weaknesses. First, the client is authenticated by the server, but the server is never authenticated by the client, making EAP-MD5 vulnerable to "rogue" servers. Second, EAP-MD5 uses hashed passwords to authenticate the users, and hashed passwords have several well-known cryptographic weaknesses. Third, EAP-MD5 has no support for dynamically assigning encryption keys, so keys are never rotated.

EAP-Cisco Wireless

EAP-Cisco Wireless is also called LEAP (Lightweight Extensible Authentication Protocol). This EAP authentication type is used primarily in Cisco wireless LAN access points and in other devices that carry the Cisco Certified Extensions (CCX) certification. LEAP provides security during credential exchange, encrypts data transmission using dynamically-generated WEP keys, and supports mutual authentication. Like EAP-MD5, cryptographic weaknesses have been found in LEAP. Specifically, the username/password exchange can be captured by an eavesdropper, and the eavesdropper can then attempt to crack the password using a dictionary attack. The username is passed across the wireless medium in clear text. Software to crack LEAP is freely available on the Internet.

EAP-TLS (Transport Layer Security)

EAP-TLS provides for certificate-based mutual authentication of the client and the network. EAP-TLS relies on client-side and server-side certificates to perform authentication, using dynamically generated per-user, per-session WEP keys and mutual authentication to secure the connection. Windows XP includes an EAP-TLS client, and EAP-TLS is also supported by Windows 2000.

Assuming that good certificate management procedures are followed, EAP-TLS is one of the most secure forms of EAP, but it also has the highest maintenance requirements. Since EAP-TLS requires both the client and server to have a certificate, it is not appropriate for sites where the user base changes regularly, such as hotspots.

EAP-TTLS

Funk Software and Certicom jointly developed EAP-TTLS (Tunneled Transport Layer Security). EAP-TTLS is an extension of EAP-TLS, which provides for certificate-based mutual authentication of the client and network. Unlike EAP-TLS, however, EAP-TTLS requires only server-side certificates, eliminating the need to configure certificates for each wireless LAN client. In addition, EAP-TTLS supports legacy password protocols such as PAP, CHAP, and MS-CHAPv2, so you can deploy it against your existing authentication system (such as Active Directory or eDirectory). EAP-TTLS securely tunnels client authentication within TLS records, ensuring that the user remains anonymous to eavesdroppers on the wireless link.

Dynamically generated per-user, per-session WEP keys and mutual authentication are used to secure the EAP-TTLS connection. The client verifies that the server's certificate is correct, and then the server verifies the client's identity after the encrypted tunnel is created. EAP-TTLS also supports fast reconnection while roaming.

PEAP (Protected EAP)

Cisco, Microsoft, and RSA developed PEAP, which is a direct competitor to EAP-TTLS. PEAP uses tunneled server-side certificates and username/password credentials for client to authenticate to a server. PEAP is supported in Windows XP with Service Pack 1 and later, and is also supported by Cisco's ACU version 5.05 and higher. PEAP supports mutual authentication as well, which adds increased security.

Some major differences between TTLS and PEAP are that PEAP has optional support for client-side certificates as well as server-side certificates, and that PEAP supports different authentication methods within the tunnel than TTLS. PEAP also supports the use of the Windows user ID and password as credentials, creating the possibility for single-sign-on authentication (i.e., the user logs onto the machine at the Windows prompt and then never has to explicitly log onto the WLAN). Like TTLS and TLS, PEAP supports fast reconnects for roaming and dynamic WEP keying.

One technical issue that arises is that there are several different implementations of PEAP. Microsoft, Cisco, and Funk each implement PEAP in a unique manner. This again brings up the need to ensure that all of the components of your EAP infrastructure support compatible EAP types.

EAP-SIM (GSM)

EAP-SIM is a mechanism for Mobile IP network access authentication and registration key generation using the GSM Subscriber Identity Module (SIM). The rationale for using the GSM SIM with Mobile IP is to leverage the existing GSM authorization infrastructure with the existing user base and the existing SIM card distribution channels. By using the SIM key exchange, no other preconfigured security association besides the SIM card is required on the mobile node. Since EAP-SIM authentication does not require any interaction on the user's part (short of inserting the SIM chip into the device), it is useful for 802.11 devices that do not have an easy way to prompt the user for authentication information, such as an 802.11-based VoIP phone handset.

EAP-FAST

EAP-FAST was developed by Cisco to support customers who "cannot enforce a strong password policy and wish to deploy an 802.1X EAP type that does not require digital certificates, supports a variety of user and password database types, supports password expiration and change, and is flexible, easy to deploy, and easy to manage." Like TTLS and PEAP, EAP-FAST performs authentication within a previously-established secure tunnel, but the creation of the tunnel is based on a Protected Access Credential (PAC) instead of an SSL certificate. One main advantage of EAP-FAST is that the protocol itself supports provisioning and management of PACs via the authentication server, eliminating much of the management overhead of certificates. In other words, when a client attempts to authenticate, the server can automatically expire its PAC, assign it a new PAC to replace its old one, and so forth. All of these things would have to be done manually under many SSL certificate-based systems.

It is likely that this list of EAP authentication types will grow as more vendors enter the wireless LAN security market and until the market chooses a standard.

 Understanding what EAP is and how it is used in general is a key element in being effective as a wireless network administrator.

WPA

The 802.11i committee was formed in 2001 to increase MAC-layer security in 802.11. Realizing that the 802.11i standard would be a long time in development, the Wi-Fi Alliance released the *Wi-Fi Protected Access* (WPA) certification. It is common for vendors to sell "pre-release" versions of products based on 802.11 standards that are still in development, but these "pre-release" products are usually not compatible with each other and may not even be compatible with the eventual final standard. WPA was a "snapshot" of the in-development 802.11i standard. Vendors could release "pre-802.11i" equipment that was compatible with the WPA certification, and vendors and customers could be assured that one vendor's products would work with any other vendor's products that were also WPA certified. This sped the adoption of stronger security measures in the wireless marketplace dramatically.

Although WPA defines advanced modes of authentication and encryption, including the use of 802.1X/EAP and TKIP, it also includes the use of WEP for backwards compatibility with non-WPA stations. If at all possible, you should configure all WPA access points to reject associations from stations using WEP (WPA requires that the AP be able to do this) and should configure all client stations to use WPA exclusively. In some cases, a WPA client might need to associate to a WEP access point – such as if the client were traveling and needed to associate to a hotspot – but this should be the exception, not the norm. If WEP is used with WPA, then the security implications are the same as if static WEP were being used.

WPA-RADIUS and WPA-PSK

Other than WEP, the WPA certification defines two main types of authentication and key management. Both types use 802.1X/EAP to authenticate the station[3], but the first type, known simply as WPA, requires a RADIUS server while the second type, known as WPA-PSK (*pre-shared key*), does not. For clarity, we will sometimes refer to the first type as WPA-RADIUS, to differentiate it from the WPA standard itself. You should remember that WPA-RADIUS is just a term we use in this text to try to avoid confusion. It is not a standard term and you should not use it outside of this book.

In the case of WPA-RADIUS, the authentication process is identical to that described in the 802.1X/EAP section of this chapter. The station first locates an access point, authenticates with the access point using Open System authentication, and associates with the access point. Once the station reaches the "authenticated and associated" state, it proceeds immediately to 802.1X/EAP authentication. Once that successfully completes, the station may send other data frames. If WPA-RADIUS is used, the authentication information that the user must present depends on the type of EAP that is being used, which will be configured in the AP and clients. For example, if the stations use EAP-MD5, then the user will have to type in a username and password; if the stations use EAP-TLS, the station will need to have been configured with an SSL certificate.

The Wi-Fi Alliance realized that home and small-office installations would probably not want or need a RADIUS server. WPA-PSK was created to allow these sites to take advantage of WPA's enhanced security. With WPA-PSK, an ASCII string is configured in all access points and stations, and this string is used to authenticate stations. Stations that are not configured with the same string as the access point cannot complete the WPA authentication. Although there are some similarities between a WPA pre-shared key and a WEP key (both are static and universal), a WPA pre-shared key is more secure than a WEP key, because the pre-shared key is not actually used to encrypt the frames. Rather, the actual encryption key is determined after the station has

---

1. Page 6 of the WPA standard, version 3.1, states that if the station or access point indicates that it will perform WPA authentication, then the device "shall perform 802.1X authentication and 802.1X key management."

verified to the AP that the station has the correct PSK. During the authentication, the access point uses EAP to assign a WEP key to each station dynamically, just as would occur if a RADIUS server were being used. This means that, even though each station is assigned a static PSK (which is cryptographically weaker than each station having a unique authentication identifier), each station encrypts data with a unique encryption key (which is cryptographically stronger than each station having the same encryption key).

WPA-PSK is not as secure as WPA-RADIUS server, but it is more secure than WEP. It is more secure than WEP because it uses more advanced forms of authentication and encryption (TKIP and AES; see below). It is less secure than WPA-RADIUS because the most secure types of EAP authentication (e.g., EAP-TLS, EAP-TTLS) aren't available without a RADIUS server, either internal or external to the AP. Regardless of which type of WPA is being used, you must configure the EAP type that the client will use, and the client and RADIUS server (if used) must all support the chosen EAP type. This issue is identical to the compatibility issue described in the 802.1X/EAP section. Whichever type of WPA you use, WPA supports automatic rekeying via standard EAP frames. This means that the clients will periodically receive a new encryption key, similar to the rekeying we described in the TKIP section.

TKIP and AES Encryption

WPA supports two types of encryption: TKIP and AES. If TKIP encryption is used, WPA requires that Michael be enabled. Remember from the TKIP section that TKIP uses the same RC4 cipher that was used in WEP. The AES encryption algorithm, on the other hand, is much stronger than RC4, but also requires much more processing power. Hardware designed for RC4 encryption simply does not have the processing power necessary to handle AES encryption. The intent of WPA is to allow older hardware to use TKIP while still maintaining the option for newer hardware to use AES. For compatibility reasons, TKIP is the default encryption method in WPA.

When deciding which of these ciphers to use, you should find out whether your hardware supports AES encryption. Many vendors have anticipated the need for AES encryption support and have released hardware capable of performing AES encryption, even though software that supports AES encryption still is not widely available. Most Wi-Fi-certified chips shipped since 2002 have the necessary hardware to support AES and can be made to support 802.11i through a firmware/driver upgrade.

WPA2/802.11i

802.11i defines "MAC Layer Security Enhancements for 802.11." 802.11i is intended to address the weaknesses in some existing forms of 802.11 authentication and encryption and to provide a single unifying standard for other forms of 802.11-related authentication and encryption. In other words, some parts of 802.11i describe technologies that are completely new to 802.11 (such as AES-based encryption), and other parts of 802.11i include technologies that existed before (such as 802.1X). The Wi-Fi Alliance has released the WPA2 certification, which is based on the completed 802.11i standard. 802.11i and WPA2 are essentially synonymous.

Several components of 802.11i existed before 802.11i. For example, 802.11i allows the use of 802.1X/EAP with EAP-TLS for authentication.[4] This architecture is identical to one that might have been in use before 802.11i was ratified. Similarly, 802.11i uses EAP messages to allow the RADIUS server to give a unique encryption key to each station.

AES and CCMP are two new terms that 802.11i introduces to the 802.11 space. As we discussed in the previous section, AES is a form of encryption that, while more secure than RC4, also requires more processing power, which means that hardware must be specifically designed to support AES. Legacy hardware that was designed just for RC4 cannot be upgraded to support AES. CCMP stands for *Counter Mode with CBC-MAC Protocol*. CCMP simply refers to a specific way of implementing AES encryption that is particularly suited for encrypting frames of data. For comparison, the terms CCMP, TKIP, and WEP are roughly analogous: they describe implementations of encryption mechanisms used by 802.11. The actual ciphers used in these mechanisms are AES, RC4, and RC4 respectively.

---

2. Actually, 802.11i allows for any valid EAP type to be used, but EAP-TLS is the de-facto standard. EAP-TLS is the only widely-deployed EAP type that meets all requirements of the 802.11i standard.

Summary

Of the security mechanisms listed in this chapter (WEP, TKIP, 802.1X/EAP, WPA, and 802.11i/WPA2), WPA is currently the simplest to implement. In WPA's most basic implementation, all the user has to do is configure the pre-shared key to achieve most of the security benefits of 802.1X/EAP and TKIP. WPA also is probably the most widespread, if only because it has replaced WEP as the "standard" security mechanism for consumer-grade access points. 802.1X/EAP is more common in enterprise installations, since they have the IT resources necessary to configure and manage the security infrastructure (installing SSL certificates on machines, for example). Enterprise installations are more likely to have an existing security infrastructure into which 802.1X/EAP can integrate. In fact, certain EAP types are specifically designed with this integration in mind.

802.11i was ratified in June 2004, but is still not widely adopted in the marketplace. Part of the reason for this slow adoption might be because consumers perceive that existing solutions (WPA or 802.1X/EAP) are good enough. Another reason might be the normal one-year wait time between ratifying an 802.11 standard and seeing products become popular in the market.

Additional Security Methods

In addition to the "802.11" solutions described previously, several security solutions are independent, or ride "on top," of 802.11. Whereas the previous solutions all operated at layers 1 and 2 of the OSI model, many of these solutions operate at layer 3 and above. Therefore, they protect the data only from the transport layer (typically TCP or UDP) headers up. Other approaches rely on restricting or redirecting the user's traffic in the infrastructure; for example, in the switches and routers.

Filtering

Wireless LANs can filter based on the MAC addresses of client stations. Almost all access points (even very inexpensive ones) have MAC filter functionality. The network administrator can compile, distribute, and maintain a list of allowable MAC addresses and program them into each access point. If a PC card or other client with a MAC address that is not in the access point's MAC filter list tries to gain access to the wireless LAN, the MAC address filter functionality will not allow that client to associate with that access point.

Although MAC filters may seem like a good security solution, you probably will not want to invest time in using them. First, they are difficult to manage, since they often must be manually configured on each AP. Second, MAC addresses are relatively easy to spoof, so the extra security gained by enabling MAC address filters is actually quite small.

Proprietary Layer 2 Encryption

In the last section, we discussed the types of layer 2 encryption that 802.11 supports: WEP, TKIP, and CCMP. We also discussed weaknesses in some of these algorithms. Some vendors have addressed these weaknesses by creating proprietary encryption methods that replace those defined in 802.11. Technically, the resulting products are not 802.11-compliant, but users of these products are more interested in security than they are in interoperability. In exchange for having to buy all of their equipment from a single vendor, they get the assurance of extremely strong authentication and encryption. These devices are sometimes called Enterprise Encryption Gateways and are discussed in more detail in chapter 7, "WLAN Infrastructure Devices." It is common for these products to use AES-based encryption, proprietary client software, and compression to make up for the loss in throughput due to high encryption.

Wireless VPNs

Wireless LAN manufacturers are increasingly including VPN server software in wireless routers (access points with routing functionality). When the VPN server is integrated into the access point, clients use off-the-shelf VPN client software and protocols, such as PPTP or IPSec, to form a tunnel directly to the access point.

To establish a VPN connection between a wireless station and a wireless router, the client would first associate with the access point (considered an integral part of the wireless router) using normal 802.11 technologies. Next, the client would obtain an IP address, whether through DHCP or statically assigned. After obtaining an IP address, the client would be required to initiate a VPN tunnel connection to the wireless router using an encryption technology specified by the administrator (IPSec or PPTP, for example). Any station that did not create a VPN connection would not be allowed to pass traffic through the wireless router onto the network backbone.

FIGURE 12.2 Wireless Router VPN solution

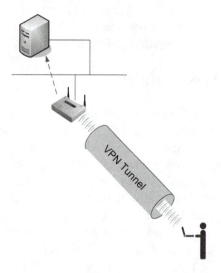

Point-to-Point Tunneling Protocol (PPTP) using shared secrets is very simple to implement, but provides only a rudimentary level of security by itself. When added to strong layer 2 encryption such as TKIP or CCMP, PPTP makes a reasonable solution for remote access over wireless links. PPTP using MPPE-128 encryption typically adds about 15 percent overhead to a wireless link. In contrast, WEP adds around 3 percent.

Consider a scenario in which a wireless user is accessing the corporate network over a wireless hotspot. If the hotspot were using layer 2 encryption, such as TKIP, the user's data would only be encrypted between the user's PC card and the AP. If the user needed to access corporate resources over the Internet, an end-to-end VPN solution would be required. Since PPTP is not much stronger than WEP, use of TKIP or CCMP on the wireless link would be desirable. However, since the link back to the corporate network is wired, PPTP might provide a reasonable level of security.

Use of IPSec with shared secrets or certificates provides a much stronger and less platform-specific encryption method than PPTP, but IPSec is more complex to configure than PPTP. If the client and server are not properly configured with compatible IPSec software, creation of the VPN tunnel will fail. Compatibly configuring IPSec software from different vendors (e.g., the AP or EWG vendor and the IPSec client software vendor) can be a challenge.

Putting the VPN server in the AP (forming a wireless router) makes sense for SOHO installations in which there will be relatively few APs. For enterprise installations, it makes more sense to use "fat" access points without this functionality and then put the VPN intelligence in an enterprise wireless gateway (EWG), as shown in Figure 12.3, or use a WLAN switch that sits upstream from "thin" APs. In these enterprise scenarios, the same VPN process takes place, except that after the client "802.11 associates" to the access point, the VPN tunnel is established with the upstream VPN device (whether WLAN switch or EWG) instead of with the access point itself.

FIGURE 12.3   Enterprise Wireless Gateway VPN solution

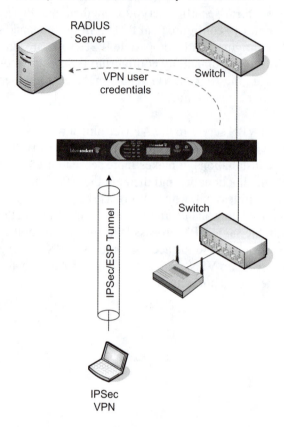

It is common to put all of the APs on a single wireless VLAN that has access to the VPN server's external port. The VPN server has its external port on the wireless VLAN and its internal port on a VLAN that has access to the rest of the network. This implementation prevents stations from gaining access to the rest of the network unless they have created a VPN tunnel.

Despite their advantages, VPN solutions are not the most popular form of wireless security. As previously discussed, WPA provides adequate security in SOHO environments, and 802.1X/EAP or 802.11i provides excellent security in enterprise environments. Given that, many sites do not want the additional management overhead and throughput degradation that VPNs create. VPNs handle multicast frames inefficiently since each multicast packet must be individually encrypted and sent as a unicast to each client. Although many VPNs do support roaming between access points and between IP subnets, the roaming is usually much slower than a layer 2 solution and can create problems for time- and latency-sensitive applications. Therefore, the most popular forms of wireless security are still WEP (unfortunately), WPA, and 802.1X/EAP.

Application-Layer Encryption (SSL & SSH)

Instead of encrypting data at layer 3, as a VPN typically does, an alternative is to encrypt data at layer 7, the application layer. Examples of this type of implementation include HTTPS, SSH (a secure form of Telnet), POP3/S (secure POP3), FTP/S (secure FTP), and so on. Application-layer encryption typically uses SSL (Secure Socket Layer) or SSH (Secure Shell) standards for encrypting IP-based conversations.

With SSL, the encrypted tunnel runs from application to application, and data is encrypted before it is handed down the network stack. That means that the data is totally protected from end-to-end. By comparison, WEP, TKIP, and CCMP only encrypt the data on the wireless network, and a layer 3 VPN only encrypts the data up to the VPN server With SSL, there is no place in the infrastructure where the data could be captured in unencrypted form.

Another advantage of SSL is its support for many different encryption algorithms. SSL supports nearly any encryption algorithm that is available on the market, from RC4 to DES to AES. This means that you can choose the right balance of security and speed for the application. For example, the RC4 cipher is relatively weak, but is very computationally simple; AES is very secure, but is computationally complex. Therefore, all other things being equal, an SSL tunnel using RC4 will have lower latency and higher throughput than one using AES, but will be more susceptible to attack.

Because the encryption is applied at the application layer, SSL has the ability to traverse any network that can carry TCP datagrams. All routers can pass IPSec and PPTP packets, but low-end NAT routers may have problems when multiple tunnels are to be created through the NAT interface. SSL, on the other hand, only requires that the appropriate TCP port be opened on the firewall or forwarded on the NAT router. At Layer 4 and below, the packets look just like any unencrypted packet.

One disadvantage of SSL encryption is a potentially less transparent user experience. With a layer 2 or layer 3 VPN, the user does not have to do anything special (beyond initial configuration of the VPN client software) to use the VPN, since the VPN is part of the network stack; however, with SSL encryption, the user might have to connect to a different port number or server, depending on the configuration of the network. This is a minor inconvenience, but it is worth remembering. An additional disadvantage of SSL is that there are potentially more attack vectors for the network than with a layer 2 or layer 3 VPN, since the infrastructure must be configured to pass TCP frames on all ports that will use SSL.

A final disadvantage of SSL is that, in order to authenticate a user, an SSL certificate must be installed on every server and every client. Management of SSL certificates is complex and can be difficult to understand. Many administrators do not consider the extra security gained to be worth the administrative hassle of installing certificates on all clients, so they choose to sacrifice some security and only install certificates on servers. This means that clients can verify that they are accessing the right server, but servers cannot verify that clients are authorized to use the server. This situation is often addressed via a two-layer authentication process in which the client verifies the server's identity by checking the server's SSL certificate, the client then sets up an SSL tunnel without presenting a client certificate, then the server prompts the client to enter a username and password within the SSL tunnel.

Figure 12.4 shows an example of using an SSL-enabled FTP client. This software has simplified the user experience as much as possible. All the user has to do differently is choose "SFTP" instead of "FTP" when he or she configures the site. If the administrator had chosen to use client-side certificates for authentication, then the user would need to have a valid SSL certificate installed on his or her machine.

FIGURE 12.4   Secure FTP using SSH2

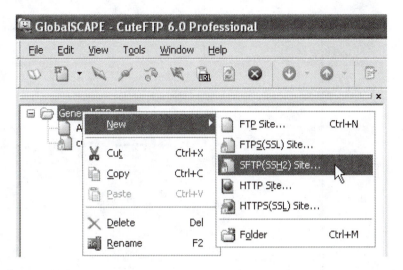

Figure 12.5 shows an example of configuring an e-mail client to use TLS v1 (which supersedes SSL v3) to check e-mail. This will ensure that the user's e-mail isn't sent clear text across the network. SSL and TLS are commonly used with SMTP, since SMTP itself does not provide any means of authenticating users – not even a username and password exchange! Using SSL in this manner, the e-mail client will verify the authenticity of the server using its certificate, set up an SSL tunnel, and then use username/password credentials to authenticate itself to the server.

FIGURE 12.5 Secure SMTP using SSL

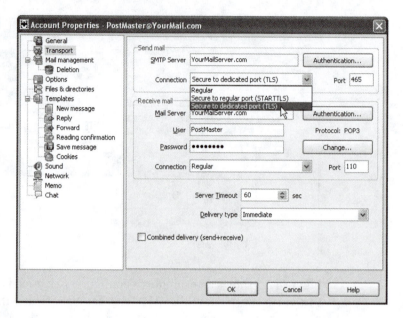

Captive Portals

A captive portal refers to a scenario in which all traffic coming through the AP is initially directed to an access control device on the wired LAN, regardless of the contents of the frame. The access control device then performs authentication and optionally allows users access to resources on the wired LAN.

You might have experienced a public captive portal at a hotel or wireless hotspot. You connect to the site's wireless network (which might be completely open), automatically get assigned an IP address, and then open your web browser. No matter what IP address or URL you put in, you are directed to the organization's authentication URL. That redirection is the essence of a captive portal. Once you authenticate (sometimes by putting in your credit card number, room number, or your previously purchased user ID), your data is allowed through to its destination.

FIGURE 12.6   Captive Portal Interface

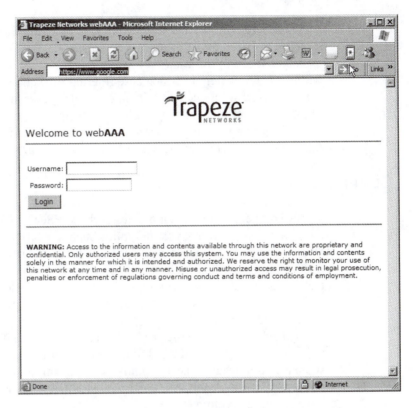

Captive portals are typically implemented via an enterprise wireless gateway or wireless LAN switch. The APs will usually be segregated onto an isolated VLAN to prevent clients from trying to circumvent the authentication server. It is common in most hotspot environments to provide no security other than using HTTPS to protect the log-on credentials. When implementing a captive portal in an enterprise environment, such as a conference room, guest area, and the like, it is common to have the captive portal also serve as a VPN end-point device, terminating IPSec tunnels, for example. In this way, not only are the log-on credentials protected, but also the data traffic is encrypted.

Profile-Based Firewalls

A profile-based firewall is a firewall that applies filtering rules selectively, based on user name, group name, or some other identifying characteristic. A profile-based firewall might be part of an EWG or wireless LAN switch, in which case filtering rules might integrate with the role-based access control. In other words, a user logs in as a member of the "sales" group, and the wireless LAN switch is configured to apply certain filtering rules to all members of that group. Different filtering rules might apply to members of the "accounting" group, and so on.

Summary

Upper-layer encryption technologies such as IPSec and SSL have some advantages over lower-layer encryption such as TKIP and CCMP. Upper-layer encryption often extends into the wired network, protecting traffic there as well as on the wireless network. Upper layer encryption technologies are generally more mature than 802.11's lower-layer technologies, so their weaknesses are more likely to have been identified and patched. On the other hand, lower-layer encryption is handled in specialized hardware on the card, which tends to make it faster than upper-layer encryption. In addition, lower-layer encryption is likely to support roaming across access points, whereas upper-layer encryption rarely supports this, and, if it does, will essentially always be slower than lower-layer encryption.

Attacks on Wireless LANs

A malicious hacker can seek to disable or attempt to gain access to a wireless LAN in several ways. Some of these methods are eavesdropping (frame capture), jamming (denial of service), man-in-the-middle, management interface exploits, encryption cracking, and connection hijacking. This list is by no means exhaustive, and some of these methods can be orchestrated in several different ways. It is beyond the scope of this book to present every possible means of wireless LAN attack. This text is aimed at giving you insight into some possible methods of attack so that security will be considered a vital part of your wireless LAN implementation.

Eavesdropping

Eavesdropping is perhaps the most simple, yet still effective, type of wireless LAN attack. Eavesdropping leaves no trace of the hacker's presence on or near the network, since the hacker does not have to actually connect to an access point to listen to frames traversing the wireless segment. Wireless LAN protocol analyzers (such as AirMagnet, AiroPeek, Observer, or CommView for WiFi) or custom applications (such as NetStumbler, MacStumbler, or Kismet) are typically used to gather information about the wireless network from a distance, as illustrated in Figure 12.7. A protocol analyzer is a completely passive device that can capture all of the data it "hears" through its antenna without being associated to the wireless network. An attacker can perform an eavesdropping attack from a great distance by attaching a high-gain antenna to a protocol analyzer and then pointing the antenna at an AP. This method of access allows the attacker to keep his distance from the facility, leave no trace of his presence, and listen to and gather valuable information. Protocol analyzers most often run on laptops or tablet PCs, but some protocol analysis and eavesdropping applications have been written to run on handheld computers and PDAs, making it easier for an eavesdropper to be surreptitious and highly mobile.

FIGURE 12.7   Passive Attack Example

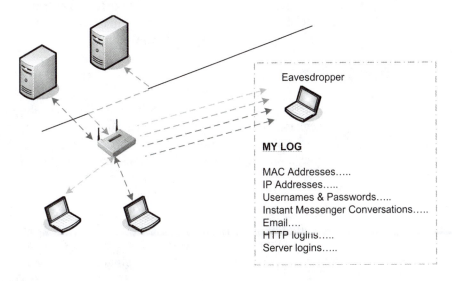

There are applications specifically geared toward the gathering of passwords from HTTP sites, e-mail, instant messengers, FTP sessions, and telnet sessions that are sent in clear text. Other applications can snatch password hashes traversing the wireless segment between client and server for log-in purposes. Any unprotected information going across the wireless segment in this manner leaves the network and individual users vulnerable to attack. Consider the impact if an intruder gained access to a user's domain log-in information and caused havoc on the network. The intruder would be to blame, but network usage logs would point directly at the user. This breach could cost a person's job. Consider another situation in which HTTP or e-mail passwords were gathered over the wireless segment and later used by a malicious intruder for personal gain from a remote site.

The main method of protecting data against eavesdropping is to use strong encryption. Encryption ensures that, even if an attacker gains access to the RF signal, he or she will not be able to do anything useful with it. Keep in mind that *completely* preventing access to the signal is essentially impossible in a wireless LAN. For example, suppose that you walk the perimeter of your site with a laptop and determine that you must be 100 feet inside the perimeter before you can even see the access point. You might feel secure, but you only verified that the signal was inaccessible with the omnidirectional antenna on your laptop's PCMCIA card. What if the attacker used a 14 dBi yagi antenna instead? Given that attackers can have access to high-gain antennas, you should assume that your signal is essentially always visible.

Encryption Cracking

Encryption cracking means finding a means of breaking the encryption mechanism (WEP, TKIP, or CCMP) in use on the network. If encryption is used, then encryption cracking is a necessary prerequisite to eavesdropping if the intruder wishes to obtain usable information. Attacks against encryption generally come in two forms: mathematical "cracks," where a weakness in the encryption algorithm itself is exploited, and social engineering attacks, where people are tricked into revealing information that allows the attacker to decrypt the data. As an example of social engineering, the attacker might call a random extension in a business, claim to be with the IT helpdesk, and ask the user to "verify" his or her WEP keys or 802.1X/EAP username and password. This section of the chapter will only cover known "cracks" against the three main encryption mechanisms used in 802.11.

There are many known cracks against the WEP algorithm. The static nature of WEP keys means that, in theory, a brute-force attack might be feasible, but in reality, weaknesses in WEP's implementation mean that there are far faster and easier ways of cracking WEP. The initialization vector of a WEP frame is not encrypted. One method of cracking a WEP key relies on "weak initialization vectors" that have mathematical qualities which make it much easier to figure out the WEP key that was used to encrypt the frame. This is not the only means of cracking WEP, but it is the most exploited.

At this point, we recommend that you not consider WEP for purposes of securing wireless LANs at all. WEP is marginally better than nothing at all, but WEP is so weak, and there are so many better alternatives out there, that there really should be no excuse to use WEP on most networks.

TKIP continues to use the RC4 cipher used by WEP, but it uses much longer initialization vectors (8 bytes instead of 4 bytes for WEP), changes WEP keys periodically, and assigns WEP keys on a per-station basis. This means that, although TKIP has some of the same cryptographic weaknesses as WEP, it is much harder to exploit those weaknesses, and the payoff for doing so is much less. The RC4 stream cipher as used by TKIP has no known exploitable weaknesses at the time of this publication.

The most likely attack vector against TKIP involves attacking the authentication mechanism and the key distribution architecture, not the encryption. When a host authenticates via TKIP, a series of 802.1X/EAP frames are exchanged between the host and the AP. Depending on the EAP type being used, this authentication might be vulnerable to attack. These attacks are more than theoretical; for example, it is known that EAP-MD5 is vulnerable to dictionary attacks; an application called *coWPAtty* can crack WPA-PSK's implementation of TKIP; and an application called *ASLEAP* can crack Cisco's LEAP using an offline dictionary attack when weak passwords are used.

These applications use a method called a dictionary attack to break the authentication. In a username/password exchange such as that used by EAP-MD5, LEAP, and WEP, the password itself is not transmitted across the network (though the username in some cases is). Instead, a *challenge string* consisting of a random string of text is sent from the authenticator to the client. The client uses its password to encrypt the challenge string and returns the result back to the authenticator. If the client has the correct password, the encryption will be correct, and the client will have demonstrated that it knows the password without ever actually exposing the password to an attacker.

A dictionary attack relies on the fact that there are a limited number of passwords available and that users tend to choose easily-guessed passwords. In a dictionary attack, the attacker captures the challenge/response exchange and then uses a computer to run through a "dictionary" of possible passwords. For each password, the computer encrypts the challenge string and tests whether the result matches the response that the client sent. When the result does match, the computer has discovered the correct password.

A dictionary attack only works if the attacker can capture the challenge/response exchange and if the password is easily guessable. Two ways of protecting against a dictionary attack are to 1) set up an encrypted tunnel before exchanging the challenge and response, and 2) use passwords that are hard to guess. Passwords can be made hard to guess by increasing their length (a longer password has more possible values for the attacker to guess) and by increasing their randomness (if a password is assumed to only contain letters, then the attacker has to guess fewer passwords than if the password contained both numbers and letters).

802.11i with CCMP uses AES encryption. Whereas TKIP might be cracked in about 100 years using today's technology, cryptography experts estimate that it would take longer than the expected lifetime of our sun to crack AES. Therefore, excluding weaknesses in 802.11i's implementation of AES, AES can be considered essentially unbreakable. Of course, weaknesses in implementation are the Achilles heel of any encryption method, and it remains to be seen whether 802.11i has any of these.

RF Jamming

Whereas an intruder would use some attacks to gain valuable information from or to gain access to your network, jamming is a technique that would be used to simply shut down your wireless network. Similar to saboteurs arranging an overwhelming denial of service (DoS) attack aimed at web servers, a wireless LAN can be shut down by an overwhelming RF signal. That overwhelming RF signal can be intentional or unintentional, and the signal may be removable or non-removable. When an intruder stages an intentional jamming attack, he could use wireless LAN equipment, but more likely, he would use a high-power RF signal generator. Figure 12.8 illustrates an example of jamming a wireless LAN.

FIGURE 12.8   RF Jamming Attack Example

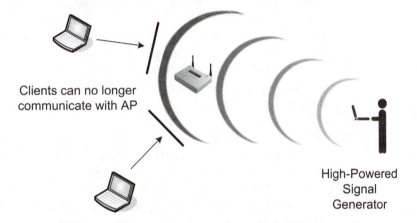

Clients can no longer communicate with AP

High-Powered Signal Generator

Removing this type of attacker from the premises first requires locating the source of the RF signal. Locating an RF signal source can be done with an RF spectrum analyzer. There are many spectrum analyzers on the market, but having one that is handheld and battery operated is quite useful. Several manufacturers make handheld spectrum analyzers, and a few wireless LAN manufacturers have created spectrum analyzer software utilities for use in wireless client devices. Using the spectrum analyzer with a directional antenna, it may be possible to locate the attacker's location. With an omnidirectional antenna, getting a directional fix can be more difficult. Keep in mind that the attacker might be located outside of the network's coverage area and might be using a high-gain antenna to "fire" the interference onto the site.

It is important to keep in mind that protecting against an active attacker with jamming equipment is difficult, if not impossible. Even shielding from outside signals might be overcome with a sufficiently high-gain antenna and a strong amplifier. This would certainly violate FCC regulations, but the attacker probably does not care. Even if you find the attacker, it may be difficult to take legal action against him or her, depending on the laws of your local jurisdiction.

When jamming is caused by a non-moveable, non-malicious source, such as a communications tower or other legitimate system, you might have to consider using a wireless LAN system that utilizes a different set of frequencies. For example, if you were responsible for the design and installation of an RF network at a large apartment complex, special considerations might be in order. If an RF interference source were a large number of 2.4 GHz spread spectrum phones, baby monitors, and microwave ovens in this apartment complex, then you might choose to implement 802.11a equipment that uses the 5 GHz U-NII bands instead of 802.11b equipment that shares the 2.4 GHz ISM band with these other devices.

Unintentional jamming occurs regularly due to many different devices across many different industries sharing the 2.4 GHz ISM band with wireless LANs. Fortunately, malicious jamming is not a common threat, at least in part because it is fairly expensive to obtain the required equipment, and the only victory that the hacker gets is temporarily disabling a network. You should keep in mind, however, that wireless networks based on license-free bands are always vulnerable to RF jamming. You should consider the implications of a complete loss of your wireless network carefully when deciding what applications to run over the network and what backup systems to install. For example, we have heard of hospitals installing wireless networks so that doctors can access patient records via their PDAs. In this case, jamming would probably be just an inconvenience, since paper records probably still exist. In other cases, we have heard of companies moving their entire phone system to VoWi-Fi. The effect of a jamming attack on this system would be much more significant.

Wireless Hijacking

A wireless hijacking attack is a situation where an attacker uses a high-powered, narrowband RF jamming device to jam the channel on which a client device is connected to a legitimate AP. When the client device roams, the hijacker is using a laptop running both AP software and DHCP server software to capture the unsuspecting user's layer 2 and layer 3 connections as shown in Figure 12.9. Once the user is connected to the hijacker, the user will not roam away from the hijacker's machine unless he goes out of range or is released manually by the hijacker.

FIGURE 12.9   Hijacking Attack

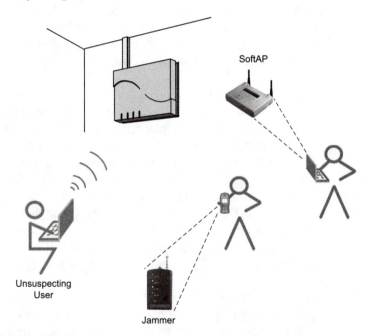

SoftAP

Unsuspecting
User

Jammer

The person perpetrating the hijacking attack would first have to know the SSID that the wireless clients are using, and, as we have discussed earlier, this piece of information is easily obtained using a protocol analyzer. This type of attack assumes that the client's utility software is using (or has configured) a profile that does not use a security method. The best remedy for hijacking attacks is use of mutual authentication and encryption. Many 802.1X/EAP types, such as PEAP-MSCHAPv2, EAP-

TTLS, and EAP-FAST, support mutual authentication and strong encryption (TKIP or CCMP).

Rogue Access Points

An unauthorized, or "rogue," access point is not, in and of itself, an attack on a network. But rogue access points are often unsecured and might attach to the internal wired network, so they often provide holes that an attacker can exploit. On the other hand, an attacker might plant a rogue AP specifically as part of a larger-scale attack on the network. For example, an attacker may gain access to the customer's premises by pretending to be a maintenance worker, and then hiding an AP in an office with a window, secretly connecting the AP to the user's Ethernet port. The attacker is then able to access the network via the wireless signal that propagates out the window of the office, using that access to attempt to penetrate the company's servers.

Preventing rogue APs completely on a long-term basis is close to impossible. Physical security of the premises is one step, since it prevents unauthorized people from "planting" rogue APs. A strong corporate policy, with well-defined penalties and a well-maintained, high-performance corporate WLAN, will remove employees' motivation to bring unauthorized WLAN equipment on-site. Enabling 802.1X/EAP authentication on all Ethernet switches, which would require APs to authenticate to the switch before they could send data through the switch, could completely prevent unauthorized APs from accessing the network. Few administrators will tolerate the management overhead this would create, since it would also require all other wired clients to authenticate.

The second step of securing your network against rogue APs is detecting them and responding to them. Fortunately, it is very difficult to hide an AP since it must advertise its presence through beacons in order for clients to detect it and associate with it. One method of detecting rogue APs is to physically walk the site with a protocol analyzer, looking for beacons from rogue APs and frames from stations that are associated with rogue APs. This method has two main weaknesses. First, walking the site is time and labor intensive. Second, since it is time and labor intensive, it is likely that it will not be performed often, meaning that a rogue AP can be on-site for a long time before it is detected.

Wireless vendors have created wireless intrusion detection systems (WIDS) with automatic rogue AP detection to address this need. These systems typically involve wireless sensors that are installed throughout the facility or campus coverage area. In some cases, the sensors are dedicated devices, but increasingly, the sensor firmware is incorporated into the APs themselves. In the best case, the AP is capable of acting both as a sensor and an AP at the same time. This requires that the AP have two radios, however, so some APs must switch out of AP mode and into WIDS mode, degrading performance.

One challenge of rogue AP detection systems is how to identify which APs are authorized and which are rogues. The simplest and most-used method is to simply create a list of authorized APs, based on their MAC addresses. Any AP that is not on the list is considered to be a rogue. This solution has the disadvantage that new APs must be manually added to the list and decommissioned APs must be removed to the list. An additional disadvantage is that it is relatively easy to spoof an AP's MAC address.

Physically locating and removing the rogue AP once it is detected is another challenge. The WIDS will report which sensor detected the rogue, which will narrow down the rogue's possible location to the coverage area of the sensor. This is one time when a good site survey will come in handy, since it will show the exact coverage area of the device. Locating the AP within the coverage area of the sensor is usually a matter of trial-and-error. You place a wireless protocol analyzer near the sensor until you detect the rogue AP, then move in a direction and see if the signal strength of the rogue AP goes up or down. If it goes up, you continue moving in that direction; if it goes down, you move in a different direction.

Most WIDS today incorporate some form of automatic rogue location, either triangulation or "fingerprinting," that can further reduce the area you have to search. Rogue triangulation works by measuring the signal strength from the rogue device to three or more wireless sensors. If the signal strength is equal in all sensors, then the rogue device must be roughly equidistant from all of them. If the signal strength is stronger on one sensor, then the rogue device must be closer to that sensor. The specifics of this technique are essentially always proprietary, and vendors advertise different degrees of accuracy and precision. "Fingerprinting" is a more sophisticated form of triangulation that takes into account the attenuation and reflection characteristics of the area in which the WLAN is installed.

Just because an AP is undocumented does not mean it is a threat to your network's security. For example, in a multi-tenant office building, a neighbor might have perfectly secure APs that are not registered with your WIDS. On the other hand, you might have recently added an AP to your network, but not registered it with the WIDS yet. In order to cut down on false positives, some WIDS systems offer more sophisticated forms of rogue detection. Rather than simply relying on the device's MAC address to determine whether the device is a rogue, the WIDS can be configured with "good" and "bad" security profiles. For example, the WIDS might be told that any AP using WEP encryption should be treated as dangerous, but any AP using EAP-TLS should be treated as secure. This is one area where development is occurring rapidly. The ability to accurately and automatically detect rogue devices while rejecting false alarms is key to successfully securing your network.

Penetration Attacks

A penetration attack occurs when an attacker gains access to the wired network through a wireless access point. A penetration attack might be used to gain access to a server to obtain valuable data, use the organization's Internet access for malicious purposes, or even change the network infrastructure configuration. By connecting to a wireless network through an access point, a user can begin to penetrate deeper into the network, or perhaps make changes to the wireless network itself. For example, if an attacker made it past a MAC filter, then he could navigate to the access points and remove all MAC filters, making it easier to gain access next time. The administrator might not even notice this change for some time.

Some examples of active attacks might be a drive-by spammer or a business competitor wanting access to your files. A spammer could queue e-mails in his laptop, then connect to your home or business network through the wireless LAN. After obtaining an IP address from your DHCP server, the hacker can send tens of thousands of e-mails using your Internet connection and your ISP's e-mail server without your knowledge. This kind of attack could cause your ISP to discontinue your connection for e-mail abuse when it is not even your fault. A business competitor might want to get your customer list with contact information, or maybe your payroll information, in order to better compete with you or to steal your customers. These types of attacks happen regularly without anyone's knowledge.

Once an attacker has an active wireless connection to your network, he might as well be sitting in his own office with a wired connection because the two scenarios are not much different. Wireless connections offer the attacker plenty of speed and access to servers, wide area connections, Internet connections, and other users' desktops and laptops. With a few simple tools, it is relatively simple to gather important information, impersonate a user, or even cause damage to the network through reconfiguration. Probing servers with port scans, creating null sessions to shared directories, and having servers dump passwords to hacking utilities (and subsequently logging into servers using existing accounts) are all things that can be done by following the instructions in off-the-shelf hacker books.

A penetration attack can occur once the attacker has cracked the encryption or authentication mechanism in use (allowing the attacker to secure a user's security credentials), but it is important to remember that there are other vectors for penetration attacks. One of the most common vectors for a penetration attack is a *management interface exploit*. Most enterprise-class access points have more than one management interface. For example, an AP might have a serial interface, a web interface, and be configurable via SNMP. Even if the administrator secures one of these methods, if the other two are left open, the attacker may be able to gain access to the LAN.

It is common for administrators to leave the serial interface unsecured as a backup in case they lock themselves out of the other interfaces. They then rely on physical security to keep attackers away from the AP. But physical security is notoriously easy to compromise: a button-down shirt, tie, and a clipboard will get you past many security stands. An administrator might lock down the web interface of the access points but forget that they are also configurable via SNMP. If an attacker can gain access to the wired LAN (which is often less secure than the wireless LAN), he or she might be able to reconfigure the AP via SNMP, allowing wireless access from off-site.

Disabling unneeded configuration interfaces is the best way to secure an access point against a management interface exploit, but, of course, you cannot disable all management interfaces. Therefore, any interface(s) that you leave enabled should only respond to secure protocols. If the interface is a web interface, HTTPS should be required with a username and password credential, at a minimum. If the management interface uses SNMP, then SNMPv3, with its integrated authentication and encryption is the most secure option. Unfortunately, not all devices support SNMPv3. If terminal emulation is required, then using SSH2 instead of TELNET is the most secure option if the AP supports it. Finally, if the management interface is a serial connection, the only option is to either disable it (not always possible, as the serial connection is sometimes considered a last-chance option if all others are locked out) or to physically secure the AP, which is always a good idea anyway.

Corporate Security Policy

A corporate security policy defines all of the parameters that should be taken into account to secure a company's network. A security policy generally contains at least three types of information.

First, it defines what measures must be taken to secure the network, such as the type of authentication and encryption that must be used on the WLAN, how often users must change their passwords, what kind of training users and administrators will receive, what type of intrusion detection system will be deployed, and so on.

Second, it defines how audits will be performed and how breaches in security, such as rogue devices, will be handled. Corporate policy might require that a manual walkabout scan for rogue equipment be performed at least once a week, or it might require that a WIDS generate reports daily for the entire network. Corporate policy also might specify that, when a rogue device is located, the best course of action might be not to remove it immediately; thus, the attackers will not be tipped off that they have been discovered. It may define who is to be contacted if a rogue AP is detected, and under what circumstances the police should be called if foul play is suspected.

Finally, a security policy defines penalties that will occur if the mandates of the policy are not followed. If a user is found to have installed a piece of rogue equipment, how will that user be penalized for breaking the policy? Although this is not a pleasant part of the policy to think about, it is necessary to prevent the WLAN administrator from being the "bad guy" when a policy violation occurs.

Security policies are divided into two categories: general security policy and functional security policy, each of which has multiple sub-categories. General policy describes items taken into consideration that do not fall into a specific technical category. Functional policy describes items that do fall into a specific technical category. This division should become clearer once we present some examples. Security policies are a complex topic, which we will not be able to fully cover in this chapter. Although we will discuss a security policy from a specifically wireless perspective, in reality, a security policy must incorporate all aspects of the network.

The benefits of having, implementing, and maintaining a solid security policy are too numerous to count. Preventing data loss and theft, preventing corporate sabotage or espionage, and maintaining company secrets are just a few. Even the suggestion that attackers could have stolen data from an industry-leading corporation may cause confidence in the company to plummet, and stock prices of that company could soon follow.

The beginning of good corporate policy starts with senior management. Recognizing the need for security and delegating the tasks of creating the appropriate documentation to include wireless LANs into the existing security policy should be top priority. First, those who are responsible for securing the wireless LAN segments must be educated in the technology. Next, the educated technology professional should interact with upper management and agree on company security needs. This team of educated individuals is then able to construct a list of procedures and requirements that, if followed by personnel at every applicable level, will ensure that the wireless network remains as safely guarded as the wired network.

General Security Policy

A general security policy begins with a risk assessment. Risk assessment begins by identifying *assets*, which are specific things that must be protected against an attack. Assets can be physical (the WLAN equipment itself) or virtual (the information stored on the company's servers). Next, all possible *threats* to the assets are enumerated. For example, an AP might be stolen or the company's customer database might be copied. Finally, the *cost* of each threat is analyzed. For example, if an AP is stolen, the cost is essentially just the cost of the AP, while the cost of losing the customer database might be millions of dollars in lost sales or legal judgments against the company. Analysis of cost is also known as *impact analysis*. The "cost" of a successful attack might be more than financial (e.g., lost time and lost customer confidence) but if possible, it is good to express the cost of an attack in terms of dollars, since that provides a standard way of comparing the severity of different attacks.

For each threat, the security analyst must next determine specific *attacks* that could manifest that threat. For example, losing an AP is a threat; a specific person sneaking onto the premises and taking an AP is an attack. Gaining unauthorized access to the customer database is a threat; a person cracking a WEP key and accessing the database via the WLAN is an attack. The identification of threats requires that the analyst be well-versed in the possible *attack vectors* of the system. It is for this reason that outside security specialists are often called in to help draft a security policy. Every part of the security policy (both general and functional) should be designed to mitigate the risks of these attacks.

The general security policy might contain these specific sections at a minimum:

- *Statement of Authority* – A statement of which authority is putting this policy in place, which managers or directors are sponsoring this policy, and who will ultimately be responsible for the effectiveness of this policy.
- *Applicable Audience* – To whom is this policy addressed. In a large organization, the IT department might have a security policy addressed specifically to it, for example. End users may have a

different set of guidelines to follow than IT staff, so different parts of the policy may apply to different audiences.

- *Violation Reporting Procedures and Enforcement* – Who will enforce the policy and what will happen when it is violated, either through an outside attack or an employee not following procedure?

- *Risk Assessment* – What assets will the policy protect, what are the threats to those assets, how likely is each of the attacks, and what is the cost of each possible successful attack?

- *Security Auditing* – How will the effectiveness of the policy be verified? How will the company make sure that the policy is being followed? This might involve an outside auditor or an internal team.

Functional Security Policy

A functional security policy describes technology-related procedures that must be followed to keep the network secure. The functional policy provides specific methods of mitigating the threats described in the general policy. For example, the general policy might describe the threat of someone stealing an AP, whereas the functional policy might mandate that all APs be mounted at least seven feet off the ground and be secured to the wall with a locking mount. A successful functional policy requires that the designer be very knowledgeable about what technological methods are available to mitigate each risk. As you can imagine, if the policy designer did not know about WEP's weaknesses, he might incorrectly conclude that WEP was acceptable to mitigate the risk of data theft. As with the general policy, it is a good idea to bring in a security specialist when designing a functional policy.

A functional policy might contain these specific sections at a minimum, but this list should not be considered comprehensive:

- *Password policies* – If passwords are used to authenticate users, then the functional policy should specify the parameters for a valid password, such as length, content, and so on. It should also specify how often the password should be changed.

- *Training requirements* – Training of users and IT personnel is critical to security. Users must understand how to properly use the network's security mechanisms as well as understand why it is important not to circumvent them in the name of security.

- *Acceptable usage* – A functional policy should specify acceptable uses of the WLAN. This might be different from the usage policy for the LAN, since WLANs typically have less bandwidth available. For example, users might not be allowed to download CD images over the WLAN due to bandwidth limitations.

- *Security configuration for devices* – This is where you put requirements for what type of encryption and authentication must be used. People sometimes make the mistake of focusing too much on authentication and encryption and forget about all the other aspects of security. As you can see, this is just one point among many in the big picture of security.

- *Asset Management* – How will wireless equipment be tracked? APs and bridges are especially susceptible to theft because they are often accessible to untrustworthy persons.

Security Recommendations

The following are some recommendations that might be included in a security policy. Some of these recommendations reiterate points made earlier in the chapter, while others are mentioned here for the first time.

Keep Sensitive Information Private

Some items that should be known only by network administrators at the appropriate levels are:

- Usernames and passwords of wireless infrastructure devices
- SNMP community strings of wireless infrastructure devices
- Encryption keys (if statically assigned, as with WPA-PSK)

The point of keeping this information only in the hands of trusted, skilled individuals, such as the network administrator, is important because a malicious user or attacker could easily use these pieces of information to gain access into the network and network devices. This information can be stored in one of many secure fashions. There are now applications on the market using strong encryption for the explicit purpose of password and sensitive data storage.

It might not be possible to keep all of this information completely secret, but that should be the goal. For example, SNMP community strings are transmitted in clear-text (in versions prior to v3), so an attacker who had physical access to the wired LAN could probably learn them. Nevertheless, keeping this information secret adds one more hurdle that the attacker must overcome, slowing him down just a little more. Remember that it is very difficult or impossible to completely prevent an attack; therefore, security measures often have the goal not of preventing an attack completely, but of slowing an attacker down long enough that he can be caught before doing significant damage. From this perspective, a security mechanism can still be useful even if it can be circumvented. The principle of "low hanging fruit" applies here. Typically attackers will go after the most easily obtained trophies.

Physical Security

Although physical security, when using a traditional wired network, is important, it is even more important for a company that uses wireless LAN technology. For reasons discussed earlier, a person who has a wireless PC card (and maybe an external antenna) does not have to be in the same building as the network to gain access to the network. Even intrusion detection software is not necessarily enough to prevent wireless attackers from stealing sensitive information. Passive attacks leave no trace on the network because no connection is ever made

Having guards make periodic scans around the company premises looking specifically for suspicious activity is effective in reducing attackers from casually loitering and eavesdropping on the WLAN. Security guards should be trained to recognize 802.11 hardware and to alert the appropriate company personnel when a wireless attack is suspected. It is very easy for an attacker to hide 802.11 hardware or to scan from a great distance; therefore, a wireless intrusion detection system usually should be installed in addition to good physical security.

Security Audits

Periodic scans of the network with protocol analyzers or WIDS in a search for rogue devices or specific attacks are a valuable way of keeping the wireless network secure. Consider if an elaborate (and expensive) wireless network solution were put in place with state-of-the-art security, and, since coverage did not extend to a particular area of the building, a user took it into his or her own hands to install an additional, unauthorized access point in the work area. In this case, this user has just provided an attacker with the necessary route into the network, completely circumventing a very good (and expensive) wireless LAN security solution.

Security audits should be well documented in the corporate security policy. The types of procedures to be performed, tools to be used, frequency of the audits, and reports to be generated should all be clearly spelled out as part of the corporate policy, so that this tedious task does not get overlooked. Managers should expect a report of this type on a regular basis from the network administrator. It is a common practice to hire an external contractor to perform security audits (sometimes called penetration tests) so that details do not get overlooked. Administrators responsible for building and supporting the network may overlook security holes due to being too familiar with the network.

Using Advanced Security Solutions

Organizations implementing wireless LANs should take advantage of some of the more advanced security mechanisms available on the market today. A security policy also should require that the implementation of any such advanced security mechanism be thoroughly documented. Because these technologies are new, often proprietary, and often used in combination with other security protocols or technologies, they must be documented so that, if a security breach occurs, network administrators can determine where and how.

Because so few people in the IT industry are educated in wireless technology, the likelihood of employee turnover causing network disruption, or at least vulnerability, is much higher when wireless LANs are part of the network. This turnover of employees is another very important reason that thorough documentation on wireless LAN administration and security functions should be created and maintained and that education for users and administrators should be kept current.

Public Wireless Networks

It is likely that corporate users with sensitive information on their company laptop computers will want to connect those laptops to public wireless LANs. It should be a matter of corporate policy that all wireless users (whether wireless is provided by the company or by the user) run both personal firewall software and antiviral software on their laptops. Most public wireless networks have little or no security. This is in order to make connectivity simple for the user, and to decrease the amount of required technical support by the public wireless network operator.

Even if upstream servers on the wired segment are protected, the wireless users are still vulnerable. Consider the situation in which an attacker is sitting at an airport next to a Wi-Fi hot spot. This attacker can "sniff" the wireless LAN using a protocol analyzer, obtain usernames and passwords, log into the system using stolen credentials, and then wait for unsuspecting users to log in also. Then, the attacker can do a ping sweep across the subnet looking for other wireless clients, find the users, and begin hacking into their laptop computer's files. These vulnerable users are considered "low hanging fruit," meaning that they are easy to hack because of their general unfamiliarity with leading-edge technology, such as wireless LANs.

Also remember that when a user is associated to a public-access network, the layer 2 security is only as good as that of the public-access network. You might use 802.1X with EAP-TLS at the office, but if your local hotspot uses only a captive portal, your data is vulnerable while you are using the hotspot. The risks of sensitive data being captured on public-access networks can be lessened by requiring layer 3 or higher VPNs for remote access into secure corporate networks, but any files shares on the computer itself are still open to attack. For this reason, a personal firewall is a necessity.

Limited and Tracked Access

Most enterprise LANs have some method of limiting and tracking a user's access on the LAN. Typically, a system supporting Authentication,

Authorization, and Accounting (AAA) services is deployed. AAA means that the enterprise can identify which user is performing actions (Authentication), that the user is allowed to perform the actions (Authorization), and track which actions the user performed (Accounting). Accounting is sometimes used in a general sense to mean "auditing," but it is sometimes used literally to mean "keeping track of how much we should charge this particular client." For example, when you make a cell phone call, your handset must go through an AAA procedure with a server at the cell company. That server tracks the number of minutes you have used and bills you accordingly.

Keeping logs of users' rights and the activities they performed while using your network can prove valuable if there is ever a question of who did what on the network. Consider if a user was on vacation, yet during the vacation the user's account was used almost every day. Keeping logs of activity such as this will give the administrator insight into what is really happening on the LAN. Using the same example, and knowing that the user was on vacation, the administrator could begin looking for where the masquerading user was connecting to the network. As another example, consider a case in which a user has been logged performing illegal actions. Accounting lets you track what the user did, but without strong authentication, the user could claim that someone else had used his or her machine to perform the actions. On the other hand, if the network's authentication architecture is strong, the logs of the user's actions can more reliably be linked directly to the user.

Key Terms

Before taking the exam, you should be familiar with the following terms:

802.11i

802.1X

AES

Application-Layer Encryption

captive portal

EAP

EAP-Cisco Wireless (LEAP)

EAP-FAST

EAP-MD-5 Challenge

EAP-SIM

EAP-TLS

EAP-TTLS

Eavesdropping

IPSec

PEAP

PPTP

RADIUS

RF Jamming

Rogue Access Point

SSL

TKIP

WEP

Wireless VPN

Wireless Hijacking

WPA

WPA2

Review Questions

1. Explain why WEP was initially chosen as the security standard for 802.11 wireless LANs, why WEP was subsequently found to be lacking in enterprise-level security, and how WPA and TKIP improve upon the security provided by WEP for both consumer and enterprise use.

2. Identify and explain five different EAP types and how each works with 802.1X port-based access control.

3. What is the key difference between EAP-TLS and EAP-TTLS? What security benefit does this difference provide, and why?

4. AES is the default encryption component in the 802.11i security standard. Explain why AES may be adopted much more slowly in the enterprise than other encryption methods.

5. Explain why preventing access to the RF signal is essentially impossible in a wireless LAN.

6. Of all the possible malicious attacks on a wireless LAN, which attack is impossible to prevent except with the use of strong physical security? Why?

7. Which compromise of wireless LAN security very often is implemented by someone internal to the organization, yet should be treated as a complete security breach? Why is this attack so common today?

8. Explain the necessity of a wireless LAN security policy prior to the implementation of a wireless LAN as well as when an organization elects NOT to implement any wireless LAN systems.

Site Survey Fundamentals

CWNA Exam Objectives Covered:

❖ Explain the importance of and processes involved in conducting a complete RF site survey

❖ Explain the importance of and proprietary documentation involved in preparing for an RF site survey

- Gathering business requirements

- Interview managers and users

- Defining security requirements

- Gathering site-specific documentation

- Documenting existing network characteristics

- Gathering permits and zoning requirements

- Indoor- or outdoor-specific information

❖ Explain the technical aspects and information collection procedures involved in an RF site survey

- Interference sources

- Infrastructure connectivity and power requirements

- RF coverage requirements

- Data capacity requirements

- Client connectivity requirements

❖ Describe site survey reporting procedures

- Customer reporting requirements

- Reporting methodology

- Security-related reporting

- Graphical documentation

- Hardware recommendations and bills of material

In This Chapter

What is a Site Survey?

Preparing for a Site Survey

Site Survey Equipment

Conducting a Site Survey

Alternative and Supplemental Site Survey Methods

Site Survey Reporting

❖ Identify the equipment, applications, and system features involved in performing automated site surveys
  - Predictive analysis / simulation applications
  - Integrated virtual site survey features
  - Self-managing RF technologies
  - Passive site-survey verification tools and/or applications
❖ Identify the equipment and applications involved in performing manual site surveys
  - Site survey hardware kits
  - Active site survey tools and/or applications
  - Passive site survey tools and/or applications
  - Manufacturers' client utilities

In this chapter, we will discuss the process of conducting a site survey, also known as a "facilities analysis." We will discuss terms and concepts that you have probably heard and used before if you have ever installed a wireless network from the ground up. If wireless is new to you, you might notice that some of the terms and concepts carry over from traditional wired networks. Concepts like throughput needs, power accessibility, extensibility, application requirements, budget requirements, and signal range will all be key components as you conduct a site survey. We will further discuss the ramifications of a poor site survey and even no site survey at all. Our discussion will cover a checklist of tasks that you need to accomplish and equipment that you will use, and we will apply those checklists to several hypothetical examples.

What is a Site Survey?

An RF site survey is a *map* to successfully implementing a wireless network. There is no hard and fast technical definition of a site survey. You, as the CWNA candidate, must learn the process of conducting the best possible site survey for the client, whether that client is internal or external to your organization. The site survey is not to be taken lightly, and can take days or even weeks, depending on the site being surveyed. The resulting information of a quality site survey can be significantly helpful for a long time to come.

 If you do not perform a thorough site survey, the wireless LAN might never work properly, and you (or your client) could spend thousands of dollars on hardware that doesn't perform the intended tasks. A site survey is the first, and most important, step in successfully implementing any wireless LAN.

A site survey is a task-by-task process by which the surveyor discovers the RF behavior, coverage, and interference, determines proper hardware placement in a facility, and determines proper output power and cabling requirements for the hardware. The site survey's primary objective is to ensure that mobile workers – the wireless LAN's "clients" – experience a continually high-quality RF connection as they move around their facility. High quality may mean different things at different times in different circumstances. In most cases, high quality relates to signal strength. Typically, the real test for the quality of WLAN connectivity is whether or not users can access appropriate network resources with the necessary bandwidth to perform their job duties. Employees who are using the wireless LAN should never have to think about the wireless LAN. Proper performance of the tasks listed in this section will ensure a quality site survey and can help achieve a seamless operating environment every time you install a wireless network.

Site surveying involves analyzing a site from an RF perspective and discovering what kind of RF coverage a site needs in order to meet the business goals of the customer. During the site survey process, the surveyor will ask many questions about a variety of topics, which are covered in this chapter. These questions allow the surveyor to gather as much information as possible to make an informed recommendation about what the best options are for hardware, installation, and configuration of a wireless LAN.

Though a surveyor may be documenting the site survey results, another individual (possibly the RF design engineer) may be doing the site survey analysis to determine the best placement of hardware, and yet a third individual might be performing the installation. When installing an access point, a difference in position of just a few feet can make a big difference in the coverage area of the AP. Therefore, all of the results of the entire survey must be thoroughly documented. Organized and accurate documentation by the site surveyor will result in a much better design and installation process.

In some cases, the equipment may be installed by individuals who have little or no knowledge of RF design principles. For example, a nationwide company might contract out the installation of the equipment to a company that primarily does LAN installations (pulling Cat5 data cable and the like). This is partly because there are not very many companies currently specializing in WLAN installation.

If that is the case for you, it is even more important that the results of the site survey be clearly and thoroughly documented. We recommend creating two versions of the survey report: a "complete" version that includes all of the information from the survey (RF contours, dead zones, etc.) and an "installation" version that contains just enough information for the installer to properly install the access points—e.g., "Install access point #12 directly across from the center-line of the doorway to room 205, at a height of seven feet above the floor. Install the AP on the wall with

the front of the AP facing into the hallway and the antennas pointing
directly up towards the ceiling."

The site survey documentation serves as a guide for the network design
and for installing and verifying the wireless communication
infrastructure. If you *don't* do a site survey, you will not have the
knowledge of your clients' needs, the sources of interference, the "dead"
spots (where no RF coverage exists), knowledge of where to install the
access point(s), and worst of all, you won't be able to estimate for the
client how much the wireless LAN will cost to implement! Although
performing RF site surveys is the only business that some firms engage
in, a good site survey can be the best sales tool that a network integration
firm has at its disposal. Performing a quality site survey can, and many
times should, lead to your organization performing the installation and
integration of the wireless LAN for which the site survey was done.

Many WLAN administrators still believe that they can install a wireless
network without performing a site survey (although, thankfully, this
number seems to have decreased significantly since 802.11 first became
popular). Even if you are just putting a wireless access point in your
home—an installation that most people would say is simple enough to not
need a site survey—a minimal site survey might help you avoid channels
that your neighbor is using. We are not suggesting that all installations
should have full RF modeling; rather, the sophistication of the site survey
should reflect the complexity of the installation.

Preparing for a Site Survey

The planning of a wireless LAN involves collecting information and
making decisions. The following is a list of the most basic questions that
must be answered before the physical work of the site survey begins.
These questions are purposely open-ended because each one results in
more information being passed from the client to the surveyor, making the
surveyor better prepared to go on-site and do the site survey. Most, if not
all, of these questions can be answered via phone, fax, or e-mail,
assuming the people with the answers to the questions are available.
Again, the more prepared the surveyor is before arriving at the site (with a
site survey toolkit), the more productive the time on-site will be. Some of

the topics you may want to question the network management about before performing your site survey are:

- Facilities Analysis
- Existing Networks
- Area Usage & Towers
- Purpose & Business Requirements
- Bandwidth & Roaming Requirements
- Available Resources
- Security Requirements

Facility Analysis

What kind of facility is it?

This question is very basic, but the answer can greatly impact the site survey work for the next several days. Consider the obvious differences between conducting a site survey of a small office with one server and 20 clients and performing a site survey of a large international airport. Aside from the obvious size differences, you must take into account the number of users, security requirements, bandwidth requirements, budget, what kind of impact jet engines have on 802.11 RF signals, coverage areas of access points or WLAN switches, and so on.

All that and more comes from the "facilities analysis" question. Your answers could come in the form of pictures, written descriptions, or blueprints, whenever possible. The more you know before you get to the facility, the better prepared you will be when you actually arrive. Depending on the facility type, there will be standard issues to be addressed. Knowing the facility type before arrival will save time on-site.

To demonstrate the standard issues, let's consider two facility types. The first example is a hospital. Hospitals are subject to an act of Congress known as HIPAA. HIPAA mandates that hospitals (and other like health care organizations) keep certain information private. This issue alone demonstrates that, when doing a site survey for a hospital, security planning must be of prime importance.

Hospitals also have radiology equipment, mesh metal glass windows, fire doors, very long hallways, elevators, mobile users (nurses and doctors), and X-ray rooms with lead-lined walls. This set of criteria shows the surveyor some obvious things to consider, like roaming across large distances, and medical applications that are often connection-oriented between the client and server. To ensure only the necessary amount of coverage for certain areas, semi-directional antennas may be used instead of omni antennas. Semi-directional antennas tend to reduce multipath, since the signal is being focused in one direction. Elevators are everywhere, and cause RF "shadows" because elevators are basically "dead" RF zones. A hospital site survey is a good "trial by fire" for individuals wanting to get immersed in wireless LAN technology.

The second facility type is a real estate office with approximately 25 agents. In this environment, security is important, but not mandated by law, so rudimentary security measures might suffice. Coverage will likely be adequate with only one or two centrally-located access points, and bandwidth requirements would be nominal since most of the access is Internet-based or transferring small files back and forth to the file server.

These two scenarios are quite different, but both need site surveys. The amount of time that it will take to perform a site survey at each facility is also very different. The real estate office may not even take a full day, whereas the hospital, depending on its size, might take a week or more. Many of the activities of the users in each facility, such as roaming, are very different. With nurses and doctors in a hospital, roaming is just part of the job. In the relatively small, multi-room facility of the real estate firm, users sit at their desks and access the wireless network from that one location, so roaming may not be necessary.

Existing Networks

Is there already a network (wired or wireless) in place?

This question is also basic, but you must know if the client is starting from scratch or if the wireless LAN must work with an existing infrastructure. If there is an existing infrastructure, what it consists of must be known. Most of the time, there are existing wired and wireless portions of the network infrastructure, which opens the door to a myriad of questions that need answering. Documentation of existing wireless

LAN hardware, frequencies being used, number of users, expected throughput, etc., must be taken into account so that decisions can be made on how the new equipment (if needed) will fit in. It also may be the case that the customer did the initial installation, and has since outgrown the initial installation. If the existing setup functions poorly, this poor performance must also be noted so the problems are not repeated.

Questions commonly asked of the network administrator or manager include:

- What client operating systems are in use?
- How many users (today and two years from now) need simultaneous access to the wireless network in a given area?
- What is the bandwidth (per user) requirement on the wireless network?
- What desktop protocols are in use over the wireless LAN?
- What spread spectrum technologies and channels are currently in use?
- What wireless LAN security measures are currently in place?
- Is there currently a WLAN security policy in place? If not, who is responsible for creating one?
- Where are wired LAN connection points (wiring closets) located in the facility?
- Do the existing edge switches support 802.3af PoE?
- What are the client's expectations of what a wireless LAN will bring to their organization?
- Is there a naming convention in place for infrastructure devices, such as routers, switches, access points, and wireless bridges? If not, who is responsible for creating one? (see Figure 13.1)

FIGURE 13.1   Naming Conventions

1: AP_North_Storage_7
2: AP_North_Storage_6
3: AP_North_Sales_23

Obtain a detailed network diagram (topology map) from the current network administrator. When one or more wireless LANs are already in place, the site survey will become all the more difficult, especially if the previous installations were not done properly. Doing a site survey with an ill-functioning wireless LAN in place can be almost impossible without the cooperation of the network administrator to disable the network where and when needed, because the existing wireless network can interfere with the probes and "test" access points that you are using to perform the site survey. Ideally, no pre-existing wireless network will exist, but if one does exist, it should be disabled (if it will not be part of the final installation) or incorporated into the design (if it will be part of the final installation). Upgrades of existing wired infrastructure devices also might be necessary to enhance throughput and security on the wireless LAN.

It may be necessary to sign a confidentiality agreement in order to obtain network diagrams or blueprints from your client.

Where are the network wiring closets located?

It is not uncommon to find that what seems like the most appropriate location for installing an access point ends up being too far from a wiring closet to allow for upstream network connectivity. Knowing where these wiring closets are ahead of time will save time later on. Locations of these wiring closets should be documented on the network topology map, blueprints, or other facility maps. There are solutions for these problems, such as using access points or bridges as repeaters, but this method of connectivity should be avoided where possible. Connecting bridges and access points directly into the wired distribution system is almost always favored.

How will the APs be powered?

If the APs are to be powered via AC adapters located near the devices, it will be necessary to ensure that an electrical outlet is within a reasonable distance of the AP. Do not assume that it will be simple to run AC power to the AP's location, since building codes apply to running high-voltage wires. If you plan to power the APs with PoE, then you can run cables wherever you like, but you must take into account Ethernet's distance limitations. In addition, you must be certain that the wiring closet to which the AP will connect has the necessary injectors or active PoE switches to provide power to the AP(s).

Has an access point/bridge naming convention been devised?

If a wireless LAN is not currently in place, a logical naming convention may need to be devised by the network manager. Using a logical naming convention with access points and bridges on the wireless network will make managing them, once they are in place, much easier. For the site surveyor, having logical names in place for each access point and bridge will facilitate the task of documenting the placement of units in the RF site survey report.

Area Usage & Towers

Is the wireless LAN going to be used indoors, outdoors, or both?

Do hurricanes or tornadoes occur frequently in this site's locale? Outdoor usage of wireless LAN gear creates many situations and potential obstacles to installing and maintaining a wireless LAN. As we discussed in prior sections, a strong wind can eliminate the signal on a long distance wireless link. If inclement weather such as ice or strong rain is often present, radomes (domelike shells transparent to radio-frequency radiation, used to house RF antennas) might be considered to protect outdoor antennas. If bridges or access points need to be mounted outdoors as well, a NEMA-compliant weatherproof enclosure might be considered, as shown in Figure 13.2.

FIGURE 13.2   NEMA Enclosure

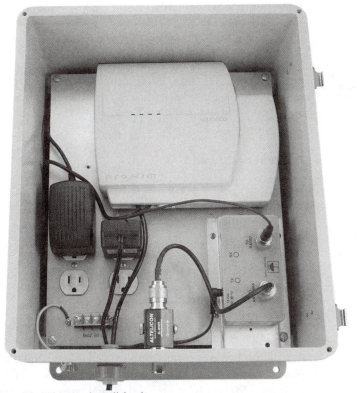

Copyright 2004 www.hyperlinktech.com

Outdoor wireless connections are vulnerable to security attacks, since the intruder would not have to be inside the building to get into the network. Once it is determined that the survey is for indoors, outdoors, or both, try to obtain any available property survey documents and diagrams. Indoors, these documents will show you the floor layout, fire walls, building structure information, wiring closets, and other valuable information.

Outdoors, these documents will show how far the outdoor wireless LAN can safely extend without significant chance of intrusion.

When outdoors, look for RF signal obstructions, such as buildings, trees, mountains, etc. Checking for other wireless LAN signals at the point where outdoor antennas will be installed is a good idea. If channel 1 in a DSSS system were to be used, and subsequently it was found that channel 1 is in use by a nearby outdoor system using an omni-directional antenna, the report should document that a channel that does not overlap channel 1 should be used for this bridge link.

Remember that trees not only pose a potential problem in regards to Fresnel Zone blockage, but also may be a source of attenuation problems during periods of rainy or freezing weather. Tree leaves collect rainwater and snow, and this will produce attenuation of your signal until the water has evaporated if the tree is in the Fresnel Zone.

Is a tower required?

When performing a site survey, a 30-foot tower might be needed on top of a building to clear some trees that are in the direct signal path of an outdoor wireless link. If a tower is required, other questions that need to be asked might include:

- If the roof is to be used, is it adequate to support a tower?
- Is a structural engineer required?
- Is a permit necessary?

A structural engineer may be required to determine if a tower can be placed on top of a building without safety risks to the occupants of the building. Municipal permits also may be necessary to install a tower.

Permits or government approval may be necessary to install a tower. For example, for towers that are more than 200 feet (61 meters) above ground level, the FCC requires that the FAA be notified prior to constructing or modifying an antenna structure (tower, pole, building, etc.). Instructions for notifying the FAA (the proper forms to fill out and where to send them) can be found in the Code of Federal Regulations, title 47, part 17, which you can find via a web search on the term "47 CFR Part 17."

A 180-foot tall building with a 21-foot tall tower would require FAA notification, for example, because the building (antenna structure) has been modified and exceeds 200 feet. However, the FCC and FAA make an exception for antenna towers that are less than 20 feet in height, which may be added to any building, regardless of the resulting height of the building. So, for example, a 20 foot tower could be added to a 190 foot building without FAA notification, even though the resulting structure would be 210 feet tall.

If the antenna structure is located fewer than 20,000 feet (6.10 km) from an airport runway, the maximum height is calculated based on an imaginary diagonal surface extending away from the nearest runway of the airport at a specified slope. The specific values can be found in part 17.7 of the Code of Federal Regulations, title 47, which you can find via a web search on the term "47 CFR Part 17."

Finally, an exception is made if the antenna structure "would be shielded by existing structures of a permanent and substantial character or by natural terrain or topographic features of equal or greater height, and would be located in the congested area of a city, town, or settlement where it is evident beyond all reasonable doubt that the structure so shielded will not adversely affect safety in air navigation." In other words, if you are in a city and are surrounded by 300 foot buildings, it is okay to put a tower onto your building that makes the tower 250 feet high.

Purpose & Business Requirements

What is the purpose of the wireless LAN? What are the business requirements?

From a temporary office to complete data connectivity for the Olympics, the answer to this question will drive many decisions. Using the extreme example and contrast of a temporary office versus the Olympics, dozens of issues might come up, such as budget, number of users, outdoor connectivity, temporary network access, and security.

Recommending a high-speed 802.11a installation for an organization that is only using a few wireless PDAs would be poor judgment because most 802.11 cards that are compatible with PDAs (CF and SD form factor) are

802.11b only. Therefore, the PDAs wouldn't be able to take advantage of 802.11a's higher speeds. As much information as can be gathered will be helpful in understanding how the wireless LAN is to be used. This information gathering may require interviews with some network users, as well as network management.

Find out exactly what the client expects to do with the wireless LAN and what applications are going to be used over this new network. There might be several distinct and independent purposes for the wireless LAN. Thoroughly documenting the client's needs enables the network architect to design a solution that will meet all of the client's needs, and also may assist the client in its network management.

For example, at a ski resort, ski instructors and their supervisors use wireless handheld PDAs to coordinate skiing classes across several slopes at once. Since these handhelds are used over a vast stretch of land, range is very important, but the small amount of data being carried over the wireless network means that many of these wireless PDAs can be used on a single access point at any given time without degraded performance. In contrast, a small group of graphic designers, sitting in one room and needing access to file servers to which they transfer large images over the wireless network, need high-speed access, but minimal range. Only a small number of this type of user (high bandwidth) should be connected to an access point at any given time. Connection-oriented applications can time out during drops in coverage if coverage is poor or intermittent, causing user complaints. Real-time applications are sensitive to delay caused by corrupted frames, whereas file transfer applications will probably recover gracefully and without the users' knowledge. These scenarios show how uses of wireless LANs can vary substantially. The site surveyor must know the business needs of the organization in order to effectively perform a site survey.

One application that deserves special mention is VoWiFi (VoIP over Wi-Fi). First, voice traffic is more sensitive to latency and frame loss, of which wireless LANs have much more than traditional LAN data transfer. Second, users are immediately aware, and are relatively intolerant, of even small degradation in voice call quality, whereas they may tolerate or not even notice degradation in data transfer quality. Suffice it to say that if VoWiFi is one of your network's applications, you should, at the very least, design the network to the widest tolerances. Users should always have the maximum data rate possible and the number of users per access point should be minimized.

One recommendation from the 802.11b-only days is to not mix data and voice on the same wireless network, and this is still the safe choice. Some vendors have proprietary protocols that allow better voice performance, even in mixed voice/data networks, but of course these protocols only work with a single vendor's APs and phones, so you cannot mix them with other vendors' equipment. It remains to be seen how successful standards-based protocols QoS (IEEE 802.11e) will be at addressing this issue, since 802.11e has not been ratified at the time of this printing.

Bandwidth & Roaming Requirements

What is the required capacity of the network?

The answer to this question will determine the technology to be implemented and the technology that will be used during the site survey. For example, if the client is a warehouse facility and the only purpose that the wireless LAN will serve is scanning data from box labels and sending that data to a central server, the throughput requirements are very small. Most data collection devices require only 2 Mbps (such as a computer on a forklift in a warehouse), but require seamless connectivity while moving (mobility). However, if the client organization requires that the wireless LAN will serve 35 software developers who need high-speed access to application servers, test servers, and the Internet, then throughput is a high priority, but roaming may not be a high priority. This is true since these software developers will probably remain in one location while working.

The capacity of the network, both in terms of simultaneous users and total expected throughput must be determined. Most vendors quote a maximum users-per-AP for adequate performance. The network should be designed to stay below this number. In addition, you can estimate the total throughput that a single AP should be able to provide (typically about 5 Mbps for 802.11b and 20 Mbps for 802.11a and 802.11g) and then determine whether a single AP can meet the anticipated throughput needs of the users. Remember that if the network is close to 100 percent capacity when it is designed, it will probably be over-utilized shortly after it is deployed, so design for more capacity than the users are actually expected to use.

What are the organization's roaming requirements?

It is important to distinguish between "roaming," as in "the ability to pick up your laptop and go to another location and have connectivity at the new location," and "the ability to maintain a connection while moving." Implementing "wireless mobility" (the latter definition) can be tricky, if only because the user may roam from one IP subnet to another, necessitating layer 3 roaming protocols in addition to 802.11's native layer 2 roaming support. Fortunately, most wireless networks do not actually need to provide "wireless mobility." As long as the user can put his laptop down anywhere in the coverage area and get coverage, then it does not matter if he has coverage *while* moving. This concession can simplify the site survey and the network installation significantly.

How many users are typically in a given area?

An understanding of how many users will be located in a given area is required to calculate how much throughput each user is going to have. If the network manager is not able to provide this information, the person doing the site survey may need to interview the actual users or to visit the customer site using a protocol analyzer during certain times of the day to be able to make an informed decision. Different departments within an organization will have different numbers of users. It is important to understand that the needs can differ from one part of a facility to another.

What type of applications will be used over the wireless LAN?

Find out if the network is being used to transmit non time-sensitive data only, time-sensitive data such as voice or video only, or both at the same time. High bandwidth applications, such as file transfers or streaming DVD-quality video, will require greater throughput per user than an application that makes infrequent network requests. Connection-oriented applications will need to maintain connectivity while roaming. Analyzing and documenting these application requirements before the site survey will allow the site surveyor to make more informed decisions when testing areas for coverage.

Are there any non-typical times in which network needs may change for a particular area?

Changes in network needs could be something as simple as more users being on a particular shift or something as difficult to discover as seasonal changes. For example, if a building-to-building bridge link were being surveyed in winter, the trees would be without leaves. In the spring, trees will fill with leaves, which in turn fill with water when it rains. This can cause problems with the wireless link. In another example, a wireless network might be designed around the assumption of few users, but an annual sales meeting might fill the conference room with many sales representatives using the wireless network, overwhelming it.

Available Resources

What are the available resources?

Among topics to discuss with the network manager regarding available resources are the project's budget, the amount of time allotted for the project, and whether or not the organization has administrators trained on wireless networks. If documentation of previous site surveys exists, and current topology and facility maps are available, the site surveyor should request copies of these plans. It is possible that the network administrator may not give access to all of these resources, citing security reasons. In this case, it might be possible to gain access by asking local staff to accompany you on the survey. If that is not possible, then the site survey may take additional time, and the cost of the site survey would probably increase.

Are facility blueprints available (electronic or printed)?

Among the first items to request from a network manager are blueprints or some kind of floor plan showing the physical layout of the facility, as shown in Figure 13.3. Without the official building or facility schematics, a diagram must be created that shows the dimensions of the areas, the offices, where the walls are located, network closets, power outlets, etc.

FIGURE 13.3 Blueprints or floor plans

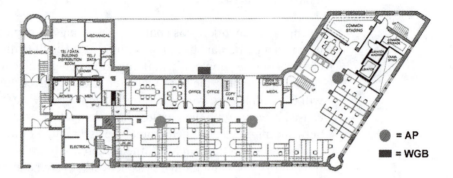

= AP

= WGB

Creating a facility drawing can be a time-consuming task. If it is necessary to manually create such a document, simple things like notebook paper with grid lines help improve efficiency as the site survey is performed. This information can later be put into Visio, AutoCAD, or other such applications for professional presentation to the customer as part of the RF Site Survey Report.

Once you have floor plans, we recommend marking on them where equipment will be placed and its approximate coverage area. If the floor plans are electronic, you might be able to place icons in software. If the floor plans are paper, then we suggest using colored stickers to represent the equipment.

Are there any previous site survey reports available?

If a company has previously had a site survey performed, having that site survey report available can cut down on the time it takes for the new survey to be completed. Be sure that the previous report does not bias the decisions made regarding the current site survey.

Is a facilities escort or security badge required?

A security badge or an escort may be required to move throughout the facility freely. When performing a site survey, every square foot of the facility is usually covered in order to answer all the questions needed to define the RF coverage. In government or other high-security facilities, this might not be possible if you are an external contractor and/or do not have the required security clearances. There are various contingencies for this case. Depending on the security requirements, the on-site administrator might perform a survey for the prohibited areas and give it to the surveyor for incorporation into the survey. Alternatively, the on-site administrator might simply decide to handle the survey for the prohibited areas entirely internally without passing along this documentation to you.

It has been said that RF site surveying is 90 percent walking and 10 percent surveying. This is usually true, so you should wear very comfortable shoes and make sure that an escort (if necessary) has plenty of time while the survey is being performed.

Is physical access to wiring closets and the roof available if needed?

Physical access to both the roof and to wiring closets may be needed to determine antenna placement and network connection points.

Security Requirements

What level of network security is necessary?

Customers may have very strict demands for data security, or in some cases, no security may be required. It should be explained to the customer that WEP should not be used because it can easily be circumvented. As we discussed in chapter 12, WPA should be the minimum level of security, with WPA2/802.11i being preferred. Briefly educating the customer on available security options is an important step in getting started with a site survey. A discussion with the customer will provide him enough information to feel informed and will allow him to better understand the solutions likely to be presented by the design engineer. After this discussion, the customer may likely have several questions involving wireless network security that may aid the site surveyor in properly documenting the customer's business needs.

What corporate policies are in place regarding wireless LAN security implementation and management?

The network manager may not have any security policies in place. If the customer already has a wireless LAN in place, the existing security policies should be reviewed before the site survey is started. If corporate security policies relating to wireless LANs do not exist, you should ask questions about security requirements regarding their installation.

During the design phase of integrating the wireless LAN (design is not part of the site survey itself), the RF design engineer could include a security report detailing security suggestions for this particular installation. The network administrator could then use this information to form a corporate policy. Security policies may differ slightly between small, medium, and enterprise installations, and can sometimes be re-used. There are general security practices that are common to all installations of wireless LANs. Examples of things that should be included in a security policy include:

- Minimum levels of security such as: "the network must use WPA2 authentication with EAP-TLS, mutual authentication, and AES encryption (or another equivalent technology)."
- Procedure for adding new devices to the network.
- Procedure for detecting and responding to a security lapse.
- Penalties for violation of the security policy.

Security policies are covered in more detail in chapter 12, "Security."

Preparation Exercises

As a thought-provoking exercise, consider some of the hypothetical examples mentioned earlier (small office wireless LAN, international airport wireless LAN, and a wireless LAN for connecting all the computers at the Olympics), and then ask the following questions:

- Are the users mobile within the facility (do they compute in place or move while computing)?
- How far – inside or outside the facility – will the users roam and still need connectivity?
- What level of access do these users need to sensitive data via the wireless network? Is security required? How secure is "secure enough?"

- Do these users use any bandwidth-intensive, time-sensitive, or connection-oriented applications?
- How often do these users change departments or locations?
- Will any or all of these users have Internet access, and what are the policies regarding file downloads?
- Does the office/work environment of these users ever change for special events that could disrupt a wireless LAN?
- Who currently supports these users on the existing network, and are they qualified to support wireless users?
- If the users are mobile, what type of mobile computing device do they use (e.g., Hand Scanner, PDA, or Laptop)?
- How often and for how long will the users with laptops work without AC power?

There are many specific questions about the users of the wireless LAN and their needs, and this information is vital to the site survey. The more information that can be gathered about who will be using the wireless LAN and for what purposes, the easier conducting the site survey will be.

Preparation Checklist

Below is a general list of items that should be obtained from or scheduled with the client prior to visiting the site to do the site survey, if possible.

- ❏ Building floor plans (including power source documentation)
- ❏ Previous wireless LAN site survey documentation
- ❏ Current network diagram (topology map)
- ❏ A meeting with the network administrator and network manager
- ❏ A meeting with the facilities manager
- ❏ A meeting with the network security manager
- ❏ Access to all areas of the facility to be affected by the wireless LAN
- ❏ Access to wiring closets and the roof (if outdoor antennas are anticipated)
- ❏ Future construction plans, if available

Many of these issues can be addressed via a pre-survey questionnaire that is filled out by the appropriate personnel before the surveyor even goes on site. This can save significant time for both the administrator and the surveyor, since the common questions are answered sooner. A sample site survey questionnaire is included in an appendix of this book.

Now that all of these questions are answered and complete documentation of the facility has been made, you are ready to leave your office and go on site.

Site Survey Equipment

There are two general types of site surveys. The "manual" method involves walking around the site with a test access point and client station, measuring the RF propagation characteristics at various locations. This was the only method of performing a site survey when 802.11 first became popular. In contrast, the "automatic" method involves using software and sensors to predict the likely coverage of equipment based on floor plans and other schematics.

This section will cover the wireless LAN equipment and tools required to perform a manual site survey. A later section will describe automatic site surveys. In some cases, you may not need to perform a full manual survey. It is often most efficient to perform an automatic survey, then to perform an abbreviated manual survey to validate the results.

In the most basic indoor cases, you will need at least one access point, a variety of antennas, antenna cables and connectors, a laptop computer (or PDA) with a wireless PC card, some site survey utility software, and *lots* of paper. Some minor things can be added to your mobile toolkit, such as double-sided tape (for temporarily mounting antennas to the wall), an uninterruptible power supply (UPS) with a charged-up battery (for powering the access point where there is no source of AC power), a digital camera for taking pictures of particular locations within a facility, a set of two-way radios if you're working in teams, and a secure case for the gear. Some manufacturers sell site survey kits already configured, but in many cases individuals prefer to select the tool kit and wireless LAN equipment piece by piece to assure that they get all of the pieces they need. A more comprehensive list of equipment required during a site survey is provided in a checklist at the end of this section.

Access Point

The access point used during a site survey should have variable output power and, if possible, external antenna connectors. The variable output power feature allows for easy sizing of coverage cells during the site survey. This tool is particularly useful for situations involving long hallways, such as in a hospital.

 It is not hard to see how changing output power in software is more convenient than adding, mounting, and then dismounting and removing antennas with different amounts of gain. If your AP does not have variable output power, a variable attenuator can be used to simulate variable output power.

One clever "trick of the trade" for performing site surveys is to carry a UPS battery-backup with you. The type of UPS that is designed to power a desktop computer and CRT monitor for five to fifteen minutes (available for under $100 at your local office supply or consumer electronics store) can easily power an AP for hours. This configuration makes the access point mobile, and able to be placed anywhere the site surveyor needs to perform testing. This group of components can be tie-strapped together, or put into a single, portable enclosure. Many times the access point will be placed on a ladder or on top of the ceiling tiles while the antenna is temporarily mounted to a wall. Having completely portable gear with no need for AC power makes the site survey go much faster than it would otherwise. If the customer plans to use external antennas, you should have one of each type of antenna, a pigtail cable, and a length of coaxial cable to attach the antenna to the AP during testing.

 Mobile access points mounted to battery packs with a UPS may look like some sort of dangerous device and may be confiscated at airports. Make sure you disclose to all security personnel exactly what this configuration is, and what it is for. Placing such devices in a hard-shell travel case and checking the case is likely a better scenario than having it as a carry-on item.

PC Card and Utilities

High quality wireless PC cards often come with site survey utility software, as shown in Figure 13.4. Site survey utilities from different manufacturers will vary in their functionality, but most offer a link speed indicator and signal strength meter at a minimum. These two tools will provide general indications of coverage. To perform a quality site survey, the following quantitative measurements should be recorded as a minimum:

- Signal strength (measured in dBm)
- Noise floor (measured in dBm)
- Signal-to-noise ratio ("SNR") (measured in dB)
- Link speed

Only a few vendors offer this complete set of tools in their client utility software. With quality site surveying software (whether using one or more wireless PC cards), site survey measurements can be efficiently completed with accuracy.

FIGURE 13.4 Site Monitor application

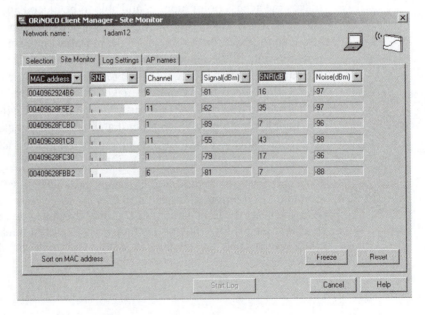

While walking around the intended coverage area, pay particular attention to the SNR measurement because it shows the strength of the RF signal versus the background noise. The SNR also shows the viability of the RF link and is a good indicator of whether or not a client will connect and remain connected. For most PC cards, a signal-to-noise ratio of 20 dB or higher will provide the maximum data rate (11 Mbps for 802.11b or 54 Mbps for 802.11g). Whether a link is actually viable or not depends on factors other than just SNR, but as long as a link is stable and the access point provides the client with a level of RF power significantly above its sensitivity threshold, the link can be considered viable.

Having a utility that can measure the signal strength, the SNR, and the background RF noise level (called the "noise floor") is very useful. Knowing the signal strength is useful for finding out if an obstacle is blocking the RF signal or if the access point is not putting out enough power. The SNR measurement lets the site surveyor know if the link is clean and clear enough to be considered viable. Knowing the noise level is useful in determining if RF interference is causing a problem in the link, or if the level of RF in the environment has changed from the time that a baseline was established. An engineer can use all three of these measurements to make design and troubleshooting determinations.

One particularly useful function of a wireless PC card is the ability to change the power output at the client station during the site survey. This feature is useful because you should test for situations in which near/far or hidden node problems might exist. Not everyone has the luxury of taking the time to do this sort of testing, but this feature is useful when time permits.

FIGURE 13.5 Client-side power adjustment

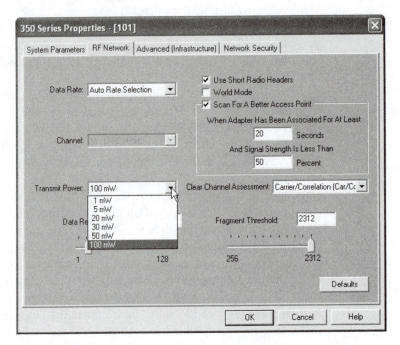

Third party utilities such as NetStumbler are valuable during a site survey in which there are already access points and bridges in place. These utilities enable you to find all of these units quickly and record their information (such as MAC address, SSID, WEP status, signal strength, SNR, noise, etc.). These utilities can replace what the driver software and manufacturer utilities often miss. Better still are full protocol analyzers like AirMagnet, AiroPeek, and Observer (if installed with "raw mode" drivers), since they show all frames that were heard on the air, while NetStumbler and similar applications only show specific, limited information.

FIGURE 13.6   WLAN Protocol Analyzer Site Survey Utility (Network Instruments Observer)

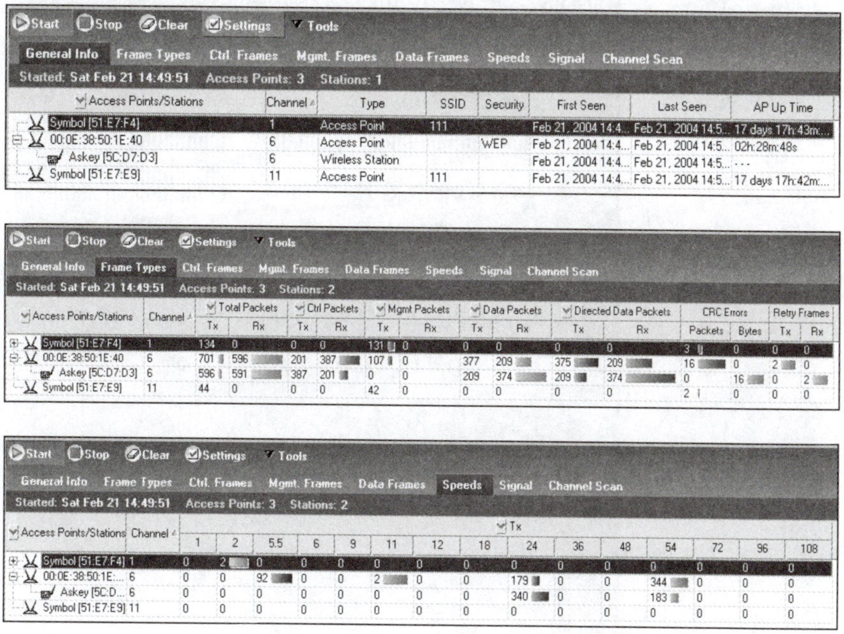

A multi-purpose utility such as the one shown in Figure 13.6 can be used to measure the wireless link speed, signal strength, signal quality, and other parameters. This information is useful in case part of the site survey requirement is to size or shape the cells for 11 Mbps usage (or some other speed) by clients.

FIGURE 13.7 Site Survey Utility

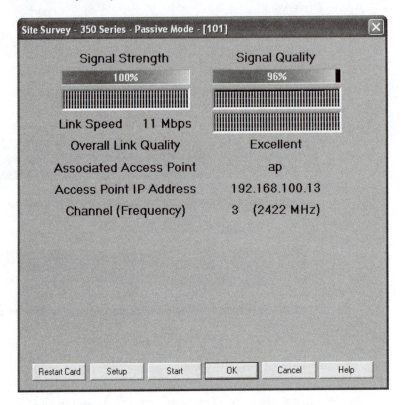

As we learned earlier, Dynamic Rate Shifting (DRS) allows a client to automatically downshift link speeds as range increases. If the business requirements are for all clients to maintain 11 Mbps connectivity while roaming, then proper coverage patterns must be documented during the site survey.

Laptops & PDAs

A laptop computer or PDA unit is used for checking for signal strength, noise floor, link speed, and coverage while roaming around the facility. Many site survey professionals have begun using PDAs instead of laptop computers to perform the site survey because of battery life and portability. PDAs can report the same information and connect to the network in the same way as the laptop without the extra 3–7 pounds of weight in a laptop. Three to seven pounds might not seem like much weight, but after carrying a laptop of this weight around a facility that measures over a million square feet (which is a common facility size), a PDA that supports the functionality you need to do your site survey may seem like a trivial purchase. Most manufacturers make Pocket PC and Windows CE drivers and utilities (including the site survey utilities) for their PCMCIA cards.

On the other hand, PDAs have the disadvantage that they probably do not realistically represent the eventual production environment. For example, the antenna on a laptop will probably be oriented differently than the antenna on a PDA. A PDA might only have drivers for 802.11b cards, whereas the production environment might use a/b/g cards. The PDA probably cannot run a sample version of the production application for the best "real-world" testing. To address these concerns, miniature laptops are available weighing as little as 1.5 pounds, which serve the same purpose of having a more portable unit for site surveying. However, these ultra-portable laptops tend to cost much more than a PDA.

Simple screen-capture software is also beneficial. For reporting purposes, screenshots show the actual results that the site surveying software displayed. These screenshots can be presented to the customer as part of the RF site survey report, which is why custom screen capture software is useful. Screen capture software packages are available for Windows, Pocket PC, and Linux operating systems.

Laptop batteries rarely last more than three hours, and a site survey might last eight to ten hours per day. Always having fresh batteries on hand will keep you productive while on site. Without the luxury of extra laptop batteries, the only alternative is to charge the batteries during a break, which might not be a good alternative since many laptop batteries charge slowly. Another solution would be to find a very small, power-efficient laptop whose batteries are specified to last much longer than the typical two-to-three hours. As mentioned before, PDA batteries tend to last longer than do laptop batteries.

Paper

Both the surveyor and the network designer should make hard copy (paper) documentation of all findings in great detail for future reference. Digital photographs of a facility make finding a particular location within the facility much easier, and serve as graphical information for the RF site survey report as well. During most surveys, scratch paper, grid paper, and copies of blueprints or floor plans are necessary. It is a good idea to make several copies of blueprints, so that you have a "clean" copy before you start marking them up. If a facility contains several mostly-identical floors, a survey of one floor can probably be applied to the other floors, and carrying floor plans for each individual floor is probably unnecessary. When added to the equipment that will be carried around, this amount of paper and documentation tends to become a burden. For this reason, a sufficiently large mobile equipment cart that can contain all the necessary gear is quite useful while moving through a facility.

There are no industry standard forms for recording all the data that will be necessary during even the smallest site survey. However, it will prove very useful to create a set of forms that suits your style of work and recording, and to use these same forms on every site survey. Not only will this type of uniformity help you communicate your findings to the client, but it will also help maintain accurate and easy to understand records of past site surveys. These forms will be used during the creation of your site survey report as a reference for all readings taken during the site survey.

Outdoor Surveys

If the area to be covered is relatively small and users all have line of site to the antenna, an outdoor site survey can be much simpler than an indoor site survey, in which there are nearly always obstructions between the users and the antennas. Site surveys of outdoor installations can be much more complex than indoor installations if a large area needs to be covered, line of sight is obstructed (by trees or buildings), or the distance of the link is very long (several miles or more).

You can determine many factors of a long-distance point-to-point link before going on site. For example, one factor that must be considered is antenna height. The two antennas must be high enough that they keep 60 percent of the first Fresnel zone free of obstructions. The simplest way to calculate this is to use a vendor's link calculator (usually in a spreadsheet) or an online calculator. One such calculator is available at http://www.connect802.com/designer. The height of the antenna might be restricted by the height of the building at either end of the link or by

FCC and FAA regulations (discussed previously). If the distance between the antennas is long enough, the horizon itself might encroach on the Fresnel zone (this is known as "earth bulge"), and the calculator that you use should take this into account.

In order to keep the Fresnel zone clear, you will need to know the height of the highest obstruction between the two antennas and the distance from that obstruction to each antenna. The link must be designed so that the Fresnel zone clears this obstruction. This can be accomplished using surveying techniques—e.g., use a laser sight to determine distance to the obstruction and triangulate the height—but that might require climbing the tower or going on top of the building where the antenna would be mounted. This might be inconvenient and potentially a safety risk. If the obstruction is a hill or mountain, the height of the obstruction can be determined using topographical maps instead. If none of these resources are available, another method is to take a GPS receiver to the location of the highest obstruction and measure its height.

Once you have calculated the proper antenna height, the next step is to obtain the appropriate antennas, amplifiers, connectors, cabling, and other equipment. With a technician at either end of the link, install the equipment and orient the antennas using the "bridge alignment" methods described in chapter 7, "WLAN Infrastructure Devices." If the antenna is to be mounted up a tower, a properly-trained climber should be employed. The technicians at either end of the link should have walkie-talkies, cell phones, or some other means of communicating as they align the antennas.

Whereas an indoor site survey can probably be done by the average WLAN administrator, an outdoor site survey requires more skills than the average WLAN administrator will likely have, such as reading a topographical map, surveying with GPS and traditional methods, tower climbing, and so on. Therefore, outdoor site surveys and installations are more likely to be performed by external contractors specializing in that specific field of work.

Spectrum Analyzer

Spectrum analyzers come in various types. The two main categories might be considered software and hardware spectrum analyzers.

Hardware spectrum analyzers are made by many different manufacturers and may cost thousands of dollars, depending on resolution, speed, frequency range, and other parameters.

FIGURE 13.8   Hardware Spectrum Analyzer (Rohde & Schwarz FSH6)

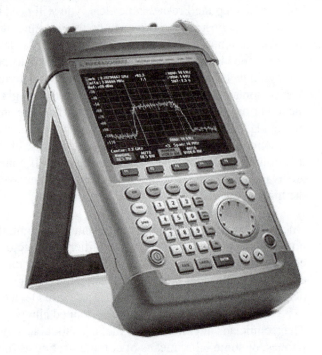

Software spectrum analyzers consist of drivers and an application that runs on a laptop computer and uses an RF radio card that attaches to the laptop, typically via PCMCIA.

FIGURE 13.9   Software Spectrum Analyzer (Proxim 7400)

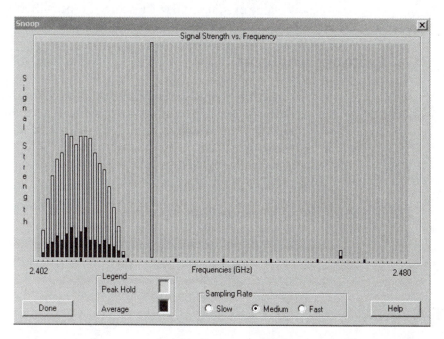

Software spectrum analyzers are capable of scanning the entire 2.4 GHz band and providing a graphical display of the results. These products give the user the effective equivalent of a hardware spectrum analyzer without the accurate quantitative measurements. This may be "good enough" in many site surveys when the spectrum analyzer is only used to locate sources and types of RF interference in a general area.

As part of the spectral analysis procedure, you may decide to have all the WLAN users turn their equipment off, if possible, so that any sources of background interference can be detected, such as low power sources of narrowband interference. Low power narrowband interference is easily located while there are no other sources of RF in use, but is quite difficult to locate when many sources of RF are in use. High power narrowband is easily located with the proper test equipment, regardless of additional RF sources.

Part of a spectrum analysis should be to locate any 802.11b or 802.11a networks in use around the implementation area of the proposed wireless LAN. If current or future plans involve installation of 802.11a products, it would be advantageous to both the site surveyor and the customer to know of any existing 5 GHz RF sources, especially if they are part of an existing wireless LAN.

Protocol Analyzer

After spectrum analysis is complete, a protocol analyzer can be used to find other wireless LANs in the area (perhaps on another floor of a building) that can affect the wireless LAN implementation. The protocol analyzer will pick up any frames being transmitted by nearby wireless LANs and will provide detailed information on channels in use, distance, and signal strength, as shown in Figure 13.10.

FIGURE 13.10 Wireless Protocol Analyzer

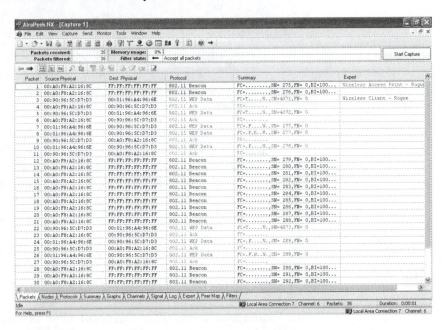

Additionally, a protocol analyzer can be invaluable for verifying that the WLAN's throughput and latency requirements are being met. Although file transfer applications typically report throughput measurements, other applications may not. By comparison, a protocol analyzer can provide utilization statistics for any application. Ping can be used as a rough measure of network latency, but a protocol analyzer can provide the actual latency of the application in question.

If the performance of the network is not matching the predictions of the site survey, an analyzer is one of the best tools to determine why. A protocol analyzer may be able to identify unauthorized or unexpected applications (depending on the encryption type that is in use), and it can definitely troubleshoot layer 1 and 2 problems, such as excessive retransmissions, use of protection mechanisms, and failed 802.1X/EAP authentication.

Site Survey Kit Checklist

A complete site survey kit should include:

- ❑ Laptop and/or PDA
- ❑ Wireless PC card with driver & utility software
- ❑ Access points or bridges as needed
- ❑ Uninterruptible Power Supply (UPS) or battery pack with DC-to-AC converter
- ❑ Site survey utility software (loaded on laptop or PDA)
- ❑ Clipboard, pen, pencils, notebook paper, grid paper, & hi-liter
- ❑ Blueprints or floor plans & network diagrams
- ❑ Indoor & outdoor RF antennas
- ❑ RF cables & connectors
- ❑ Binoculars and two-way radios
- ❑ Umbrella and/or rain suit
- ❑ Specialized software or hardware such as a spectrum analyzer or protocol analyzer
- ❑ Tools, double-sided tape, tie straps, and other items for temporarily mounting hardware
- ❑ Secure and padded equipment case for housing computers, tools, and secure documents during the survey and travel to and from the survey site

❑ Digital camera for taking pictures of particular locations within a facility

❑ Battery chargers

❑ Variable attenuator (Figure 13.11)

❑ Distance measuring wheel (Figure 13.12)

❑ Appropriate cart or other mechanism for transporting equipment & documentation throughout the facility

FIGURE 13.11 Variable attenuator

FIGURE 13.12 Distance wheel

If frequent site surveys are part of your business, create a toolkit with all this gear (and likely much more) in it, so that you will always have the necessary site survey tools on hand. The last item in the above list – a cart – will become a valued possession after you make a few dozen trips back and forth across a large facility moving the hardware and site survey support gear. Figure 13.13 shows the type of cart that can be used to carry equipment, and Figure 13.14 shows a travel case used to transport the equipment to and from the facility.

FIGURE 13.13 Mobile equipment cart

FIGURE 13.14 Site survey travel case

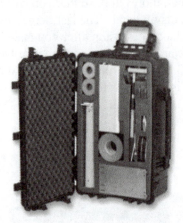

Conducting a Site Survey

Once on site with a complete site survey toolkit, walking several miles throughout the client's facility is common. However, the general task has not changed: collecting and recording information. Beginning your site survey with the more general tasks of recording non-RF related information is usually the best course of action. The following two lists show preparatory steps that should be done before beginning your site survey.

Indoor Surveys

For *indoor* surveys, locate and record the following items (as a minimum) on a copy of the facility blueprints or a drawing of the facility.

- AC power outlets and grounding points
- Wired data network connectivity points
- Ladders or lifts that will be needed for mounting access points
- Potential RF obstructions, such as fire doors, metal blinds, metal-mesh windows, etc.
- Potential RF sources such as microwave ovens, elevator motors, baby monitors, 2.4 GHz cordless phones, etc.

- Cluttered areas such as office cubical farms, document storage areas with many filing cabinets, etc.

Outdoor Surveys

For *outdoor* surveys, record the following items on a copy or sketch of the property:

- Trees, buildings, lakes, or other obstructions between link sites
- If in winter, locate trees that will grow leaves during other seasons and may interfere with the RF link
- Visual and RF line-of-sight between transmitter and receiver
- Link distance (note: if greater than 7 miles [11.7 km], calculate compensation for Earth bulge)
- Weather hazards (wind, rain, snow, ice, lightning) common to the area
- Tower accessibility and height or the need for a new tower
- Roof accessibility and height

Before You Begin

Once these preparatory items are checked and recorded, the next step is either to begin the RF site survey or to obtain more information. There are several sources from the above items that could require further information from the client, including:

- Who will provide ladders and/or lifts for mounting access points on high ceilings?
- Is the client willing or able to remove trees that interfere with the Fresnel zone?
- If a new tower is needed, does the client have the necessary permits?
- Does the client have the necessary permission to install antennas on the roof, and will the roof support a tower if needed?
- Do the building codes require plenum-rated equipment to be used?

Weather hazards may be easier to compensate for if you also reside in the area, because you may be familiar with the area's weather patterns. If you do not live there, gathering more detailed information about local weather patterns, like winds, rain, hail, tornadoes, hurricanes, and other potentially severe weather, may be necessary. Remember from our troubleshooting discussion that for the most part, only severe weather causes disruption to wireless LANs. However, you must be aware of, and prepare and compensate for, these types of weather before the implementation of the wireless network.

Lifts and ladders could be needed for an area where a trade show or other similar function is going to take place. The event's location may have 40-foot ceilings, and the access points may need to be mounted in the ceiling for proper coverage. OSHA has many regulations regarding ladders and ladder safety, and the local labor union might have rules of its own that must be followed.

If a facility such as a convention center is able to provide the personnel, ladders, and lifts, it is typically best to let these individuals perform the installation. These individuals are familiar with OSHA regulations and have processes in place to obtain the proper permits. The RF site survey report will need to reference any lifts, ladders, or permits required for installation of the wireless LAN. In some cases, a sturdy six-foot ladder for climbing into drop-ceilings is all that is needed.

If an RF cable, Cat5 cable, access point, or any other device must be placed in the plenum (the space between the drop ceiling [false ceiling] and the hard-cap ceiling), then the item must be rated to meet building codes without being placed in a metal protective shell. Figure 13.15 illustrates common plenum areas.

FIGURE 13.15 Plenum Areas

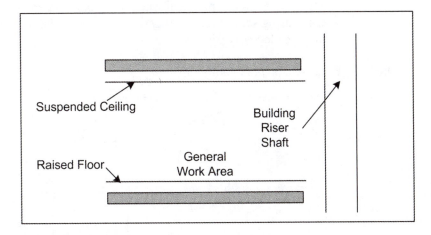

RF Information Gathering

The next task will be to gather and record data on RF coverage patterns, coverage gaps (also called "holes" or "dead spots"), data rate capabilities, and other RF-related criteria for your RF site survey report.

- Range & coverage patterns
- Data rate boundaries
- Documentation
- Throughput tests and capacity planning
- Interference types and sources
- Wired data connectivity & AC power requirements
- Outdoor antenna placement

Gather and record data for each of these areas by slowly and systematically surveying and measuring the entire facility. The sections below will describe some of these areas in more detail.

Range and Coverage Patterns

Start by placing an access point in what should be a logical location. This may not be the final location, but you have to start somewhere. The access point may get moved many times before the proper location is found, as shown in Figure 13.16. Generally speaking, starting in the center of an area is practical when using omni antennas. In contrast, when using semi-directional antennas, consider being toward one end of the intended coverage area.

FIGURE 13.16 Access point coverage testing

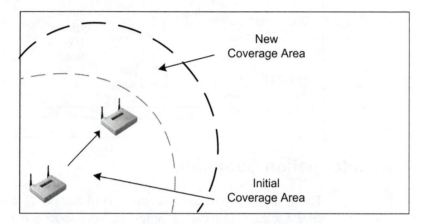

When the best locations for access points are determined, mark the locations for access points and bridges with brightly-colored, easily removable tape as shown in Figure 13.17. Take a digital picture of the location for use in the site survey report. Do not make location references in the report to temporary objects such as a desk, table, or plant that may be moved and can no longer provide a reference for positioning an access point. Make sure to note the orientation of your antennas because not all wireless LAN installers are familiar with antennas.

FIGURE 13.17 Marking tape

Various types of antennas can be used for site survey testing, including highly-directional, semi-directional, and omni-directional. When using semi-directional antennas, be sure to take into account the side and back lobes, both for coverage and security reasons. Sites may require the use of multiple antenna types to get the appropriate coverage. Long hallways might benefit from Yagi, patch, or panel antennas, while omni-directional antennas would more easily cover large rooms.

There are differing opinions as to where measuring coverage and data speeds should begin. Some experts recommend starting in a corner, while some say starting in the middle of the room is best. It does not matter where the measurements *start* so long as every point in the room is measured during the survey and covered after installation. Pick a starting point in the room, and *slowly* walk with your laptop, PC card, and site survey utility software running. While walking, record the following data for every area of the room.

- Link speed (measured in Mbps)
- Signal strength (measured in dBm)
- Noise floor (measured in dBm)
- Signal-to-noise ratio ("SNR") (measured in dB)

Walking quickly will speed up the survey process, but may cause you to miss dead spots or potential interference sources. Using a very simple example, Figure 13.18 illustrates what the recordings might look like on a simple floor plan.

FIGURE 13.18 Marked up floor plan

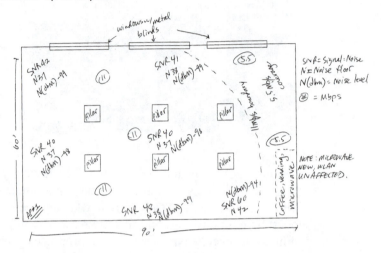

For outdoor coverage areas, be prepared to walk farther and record more. When planning an outdoor installation of an access point (to cover areas between campus buildings for example), there usually are a very limited number of places where the access point may be mounted. For this reason, moving the access point around is rarely required. Sitting atop a building is the most common place in such an installation. There are potentially many more sources of interference or blockage to a wireless LAN signal outdoors than indoors.

Site surveying is not an exact science, which is why thoroughness and attention to detail are required. Record the measurements for the general areas of the room, including measuring the farthest point from the access point, every corner of the room, and every point in the room at which there is no signal or the data rate changes (either increases or decreases). Points of measurement should be determined by the answers to the questions that were asked before you arrived on site to do the survey. Information such as where users will be sitting in a room, where users will be able to roam, the types of users (heavy file transfer or bar-code scanning, for example), and locations of break rooms with microwave ovens in them, will all help determine for which points data rate and range should be recorded.

Data Rate Boundaries

Data rate boundaries are the theoretical concentric rings (or zones) of coverage around an access point, and their coverage pattern and the rates associated with each concentric ring should be recorded. If you are using an 802.11b wireless LAN, for example, record where the data rate decreases from 11Mbps to 5.5Mbps to 2Mbps to 1Mbps, as shown in Figure 13.19. These boundaries should somewhat resemble concentric areas, with the slower data rate areas farther from the access point than the higher data rates. We often represent these boundaries as circles in examples, but in real life, they are almost never circle-shaped because obstructions limit the propagation of the AP's signals. Only where there are no obstructions are the data rate boundaries remotely circle-shaped. The client organization must be informed "when a user roams past the coffee machine and into the mailroom," that the user will not get the highest possible throughput due to the data rate decrease, which, in turn, is due to the distance increase.

FIGURE 13.19 Data rate boundaries

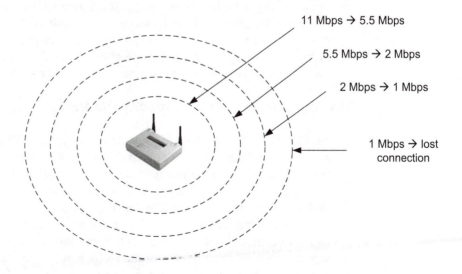

Documentation

By this point, the copy (or copies) of the facility blueprint should be well marked up, with concentric coverage zones, dead spots, data rates, and signal strength measurements in key spots. Now another location within the facility can be documented, and the process begins again. When surveying a small office and the entire office has facility-wide coverage with maximum throughput from the first testing location chosen, the process does not need to be repeated; the survey is finished. However, that will rarely be the case, so this chapter prepares you for the worst-case scenario of site surveying.

Be prepared to survey and move, survey and move, again and again, until the optimum coverage pattern for a particular area has been determined. This repetition is the reason for making multiple copies of the facility blueprint or floor plan and bringing lots of paper.

The end result of this portion of the exercise should be a map of the range and coverage of the access point from various locations, with the best results and worst-case results noted. Certainly it saves much time to document only the best possible coverage pattern, so in the interest of efficiency, it is a general practice to quickly test until a "somewhat optimum" location for the access point is found. Then you would do a complete documentation set (drawings, recording of data, etc.) for the customer. Site surveying, like anything else, takes practice to become efficient. Making decisions that affect the use of time are very important because site surveying is a very time-consuming task.

Throughput Tests and Capacity Planning

Another type of measurement (outside of the typical SNR, noise, and signal strength that we've discussed thus far) can be performed to yield valuable information to the wireless network design engineer: doing throughput testing from various points throughout the facility. The point of doing all of this coverage and data rate documentation is to understand and control what the user's experience will be on the wireless LAN. Doing live throughput tests, such as file transfers to and from an FTP server, will give you a more thorough look at what the user might experience. Sometimes this test is not possible due to a lack of wired infrastructure connectivity, but it is a valuable option when it is available.

Planning for user capacity is very important if the user is to make productive use of the wireless LAN. From the answers provided by the network manager or administrator, you will know to look for locations within the facility where there are different types of user groups present. For example, if one 50-foot by 50-foot area were to house 20 people who work from desktop PCs using client/server applications, you should determine whether one access point could provide the necessary capacity. You also should determine if co-located access points would be required to provide for these users' networking needs. In this scenario, it is likely that at least two access points would be required. In contrast, if there were 30 doctors using wirelessly connected PDAs all operating through a single access point, co-located access points probably would not be needed, due to the fact that a PDA cannot transmit large amounts of data across the network very quickly.

These pieces of information will add to the markings on the blueprint in the form of specific data rates, throughput measurements, and capacity notes. Choose the minimum data rate that the users will tolerate and then estimate the coverage area of each AP, based on the range of the AP at that data rate. The estimate of the AP's coverage should be based on either real-world tests of the AP's performance on site, or predictions from predictive site-survey software (covered later). Then, determine how many people will need coverage within that area and how much throughput they will need. For example, it might be determined that there are ten people in the coverage area of a certain AP who need a minimum of 500 kbps throughput at all times. Ten times 500 kbps = 5 Mbps, which is just about the maximum capacity of an 802.11b access point using the 11 Mbps data rate. If the AP's coverage area is drawn based on a data rate of less than 11 Mbps, more than one AP will be needed to support these users, or the coverage area will need to be redrawn using a higher data rate (which might result in less coverage area per AP).

Of course, this analysis is somewhat oversimplified when compared to real life scenarios. For example, users closer to the AP will get higher data rates than those farther away from the AP, so performance will be better for the users who are closer than the ones farther away. Users using OFDM will probably get better performance than those using DSSS, due to both higher data rates and more corruption-resistance. This analysis should provide a "worst-case" scenario that acts as a starting point for the design.

Interference Types and Sources

In this phase of the site survey process, questions are asked about potential sources of narrowband and spread spectrum RF interference.

Are there any existing wireless LANs in use in or near the facility?

Existing wireless LANs can cause hardship on a site-surveyor if permission is not provided to disable existing radios as needed. Disabling existing wireless LAN gear may not be possible due to production environments, or the surveyor may have to conduct the site survey during non-production hours.

Are there any plans for future wireless LAN installations other than the one in question?

Determine if there is another wireless LAN project that needs to be included in the analysis. These projects could affect implementation of the wireless LAN for which this site survey is being performed. For example, if the survey is for a planned VoIP wireless network and there is an existing data wireless network, the VoIP survey must take this into account. You might make different recommendations depending on whether the customer wanted to keep the two networks separate or merge the VoIP into the data network. In the former case, you might recommend exclusively 802.11a voice equipment if the data network used 802.11b/g; in the latter case, you might recommend expanding the existing 802.11b/g network with additional access points to minimize the number of users per access point.

If this is a multi-tenant building, are there any other organizations within the building that have wireless LANs or sources of RF? Are any other organizations planning wireless LAN implementations?

For multi-tenant buildings, it is possible that another organization within the same building is also planning to build a wireless LAN in the future that would impact the site survey, as shown in Figure 13.20.

Organizations within the same multi-tenant office building could have wireless LANs in place that disrupt each other's communications.

FIGURE 13.20 Multi-tenant Office Buildings

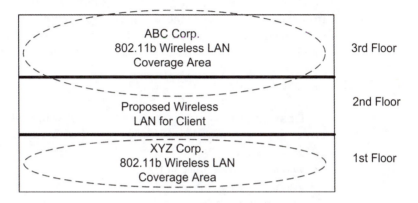

Are there any other common sources of RF interference in the 2.4 GHz band in use in the facility?

Microwave ovens, 2.4 GHz and 5 GHz cordless phones, radiology equipment, and baby monitors are common sources of RF interference. These potential interference sources need to be documented in the survey as potential problems with the installation. Microwave ovens can easily be replaced, though radiology equipment in a hospital installation may not be. Cordless phones running on the same channel as the wireless LAN can render a wireless LAN useless.

In case 802.11a networks are to be installed, are there any RF sources in the 5 GHz range?

If there were many other organizations in the area already using 802.11b or 802.11g, using 802.11a would avoid the problem of trying to coexist with another 802.11b/g network. However, it should be noted whether or not other 802.11a networks exist in the area that could interfere with an 802.11a implementation.

Obstacle-Induced Signal Loss

The chart in Figure 13.21 provides estimates on RF signal losses that occur for various objects. Using these values as a reference will save you from having to calculate these values. For example, if a signal must penetrate drywall, the strength of the signal would be reduced by 3 dB. The loss is indicated in decibels, and the resulting range effect is shown.

FIGURE 13.21 Signal Loss Chart

Obstruction	Additional Loss (dB) at 2.4 GHz
Open Space	0
Window (non-metallic tint)	3
Window (insulation-doped)	10
Sheetrock or drywall	3
Plywood (single sheet)	1
Brick or concrete blocks	15
Elevator shaft	10
Concrete floor	20
Wooden door or equivalent	3

Find and record all sources of interference as you map your range and coverage patterns, as shown in Figure 13.22. When measuring the coverage in the break room, for example, measure both when the microwave is running and when it is off. In some cases, the microwave could impact the entire wireless LAN infrastructure if the microwave is an older model and leaks significant RF power. If this is the case, advise the client to purchase a new microwave oven and not to use the existing unit. The client and the users need to be aware of the potential interference and possible lack of connectivity from the break room (or wherever a microwave oven or other interference source is operated).

FIGURE 13.22 RF Obstacles

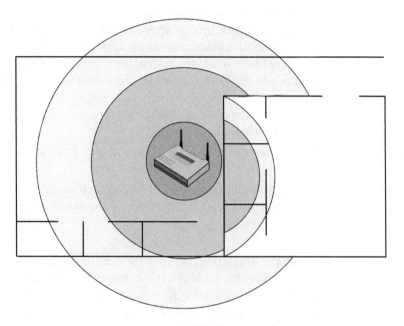

Other common sources of indoor interference to look for include metal-mesh cubicles, metal-mesh glass windows, metal blinds, inventory (what if the client *manufactures* metal blinds?), fire doors, cement walls, elevator motors, telemetry equipment, transformers, fluorescent lights, and metal-studded walls (as opposed to wood studs). Piles of objects made of paper, wood, and other similar products also serve to block RF signals.

There are standards for how a fire wall (a physical fire barrier) may be penetrated. It is important to find fire walls during the site survey because they should be noted in the site survey report. When fire walls prevent Cat5, RF, or power cabling from going wherever they are needed, it should be documented. Fire walls also can hamper the RF signal due to their physical construction, and some fire walls have fire doors directly underneath. Do the site survey with the fire doors closed because there are facilities that require fire doors to remain shut any time a person is not passing through them. Poured concrete walls and hardcap ceilings pose similar RF problems as fire walls.

In a multi-tenant office building, interference could be caused by a microwave oven belonging to a company located on the same floor or possibly on floors directly above or below you. This situation can pose a difficult problem since you have no jurisdiction over the microwave oven. There are many outdoor interference sources, and some can change just by their nature. Seek out and record the effects of the following:

- Trees, buildings, lakes, hills, or other obstructions or reflective objects
- Trees without leaves that will later have leaves or that will grow to interfere with the Fresnel zone.
- Automobile traffic – if linking two buildings at first-story height across a road, a large truck or bus could disable the link or make it erratic.

Record the interference source, its location, and its effect and potential effect on wireless LAN coverage, range, and throughput. This data should be recorded both on your copy of the blueprint as well as in a separate list for easy future reference. Taking pictures of interference sources that are permanent (e.g., lakes and buildings) will serve as a visual reference to the client. Pictures of *potential* sources of interference, like young trees or future building sites, also will help the client's decision-making for the future.

Wired Data Connectivity and AC Power Requirements

While moving the access point around the site, indoors and out, the access point may not be able to be located in the best positions. Rather, the location will be constrained to where AC power sources exist and network connectivity is within a given distance. Record on the blueprint or floor plan the locations of each AC power source and network connection point. These points will lead to the easiest (not necessarily the best) locations for access points. Document and make recommendations for the best locations for all access points. Preferred access point locations may be a solid reason for the client to install new AC power sources, as well as new network connectivity points. Remember that many brands of access points can utilize Power over Ethernet (PoE).

Some questions to consider when looking for the best place to install wireless LAN hardware are:

Is AC power available?

Without an available source of AC power, access points will not function. If AC power is not available in a particular location, an electrician's services may be required (added cost) or Power over Ethernet (PoE) can be used to power the unit. Running a power cabling drop may cost twice as much (or more) as a Cat5 data cabling drop.

Is grounding available?

Proper grounding for all wireless LAN equipment will provide added protection against stray currents from lightning strikes or electrical surges.

Is wired network connectivity available?

If network connectivity is not available, a wireless bridge may be required or an access point may need to be operated in repeater mode to provide network connectivity. Using access points as repeaters is not a desirable scenario, and the network performance would be much better if the access point could be wired to the network.

If the distance between the access point and the network connection is more than 100 meters, shielded twisted-pair (STP) cabling or an access point that supports a fiber connection can be used. However, using an access point that has fiber network connectivity negates the use of PoE and would require a source of AC power nearby. Media converters can be used when fiber runs are necessary. These powered devices can connect Cat5 copper to fiber and vice versa. When using an access point that has only a Cat5 connector, and its nearest network connection is more than 100 meters way, a media converter can solve the problem. Remember that in this configuration, PoE cannot be used end to end.

If an external RF antenna is to be used, cable lengths in the site survey report should be estimated, but never "as the crow flies." Rather, estimate RF coaxial cable lengths using straight runs with 90-degree turns. Try to keep RF cable runs under 300 feet (91.4 m), but remember to add an extra few feet of cable in case extra length is needed in the future to move the access point or bridge.

Are there physical obstructions?

Doorways, cement ceilings, walls, or other obstructions can result in some construction costs if they need to be altered to allow for power connections or to run power or data cabling to the access points or antennas.

Outdoor Antenna Placement

For outdoor antenna placement, record the location and availability of grounding points, towers, and potential mounting locations. Outdoor antennas require lightning arrestors, which require grounding. Grounding is an easy point to miss, and the client may not be aware of this necessity. Make notes of where antennas could best be mounted and whether any special mounting materials may be required.

Keep in mind that adding network connectivity *outdoors* will be a very new concept to most companies implementing wireless LANs. Specify exactly what is required to bring the network outside the building, including cables, power, weather protection, and physical protection from vandalism and theft.

Post-Installation Verification

After a wireless LAN is installed, the next step is to verify that it is performing as predicted by the site survey. Spot-checking by the site surveyor after installation is complete is most helpful in avoiding troubleshooting situations during production use of the network. A thorough site survey should catch the majority of potential problems, so it is possible that no problems will be found. Items that should be checked are:

- Does actual coverage match predicted coverage? Actual signal strength should be verified (e.g., if the survey predicted that clients would get at least -65 dBm within an area, confirm that that is the case).

- Are client stations able to roam as predicted? If seamless roaming is required, you should verify that stations' active conversations are not interrupted during roaming. A protocol analyzer can be used to verify how long roaming is taking.

- Does actual throughput match the predicted throughput? This should be verified in situations with just a few users and with many users, since throughput will change in these scenarios. If actual throughput does not match the predicted throughput, a WLAN analyzer can help detect problems such as interference, frame corruption, and more.

In some cases, the post-installation verification is skipped. If the site survey is performed by an outside company, consider adding a post-installation verification and procedures for rectification if the installed network does not match the predicted results to the contract. On the other hand, some companies offer an "as-is" site survey. This type of survey is intended to represent the best effort of the surveying company, but includes no guarantees. Although an "as-is" survey might sound like a losing proposition for the WLAN administrator, it is much cheaper than full site-survey and post-installation follow up. An experienced WLAN administrator might decide to pay for an "as-is" survey as a starting point and then rely on his or her own expertise to implement and verify the WLAN.

No site survey is going to be perfect, but a reputable and experienced surveyor should be able to either design a production network that meets your requirements or identify up front any contingencies that might make that impossible. Cases where an insurmountable and unpredictable surprise occurs after installation are rare.

Alternative and Supplemental Methods

Until now, we have described what might be called a "traditional" site survey, in which you physically walk around the area to be surveyed. This method has some significant disadvantages. It requires a significant amount of time since one or more RF engineers must physically visit all areas to be covered, but a far more important downside is that RF energy does not travel in ways that are intuitive to humans. We do not consciously interact with RF. We cannot see RF. Therefore, even a very thorough site survey may miss a particular area that has bad connectivity, and a cursory site survey is certain to miss some areas.

For example, Figure 13.23 shows picture that we typically draw when we represent RF coverage:

FIGURE 13.23 Typical picture of RF coverage

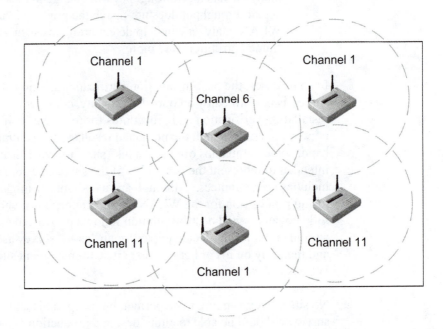

Compare that to Figure 13.24, which shows a prediction of a real AP's coverage, created based on a CAD floor plan and sophisticated mathematical modeling techniques:

FIGURE 13.24 LANPlanner Predictive Modeling Software (www.wirelessvalley.com)

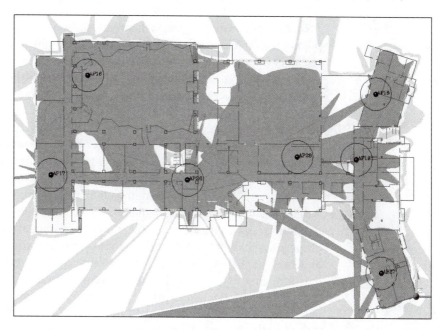

Notice that at the AP's current location, there is an area of low signal strength in the middle of the auditorium, right where you might guess that signal strength would be fine (since the signal can travel through the hallway into the auditorium). A "traditional" site survey might miss this deficiency.

The point is that coverage patterns from APs in indoor environments *never* look like circles. Incidentally, whenever you see a site survey of an indoor environment, and the APs' coverage looks like circles, you should *immediately* become suspicious of the survey's veracity. In indoor environments, RF coverage always has weird, non-intuitive "nooks and crannies" that are very difficult to detect, even with a thorough "traditional" site survey. This RF phenomenon has led to the development of "alternative" site survey methods that might be used instead of a "traditional" site survey. These methods are sometimes also used in a "supplemental" manner to verify the conclusions of the "traditional" site survey.

Predictive Software

Predictive software uses experimentally-derived attenuation values to predict the coverage of an AP based on a CAD blueprint. The RF engineer imports a blueprint into the predictive software and then tells the software what type of material each object consists of (drywall over wood studs, drywall over steel studs, brick, glass window, glass door, wooden door, etc.). Then, the engineer places access points within the floor plan and the software predicts the coverage of the AP. Depending on the expected use of the network, the engineer might do separate predictions for 802.11b, 802.11g, and 802.11a clients. This is necessary because 802.11a's 5.8 GHz signals attenuate about twice as much as 802.11b/g's 2.4 GHz signals. If signal strength is the primary factor in the prediction (which it usually is), 802.11b and 802.11g can be combined into a single prediction, since they both use the 2.4 GHz frequency band and their propagation characteristics are the same. In other words, an 802.11b and 802.11g client should see roughly the same signal strength at a given location, although they will have different data rates. On the other hand, if expected data rate is the primary factor in the prediction, it will be necessary to do a separate prediction for 802.11b and 802.11g, since 802.11g clients can achieve higher data rates farther from the AP than 802.11b clients.

One advantage of predictive modeling software is that it is easy to try out various locations to see which one works best. Predictive analysis software typically allows you to drag an AP around the floor plan and see the AP's coverage update in real-time. This makes it easy and fast to find the best location for the APs. Even though the prediction may only be 85 or 90 percent accurate, the predicted "best" locations can be used as starting points and then fine-tuned once the equipment is installed. In addition, it is common to design in a fade margin – an extra few dBm of signal strength – so that if the prediction is slightly off, the users will still get adequate coverage. For example, if users need a minimum signal strength of -75 dBm to get adequate performance, the predictions might be based on a minimum strength of -65 dBm. This might result in the purchase of a little bit of extra equipment, but the time saved by the virtual site survey more than balances this out.

FIGURE 13.25 RingMaster Integrated Planning, Configuration, and Management Software (www.TrapezeNetworks.com)

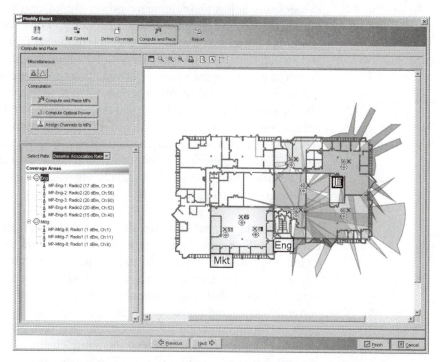

Based on the prediction, APs are purchased and installed, and then traditional site survey techniques are used to fine-tune the installation and verify the theoretical predictions. Wireless Valley (http://www.wirelessvalley.com) is an example of a vendor that makes predictive software. In addition to third party vendors like Wireless Valley, some infrastructure equipment manufacturers have available proprietary predictive modeling software that works with their equipment as an additional product. Trapeze Networks' RingMaster (http://www.trapezenetworks.com) is an example of this, and is pictured in Figure 13.25.

Self-Managing RF Technologies

In the self-managing approach, the administrator is encouraged to place APs in any location where coverage is necessary, without worrying about overlap between the APs' coverage cells. This approach might normally cause unacceptable overlap between the APs' coverage, resulting in poor performance, but in a self-managing network, the clients and APs dynamically adjust their channels, power output, and association to minimize overlap and maximize performance. For example, an AP might power up, detect that there is another AP in the area on the same channel, and switch to another channel, or both APs might reduce their power output to minimize the overlap between their coverage areas. When a station powers up and searches for an AP to associate with, it might take into account not just the AP's signal strength, but also the number of clients associated with the AP, in order to minimize the load on any one AP. The goal of a self-managing network is that the administrator can simply deploy equipment without worrying about coverage overlaps or channel allocation, and the APs and clients will dynamically adjust their parameters for best performance.

In a self-managing network, the firmware and drivers in the AP and the clients handle the management. In some cases, vendors themselves have added proprietary extensions to 802.11 that incorporate some of this functionality. For example, one vendor's APs add an information element to their beacons that tells prospective clients how many stations are currently associated to the AP. A prospective client can take that into account if more than one AP is available. Another vendor's APs are capable of automatically scanning the entire channel range and choosing a channel that is minimally utilized. These proprietary extensions improve 802.11's efficiency, but fall short of what we might call a truly "self-managing" network. A truly "self-managing" network should automatically manage channel allocation, power levels, and load-balancing of clients across access points for all devices.

Propagate Networks (www.propagatenetworks.com) writes code that integrates with the firmware in popular client cards, access points, and WLAN switches and allows them to become self-managing. Propagate's solution is based on a "swarm," or distributed approach, which means that each device manages itself based on its perception of the network. This approach is opposed to a centralized approach in which a central device manages the clients and APs. Self-management has the effect of dramatically improving performance on the WLAN while freeing the administrator from the work of managing the RF characteristics of the network. The only item the administrator then would need is a utility to view what is happening on the network for verification purposes. Utilities such as this are available.

Passive Site Survey Tools

Passive site survey tools attempt to make the traditional site survey method easier. They also provide a much more accurate means of verifying the accuracy predictive modeling surveys. For example, the passive site survey software might allow you to import a floor plan, and then describe a path through the floor plan. The software automatically records the signal strength, signal-to-noise ratio, and other characteristics as you walk the path on the imported floor plan.

FIGURE 13.26 Site Survey Software (Ekahau Site Survey)

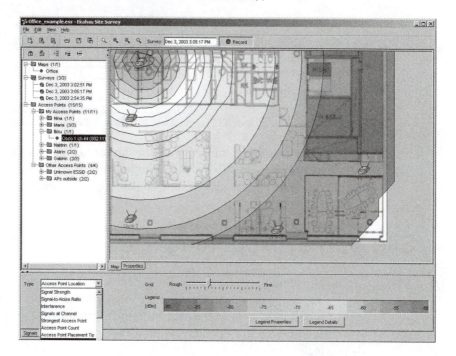

FIGURE 13.27 Site Survey Software (AirMagnet Surveyor)

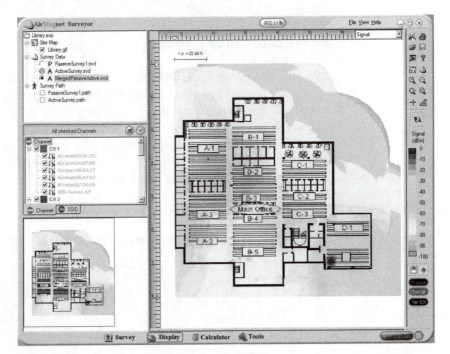

The accuracy of this software far surpasses that of traditional manual recordings, but still has the same fundamental deficiency of the traditional site survey method: it is time consuming, and you must walk the entire site.

Site Survey Reporting

Now that you have thoroughly documented the client's facility, the necessary data is available to prepare a proper report for the client. The report will serve as the map for implementation of the wireless LAN and future reference documentation for the network's administrators and technicians.

The site survey report is the culmination of all the effort thus far, and might take days to complete. It may be necessary to revisit the site to gather more data or to confirm some of the initial findings. Several more conversations may be needed with the decision makers and some of the people with whom you were unable to meet when you were on site.

Report Format

No standard defines how a site survey report should look. The following are recommendations that will serve as a starting point and guideline. First, remember that this report that this report is what the client will have after you leave. This work will represent both your knowledge and that of your company. Second, you may be doing the wireless LAN implementation and, if so, you will be working from your own documentation. If the report is inaccurate or incomplete, the implementation will not go smoothly. Third, save every piece of data collected, and include everything with the report as an attachment, appendix, or another set of documentation. This information may be needed in the future.

Once the site survey is delivered and reviewed by the client, you should consider having the client sign a simple form (the site survey report is your only deliverable) that states that the client has both received and reviewed the report, and that the report is acceptable. The client may ask for additional information and time to review before signing off. Below are some suggested sections of documentation that, at a minimum, should be provided to the client in a site survey report. Include graphics that may help illustrate the data when appropriate.

Purpose and Business Requirements

The site survey report should include all contact information for the site survey company and the client company. Both the site survey company and the customer get copies of the report. It is common for the report to be submitted to the customer electronically and in printed format. Since the electronic format of a report may be many megabytes of data (due partially to digital photos), it is typical to compress all documents and supporting information into a single .zip file (or similar) and making the report available to the customer via an FTP server.

As part of the report, restate the customer's wants, needs, and requirements, and then provide details on how these wireless LAN requirements can be met (item-by-item) as a result of using the site survey as a roadmap to implementing the new wireless LAN. Supplement this section with graphical representations (either sketches, or copies of actual blueprints) to *show* the client what types of coverage and wireless connectivity to expect and whether it will meet the requirements. This section may include an application analysis in which the site surveyor has tested the client's application to assure that the proper implementation of the new wireless LAN will provide appropriate coverage and throughput for wireless nodes.

Methodology

Discuss in detail the methodology for conducting the site survey. Tell the customer exactly what was done, how it was done, and why it was done.

RF Coverage Areas

Detail RF coverage patterns and ranges specific to the requirements that were collected. If the client said 5 Mbps was needed for all users in one particular area, correlate the findings and suggestions against that particular requirement. The concentric rings on the floor plan will be the center of attention here. It also may be helpful at this point to detail access point placements that did *not* work. Document and explain any coverage gaps.

Throughput

Detail bandwidth and throughput findings, showing exactly where in the facility there will likely be the greatest and the least of each, also using the drawings made on floor plan copies. Be sure to include screenshots of the actual numeric measurements that were recorded if not using a passive site survey tool that records them for you. These exact numbers help determine the proper solution, and proof of the measurements you took might help later in a dispute.

Interference

Detail RF interference and obstruction findings, correlating them to the particular requirements that were collected during the network management interview. Include the location and other details, such as pictures, about each source of interference. Include suggestions for removing RF interference sources where possible, and explain how the RF interference sources will affect the wireless LAN, once installed.

Problem Areas

Discuss in depth the best possible solutions to the RF (and other networking) problems that were found and documented. The client may not be aware of problems that can surface in a thorough site survey. This section should include recommendations for technologies and equipment that will best serve the customer's needs. There is rarely one solution to any technology situation. If possible, present two or three solutions so the customer will have options. It is possible that while performing a site survey, you may find problems with the customer's wired LAN. Tactfully mention any problems you find to the network administrator, especially if those problems will directly affect implementation of the wireless LAN.

Drawings

Provide Visio, CAD, or other types of drawings and graphical illustrations of how the network should be configured, including a topology map. All of the survey findings should be documented in words and pictures. It will be much easier to present a range of coverage using a floor plan rather than only words. Provide floor plan drawings or marked-up blueprints to the customer to graphically show RF findings and recommendations. Figure 13.28 illustrates where access points might be placed on a floor plan.

FIGURE 13.28 Access point placement and coverage

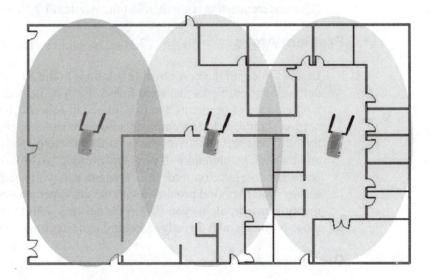

As mentioned earlier in this section, the site survey report could take days to complete and may require return visits to the site. The site survey report should be a professional technical documentation of your investigation and findings of the client's site, which can serve as a technical reference for the wireless LAN design and future network implementations.

Hardware placement and configuration information

The report should answer the following questions about hardware placement and configuration as a minimum:

- Where and how should each access point, or bridge, be mounted for maximum effectiveness? You should describe this in enough detail that a person completely unfamiliar with RF or 802.11 could install the AP. Even if the installer is familiar with RF and 802.11, this will minimize the risk of mistakes.
- What type and length of cable and connectors are necessary for each access point?
- What antenna type will be used by the device? Be as specific as possible about the antenna's characteristics.

- How will the antenna be mounted? As with the AP, this should be detailed enough that a person completely unfamiliar with RF or 802.11 could perform the installation.
- What channels should each access point be on? If the network is self-managing, this can be omitted.
- How much output power should each access point deliver? If the network is self-managing, this can be omitted.
- What will be the name of the device, if the device supports one?
- What will be the IP address of the device? This can be omitted if the device will use dynamic IP addresses, but in that case, you should have an automatic discovery and management solution. If you will be managing the devices manually, they probably should have static IPs so you can consistently reach them.
- How will the unit be powered (typically AC power or PoE)?
- How will the unit uplink to the distribution system. Typically, this will be an Ethernet link, but special considerations might apply. For example, a fiber uplink might be required, or a wireless backhaul made up of mesh routers. In some cases, perhaps a phone line or power line network might be the best option.

Additional Reporting

The site survey report should be focused on informing the customer of the best coverage patterns available in the facility. Additional pieces of information that belong in the site survey report are interference findings, equipment types needed, and equipment placement suggestions.

A site survey report should not be turned into a consulting report for implementation and security. A wireless consulting firm should be able to come in, read the site survey report, and then be able to provide effective information on equipment purchasing (including vendor selection) and security solutions. The site survey report should be kept separate from implementation and security reports, which can be equally as involved as the site survey and require as much time to complete. Often, the company that does quality work during the site survey is asked to return to perform the equipment recommendations, installation, security audits, and subsequent security solution implementations. In many cases, all of these reports will be performed under a single contract.

Consultants may charge additional fees for a report that includes information about one or more of the following:

- Which manufacturers make appropriate products for this environment, and what those particular products are.
- Which security solution makes sense for this environment and how to implement that solution.
- Detailed diagrams and drawings on how to implement the suggested solutions.
- Cost and time involved to implement the suggested solutions.
- Details of how each wireless LAN requirement listed in the RF site survey report will be met (item-by-item) in the suggested solution.

Recommendations for equipment vendors are very important, and require:

- Knowing what each vendor specializes in, their strengths and weaknesses.
- What level of support is available from a vendor and how easy it is to get replacement hardware.
- The costs and part numbers of the appropriate hardware.
- The financial stability and longevity of a company to assure long-term support.

In creating a report for the purpose of equipment recommendations and installation, create a detailed equipment purchase list (bill of materials) that covers everything needed to implement a solution that meets the customer's requirements as stated in the site survey. If you recommend three solutions (inexpensive, moderate, and full-featured, for example), three complete equipment lists should be provided. Do not omit anything, because it is better to overestimate the potential cost of a solution, and then provide ways to come in under budget. An important note here is that some customers have contractual obligations to buy a particular brand of wireless LAN hardware. In order to identify this situation, you may choose to ask this question as part of the network manager's interview. If not, then this fact should be disclosed during the implementation consultation.

Key Terms

Before taking the exam, you should be familiar with the following terms:

data boundary

data rate

dead spot

interference source

link speed

noise floor

RF coverage

signal-to-noise ratio

signal strength

site survey utility software

protocol analyzer

spectrum analyzer

Review Questions

1. Explain in your own words why a site survey (facilities analysis) is the first and most important step in installing a wireless LAN.

2. Name and explain five major items that are discovered during the site survey process.

3. What is the long term purpose of creating thorough and complete site survey documentation?

4. In performing an RF site survey, is it necessary to understand what the wireless LAN will be used for, e.g., what users will be using what applications? Why or why not?

5. Name and explain five main differences between performing an indoor site survey and an outdoor site survey.

6. Name five essential site surveying tools, and explain why each one is important.

7. Why is knowing where all sources of AC power are located important to conducting a site survey?

8.   What role can a wireless protocol analyzer play in performing a site survey?

9.   Explain the differences, advantages, and disadvantages between doing a site survey manually (e.g., walking around) and using predictive RF software. How do you know when to use one or the other?

Site Survey Access Point Form

Engineer Name: _____

Engineer Email: _____

Customer Name: _____

Job Number: _____

AP Name / Number: _____

AP Make/Model: _____

AP Type:

☐ 802.11a   ☐ 802.11b only   ☐ 802.11b/g   ☐ 802.11g only

☐ Other _____

AP Role in Network:

☐ Root   ☐ Repeater

Wiring Closet

Name / Location / Number _____

Data Cabling

Cable path (from AP to Wiring Closet) _____

Cable Type / Length _____

Existing Network Connectivity Type:

☐ 10baseTx Hub   ☐ 10/100baseTx Switch

☐ 100baseTx Hub   ☐ 10/100baseFx Switch

☐ 10baseTx Switch   ☐ 10/100/1000baseTx Switch

☐ 100baseTx Switch

Ethernet Switch/Hub

Mfr. / Model _____

IP Address (if managed) _____

Name / Location _____

Port Number _____

Survey Data Rate(s):

☐ 1 Mbps   ☐ 2 Mbps   ☐ 5.5 Mbps   ☐ 11 Mbps

☐ 6 Mbps   ☐ 9 Mbps   ☐ 12 Mbps   ☐ 18 Mbps

☐ 24 Mbps   ☐ 36 Mbps   ☐ 48 Mbps   ☐ 54 Mbps

☐ Proprietary _____

Total Throughput Required from AP (if known) _____

Prevailing Traffic Types (for QoS purposes)

☐ FTP   ☐ File Sharing   ☐ Instant Messaging

☐ HTTP   ☐ POP/SMTP   ☐ Non-IP Protocols

☐ VoIP   ☐ Data Backup   ☐ Routing Protocols

☐ Video   ☐ Database Access

☐ Telnet/SSH   ☐ Warehouse Data

Types of Clients that will connect:

☐ Mobile Scanners   ☐ PDA

☐ Laptop PC   ☐ VoIP Phones

☐ Desktop PC   ☐ Mobile Printers

☐ Other _____

Channel(s):

☐ 1 ☐ 2 ☐ 3 ☐ 4 ☐ 5 ☐ 6 ☐ 7 ☐ 8 ☐ 9 ☐ 10

☐ 11 ☐ 12 ☐ 13 ☐ 14 ☐ 36 ☐ 40 ☐ 44 ☐ 48 ☐ 52 ☐ 56

☐ 60 ☐ 64 ☐ 149 ☐ 153 ☐ 157 ☐ 161 ☐ 165

Output Power (mW or dBm): . _____

Antenna Type & Gain: _____

Pigtail Cable (if external antenna): _____

Power Cabling: _____

Surge Protection - ☐ YES ☐ NO

PoE Injector (single, multiple) _____

Lightning Protection (type, ohms) _____

RF Cabling & Connectors (type, length, ohms) _____

Mounting Location: _____

Building / Floor: _____

Floor Plan / Map Grid Reference: _____

Mounting Height: _____

Mounting Gear Required: _____

Identifying Landmarks / Items around AP: _____

Plenum Rating Required?

☐ YES   ☐ NO

AP Housing Type

☐ NEMA Enclosure   ☐ Lockable Enclosure   ☐ None

☐ Other _____

AP Mounting Information

☐ Wall   ☐ Mast   ☐ Ceiling   ☐ Tower   ☐ Enclosure

☐ Roof   ☐ Other: _____

☐ Ladder Required

☐ Lift Required

☐ Tower Climber Required

Polarization: ☐ Vertical   ☐ Horizontal   ☐ Circular   ☐ Phased-Array   ☐ Other

Orientation/Alignment _____

Mounting Gear Required _____

Notes: _____

Measurement Points:

Point 1: _____

Values: Signal _____ Noise _____ SNR _____ Other _____

Interference: ☐ Narrowband   ☐ WLAN ☐ ISM Equipment

☐ Other _____

Notes: _____

Point 2: _____

Values: Signal _____ Noise _____ SNR _____ Other _____

Interference: ☐ Narrowband   ☐ WLAN ☐ ISM Equipment

☐ Other _____

Notes: _____

Point 3: _____

Values: Signal _____ Noise _____ SNR _____ Other _____

Interference: ☐ Narrowband ☐ WLAN ☐ ISM Equipment

☐ Other _____

Notes: _____

Known Dead Spots:

Point 1: _____

Caused by: _____

Suggestions: _____

Point 2: _____

Caused by: _____

Suggestions: _____

Point 3: _____

Caused by: _____

Suggestions: _____

Obstacles in the immediate environment:

☐ Metal blinds   ☐ Fire doors   ☐ Metal mesh windows

☐ HVAC   ☐ Duct Work   ☐ Fire Wall

☐ Elevator   ☐ Machinery   ☐ Warehouse shelves / goods

☐ Pipes

☐ Other _____

Environment where AP will be placed

☐ Open office space   ☐ Office with cubicles   ☐ Warehouse / Distribution

☐ Retail Sales   ☐ Freezer/Cold Storage   ☐ Hallway / Corridor

☐ Manufacturing   ☐ Outdoors

☐ Other _____

Elements to which the AP will be exposed

☐ Heat   ☐ Cold   ☐ Fluctuating Temperature

☐ Rain / Snow ☐ Dirt / Dust   ☐ Grease

☐ Chemicals   ☐ Sunlight   ☐ Vibration

☐ Wind

☐ Other _____

Notes:

_____

_____

_____

Configuration Information

AP Management Information:

☐ HTTP _____

☐ Telnet _____

☐ SSH/SSH2 _____

☐ SNMP _____

☐ Console/Serial Port _____

☐ Custom Application _____

Wireless VLANs:

ESSID _____ → VLAN _____   ESSID _____ → VLAN _____

ESSID _____ → VLAN _____   ESSID _____ → VLAN _____

ESSID _____ → VLAN _____   ESSID _____ → VLAN _____

ESSID _____ → VLAN _____   ESSID _____ → VLAN _____

ESSID _____ → VLAN _____   ESSID _____ → VLAN _____

ESSID _____ → VLAN _____   ESSID _____ → VLAN _____

IP Address: _____

MAC Address (Ethernet): _____

MAC Address (802.11a): _____

MAC Address (802.11g): _____

ESSID: _____

Authentication/Encryption:

☐ 802.1X/LEAP   ☐ 802.1X/EAP-TLS   ☐ 802.1X/PEAP

☐ IPSec VPN   ☐ 802.1X/EAP-TTLS   ☐ 802.1X/EAP-MD5

☐ WEP Plus   ☐ PPTP VPN   ☐ L2TP VPN

☐ KeyGuard   ☐ TKIP/RC4   ☐ EAP-Kerberos

☐ WPA-PSK   ☐ WPA-RADIUS   ☐ WPA2/802.11i

☐ CCMP/AES   ☐ Other _____

Authentication Server Type:

☐ RADIUS   ☐ LDAP   ☐ Active Directory/Kerberos

☐ eDirectory/NDS ☐ Other _____

Pictures of Access Point Mounting

In the following fields, record the name and description of each digital photograph taken.

Name: _____

Description: _____

Name: _____

Description: _____

Name: _____

Description: _____

Pictures of Custom Mounting Equipment (if required)

In the following fields, record the name and description of each digital photograph taken.

Name: _____

Description: _____

Name: _____

Description: _____

Name: _____

Description: _____

Site Survey Questionnaire

Customer Name: _____

Point of Contact: _____

Address: _____

_____

**Main Facility
Phone Number:** _____

**Contact Direct
Phone Number:** _____

**Contact Cell
Phone Number:** _____

**Contact Email
Address:** _____

**Contact Fax
Number:** _____

Interview type: ☐ In Person   ☐ Phone   ☐ Email

Site Survey Definition

A site survey is a task-by-task process by which the surveyor discovers and records the RF behavior throughout a facility. This information includes coverage, interference, and proper hardware placement within the facility. Site surveying involves analyzing a site from an RF perspective to determine what kind of RF coverage and hardware is required for a facility to meet the business goals of the customer.

Existing RF Network Information

Has a site survey ever been performed at this facility prior to today?

☐ YES   ☐ NO

Will any previous site surveys be made available to our staff?

☐ YES   ☐ NO

Existing Equipment at customer premises (Choose all that apply)

☐ 802.11B   ☐ 802.11A   ☐ 802.11G

☐ Other _____

How many existing users on the Wireless LAN? _____

What is the maximum users that are expected to be on the WLAN in the near future?

6 months   _____

12 months   _____

24 months   _____

Are there any peak and/or off-peak times at which certain users access the wireless LAN more than other times?

☐ YES   ☐ NO

What are the peak times?   _____ to _____ AM / PM

What are the off peak times?   _____ to _____ AM / PM

How many users does a typical access point support during peak use?

_____

How many access points are currently in place? _____

What brand(s) of access points and wireless bridges are currently in place?

_____

_____

_____

_____

_____

Are there any existing contracts for certain brands of wireless LAN hardware in place?

☐ YES   ☐ NO

Are the existing access points performing load balancing?

☐ YES   ☐ NO

What kind of Wireless LAN security solution(s) are currently in place? (Select all that apply)

☐ None	☐ Kerberos	☐ EWG
☐ WEP	☐ RADIUS	☐ EEG
☐ LEAP	☐ LDAP	☐ Firewall
☐ EAP-TLS	☐ Active Directory	☐ Router/L3 Switch
☐ EAP-TTLS	☐ NDS	☐ Other _____
☐ PEAP	☐ VLANs	
☐ VPN	☐ WVPN	

What type of wireless LAN environment is currently in place? (Choose all that apply)

☐ Campus

☐ In-building

☐ Building-to-Building

☐ MAN

☐ Other _____

Current problems with the existing wireless LAN? (Choose all that apply)

☐ Slow throughput

☐ Frequent disconnects

☐ Difficulty roaming

☐ Logon problems

☐ Other (explain thoroughly, and include documentation if available)

_____

_____

_____

_____

If the existing WLAN is having problems, has any troubleshooting of the existing problems been performed yet?

☐ YES ☐ NO

Are there any known sources of RF in or around the facility?

☐ YES ☐ NO

Source 1: _____

Source 2: _____

Source 3: _____

Are there any known RF dead zones?

☐ YES ☐ NO

If yes, attach documentation showing location(s) of dead zone(s).

RF Network Design

What applications are/will be used over the wireless LAN?

☐ Voice

☐ Video

☐ Connection-oriented Data

☐ Connectionless Data

☐ Other _____

Do users need to roam across routed (layer 3) boundaries?

☐ YES   ☐ NO

What types of wireless client devices will be used?

☐ Laptops

☐ Desktops

☐ Handheld / PDA

☐ Scanners

☐ Thin Clients / Terminals

☐ Other _____

Are clients mounted on vehicles of any type?

☐ YES   ☐ NO

Explain _____

Is wireless printing a requirement?

☐ YES ☐ NO

Explain _____

What network protocols and traffic types are in use over the wireless LAN?

☐ IP

☐ IPX

☐ Routing protocols

☐ Internet traffic

☐ Other _____

Are switches or hubs used for network access?

☐ Switches

☐ Hubs

Are there enough available network access ports to accommodate the access points?

☐ YES ☐ NO

Are access points to be powered directly by AC power sources or is Power over Ethernet going to be used?

☐ AC ☐ PoE

What subnet(s) will be assigned to the wireless network?

☐ Private IP subnet

☐ Public IP subnet

☐ Subnet Information:

_____

Will a naming scheme for wireless infrastructure devices be provided by the customer?

☐ YES   ☐ NO

Describe the naming conventions, and/or provide examples or naming convention documentation.

_____

_____

How will the wireless network be managed?

☐ SNMP

☐ HTTP / HTTPS

☐ Telnet

☐ Console / Serial port

☐ Custom application

Site Survey Request

What type of site survey is necessary?

☐ Indoor   ☐ Outdoor

Will production application analysis be required? (Without this analysis, proper application functionality cannot be guaranteed.)

☐ YES   ☐ NO

Application(s): _____

If indoors, what kind of facility?

☐ Warehouse

☐ School

☐ Multi-tenant Office Building

☐ Manufacturing Plant

☐ Hospital

☐ Other _____

If outdoors, is this a point-to-point or point-to-multipoint connection? What distance(s)?

☐ Point-to-Point

_____

☐ Point-to-Multipoint

_____

Are there other organizations in or around your building using wireless LANs?

☐ YES   ☐ NO

Need verification _____

Are Blueprints, Floor Plans, Campus Map, or other Topology Map available?

☐ YES   ☐ NO

Which technology is the customer considering for the new installation? (Choose all that apply)

☐ 802.11A

☐ 802.11B

☐ 802.11G

☐ Other _____

Expected or Required Data rate (in Mbps)

802.11A

☐ 6 ☐ 9 ☐ 12 ☐ 18 ☐ 24 ☐ 36 ☐ 48 ☐ 54 ☐ Proprietary _____

802.11B

☐ 1 ☐ 2 ☐ 5.5 ☐ 11

802.11G

☐ 1 ☐ 2 ☐ 5.5 ☐ 11 ☐ 6 ☐ 9 ☐ 12 ☐ 18 ☐ 24 ☐ 36 ☐ 48 ☐ 54

☐ Other _____

Additional information:

_____

_____

Special Stipulations

☐ HIPAA:

_____

_____

_____

☐ US Government

_____

_____

_____

☐ State Government:

_____

_____

_____

☐ Worker's Union

_____

_____

_____

☐ OSHA

_____

_____

_____

☐ Other:

_____

_____

_____

1:1 rule, 306–308
2.4 GHz
    ISM band, 304
    PtMP, 305–307
    PtP, 308–309
3:1 rule, 308
5.8 GHz
    ISM band, 304
    PtMP, 307–308
    PtP, 309
    UNII band, 307–309
6 dB rule, 97–98
10s and 3s, rule of, 54
60 percent unobstructed radius, 90
802.11
    802.1x/EAP. *see* EAP (Extensible Authentication Protocol)
    access point standards, 232–233
    antennas measured in dBi, 63–64
    authentication methods, 339–342
    channel definitions, 188
    clause summary, 319
    co-located systems, 208–210
    FHSS and, 185
    frames, 364–365
    narrowband interference, 205–207
    network architecture. *see* network architecture, 802.11
    overview, 312–313
    PDA compatibility, 489–490
    PN (pseudorandom number) code, 191–193
    range, 212
    RSSI and, 65
    security, 213, 230–231
    security methods, 426, 442
    signal strength measurements, 64–65
    state machine, 343–344
    system cost, 205–206
    throughput, 211–212, 409
    TKIP. *see* TKIP (Temporal Key Integrity Protocol)
    WEP. *see* WEP (Wired Equivalent Privacy)
    wireless bridge support, 252
    WPA. *see* WPA (Wi-Fi Protected Access)
802.11a
    channel definitions, 188
    co-located systems, 211
    equipment compatibility/availability, 211
    interference, 525
    narrowband interference, 207
    OFDM and, 199–201
    overview, 314
    range, 212
    system cost, 206
    throughput, 211–212, 409, 413
    UNII bands, 199–200
802.11b

    channel definitions, 188
    co-located systems, 208–211
    delay spread, 175
    DSSS channels, 187
    equipment compatibility/availability, 211
    HR-DSS (high-rate DSSS), 186
    IEEE ratification, 3
    narrowband interference, 206–207
    overview, 313–314
    range, 212
    system cost, 206
    throughput, 211–212, 409, 411–412
802.11d, 318
802.11e, 315, 379
802.11F
    overview, 315–316
    protocol sequences, 349–350
    roaming, 347
802.11g
    channel definitions, 188
    co-located systems, 210–211
    delay spread, 175
    equipment compatibility/availability, 211
    narrowband interference, 206–207
    OFDM and, 186, 201
    operating modes, 201–202
    overview, 314–315
    range, 212
    system cost, 206
    throughput, 211–212, 409, 411–412
802.11h, 316–317
802.11i
    access point security, 231
    overview, 316
    WPA2, 441
802.11j, 317–318
802.11s, 318–319
802.1x/EAP. *See* EAP (Extensible Authentication Protocol)
802.3af, 292
915 MHz, ISM bands, 303–304

A

A (amperes), 48
AAA (authentication, authorization, and accounting), 432–433, 470
absorption, 35, 39
AC (alternating current)
    compared with DC, 25
    lightning and, 147
    power requirements in site surveys, 528–530
    RF signals and, 22
acceptable use policy, 468
access categories, WMM, 381–382
access control

limiting and tracking user access, 471–472

RBAC (Role-Based Access Control), 276

access points. *See* APs (access points)

accounting, in AAA, 432–433, 470

ACK (acknowledgement), 370–372, 375

acknowledgement (ACK), 370–372, 375

active gain, 73–74, 132–133

active mode, WLAN power management, 352–353

active scanning, 336–338

ad-hoc traffic indication message (ATIM), 358–359

administrators

  penetration attacks and, 463

  site survey questions, 484

Advanced Encryption Standard. *See* AES (Advanced Encryption Standard)

AES (Advanced Encryption Standard)

  access point security, 231

  encryption cracking attacks and, 456

  RC4 compared with, 447

  Rijndeal algorithm in, 278

  WPA support, 440–441

AID (association identifier), 354

air stratification, weather-related interference, 417

AirMagnet, site survey utility, 502, 538

AiroPeek, site survey utility, 502

algorithms. *See also* encryption

  comparing, 447

  mixing, 430

alignment, antenna, 117–118, 245–246

alignment utilities, wireless bridges, 249–251

all-band interference, 415

ALOHAnet, 19

alternating current. *See* AC (alternating current)

AM (Amplitude Modulation)

  modulation types, 196

  not used in wireless networks, 193

  phase and, 28

amperes (A), 48

amplification. *See* gain (amplification)

amplifiers, RF, 132–141

  active gain added by, 132–133

  configuring and managing, 136

  DC power injection, 133

  FCC specifications, 137–141

  fixed-gain vs. fixed output, 134

  options, 135

  types of, 134

amplitude

  loss of power, 33

  multipath causing decrease in signal amplitude, 395–396

  multipath causing increase in signal amplitude, 398–399

  overview, 23–24

  phase and, 27

  practical uses of, 24–25

Amplitude Modulation. *See* AM (Amplitude Modulation)

antenna accessories, 131–168

  exam objectives, 131

  frequency converters, 163–164

  grounding rods/wires, 144–145

  key terms, 167

  lightning arrestors. *see* lightning arrestors

  overview, 132

  review questions, 168

  RF amplifiers. *see* amplifers, RF

  RF attenuators, 141–143

  RF cables, 160–162

  RF connectors, 157–159

  RF "pigtail" adapter cables, 162–163

  RF splitters. *see* splitters, RF

  test kits, 165–166

antenna installation, 103–124

  alignment, 117–118

  appropriate use of antennas, 117

  diagnostics, 123–124

  mounting. *see* mounting antennas

  orientation, 117

  overview, 103

  placement by type, 103–105

  preventative maintenance, 121–123

  safety, 119–121

antenna reciprocity, 419

antennas

  6 dB rule, 97–98

  diversity as solution to multipath, 400–401

  Earth bulge and, 95–96

  EIRP, 42–43, 305

  exam objectives, 69–70

  fade margin, 101–103

  FCC specifications, 125–128

  fixed or detachable antennas for APs, 227–228

  Free Space Path Loss, 96–97

  Fresnel Zone, 88–89

  gain measurement, 63–64

  highly-directional. *see* highly-directional antennas

  isotropic radiators, 59–61

  key terms, 129

  link budget, 98–101

  LOS, 87, 89–95

  omnidirectional. *see* omnidirectional antennas

  outdoor placement, 530

  overview, 71

  PCMCIA and, 258

  polarization, 30–31

  preferred direction, 60–61

  range, 418

  review questions, 130

  semi-directional. *see* semi-directional antennas

  site survey tests, 519

  types of, 72

  wavelengths and, 27

Applicable Audience, in general security policy, 466–467
application layer encryption, 447–450
applications, site surveys, 492
applications, WLAN, 5–19
  bridging, 9–10
  corporate data access and end-user mobility, 6–7
  educational/classroom use, 7
  health care, 8
  industrial -warehousing and manufacturing, 9
  key terms, 18
  main roles, 5–6
  metro area, 15–16
  mobile office networking, 14–15
  mobility, 12–13
  network extension to remote areas, 8
  public hotspots, 16
  SOHO, 13–14
  Wireless Internet Service Providers, 11–12
APs (access points), 220–243
  antennas, 27
  association with, 342
  bridge mode, 223–225
  connectivity options, 229–230
  coverage testing, 518
  data rate boundaries, 521
  filtering, 228
  fixed or detachable antennas, 227–228
  IEEE standards, 232–233
  management features, 231–232
  modes, 222, 233
  mounting, 233–242
  naming conventions, 486
  NEMA enclosures, 241–242
  options, 227
  overview, 220–221
  phased array antennas and, 284–286
  placement, 238–240
  PoE support, 230
  power balanced between client and, 418
  power sources, 486
  removable radio cards, 228–229
  repeater mode, 225–227
  root mode, 222–223
  rouge access points, 460–462
  security, 230–231
  semi-directional antennas and, 84
  site surveys and, 499
  summary, 242–243
  variable power output, 229
  wireless bridges compared with, 243
  wireless LAN switches and, 280–281
area usage, in site survey preparation, 486–488
ARIB (Association of Radio Industries and Businesses), 311
ASLEAP, 455

assets
  management policy, 468
  protection policy, 466
association
  802.11 state machine, 343–344
  with access points, 342
association identifier (AID), 354
Association of Radio Industries and Businesses (ARIB), 311
ATIM (ad-hoc traffic indication message), 358–359
attack vectors, in security policy creation, 466
attacks
  eavesdropping, 453–454
  encryption cracking, 454–456
  overview, 452
  penetration attacks, 462–464
  replay attacks, 428
  RF jamming, 457–458
  rouge access points, 460–462
  wireless hijacking, 459–460
attenuation. *See* loss (attenuation)
attenuators, RF, 141–143
  fixed-loss vs. variable-loss, 142–143
  options, 143
  overview, 141–142
  placement, 143
auditing, security, 467, 470
authenticated and associated state, 802.11 state machine, 344
authenticated and unassociated state, 802.11 state machine, 343
authentication
  in AAA, 432–433, 470
  clients devices, 269–270
  EAP, 431–434
  EWGs, 274, 276
  joining WLANs, 339
  Open System, 339–341
  preventing wireless hijacking, 459
  Shared Key, 341–342, 431
authorization, in AAA, 432–433, 470
automatic rekeying, TKIP, 429
availability
  comparing 802.11 technologies, 211
  resource availability, 493–495
  wireless mesh routers and, 286
azimuth and elevation charts, semi-directional antennas, 80–82

B

baby monitors, interference from, 525
backoff timer, 371
bandwidth
  semi-directional antennas, 79–80

site survey preparation, 491–493
spread spectrum, 171
Barker Coding, 191–192
basic service set (BSS). *See* BSS (basic service set)
beacons
functions of, 334–335
overview, 333–334
time synchronization, 334
beams, RF fields emitted from antennas, 72
beamwidth
highly-directional antennas, 86
semi-directional antennas, 79–80
behaviors, RF
absorption, 39
diffraction, 36–37
gain, 33
loss, 33–35
reflection, 35
refraction, 36
scattering, 38
bidirectional RF amplifiers, 134
blueprints
facility, 493
predictive software and, 534
bridge mode, APs, 223–225
bridges, wireless, 243–253
aligning, 245–246, 249–251
calculating path, 249–251
fixed vs. detachable antennas, 251
managing, 253
modes, 244
mounting, 253
naming conventions, 486
options, 246–249
overview, 243
security features, 252
standards, 252
bridging WLAN applications, 9–10
brute force attacks, 455
BSS (basic service set), 329–333
access points, 220
extended service set identifier, 332–333
identifier, 331–332
Power Save mode and, 353–358
types of, 329–330
BSSID (BSS Identifier), 331–332
building-to-building connectivity, WLANs, 9–10

C

cables, 160–162
attenuation ratings, 161
choosing, 160
drip loop, 123
loss calculation, 161–162

moisture protection, 122
"pigtail" adapter cables, 162–163
testing, 123
calibration report, RF splitters, 156
CAM (continuous aware mode), 352
capacity planning, 522–524
captive portals, 450–451
carrier sense, 367–368, 383
Carrier Sense Multiple Access/Collision Avoidance. *See* CSMA/CA (Carrier Sense Multiple Access/Collision Avoidance)
Cat5 cable
choosing, 160–161
connectivity and, 230
PoE and, 290–291, 295–296
CCA (clear channel assessment), 367, 374
CCK (Complementary Code Keying), 195–196
CCMP, 456
CCX (Cisco Certified Extensions), 435
ceiling mounts
antennas, 107
APs (access points), 234–237
ceiling tile antenna, 115–116
Certified Wireless Network Administrator exam. *See* CWNA (Certified Wireless Network Administrator) exam
CF (compact flash), 259
CFP (Contention Free Period), 376–378
CFR (Code of Federal Regulations)
CFR 15.203, 125–126
CFR 15.204, 126, 137–141
CFR 15.407, 125–126
CFR 47, 176, 489
overview, 176
channels
DSSS, 186–190
FHSS, 181–182
OFDM, 197
CHAP password protection, 435–436
chips, Barker Code, 192
ciphertext, WEP, 426
Cisco 1400 wireless bridge, 247
Cisco Certified Extensions (CCX), 435
Cisco link status monitoring, 267–268
classroom use, WLANs, 7
clear channel assessment (CCA), 367, 374
clients devices, 257–271
driver installation, 264
Ethernet and serial converters, 264
manufacturer utilities, 264–270
options, 264
overview, 257
PC, CF, and SD cards, 258–260
PCI adapters, 260–262
PCMCIA-to-PCI adapters, 263
USB adapters, 262–263

Windows XP Wireless Zero Config, 271
co-located systems
  comparing 802.11 technologies, 208–211
  FHSS, 182–184
co-location throughput, 410–413
Coax-Seal, 121–122
coaxial cable, 161
Code of Federal Regulations. *See* CFR (Code of Federal Regulations)
collision handling, 375
compact flash (CF), 259
Complementary Code Keying (CCK), 195–196
configuration
  device security configuration, 468
  EEGs, 280
  EWGs, 276–278
  hardware, 542–543
  RF amplifiers, 136
  wireless mesh routers, 289–290
  wireless residential gateways, 273–274
  WLAN switches, 283–284
connectivity modes, APs, 222, 233
connectivity, wired options for APs, 229–230
connectors, 157–159
  choosing, 158–159
  FCC specifications requiring unique connectors, 125–126
  lightning arrestors, 149
  moisture protection, 122
  N-type, 157
  RFamplifers, 135
  SMA, 158
  TNC, 158
  types of, 156, 157
consultants, 544
Contention Free Period (CFP), 376–378
contention window, 371–374
  how it works, 371–372
  length, 374
  overview, 371
  SIFS and DIFS frames and, 373
continuous aware mode (CAM), 352
control frames, 365–366
convolution coding, OFDM, 198–199
cordless phones, interference from, 525
corporate data access, WLANs, 6–7
corporate security policy
  advanced mechanisms, 470–471
  functional security policy, 467–468
  general security policy, 466–467
  limiting and tracking user access, 471–472
  overview, 464–465
  physical security, 469
  privacy of sensitive information, 468–469
  public wireless networks, 471
  security auditing, 470

site surveys and, 495–496
corrupted signals, 396–397, 403
costs, 802.11 technologies, 205–206
coverage
  azimuth and elevation charts, 80–82
  illustration of, 532
  omnidirectional antennas, 74–75
  post-installation verification, 530
  semi-directional antennas, 78–79
  site surveys, 517–521, 540
coWPAtty, 455
CSMA/CA (Carrier Sense Multiple Access/Collision Avoidance)
  collision handling, 375
  DCF (Distributed Coordination Function) and, 375–376
  near/far problems, 408
  overview, 367
CTS-to-Self, 387
CWNA (Certified Wireless Network Administrator) exam
  how to get certified, xxxiii
  reasons for certification, xxxi–xxxii
  tips for succeeding, xlv

D

data frames, 365–366
data rate
  boundaries, 521
  comparing 802.11 technologies, 211–212
  utilities for monitoring, 266
Data Terminal Equipment (DTE), 292
dB (decibels), 50–52, 56
dBd, 63–64
dBi, 59–62
dBm, 55–59
DC (direct current)
  AC compared with, 25
  lightning and, 147
  PoE devices and, 292–294
  RF amplifiers, 133
  RF splitters, 157
DCF (Distributed Coordination Function), 375–376
dead spots, 517, 519, 521
decibels (dB), 50–52, 56
degrees, phase measurement, 27
delay spread
  802.11, 175
  multipath and, 394
  spread spectrum technology, 174
delivery traffic indication message (DTIM), 355–358
Denial of Service (DoS), 457. *See also* jamming
DES, 447
detachable antennas
  APs, 227–228
  wireless bridges, 251

workgroup bridges, 255

devices
clients devices. *see* clients devices
exam objectives, xxxviii–xl
infrastructure devices. *see* infrastructure devices
security configuration, 468

DFS (dynamic frequency selection), 316–317

diagnosing. *See* troubleshooting WLANs

dictionary attacks, 455–456

Differential Phase Shift Keying (DPSK), 194

Differential Quaternary Phase Shift Keying (DQPSK), 195, 201

diffraction, 36–37

DIFS (Distributed Coordination Function Interframe Space), 371, 377–378

dipole antennas
as example of omnidirectional antenna, 72–73
magnetic mounts, 107
placement, 103–104
U-bolt mounts, 106
uses of, 77

direct current. *See* DC (direct current)

Direct Sequence Spread Spectrum. *See* DSSS (Direct Sequence Spread Spectrum)

dish/grid antennas
as example of highly-directional antenna, 85
mounting, 112
placement, 105
tilt-and-swivel mounts, 112

distance wheel, 512

Distributed Coordination Function (DCF), 375–376

Distributed Coordination Function Interframe Space (DIFS), 371, 377–378

Distribution System (DS), 344–346

Distribution System Medium. *See* DSM (Distribution System Medium)

Distribution System Services (DSS), 344

documentation, site surveys, 505–506, 522

DoS (Denial of Service), 457. *See also* jamming

downfade, 395–396

downtilt
dipole antennas, 77
semi-directional antennas, 84

DPSK (Differential Phase Shift Keying), 194

DQPSK (Differential Quaternary Phase Shift Keying), 195, 201

drawings/illustrations, site surveys, 541–542

drip loop, in antenna cables, 123

driver installation, WLAN cards, 264

DRS (Dynamic Rate Selection), 389–390, 504

DS (Distribution System), 344–346

DS parameter sets, beacon functions, 334

DSM (Distribution System Medium)
Ethernet as DSM, 344–345
overview, 344

Powerline networking as DSM, 345–346

DSP (digital signal processing), 197

DSS (Distribution System Services), 344

DSSS (Direct Sequence Spread Spectrum), 186–196
in 802.11, 312–313
CCK (Complementary Code Keying), 195–196
channels, 186–190
co-located systems, 208–211
data rate and throughput, 211–212
DRS (Dynamic Rate Selection) and, 389
encoding, 191–192, 196
encoding vs. modulation, 196
FCC specifications, 176–177
narrowband interference, 206–207
overview, 186
processing gain, 192–193
PSK (Phase Shift Keying), 193–195
range, 212
security, 213

DTE (Data Terminal Equipment), 292

DTIM (delivery traffic indication message), 355–358

dwell time, FHSS, 179–181

dynamic frequency selection (DFS), 316–317

Dynamic Rate Selection (DRS), 389–390, 504

E

E-planes, polarization, 30

EAP (Extensible Authentication Protocol), 431–438
authentication, 431–434
EAP-Cisco Wireless (LEAP), 431, 435
EAP-FAST, 276, 437–438
EAP-MD-5 Challenge, 435
EAP-SIM (GSM), 437
EAP-TLS (Transport Layer Security), 435–436
EAP-TTLS (Tunneled Transport Layer Security), 276, 436
encryption cracking attacks, 455–456
PEAP (Protected EAP), 436–437
preventing wireless hijacking, 459–460
WPA and, 322

Earth bulge, antennas and, 95–96

eavesdropping, 453–454

EDCAF (Enhanced Distributed Channel Access Function), 379–381

educational use, WLANs, 7

EEGs (Enterprise Encryption Gateways), 278–280
configuring and managing, 280
overview, 278–279
proprietary layer 2 encryption, 443

effects, multipath, 395

effects, VSWR, 41

EIFS (Extended Interframe Space), 371

EIRP (Equivalent Isotropically Radiated Power)
overview, 42–43

point-to-multipoint links, 306–308
point-to-point links, 308–309
power radiated by antennas, 305
Ekahau Site Survey, 537
electromagnetic fields, 30
electromagnetic waves, 23, 35
elevation and azimuth charts, semi-directional antennas, 80–82
encoding
  Barker Coding, 191–192
  CCK (Complementary Code Keying), 195–196
  DSSS, 191–192, 196
  OFDM, 203–204
  types of, 196
encryption
  access point security, 231
  application layer, 447–450
  EEGs, 278–279
  layer 2, 278, 443
  MPPE-128, 444
  preventing wireless hijacking, 459
  protecting encryption keys, 468–469
  strong encryption as protection against eavesdropping, 454
  throughput and, 408–409
  wireless bridges, 252
  WPA supported, 440–441
encryption cracking attacks, 454–456
end-span, PoE devices, 292
Enhanced Distributed Channel Access Function (EDCAF), 379–381
Enterprise Encryption Gateways. *See* EEGs (Enterprise Encryption Gateways)
enterprise wireless gateways. *See* EWGs (enterprise wireless gateways)
environmental factors, range, 419
equipment cart, 513
equipment compatibility/availability, 802.11 technologies, 211
Equivalent Isotropically Radiated Power. *See* EIRP (Eqivalent Isotropically Radiated Power)
error correction, convolution coding, 198–199
ESS (extended service set), 332
ESSID (extended service set identifier), 333
Ethernet
  AP connectivity and, 229–230
  as DSM, 344–345
  EWGs and, 274
  PoE capable Ethernet switches, 294–295
Ethernet converters, 264
ETSI (European Telecommunications Standards Institute), 311
EWGs (enterprise wireless gateways), 274–278
  captive portals, 451
  configuring and managing, 276–278

overview, 274–275
  VPN solutions, 445–446
  WLAN switches and, 282
exam objectives, xxxv–xliv
  antenna accessories, 131
  antennas, 69–70
  frame transmission, 363
  infrastructure devices, 217
  network architecture, 802.11, 327–328
  network implementation, xl–xli
  network security, xli–xliii
  protocols and devices, xxxviii–xl
  regulations and standards, xxxvi–xxxviii
  RF mathematics, 47
  RF (radio frequency), 21
  RF technologies, xxxiv–xxxvi
  security, 423–424
  site surveys, 477–478, xliii–xliv
  spread spectrum technology, 169–170
  standards, 299–300
  troubleshooting WLANs, 393
  WLANs, 1
exponential growth, 50
Extended Interframe Space (EIFS), 371
extended service set (ESS), 332
extended service set identifier (ESSID), 333
Extensible Authentication Protocol. *See* EAP (Extensible Authentication Protocol)

F

FAA, tower regulations, 488–489
facility
  analysis, 482–483. *see also* site surveys
  blueprints, 493–494, 514
  documenting, 505
fade margin, antennas, 101–103
failover, wireless mesh routers, 286–287
fault protection, PoE, 295–296
FCC (Federal Communication Commission), 301–310
  antenna rules, 125–128
  FHSS, 184–185
  frequency ranges, 26
  intentional radiators, 41
  ISM bands, 303–304
  license-free bands, 302–303
  overview, 301
  power output, 305–310
  PtMP 2.4 GHz ISM, 305–307
  PtMP 5.8 GHz UNII, 307–308
  PtP 2.4 GHz ISM, 308–309
  PtP 5.8 GHz UNII, 309
  RF amplifiers, 137–141
  sector and phased array antennas, 309–310
  spread spectrum technology, 176–177

tower regulations and permits, 488–489
UNII bands, 304–305
UNII-I devices, 125–126
wattages regulations for antennas, 49
FH parameter sets, beacon functions, 334
FHSS (Frequency Hopping Spread Spectrum), 178–185
802.11, 312–313
802.11d, 318
co-located systems, 182–184, 208–210
data rate and throughput, 211–212
dwell time limits, 180–181
dwell time vs. hop time, 179
equipment compatibility and availability, 211
FCC specifications, 176–177, 184–185
hop sequences and channels, 181–182
IEEE standards, 184
narrowband interference, 205–206
overview, 178
range, 212
security, 213
system cost, 205–206
fiber optic cable, 150–151
filtering
EWG support for, 277
MAC filters, 442–443
MAC or protocol filtering for APs, 228
workgroup bridges, 256
fingerprinting, 461–462
firewalls, profile-based, 452
fixed antennas
APs, 227–228
wireless bridges, 251
workgroup bridges, 255
fixed-gain vs. fixed output, RF amplifiers, 134
fixed-loss vs. variable-loss, RF attenuators, 142–143
forgeries, WEP and, 428
fragmentation
of frames, 387–388
throughput and, 409
frame transmission (MAC/PHY layers), 363–392
802.11 frames, 364–365
carrier sense, 367–368
collision handling, 375
contention window, 371–374
CSMA/CA, 367
CTS-to-Self, 387
DCF (Distributed Coordination Function), 375–376
DIFS (distributed coordination function interframe space), 371
DRS (Dynamic Rate Selection), 389–390
EIFS (extended interframe space), 371
exam objectives, 363
fragmentation, 387–388
interframe spacing, 368–369
key terms, 391

maximum frame size, 366–367
overview, 364
PCF (Point Coordination Function), 376–378
PIFS (point coordination function interframe space), 370
QoS, 378–382
review questions, 392
RTS/CTS (Request to Send/Clear to Send), 383–386
SIFS (short interframe space), 369–370
slot time, 374
wireless frame types, 365–366
frames
802.11, 364–365
Ethernet compared with wireless, 366–367
fragmentation of, 387–388
maximum size, 366–367
wireless types, 365–366
Free Space Path Loss, 96–97, 399
frequency
formula for calculating, 26–27
overview, 25–26
physical dimensions of antennas and, 71
practical uses of, 25–26
frequency converters, 163–164
Frequency Hopping Spread Spectrum. See FHSS (Frequency Hopping Spread Spectrum)
frequency modulation, 196
frequency response
lightning arrestors, 149
RF amplifiers, 135
RF cables, 160
RF connectors, 159
RF splitters, 155
Fresnel Zone
Earth bulge and, 95–96
LOS and, 88–89
obstructions and, 89–95
site surveys and, 507
FSL. See Free Space Path Loss
functional security policy, 467–468

G

gain (amplification). See also amplifers, RF
dBi and dBd and, 63
dipole antennas, 73
effect of passive gain on coverage in omnidirectional antennas, 74–75
high gain antennas, 86–87
measuring in dB, 52–53
overview, 33
passive vs. active in omnidirectional antennas, 73–74
RF amplifiers and, 132–133
gateways
enterprise encryption. see EEGs (enterprise encryption gateways)

enterprise wireless. *see* EWGs (enterprise wireless gateways)
   wireless residential. *see* wireless residential gateways
Gaussian Frequency Shift Keying (GFSK), 178
general security policy, 466–467
GFSK (Gaussian Frequency Shift Keying), 178
GPS Receiver, 248, 507
grid antennas. *See* dish/grid antennas
ground blocks, 120
grounding rods, 144–145
grounding system
   antennas, 120–121
   purposes of, 144
   site surveys and, 529
   using grounding rods/grounding wires, 144–145
grounding wires, 144–145
guards, security, 469

H
H-planes, polarization, 30
hackers. *See* attacks
hardware, 542–543. *See also* devices
harmonics, OFDM channels, 197
HCF (Hybrid Coordination Function), 379, 381
health care, WLANs, 8
hertz (Hz), 25
hidden nodes
   diagnosing, 403–404
   overview, 402–403
   problem with, 368, 383–384
   solutions for, 404–406
high-rate DSSS (HR-DSSS)
   802.11b, 186, 313–314
   channels, 189–190
highly-directional antennas
   overview, 84–85
   radiation pattern of, 85
   safety, 119
   uses of, 86–87
hijacking, wireless, 459–460
history, WLANs, 2–4
hops, FHSS
   defined, 178
   hop sequences, 181–182
   hop time, 179
horizontal polarization, antennas, 31
hotspots, WLANs, 16
HR-DSS (high-rate DSSS)
   802.11b, 186, 313–314
   channels, 189–190
HTTP, 228
HTTPS, 447
Hybrid Coordination Function (HCF), 379, 381
Hz (hertz), 25

I
IAPP (inter-access-point protocol), 315–316, 347
IBSS (independent basics service set), 329, 358
IC (Industry Canada), 311
IDS (intrusion detection systems), 461–462
IEEE (Institute of Electrical and Electronics Engineers), 311–319
   802.11. *see* 802.11
   802.11 clause summary, 319
   802.11a. *see* 802.11a
   802.11b. *see* 802.11b
   802.11d, 318
   802.11e, 315
   802.11F. *see* 802.11F
   802.11g. *see* 802.11g
   802.11h, 316–317
   802.11i. *see* 802.11i
   802.11j, 317–318
   802.11s, 318–319
   APs, 232–233
   FHSS, 184
   lightning arrestors, 148
   overview, 311–312
IFS (interframe spacing)
   DIFS (Distributed Coordination Function Interframe Space), 371
   EIFS (Extended Interframe Space), 371
   overview, 368–369
   PIFS (Point Coordination Function Interframe Space), 370
   SIFS (Short Interframe Space), 369–370
illustrations/drawings, site surveys, 541–542
impact analysis, in security policy creation, 466
impedance
   lightning arrestors, 149
   loss of power, 33–34
   matching in cabling and connectors, 41
   RF connectors, 159
   RF splitters, 155
   RFamplifers, 135
   VSWR and, 39, 40
in-phase signals, 28
independent basics service set (IBSS), 329, 358
indoor surveys, 514–515
industrial roles, WLANs, 9
Industrial, Scientific, and Medical bands. *See* ISM (Industrial, Scientific, and Medical) bands
Industry Canada (IC), 311
information gathering, site surveys, 517
infrastructure devices, 217–298
   APs (access points). *see* APs (access points)
   APs with phased array antennas, 284–286
   clients devices. *see* clients devices

enterprise encryption gateways, 278–280
enterprise wireless gateways, 274–278
exam objectives, 217
key terms, 297
overview, 219–220
Power over Ethernet devices. *see* PoE (Power over Ethernet)
review questions, 298
wireless bridges. *see* bridges, wireless
wireless mesh routers, 286–290
wireless residential gateways, 271–274
wireless routers, 256–257
WLAN switches, 280–284
workgroup bridges, 253–256
Initialization Vector (IV), WEP, 427, 430
insertion loss
lightning arrestors, 149
RF connectors, 159
RF splitters, 154
Institute of Electrical and Electronics Engineers. *See* IEEE (Institute of Electrical and Electronics Engineers)
intentional radiators
flexibility in antenna choice allowed by FCC specifications, 126–127
overview, 41–42
unique connectors required by FCC specifications, 126
inter-access-point protocol (IAPP), 315–316, 347
inter-symbol interference (ISI), 174–176
interference
all-band, 415
narrowband, 413–415
overview, 413
site surveys, 524–525, 540–541
weather, 415–418
interframe spacing. *See* IFS (interframe spacing)
interoperability
802.11 devices, 211
Wi-Fi Alliance and, 320–321
intrusion detection, access points, 231
intrusion detection systems (IDS), 461–462
IP addresses, access point management, 232
IPSec (IP Security), 278, 443–445
ISI (inter-symbol interference), 174–176
ISM (Industrial, Scientific, and Medical) bands, 303–304
2.4 GHz, 304
5.8 GHz, 304
915 MHz, 303–304
overview, 302
PtMP links, 305–307
PtP links, 308–309
isotropic radiators, 59–61
IV (Initialization Vector), WEP, 427, 430

J

jamming
defined, 172–173
narrowband signals, 172
RF jamming attacks, 457–458
spread spectrum signals, 173–174

K

keystreams, 426

L

LANPlanner Predictive Modeling Software, 533
laptops, site surveys, 504–505
last mile data delivery, WISPs, 11–12
layer 2 encryption, 278, 443
LDAP (Lightweight Directory Access Protocol), 276, 432
LEAP (Lightweight Extensible Authentication Protocol), 431, 435, 455
LEDs, bridge alignment, 245
left-hand mounts, antennas, 110
license-free bands, FCC, 302–303
disadvantages of, 303
ISM and UNII, 302
light, speed of, 26
lightning
DC and AC current generated by, 147
grounding system and, 144
lightning arrestors and, 145
lightning arrestors, 145–151
fiber optic cable, 150–151
how they work, 145–146
installed on wireless LAN, 147
installing, 150
options, 147–150
overview, 145
physical design, 146
Lightweight Directory Access Protocol (LDAP), 276, 432
Lightweight Extensible Authentication Protocol (LEAP), 431, 435, 455
line of sight. *See* LOS (line of sight)
link budget, 98–103
calculating, 100–101, 103
determining multipath with, 399–400
fade margin and, 102
overview, 98
receive sensitivity and, 99–100
RF amplifiers and, 132, 135
link calculator, 506
link speed, site surveys, 519
link status monitoring, 267–268
Linksys WET54GS5, 247
Linksys WGA54G game console bridge, 248
Linksys WMP55AG, 261
Linksys WPC55AG PCMCIA radio card, 258
Linksys WUSB12 & WUSB54GP, 263

load balancing, 351–352
lobes, RF fields emitted from antennas, 72
logarithmic decay, 50
LOS (line of sight)
  60 percent unobstructed radius, 90
  Earth bulge and, 95–96
  Fresnel Zone and, 88–89
  obstructions, 89–95
  outdoor surveys, 506
  overview, 87
  types of, 394
loss (attenuation)
  measuring in dB, 50, 52–53
  overview, 33–35
  return loss caused by VSWR, 39
  RF attenuators, 141–142
  RF cables, 160, 161
  "rule of 10s and 3s", 55
  signal loss chart, 526

M

MAC filters
  APs, 228
  penetration attacks and, 462
  WLAN security and, 442–443
MAC headers, 366
MAC layer. *See* frame transmission (MAC/PHY layers)
magnetic mounts, antennas, 107
maintenance, antennas
  diagnostics, 123–124
  preventative, 121–123
management
  APs, 231–232
  EEGs (enterprise encryption gateways), 280
  EWGs (enterprise wireless gateways), 276–278
  interface exploits, 463–464
  RF amplifiers, 136
  wireless bridges, 253
  wireless mesh routers, 289–290
  wireless residential gateways, 273–274
  WLAN switches, 283–284
  workgroup bridges, 255–256
management frames, 365
mathematics, RF. *See* RF mathematics
maximum transmission unit (MTU), 366
MDI (Media Dependent Interface), 292
measurements
  accuracy of, 62–63
  dB, 50–52
  dBd, 63–64
  dBi, 59–62
  dBm, 55–59
  degrees of phase, 27
  hertz (Hz), 25

milliwatts (mW), 49–50
  ohms, 39
  signal strength, 64–65
  VSWR, 40
  watts (W), 48–49
Media Dependent Interface (MDI), 292
mesh networks, 318–319
mesh routers, 286–290
  configuring and managing, 289–290
  overview, 286–289
  typical use of, 289
message integrity checksum (MIC), 430
methodology section, site survey reports, 540
metro areas, WLANs, 15–16
MIC (message integrity checksum), 430
Michael, 430
microwave ovens, interference from, 525
mid-span, PoE devices, 292
milliwatts (mW), 49–50, 51
MIMO (Multiple-in/Multiple-out), 401
mini-PCI radio card, 261–262
mixing algorithm, 430
mobile office networking, WLANs, 14–15
mobile subnets, 351
mobility, WLANs, 6–7, 12–13
modes
  APs (access points), 222, 233
  wireless bridges, 244
  workgroup bridges, 256
modulation
  amplitude modulation, 28, 193, 196
  frequency modulation, 196
  phase modulation, 28
  QAM (Quadrature Amplitude Modulation), 203–204
  types of, 196
moisture, protecting antennas from, 121–122
mounting
  APs, 233–242
  RF amplifiers, 136
  RF splitters, 156
  wireless bridges, 253
mounting antennas
  aesthetics, 115–117
  dish/grid antennas, 112
  magnetic mount, 107
  omnidirectional antennas, 76
  right and left-hand mounts, 110
  sector antennas, 113–114
  suction mounts, 110
  tilt-and-swivel mounts, 108–109
  tips for, 115
  U-bolt mounts, 106
  universal mount, 107–108
  yagi antennas, 111–112
MPPE-128, 444

MS-CHAPv2, 436
MTU (maximum transmission unit), 366
multi-port DC voltage injectors, PoE, 293–294
multipath, 394–401
  corrupted signals, 396–397
  decreased signal amplitude, 395–396
  defined, 35
  effects of, 395
  increased signal amplitude, 398–399
  metal obstructions and, 119
  nulling, 397–398
  overview, 394–395
  solutions for, 400–401
  spread spectrum technology and, 174–176
  troubleshooting, 399–401
Multiple-in/Multiple-out (MIMO), 401
mW (milliwatts), 49–50, 51

N

N-type connectors
  pigtail adapters for, 163
  RF connectors, 157
  RF splitters, 152
naming conventions
  APs and bridges, 486
  networks, 484–485
narrowband interference, 205–207, 413–415
narrowband transmission, 171–174
NAT (network address translation), 271
National Electronics Council (NEC), 144
near/far, 406–408
  overview, 406–407
  solutions for, 408
  troubleshooting, 407–408
NEC (National Electronics Council), 144
NEMA enclosures, access points, 241–242, 487
NetGear, site survey utilities, 265
NetStumbler, site survey utilities, 502
network address translation (NAT), 271
network architecture, 802.11, 327–361
  BSS (basic service set), 329–333
  DS (Distribution System), 344–346
  exam objectives, 327–328
  joining WLANs. *see* WLANs (wireless LANs), joining
  key terms, 360
  overview, 329
  power management. *see* WLANs (wireless LANs), power management
  review questions, 361
  roaming. *see* roaming
  scanning WLANs. *see* WLANs (wireless LANs), locating
network implementation, xl–xli
network security, xli–xliii
nodes. *See also* hidden nodes

balancing power on local/remote, 408
increasing power to, 405
moving, 406
noise floor
  defined, 172
  measuring, 501
  site surveys and, 519
nulling, 397–398, 403

O

Observer, site survey utility, 502
obstructions
  hidden node problem and, 403
  identifying in site surveys, 526–528
  LOS and, 89–95
  metal obstructions, 119
  outdoor surveys, 488
  removing obstacles as solution to hidden nodes, 405
OFDM (Orthogonal Frequency Domain Multiplexing), 197–204
  802.11a, 199–201, 314
  802.11g, 201–202, 314–315
  co-located systems, 210–211
  convolution coding, 198–199
  data rate and throughput, 211–212
  delay spread, 175
  DRS (Dynamic Rate Selection) and, 389
  encoding, 203–204
  FCC specifications, 176–177
  how it works, 197–198
  narrowband interference, 207
  overview, 197
  range, 212
  security, 213
"Ohmic heating", 144
Ohms, as measure of resistance, 39
omnidirectional antennas
  effect of passive gain on coverage, 74–75
  examples of, 74
  mounting, 76, 115
  overview, 72–73
  passive vs. active gain, 73–74
  PtMP links, 306
  uses of, 76–77
one-to-one rule, 306–308
Open System authentication, 339–341
operating modes, 802.11g, 201–202
orientation, antennas, 117
Orthogonal Frequency Domain Multiplexing. *See* OFDM (Orthogonal Frequency Domain Multiplexing)
oscillation, 30
OSHA compliance, 121
out-of-phase signals, 28, 397–398
outdoor surveys

conducting, 515
obstructions, 488
site survey equipment, 506–507

P

PAC (Protected Access Credential), 437
Packet Binary Convolutional Code (PBCC), 204–205
panel antennas
  as example of semi-directional antenna, 77–78
  mounting aesthetics, 115
  placement, 104
  tilt-and-swivel mounts, 108–109
  universal mounts, 107–108
  uses of, 82–83
  window and wall mounts, 110
PAP, 436
parabolic dish antennas, 84–85
passive gain
  antennas, 132
  compared with active gain, 73–74
  effect on coverage of omnidirectional antennas, 74–75
passive scanning, beacons, 335–336
passive tools, site surveys, 537–538
passwords
  CHAP, 435, 436
  MS-CHAPv2, 436
  PAP, 436
  policies, 467
  protecting sensitive information, 468
PAT (Port Address Translation), 273
patch antennas
  as example of semi-directional antenna, 77–78
  mounting aesthetics, 115
  placement, 104
  tilt-and-swivel mounts, 108–109
  universal mounts, 107–108
  uses of, 82–83
  wall mounts, 110
path calculation utilities, wireless bridges, 249–251
Path Loss. See Free Space Path Loss
PBCC (Packet Binary Convolutional Code), 204–205
PC cards. See PCMCIA
PCF (Point Coordination Function), 376–378
  overview, 376
  PIFS and DIFS interaction, 377–378
  process of, 376–377
PCI
  PCI and mini-PCI adapters, 260–262
  PCMCIA-to-PCI adapters, 263
PCMCIA, 258 260
  antennas, 258
  overview, 258
  PCMCIA-to-PCI adapters, 263
  site surveys and, 500–504

slots on APs, 228
PDAs
  802.11 compatibility, 489–490
  site survey equipment, 504–505
PEAP (Protected EAP)
  EWGs and, 276
  overview, 436–437
  preventing wireless hijacking, 459
penetration attacks, 462–464
penetration tests, 470
per-packet key mixing, TKIP, 429
performance tuning, clients devices, 268
phantom voltage, 133
phase
  nulling causing out-of-phase signals, 397–398
  overview, 27–29
  practical uses of, 29
Phase 1 intermediate keys, TKIP, 429
Phase Modulation, 28
phase, of signals, 193
Phase Shift Keying. See PSK (Phase Shift Keying)
phased array antennas, 127–128
  APs (access points) and, 284–286
  FCC power output specifications, 309–310
photographs, documentation of facilities, 505
PHY layer, 374. See also frame transmission (MAC/PHY layers)
physical carrier sense, 383
physical security, 469
PIFS (Point Coordination Function Interframe Space), 370, 377–378
"pigtail" adapter cables, 162–163
pilot carriers, OFDM, 200–201
plaintext, WEP, 426
PN (pseudorandom number) code, 191–193
PoE (Power over Ethernet)
  APs supporting, 230
  EWGs and, 275
  fault protection, 295–296
  multi-port DC voltage injectors, 293–294
  options, 291–292
  overview, 290–291
  PoE capable Ethernet switches, 294–295
  single-port DC voltage injectors, 292–293
Point Coordination Function. See PCF (Point Coordination Function)
Point Coordination Function Interframe Space (PIFS), 370, 377–378
point-to-multipoint. See PtMP (point-to-multipoint)
point-to-point. See PtP (point-to-point)
Point-to-Point Tunneling Protocol (PPTP), 443–445
polarization
  antenna orientation and, 117
  overview, 29–32
  practical uses of, 32

policies. *See* security policies
polling process, PCF, 376
Port Address Translation (PAT), 273
portals, captive, 450–451
power
  increasing power to nodes, 405
  over Ethernet. *see* PoE (Power over Ethernet)
  ratings of RF splitters, 156
  transmission power effecting range, 418
  utilities for monitoring, 265–266
  variable power output for APs, 229
power dividers. *See* splitters, RF
power level chart, 58
power lines, antennas and, 120
power management, 352–359
  Active mode, 352–353
  overview, 352
  Power Save mode in BSS, 353–358
  Power Save mode in IBSS, 358
power meters, 153, 165–166
power output rules, FCC, 305–310
  PtMP 2.4 GHz ISM, 305–307
  PtMP 5.8 GHz UNII, 307–308
  PtP 2.4 GHz ISM, 308–309
  PtP 5.8 GHz UNII, 309
  sector and phased array antennas, 309–310
Power over Ethernet. *See* PoE (Power over Ethernet)
power save mode
  in BSS, 353–358
  in IBSS, 358
power save polling (PSP), 352
Powerline networking as DSM, 345–346
PPTP (Point-to-Point Tunneling Protocol), 443–445
pre-shared keys (PSK)
  access point security, 230–231
  WPA and, 322, 439–440
predictive software, site surveys, 534–535
preferred direction, antennas, 60–61
preventative maintenance, antennas, 121–123
privacy of sensitive information, 468–469
PRNG (pseudorandom number generator), 426
processing gain, DSSS, 191–193
profile-based firewalls, 452
profile management utility, 266–267
Propagate Networks, 536
properties, RF
  amplitude, 23–25
  frequency, 25–26
  phase, 27–29
  polarization, 29–32
  wavelength, 26–27
Protected Access Credential (PAC), 437
protection mechanisms
  clients devices, 268
  CTS-to-Self, 387

protective equipment, for weather-related interference, 417–418
protocol analyzers
  eavesdropping, 453
  security auditing, 470
  site surveys, 502, 510–511
  troubleshooting near/far, 407
protocol filtering, 228
protocols, exam objectives, xxxviii–xl
Proxim AP-700, 221
Proxim profile management utility, 267
pseudorandom number generator (PRNG), 426
pseudorandom number (PN), 191–193
PSK (Phase Shift Keying)
  DPSK (Differential Phase Shift Keying), 194–195
  DQPSK (Differential Quaternary Phase Shift Keying), 195
  overview, 193
  as type of modulation, 196
PSK (pre-shared keys)
  access point security, 230–231
  WPA and, 322, 439–440
PSP (power save polling), 352
PtMP (point-to-multipoint)
  2.4 GHz ISM, 305–307
  5.8 GHz UNII, 307–308
  APs, 223
  omnidirectional antennas, 76
  wireless bridges, 244
PtP (point-to-point)
  2.4 GHz ISM, 308–309
  5.8 GHz UNII, 309
  APs, 223
  highly-directional antennas, 86–87
  semi-directional antennas, 82
  wireless bridges, 244
public wireless networks, 471
purpose and business requirements, site surveys, 489–491, 539–540

Q

QAM (Quadrature Amplitude Modulation), 203–204
QoS (Quality of Service), 378–382
  802.11e, 315, 379
  EDCAF (Enhanced Distributed Channel Access Function), 379–381
  HCF (Hybrid Coordination Function), 381
  WMM (Wi-Fi Multimedia), 381–382

R

radiation pattern, highly-directional antennas, 85
radio cards
  Linksys WMP55AG PCI radio card, 261
  Linksys WPC55AG PCMCIA radio card, 258

mini-PCI radio card, 261–262
removable radio cards for APs, 228–229
SanDisk SD Wi-Fi, 260
Symbol Mobile Networker CF radio card, 259
radiology equipment, interference from, 525
RADIUS (Remote Authentication Dial-In User Service)
access point security, 230–231
EWGs and, 276
remote authentication with, 432
WPA-RADIUS, 439–440
radomes, 417–418, 487
range
802.11 technologies, 212
antenna type and, 418
environmental factors, 419
overview, 418
site surveys, 517–521
transmission power and, 418
RBAC (Role-Based Access Control), 276
RC4
access point security, 231
AES compared with, 447
encryption cracking attacks, 455
TKIP and, 429
WEP and, 426, 427
reassociation
overview, 347–348
problems with, 349
process of, 348
receive sensitivity, link budget, 99
Received Signal Strength Indicator (RSSI), 65, 245
reflection
as cause of multipath, 400
danger of reflecting high power signals, 119
overview, 35
refraction, 36
regulations, exam objectives, xxxvi–xxxviii
remote areas, WLANs, 8
Remote Authentication Dial-In User Service. See RADIUS (Remote Authentication Dial-In User Service)
repeater mode, APs, 225–227
replay attacks, 428
Report & Order 04-165, 125–126, 128, 310
Request to Send/Clear to Send. See RTS/CTS (Request to Send/Clear to Send)
resistance. See impedance
resource availability, site surveys, 493–495
return loss, VSWR, 39
reusability, lightning arrestors, 148
review questions
antenna accessories, 168
antennas, 130
frame transmission, 392
infrastructure devices, 298
network architecture, 802.11, 361

RF mathematics, 68
RF (radio frequency), 45
security, 475–476
site surveys, 546–547
spread spectrum technology, 215
standards, 325
troubleshooting WLANs, 421
WLANs (wireless LANs), 19
RF mathematics, 48–68
accuracy of measurements, 62–63
dB, 50–52
dBd, 63–64
dBi, 59–62
dBm, 55–59
exam objectives, 47
gain and loss measurements, 52–55
key terms, 65
milliwatts (mW), 49–50
overview, 48
review questions, 68
RSSI, 65
signal strength measurements, 64–65
watts (W), 48–49
RF (radio frequency)
absorption, 39
amplifiers. see amplifers, RF
amplitude, 23–25
attenuators. see attenuators, RF
cables. see cables
connectors. see connectors
corrupted signals, 396–397
coverage. see coverage
diffraction, 36–37
dividers. see splitters, RF
EIRP, 42–43
exam objectives, 21
frequency, 25–26
gain, 33
intentional radiators, 41–42
jamming. see jamming
key terms, 44
LOS, 394
loss, 33–35
multipath causing decrease in signal amplitude, 395–396
multipath causing increase in signal amplitude, 398–399
phase, 27–29
polarization, 29–32
reflection, 35
refraction, 36
review questions, 45
scattering, 38
shadows, 483
signal strength, 501, 537
signals, 22–23
site surveying, xliii–xliv

splitters. *see* splitters, RF
technologies, xxxiv–xxxvi
VSWR, 39–41
wavelength, 26–27
RG-58 cable, 161
right-hand mounts, antennas, 110
rights, user, 472
Rijndeal algorithm, 278
RingMaster Integrated Planning, Configuration, and
Management Software, 535
risk assessment, 466, 467
roaming, 346–352
  802.11F, 349–350
  load balancing, 351–352
  mobile subnets, 351
  overview, 346–347
  post-installation verification, 531
  reassociation, 347–349
  site survey preparation, 491–493
  standards, 347
  VPNs not supporting, 447
Role-Based Access Control (RBAC), 276
roles, WLANs, 5–6
root mode
  APs, 222–223
  wireless bridges, 244
rouge access points, 460–462
routers, wireless. *See also* wireless residential gateways
  overview, 256–257
  wireless mesh routers, 286–290
RSSI (Received Signal Strength Indicator), 65, 245
RTS/CTS (Request to Send/Clear to Send)
  diagnosing hidden nodes, 404
  overview, 383–386
  solutions for hidden nodes, 405
  throughput and, 409
rules
  1:1 rule, 306–308
  3:1 rule, 308
  6 dB rule, 97–98
  "10s and 3s", 54–55

S

safety, 119–121
  courses in, 121
  grounds and, 120–121
  high gain antennas and, 119
  metal obstructions and, 119
  power lines, 120
  using professional installers, 119
SanDisk SD Wi-Fi, 260
scanning. *See also* WLANs (wireless LANs), locating
  active scanning, 336–338
  overview, 333

passive scanning, 335–336
scattering, 35, 38
SD (secure digital), 259–260
sector antennas
  FCC power output specifications, 309–310
  mounting, 114
  overview, 113–114
secure digital (SD), 259–260
Secure Shell. *See* SSH (Secure Shell)
Secure Socket Layer (SSL), 278, 447–450
security, 423–476. *See also* attacks; authentication;
encryption
  802.11 methods, 426
  application layer encryption, 447–450
  APs, 230–231
  auditing, 467, 470
  captive portals, 450–451
  clearance for site surveys, 494–495
  comparing 802.11 technologies, 213
  corporate policies for. *see* corporate security policy
  device security configuration, 468
  EAP. *see* EAP (Extensible Authentication Protocol)
  exam objectives, 423–424
  filtering, 442–443
  key terms, 473–474
  layer 2 encryption, 443
  overview, 425
  profile-based firewalls, 452
  review questions, 475–476
  site surveys and, 495–496
  WEP. *see* WEP (Wired Equivalent Privacy)
  wireless bridges, 252
  wireless VPNs, 443–447
  workgroup bridges, 255
  WPA (Wi-Fi Protected Access). *see* WPA (Wi-Fi
Protected Access)
security guards, 469
security policies
  functional security policy, 467–468
  general security policy, 466–467
  site surveys and, 495–496
self-managing RF technologies, 535–537
semi-directional antennas
  azimuth and elevation charts, 80–82
  bandwidth of, 79–80
  coverage area, 78–79
  overview, 77–78
  uses of, 82–84
sensitive information, privacy of, 468–469
service set identifiers. *See* SSIDs (service set identifiers)
Shared Key authentication, 341–342, 431
Short Interframe Space (SIFS), 369–370, 373
SIFS (Short Interframe Space), 369–370, 373
signal generators, 123–124, 165–166
signal loss. *See* loss (attenuation)

signal splitters. *See* splitters, RF
signal strength
  measuring, 64–65, 500–501, 537
  RSSI and, 245
  site surveys and, 519
signal to noise ratio. *See* SNR (signal to noise ratio)
signals
  RF. *see* RF (radio frequency)
  spread spectrum, 171
SIM (Subscriber Identity Module), 437
single-port DC voltage injectors, PoE, 292–293
site surveys, 477–547
  alternative/supplemental methods, 531–533
  data rate boundaries, 521
  documentation, 522
  exam objectives, 477–478
  indoor surveys, 514–515
  interference sources, 524–525
  key terms, 545
  multipath determination, 400
  obstructions, 526–528
  outdoor antenna placement, 530
  outdoor surveys, 506–507, 515
  overview, 479–481
  passive tools, 537–538
  post-installation verification, 530–531
  predictive software, 534–535
  range and coverage patterns, 517–521
  review questions, 546–547
  RF information gathering, 517
  self-managing RF technologies, 535–537
  throughput testing/capacity planning, 522–524
  utilities, 265
  wired data connectivity and AC power requirements, 528–530
  before you begin, 515–517
site surveys, equipment, 498–499
  access point, 499
  documentation, 505–506
  laptops and PDAs, 504–505
  for outdoor surveys, 506–507
  overview, 498–499
  PC cards and utilities, 500–504
  protocol analyzers, 510–511
  spectrum analyzers, 507–510
  survey kit checklist, 511–514
site surveys, preparation
  area usage, 486–488
  bandwidth and roaming requirements, 491–493
  checklist, 497–498
  exercises, 496–497
  existing network in place, 483–486
  facility analysis, 482–483
  overview, 481–482
  purpose and business requirements, 489–491

resource availability, 493–495
security requirements, 495–496
towers, 488–489
site surveys, reports
  additional information in, 543–544
  drawings/illustrations, 541–542
  format, 539
  hardware placement and configuration, 542–543
  interference, 540–541
  methodology section, 540
  overview, 538–539
  problem areas, 541
  purpose and business requirements, 539–540
  RF coverage areas, 540
  throughput, 540
SiteSafe, 121
slot time, 374, 382
SMA connectors, 158, 163
Small Office, Home Office (SOHO), 13–14
"smart antennas", 127–128
SMTP, 449–450
SNMP, 231, 464, 468
SNR (signal to noise ratio)
  corrupted signals and, 397
  defined, 172
  environmental factors, 419
  measuring, 501
  passive site surveys, 537
  site surveys and, 519
SOHO (Small Office, Home Office), 13–14
solutions. *See* troubleshooting WLANs
spectrum analyzers
  diagnosing interference, 414
  diagnosing RF jamming attacks, 457–458
  site surveys and, 509–510
  types of, 507–509
spectrum mask, DSSS channels, 187
splitters, RF, 151–157
  checklist for choosing, 154–157
  examples of, 152
  monitoring power on wireless LAN links, 153–154
  overview, 151–152
spread spectrum technology, 169–215
  DSSS. *see* DSSS (Direct Sequence Spread Spectrum)
  exam objectives, 169–170
  FCC specifications, 176–177
  FHSS. *see* FHSS (Frequency Hopping Spread Spectrum)
  key terms, 214
  multipath and inter-symbol interference and, 174–176
  narrowband transmission and, 171–174
  OFDM. *see* OFDM (Orthogonal Frequency Domain Multiplexing)
  overview, 171
  PBCC, 204–205
  review questions, 215

throughput, 409
uses of, 176
SSH (Secure Shell)
access point management, 231
application layer encryption, 447–450
penetration attacks and, 464
as VPN technology, 278
SSIDs (service set identifiers)
beacon functions, 334
overview, 332–333
wireless hijacking, 459
SSL (Secure Socket Layer), 278, 447–450
standards, 299–325
ARIB (Association of Radio Industries and Businesses), 311
ETSI (European Telecommunications Standards Institute), 311
exam objectives, 299–300, xxxvi–xxxviii
FCC. *see* FCC (Federal Communication Commission)
IC (Industry Canada), 311
IEEE. *see* IEEE (Institute of Electrical and Electronics Engineers)
key terms, 324
review questions, 325
roaming, 347
Wi-Fi Alliance. *see* Wi-Fi Alliance
wireless bridges, 252
WLANs, 4–5
star topologies, 305. *See also* PtMP (point-to-multipoint)
Statement of Authority, general security policy, 466
subcarriers, OFDM, 198, 200–201
Subscriber Identity Module (SIM), 437
suction mounts, antennas, 110
switches, Ethernet, 280, 294–295
switches, WLANs, 280–284
configuration and management, 283–284
overview, 280–283
Symbol Mobile Networker CF radio card, 259
system cost, 802.11 technologies, 205–206
system operating margin. *See* link budget

T

telnet, 231
Temporal Key Integrity Protocol. *See* TKIP (Temporal Key Integrity Protocol)
temporal keys, WEP and TKIP, 429
test kits, antennas, 165–166
testing
cables, 123
coverage, 518
ground, 120–121
penetration, 470
throughput, 522–524
threat analysis, in security policy creation, 466

three-to-one rule, 308
throughput, 408–413
802.11 technologies, 211–212
co-location throughput, 410–413
monitoring, 266
overview, 408–409
post-installation verification, 531
site surveys, 540
testing, 522–524
tilt-and-swivel mounts, antennas, 108–109
TIM (traffic indicator map), 334–335, 354
time synchronization, beacon functions, 334
TKIP (Temporal Key Integrity Protocol), 428–431
addressing weaknesses in WEP, 428–431
encryption cracking attacks, 455
LEAP and, 431
WPA and, 322, 440–441
TNC connectors
pigtail adapters for, 163
RF connectors, 158
RF splitters, 152
Token Ring, 229–230
topographical software, 250
topology map, site surveys, 485
towers, 488–489
tracking user access, 471–472
traffic indicator map (TIM), 334–335, 354
traffic patterns, 409
training policies, 467–468
transmission power effecting range, 418
transmitters, in test kits, 165–166
Trapeze Networks' RingMaster, 535
troubleshooting WLANs, 393–421
all-band, 415
antennas, 123–124
exam objectives, 393
hidden nodes, 404–406
key terms, 420
multipath, 399–401
narrowband interference, 413–415
near/far, 407–408
overview, 394
range-related issues, 418–419
review questions, 421
throughput, 411–413
weather/environmental factors, 415–418
tunnels, 277

U

U-bolt mounts, 106, 136
UHF antennas, 64
unauthenticated and unassociated state, 802.11 state machine, 343
unidirectional RF amplifiers, 134

UNII (Unlicensed National Information Infrastructure) bands, 304–305
  lower (UNII-1), 125–126, 304–305
  middle (UNII-2), 305
  OFDM, 199–200
  overview, 302
  PtMP links, 307–308
  PtP links, 309
  upper (UNII-3), 305
universal mounts, antennas, 107–108
upfade, 398–399
UPS battery backup, 499
USB adapters, 262–263
users
  capacity planning, 523–524
  limiting and tracking user access, 470
  protecting usernames, 468
  rights, 472
  site surveys, 492
  WLANs, 6–7
utilities, client, 264–270
  authentication, 269–270
  data rate, 266
  link status monitoring, 267–268
  performance tuning, 268
  power monitoring, 265–266
  profile management, 266–267
  protection mechanisms, 268
  site survey, 265
  Windows XP Wireless Zero Config, 271
utilities, site survey, 500–504
  measuring SNR, noise floor, signal strength, 500–501
  NetStumbler, 502
  protocol analyzers, 502
  third-party, 502–504

V

V (volts), 48
variable attenuator, 512
variable power output, APs, 229, 499
vendor/product recommendations, 544
vertical polarization, antennas, 31
VHF antennas, 64
Violation Reporting and Enforcement, general security policy, 467
virtual carrier sense, 368, 383
visual LOS, 394. *See also* LOS (line of sight)
VLANs, 281
VoIP over WiFi (VoWiFI), 490–491
voltage breakdown, 148–149
Voltage Standing Wave Radio. *See* VSWR (Voltage Standing Wave Radio)
voltmeters
  antenna alignment, 118

bridge alignment, 245–246
volts (V), 48
VoWiFI (VoIP over WiFi), 490–491
VPNs
  EWGs and, 277
  technologies, 278
  wireless, 443–447
VSWR (Voltage Standing Wave Radio), 39–41
  effects of, 41
  lightning arrestor VSWR rating, 147
  moisture effecting, 122
  overview, 39–40
  RF splitter VSWR rating, 155
  solutions to, 41
  VSWR measurements, 40
  VSWR rating of lightning arrestors, 150

W

W (watts), 48–49
wall mounts, antennas, 110
warranty, lightning arrestors, 150
water/snow, weather-related interference, 415–416
watt meters, 123–124
watts (W), 48–49
wavelength
  formula for calculating, 26–27
  overview, 26–27
  practical uses of, 27
weather, 415–418
  air stratification, 417
  outdoor surveys and, 516
  overview, 415
  protective equipment, 417–418
  site surveys and, 486–487
  water/snow, 415–416
  wind, 416–417
WECA, 3
WEP (Wired Equivalent Privacy), 426–431
  802.11i, 316
  access point security, 230
  encryption, 278
  encryption cracking attacks, 455
  overview, 426–427
  Shared Key authentication, 341–342
  TKIP and, 428–431
  weaknesses of, 427–428
  WEP keys, 428
WGB (workgroup bridges), 253–256
  filtering, 256
  fixed vs. detachable antennas, 255
  management, 255–256
  modes, 256
  number of clients supported, 256
  options, 255

overview, 253–255
security, 255
Wi-Fi Alliance, 320–323
equipment compatibility/availability, 211
formation of, 3
overview, 320–321
WMM (Wi-Fi Multimedia), 322–323
WPA (Wi-Fi Protected Access), 321–322
Wi-Fi Multimedia. *See* WMM (Wi-Fi Multimedia)
Wi-Fi Protected Access. *See* WPA (Wi-Fi Protected Access)
WIDS (wireless intrusion detection systems), 461–462, 470
wind, weather-related interference, 416–417
window mounts, antennas, 110
Windows XP Wireless Zero Config, 271
wired connectivity, site surveys, 528–530
Wired Equivalent Privacy. *See* WEP (Wired Equivalent Privacy)
wireless bridges. *See* bridges, wireless
wireless frames, 365–366
wireless hijacking, 459–460
Wireless Internet Service Providers (WISPs), 11–12
wireless intrusion detection systems (WIDS), 461–462, 470
wireless LAN switches. *See* switches, WLANs
wireless LANs. *See* WLANs (wireless LANs)
wireless mesh routers. *See* mesh routers
Wireless Metropolitan Area Networks (WMANs), 176
Wireless Personal Area Networks (WPANs), 176
wireless repeaters, 225
wireless residential gateways, 271–274
configuration and management, 273–274
options, 273
overview, 271–272
wireless routers. *See* routers, wireless
Wireless Valley, 535
Wireless Wide Area Networks (WWANs), 176
Wireless Zero Config, Windows XP, 271
wiring closets, 485–486, 495
WISPs (Wireless Internet Service Providers), 11–12
WLANs (wireless LANs)
antenna accessories, 163–164
applications. *see* applications, WLAN
clients devices. *see* clients devices
exam objectives, 1
history of, 2–4
infrastructure devices. *see* infrastructure devices
key terms, 18
lightning arrestors installed on, 147
monitoring power with RF splitters, 153–154
power management. *see* power management
review questions, 19
RF amplifier placement in, 136
security. *see* security
today's standards, 4–5
troubleshooting. *see* troubleshooting WLANs

WLANs (wireless LANs), joining, 338–344
802.11 state machine, 343–344
association, 342
authentication, 339–342
overview, 338
WLANs (wireless LANs), locating, 333–338
active scanning, 336–338
beacons, 333–334
FH or DS parameter sets, 334
overview, 333
passive scanning, 335–336
SSIDs, 334
supported rates, 335
time synchronization, 334
traffic indicator map (TIM), 334–335
WMANs (Wireless Metropolitan Area Networks), 176
WMM (Wi-Fi Multimedia)
access categories, 381–382
overview, 322–323
QoS (Quality of Service), 381–382
wireless bridges, 252
workgroup bridges. *See* WGB (workgroup bridges)
WPA (Wi-Fi Protected Access), 438–441
access point security, 230–231
encryption, 278, 440–441
overview, 321–322, 438
WPA-PSK, 439–440, 455–456
WPA-RADIUS, 439–440
WPA2/802.11i, 441
WPA2/802.11i, 441
WPANs (Wireless Personal Area Networks), 176
WWANs (Wireless Wide Area Networks), 176

Y

yagi antennas
as example of semi-directional antenna, 77–78
mounting, 111–112
placement, 104–105
radome as protective device for, 417–418
tilt-and-swivel mounts, 112
U-bolt mounts, 111
uses of, 82–83

Z

zip ties, for mounting APs, 238

INTERNATIONAL CONTACT INFORMATION

AUSTRALIA
McGraw-Hill Book Company Australia
Pty. Ltd.
TEL +61-2-9900-1800
FAX +61-2-9878-8881
http://www.mcgraw-hill.com.au
books-it_sydney@mcgraw-hill.com

CANADA
McGraw-Hill Ryerson Ltd.
TEL +905-430-5000
FAX +905-430-5020
http://www.mcgraw-hill.ca

GREECE, MIDDLE EAST, & AFRICA
(Excluding South Africa)
McGraw-Hill Hellas
TEL +30-210-6560-990
TEL +30-210-6560-993
TEL +30-210-6560-994
FAX +30-210-6545-525

MEXICO (Also serving Latin America)
McGraw-Hill Interamericana Editores
S.A. de C.V.
TEL +525-117-1583
FAX +525-117-1589
http://www.mcgraw-hill.com.mx
fernando_castellanos@mcgraw-hill.com

SINGAPORE (Serving Asia)
McGraw-Hill Book Company
TEL +65-863-1580
FAX +65-862-3354
http://www.mcgraw-hill.com.sg
mghasia@mcgraw-hill.com

SOUTH AFRICA
McGraw-Hill South Africa
TEL +27-11-622-7512
FAX +27-11-622-9045
robyn_swanepoel@mcgraw-hill.com

SPAIN
McGraw-Hill/Interamericana de España,
S.A.U.
TEL +34-91-180-3000
FAX +34-91-372-8513
http://www.mcgraw-hill.es
professional@mcgraw-hill.es

UNITED KINGDOM, NORTHERN,
EASTERN, & CENTRAL EUROPE
McGraw-Hill Education Europe
TEL +44-1-628-502500
FAX +44-1-628-770224
http://www.mcgraw-hill.co.uk
computing_neurope@mcgraw-hill.com

ALL OTHER INQUIRIES Contact:
Osborne/McGraw-Hill
TEL +1-510-549-6600
FAX +1-510-883-7600
http://www.osborne.com
omg_international@mcgraw-hill.com